Learning from *All* the Faithful

Learning from *All* the Faithful

A Contemporary Theology of the *Sensus Fidei*

EDITED BY
Bradford E. Hinze
AND
Peter C. Phan

☙PICKWICK *Publications* · Eugene, Oregon

LEARNING FROM *ALL* THE FAITHFUL
A Contemporary Theology of the *Sensus Fidei*

Copyright © 2016 Wipf and Stock Publishers. All rights reserved. Except for brief quotations in critical publications or reviews, no part of this book may be reproduced in any manner without prior written permission from the publisher. Write: Permissions, Wipf and Stock Publishers, 199 W. 8th Ave., Suite 3, Eugene, OR 97401.

Pickwick Publications
An Imprint of Wipf and Stock Publishers
199 W. 8th Ave., Suite 3
Eugene, OR 97401

www.wipfandstock.com

PAPERBACK ISBN: 978-1-4982-8021-1
HARDCOVER ISBN: 978-1-4982-8023-5
EBOOK ISBN: 978-1-4982-8022-8

Cataloguing-in-Publication data:

Names: Hinze, Brandford E. | Phan, Peter C.

Title: Learning from all the faithful : a contemporary theology of the sensus fidei / edited by Brandford E. Hinze and Peter C. Phan.

Description: Eugene, OR: Pickwick Publications, 2016. | Includes bibliographical references.

Identifiers: ISBN 978-1-4982-8021-1 (paperback) | ISBN 978-1-4982-8023-5 (hardcover) | ISBN 978-1-4982-8022-8 (ebook).

Subjects: LSCH: Catholic Church—Doctrines. | Sensus fidelium.

Classification: BX1746 L385 2016 (print) | BX1746 (ebook).

Manufactured in the U.S.A.   10/19/16

Portions of chapter 17 were published as "Weaving Memory, Structuring Ritual, Evoking Mythos: Commemoration of the Ancestors," M. Shawn Copeland, *Invitation to Practical Theology: Catholic Voices and Visions*, edited by Claire E. Wolfteich (Paulist, 2014) 125–48.

An earlier version of chapter 9 was published as "The *Sensus Fidelium:* Old Questions, New Challenges," John J. Burkhard, *CTSA Proceedings* 70 (2015) 27–43.

Chapter 23 was published as "The Sensus Fidei in the Recent History of the Latin American Church," Maria Clara Luchetti Bingemer, *CTSA Proceedings* 70 (2015) 48–59.

Chapter 24 was published as "Theology as Conversation: Sensus Fidelium and Doing Theology on/from the Margins," Gemma Cruz, *CTSA Proceedings* 70 (2015) 60–65.

Chapter 25 was published as "How Are Theologians Challenged and Informed by their Engagement with the Sense of the Faithful in the Local / Global Church," Anne Arabome, SSS, *CTSA Proceedings* 70 (2015) 60–71.

Contents

Contributors / xi

Acknowledgments / xiii

Abbreviations / xiv

Introduction / xv

Part 1: Historical Perspectives

1. The *Sensus Fidelium* in Augustine / *Andrew Salzmann* / 3
2. St. Thomas Aquinas and the Foundations of the *Sensus fidelium* / *Jonathan M. Kaltenbach* / 18
3. Sensuous History: The Medieval Feast of Corpus Christi as an Expression of the *Sensus Fidelium* / *Thomas Ryan* / 27
4. John Henry Newman on Consulting the Faithful: An Idea in Need of Development / *Ryan Marr* / 42
5. Supremacy in the Sense of the Faith: Theological Anthropology and the "Various Ranks" (*Lumen Gentium* 13) / *Jeannine Hill Fletcher* / 53
6. *Sensus Fidelium* and the International Theological Commission—Has Anything Changed Between 2012 and 2014? / *Gerard Mannion* / 69

Part 2: Disputed Questions on the Use of Social Sciences

7. *Sensus Fidei* and Sociology: How Do We Find the Normative in the Empirical? / *Neil Ormerod* / 89

8. The Use of Sociology in the Study of the *Sensus Fidelium*: An Evaluation of the Contribution of Jerome Baggett / *Robert Cortegiano* / 103

Part 3: Systematic Theology and Social Ethics

9. The *Sensus Fidelium*: Old Questions, New Challenges / *John J. Burkhard* / 125

10. The Church as a Hermeneutical Community and the Eschatological Function of the *Sensus Fidelium* / *Ormond Rush* / 143

11. Whose *Sensus*? Which *Fidelium*? Justice and Gender in a Global Church Cristina / *Cristina L. H. Traina* / 155

12. Beyond "Who Am I To Judge?" The *Sensus Fidelium*, LGBT Experience, and Truth-Telling in the Church / *Brian N. Massingale* / 170

13. Who Are the *Fideles* and What Is their *Sensus*? Insights from Bernard Lonergan / *William P. George* / 184

14. A Rahnerian Reading of *Sensus Fidei* in the Life of the Church / *Michael M. Canaris* / 196

Part 4: Insights on the *Sensus Fidei* for World Christianity

15. *Sensus Fidelium, Dissensus Infidelium, Consensus Omnium*: An Interreligious Approach to Consensus in Doctrinal Theology / *Peter C. Phan* / 213

16. A Mosaic of Identities of the *Sensus Fidelium*: The Realities of African Ecclesial Communities in Diaspora / *SimonMary A. Aihiokhai* / 226

17. The Institute for Black Catholic Studies: Culture, the *Sensus Fidelium*, and Practical Theological Agency / *M. Shawn Copeland* / 237

18. Learning to Discern the *Sensus Fidelium Latinamente*: A Dialogue with Orlando Espín / *Edward Hahnenberg* / 255

19. Latina Lives, Latina Literature: A Narrative Camino in Search of the *Sensus Fidelium* / *Natalia Imperatori-Lee* / 272

20. "Who Do You Say That I Am?" Uncovering the Chinese *Sensus Fidelium* in Images of Jesus in Pre-Communist Chinese Catholic Devotional Art from the 1930s–1940s / *Jonathan Y. Tan* / 281

21. Discerning the *Sensus Fidelium* in Asia's Narrative Theologies / *Edmund Kee-Fook Chia* / 295

22. Storytelling as an Expression of *Sensus Fidelium*: A Korean-American Catholic Perspective / *Hoon Choi* / 312

23. The *Sensus Fidei* in the Recent History of the Latin American Church / *Maria Clara Luchetti Bingemer* / 329

24. Theology as Conversation: *Sensus Fidelium* and Doing Theology on/from the Margins / *Gemma Cruz* / 344

25. How Are Theologians Challenged and Informed by their Engagement with the Sense of the Faithful in the Local / Global Church / *Anne Arabome* / 360

Selected Bibliography / 367

Topical Index / 371

Personal Name Index / 377

Contributors

SimonMary Asese Aihiokhai, Visiting Assistant Professor of Theology, Valparaiso University, Valparaiso, Indiana

Anne Arabome, SSS, Visiting Scholar, Claremont School of Theology, Claremont, California

Maria Clara Bingemer, Professor of Systematic Theology, Pontifical Catholic University, Rio de Janeiro, Brazil

John J. Burkhard, OFM Conv., Emeritus Professor of Systematic Theology at the former Washington Theological Union, Washington, DC

Michael M. Canaris, Assistant Professor of Systematic Theology and Ecclesiology at the Institute of Pastoral Studies, Loyola University Chicago

Edmund Chia, Senior Lecturer and Coordinator of Interreligious Dialogue, School of Theology at Australian Catholic University

Hoon Choi, Assistant Professor of Theology, Bellarmine University, Louisville, Kentucky

M. Shawn Copeland, Professor of Systematic Theology at Boston College, Chestnut Hill, Massachusetts

Robert J. Cortegiano, PhD candidate in Systematic Theology, Fordham University, Bronx, New York

Gemma Tulud Cruz, Senior Lecturer in Theology at Australian Catholic University, Melbourne

Jeannine Hill Fletcher, Professor of Theology at Fordham University, Bronx, New York

CONTRIBUTORS

William P. George, Professor of Theology at Dominican University, River Forest, Illinois

Bradford E. Hinze, The Karl Rahner, SJ, Professor of Theology, Fordham University, Bronx, New York

Jonathan M. Kaltenbach, PhD candidate in Theology, University of Notre Dame, Notre Dame, Indiana

Gerard Mannion, Amaturo Chair in Catholic Studies, Georgetown University, Washington, DC

Ryan J. Marr, Assistant Professor of Philosophy, Mercy College of Health Sciences, Des Moines, Iowa

Bryan N. Massingale, Professor of Theological Ethics, Fordham University, New York, New York

Neil Ormerod, Professor of Theology, Institute for Religion & Critical Inquiry, Faculty of Theology and Philosophy, Australian Catholic University, Strathfield, Australia

Peter C. Phan, The Ignacio Ellacuría Chair of Catholic Social Thought, Georgetown University, Washington, DC

Ormond Rush, Associate Professor, Australian Catholic University, Brisbane, Australia

Andrew Benjamin Salzmann, Assistant Professor of Theology, Benedictine College, Atchison, Kansas

Jonathan Y. Tan, The Archbishop Paul J. Hallinan Professor of Catholic Studies at Case Western Reserve University, Cleveland, Ohio

Cristina L.H. Traina, Professor of Religious Studies, Northwestern University, Evanston, Illinois

Thomas Ryan, Professor of Theology and Ministry, Loyola University New Orleans

Acknowledgments

THE EDITORS WISH TO express their sincerest thanks to all the contributors who have generously and graciously agreed to work for this volume.

We are also deeply thankful to Lynne Moss Bahr, PhD candidate, Christianity in Antiquity, Fordham University, for her expert and prompt editorial work. Without her help we would not have been able to meet the deadline for submitting the manuscript to the publisher, which is a rare feat for a book with so many authors! Our sincere gratitude as well go to Amy Phillips from the Woodstock Library at Georgetown University for your excellent work in preparing the index.

Abbreviations

CDF	Congregation for the Doctrine of the Faith
EG	*Evangelii Gaudium*
ITC	International Theological Commission
LD	John Henry Newman, *The Letters and Diaries of John Henry Newman*
LG	*Lumen Gentium*
OCTF	John Henry Newman, *On Consulting the Faithful in Matters of Doctrine*
SFLC	Sensus Fidei in the Life of the Church
ST	Thomas Aquinas, *Summa Theologiae*
TI	Karl Rahner, *Theological Investigations*

Introduction

Do various members of the church—regardless of their generation, gender, race, sexual orientation, and country of origin, and whatever their doubts are about official church teachings and policies—have any role in determining, safeguarding, and assessing the authentic teaching of the faith of the church? Over the last fifty years this question has received increased attention by Christians, especially among Roman Catholics, ever since the issue was addressed at the Second Vatican Council. Before the council it was commonly assumed that it was the bishops in union with the pope that articulated authentic church doctrine and it was expected the faithful would adhere to it.

The term sense of the faith, in Latin *sensus fidei*, attributed to an individual believer, and by inference the collective designation, sense of the faithful, *sensus fidelium*, surfaced in the Second Vatican Council's description of the church as the pilgrim people of God who are called to share in the messianic mission of Jesus Christ as priest, prophet, and king. Through baptism individuals and by extension all the faithful of the church are gifted with a particular instinct or perceptive ability by which they are able to receive and recognize the revealed word of God and through the use of their imagination and practical judgment apply the faith of the church in their daily lives and thus become a Christian disciple and participate in the mission of the church. The particular formulation found in Vatican II's *Lumen Gentium, the Dogmatic Constitution on the Church*, speaks of "the supernatural sense of the faith of the entire people of God." This phrase was introduced to shed light how all of the people of God through the baptismal anointing of the Spirit come to participate in the prophetic office of Jesus Christ in truthful witness and missionary outreach. While *Lumen Gentium* gave unprecedented attention to this formula, the expression invokes a classic theme central in the Christian life of faith. This motif can be traced back to the earliest period of the church, and became especially pronounced in the debates in Christianity leading up to the Council of Nicaea, where many of the faithful recognized the core Christological faith of the church at a time when many bishops did not.

In the years since the council, the sense of the faithful became a disputed topic. Some discredited the idea for being based on sociological reasoning and equated it with poll results, and not genuinely theological. The influence of such criticisms in certain circles led some to fear that this classic and now urgent doctrine was being undermined and as a result falling into disuse. Yet what appeared threatened was still operative. The council's retrieval of the local church, of the importance of church synods, and of the shared participation of all the baptized in the life and mission of the church, all find a vital source and orientation in the sense of the faithful. Just as Vatican II's teaching has provided a challenge to bishops to immerse themselves in, and have their understanding of the faith informed by the sense of the faithful, so too theologians are being summoned to learn from the sense of the faithful in local churches and communities, and among populations on the periphery of the church around the world.

The theme of the sense of the faithful has been particularly important for Pope Francis as is evident in his interviews and his writings. He speaks of this notion when he promotes consultation with the faithful by bishops, priests, and theologians in the practice of synod of bishops, national and regional episcopal conferences, and in the local churches. This was particularly pronounced in his call for bishops from around the world to prepare for the back-to-back synods of bishops held in 2014 and 2015 on the theme of the family.

This book brings together essays by a wide range of scholars with different areas of expertise. They come from diverse generational, gender, racial, and ethnic backgrounds in Catholic theology today. These essays provide a particularly wide range of offerings from scholars who come from geographical areas in the Global South, from Africa, Latin America, Asia, as well as from the United States.

This volume begins with a section devoted to the contributions of major theologians, official Catholic documents, and one major feast; Augustine of Hippo, Thomas Aquinas, John Henry Newman, and the documents of Vatican II; the treatment of this topic by the International Theological Commission in its 2014 document "*Sensus Fidei* in the Life of the Church" receives extended analysis and reflection; and there is an analysis of the medieval feast of Corpus Christi. The second section of the volume includes two essays that explore a range of issues that pertain to the use of sociological methods in the determination of the sense of the faithful since this has been a disputed question in theology since Vatican II. Section three has essays reviewing the basic issues in systematic theology pertaining to matters of faith, doctrinal development, theological hermeneutics, and the church; essays exploring the role of the sense of the faithful in the disputed areas of gender and sexual orientation in theological ethics; this section also includes essays devoted to the influential work of Karl Rahner and Bernard Lonergan. The final section of the volume introduces widely unknown sources and insights from Africa, Asia, Caribbean, and Latin America, including African American and Latino/a voices. It is all the more important to note these new voices in the chorus of the *sensus fidei/fidelium* as Christianity is becoming a "World Christianity."

Part 1

Historical Perspectives

1

The *Sensus Fidelium* in Augustine

— Andrew Benjamin Salzmann —

Introduction

THE INFLUENCE OF AUGUSTINE of Hippo (354–430), a theologian and bishop from Romanized Africa, is difficult to overstate. One of the four great "doctors" of the Latin church, Augustine became a fundamental source for Catholic theology and a perduring influence on Western thought. No less than Jaroslav Pelikan commented that, in the centuries after Augustine's death and until the rise of scholasticism, the construction of an "Augustinian synthesis" provided the very basis of "the integrity of the catholic tradition."[1] Already attentive to a desire to return to the "sources" of Catholic thought, the Second Vatican Council (1962–1965) understandably turned to Augustine in *Lumen Gentium*'s articulation of the *sensus fidei*, the supernatural "instinct" that the faithful have for discerning the content of the Catholic faith. A modern term, "*sensus fidei*," does not appear in Augustine's own lexicon. A study of the *sensus fidei* in Augustine's thought has to be content to look for ideas that are relatively analogous to the contemporary understanding of *sensus fidei*, which has developed considerably in the relatively short time since the publication of *Lumen Gentium*.[2] The

---

1. Jaroslav Pelikan, *The Growth of Medieval Theology (600–1300)* (Chicago: University of Chicago Press, 1978) 49–50. Even as the introduction of Aristotelian logic upended that "Augustinian synthesis" of the early Middle Ages, the *Sententiae* of Peter Lombard, a systematic arrangement of doctrinal themes that drew heavily on Augustine, provided an important foundation for the subsequent rise of Scholasticism.

2. As the International Theological Commission (ITC) notes, "The phrase *sensus fidei* is found neither in the Scriptures, nor in the formal teaching of the Church until Vatican II."

ITC, *Sensus fidei in the Life of the Church*. 2014, 7, www.vatican.va/roman_curia/

search for these analogues has to be grounded in a clear definition of what "*sensus fidei*" meant at Vatican II and what it entails today.

Defining *Sensus fidei*

"The holy people of God," *Lumen Gentium* begins, "shares also in Christ's prophetic [i.e., teaching] office."[3] It continued, referencing Augustine's *On the predestination of the saints*:

> The entire body of the faithful, anointed as they are by the Holy One (cf. Jn. 2:20, 27), cannot err in matters of belief. They manifest this special property by means of the whole peoples' supernatural discernment of the faith (*supernaturali sensu fidei*) when, "from the Bishops down to the last of the lay faithful" (*praed. sanct.* 14:27), they show universal agreement in matters of faith and morals . . . [a sense or discernment] aroused and sustained by the Spirit of truth.

While this *sensus fidei* is, therefore, a communal prerogative, this communal dimension of the *sensus fidei* is rooted in the gift of the Holy Spirit to each member of the Body. And so *Lumen Gentium* continues: Through this very sense, "the people of God . . . penetrates [the faith] more deeply with right thinking, and applies it more fully in its life." The International Theological Commission (ITC), reflecting on this passage in an important 2014 document, understands the *sensus fidei* as an active participation in the teaching office of the church by all believers, empowered by the individual gift of the Holy Spirit, so that the people of God "have their own, active role to play in conserving and transmitting the faith," a role distinct from—if ultimately harmonious with (ITC, 38–39)—that of their pastors (ITC 4 and 2, respectively).[4] The *sensus fidei*, then, is defined as "a supernatural appreciation of the faith, aroused by the Holy Spirit, by which people guided by their pastors adhere unfailingly to the faith" (ITC, 46). The document goes on to formalize the distinction implicit in *Lumen Gentium* between the broad

---

congregations/cfaith/cti_documents/rc_cti_20140610_sensus-fidei_en.html.

3. Second Vatican Council, *Dogmatic Constitution on the Church—Lumen Gentium*, November 21, 1964, 12, http://www.vatican.va/archive/hist_councils/ii_vatican_council/documents/vat-ii_const_19641121_lumen-gentium_en.html.

4. But the ITC insists on the "freedom of the *Ecclesia docens* vis-à-vis the *Ecclesia discens*," so that the consensus of the faithful or the perpetual sense of the church, particularly in its piety and devotion, is only one source of that doctrine which pastors teach, along with "Holy Scripture, venerable Tradition . . . the remarkable agreement of Catholic bishops and the faithful, and the memorable Acts and Constitutions" of the popes (38, 40).

consensus of the body of the faithful (termed *sensus fidei fidelium*) and the individual believer's instinctive sense for the truth of the faith (termed *sensus fidei fidelis*), even if that individual's intellectual formation in the content of the faith may be lacking. The example of *sensus fidei fidelium* made famous by John Henry Newman is the communal confession of Christ's divinity or Mary's divine maternity by the body of believers, even in the face of the dissension of bishops and theologians.[5] Examples of the "*sensus fidei fidelis*" might include the uneducated believer who instinctively knows the content or implications of the faith. In either case, the *sensus fidei* is viewed as more than the "passive infallibility" of the laity that was discussed in pre-conciliar textbooks; Vatican II's understanding of the *sensus fidei* includes the people of God's ability to actively discern the content of the faith and to apply its moral demands to their various contexts.

Augustine and the *Sensus Fidei Fidelium*

As mentioned, the sole authority from the tradition cited by *Lumen Gentium* in its description of the *sensus fidei* is Augustine's *On the Predestination of the Saints*: The *sensus fidei* is manifest "when, 'from the Bishops down to the last of the lay faithful' (*praed. sanct.* 14:27), they show universal agreement in matters of faith and morals." Augustine is thus invoked to demonstrate the *sensus fidei fidelium*—the whole people's sense of the faith—which is ultimately rooted in the presence of the Holy Spirit to each. The context from which this line emerges is both interesting and complicating: The Pelagians, in arguing that an individual's own effort can be sufficient for salvation, suggest that the Christian can be certain of salvation. Augustine, in arguing that human nature remains too weak for holiness without the assistance of divine grace, also argues that the continuing weakness of the human heart means that salvation is never certain—one always faces the risk of falling back into sin. Thus, Augustine argues, death is advantageous to the Christian, as death and death alone removes the possibility of a lapse into sin. In the course of making this argument, Augustine (following Cyprian) appealed to a line from the Book of Wisdom: The one loved by God is "snatched away" by death, "lest wickedness pervert his mind or deceit beguile his soul" (4:11). Augustine's interlocutors rejected this appeal to the Book of

---

5. John Henry Newman, *On Consulting the Faithful in Matters of Doctrine* (New York: Sheed & Ward, 1961) 76–77.
Cf. Ryan Marr's contribution to this volume, which considers complications to the validity of Newman's claim.

Wisdom because they did not accept it as an authority (*praed. sanct.* 14:26).[6] To defend its canonicity, Augustine explains that this book "has merited to be read over a long period of time from the platform of the lectors of the Church of Christ, and to be heard by all Christians, from the bishops down to the lowliest faithful laity, penitents, and catechumens, with the respect that is owed to the divine authority" (*praed. sanct.* 14:27).[7] This defense of Wisdom's canonicity could demonstrate a belief in the passive infallibility of the people of God (*ecclesia discens*): The people of God have recognized, received, and in so doing "ratified" the Book of Wisdom as authoritative. On the other hand, his argument may also have less to do with its "ratification by the faithful" than with an appeal to tradition and a traditional practice of which everyone is aware: The Book of Wisdom constitutes a valid source for theological debate because it is canonical, not secret *gnosis*; it has always been read in the churches, as everyone knows. It is not clear that Augustine was here expressing the belief that the faithful as a whole have an instinctive sense for the content or application of the faith.[8]

Lumen Gentium's reference to the debate over the canonicity of the Book of Wisdom is only one of four examples of Augustine's appeal to global consensus identified by Yves Congar, OP, in an appendix to his 1956 book *Lay People in the Church*, written in the years leading up to Vatican II. Congar also refers to the practice of not rebaptizing heretics, the practice of praying for the conversion of sinners, and the role of baptism in salvation, particularly the baptism of infants, as beliefs defended by appeal to the beliefs and practices of the body of the laity.[9] Subsequent theological reflection on Augustine and the *sensus fidei fidelium* has largely continued attending

---

6. The Latin abbreviations used to cite the works of Augustine follow standard practice. A table codifying these abbreviations can be found in the front matter of Allan D. Fitzgerald, OSA, ed., *Augustine through the Ages: An Encyclopedia* (Grand Rapids, MI: Eerdmans, 1999). Thus, *praed. sanct.* refers to *De praedestinatione sanctorum*; *mag.* refers to *De magistro*; *s.* refers to *Sermones*, etc.

7. FC 86 (1992).
For translations of Augustine's work, I have drawn from two major multi-volume series: The *Fathers of the Church* (FC), ed., R. J. Deferrari (Washington, DC: Catholic University Press, 1947–present) and the *Works of Saint Augustine: A Translation for the 21st Century* (WSA), ed., J. E. Rotelle (New York: New City, 1990–present). For the sake of simplifying citations, I cite these translations by series abbreviation, volume number, and year.

8. This discussion of Augustine's intention in this passage of *On the Predestination of the Saints* should not, however, be interpreted as an attempt to assess the validity of the argument made in *Lumen Gentium*, whose validity as a conciliar constitution is not dependent upon scholarly assessments of its use of Augustine.

9. Yves Congar, OP, *Lay People in the Church*, trans. Donald Attwater (Westminster, MD: Newman, 1959), 441–43.

to these themes.[10] The association between Augustine's teaching on the infallible consensus of the church and the modern articulation of *sensus fidei fidelium*, however, has to negotiate a double slipperiness of terms.

First, the definition of *sensus fidei fidelium* sometimes slips between the pre-conciliar idea of the passive infallibility of the *ecclesia discens*, which can be consulted as a reliable source for the content of the deposit of the faith, and the conciliar idea of the laity's corporate sense for actively penetrating the faith "more deeply with right thinking, and appl[ying] it more fully in its life" (*Lumen Gentium*, 12). Certainly, Augustine believed that the practice of the whole Church could be a witness to the content of the deposit of the faith; in fact, he states that one of these examples, infant baptism, is not merely a development of lay piety but a matter of invariable custom rooted, not in the decree of any church council but rather in apostolic authority (*bapt.* 4.23.31-4.24.32). This appeal to the *dogma populare* is an appeal to the body of the church as a witness to unchanging tradition, but it cannot be used to ascribe to Augustine a belief in the *sensus fidei fidelium* as a kind of instinct for a communal development of, or fuller application of, the understanding of the Christian faith by the people.

Second, the function of the consensus of the Church in Augustine is similarly slippery, shifting from a sort of passive infallibility of the whole church to an apologetic for the importance of humility in the face of authority. In one place, Augustine notes that while the resurrection of the body has gained general acceptance, a few among the most and least learned continue to deny it (see *civ. Dei* 22.5). This global consensus on the resurrection of the body illustrates that either the holdouts are quite stupid or quite prideful. Augustine incorporates his treatment of miracles into this debate, to make the point that the existence of many improbable events should move the crass obstinacy of the hold-outs to accept the authority of the church with humility (see also *vera rel.* 25.47). The theme of the authority of consensus sometimes functions as a corrective for pride. In any event, Augustine believes that the general consent of Christians "functions as a sure norm for determining the apostolic faith," but that is not identical with the contemporary articulation of *sensus fidei fidelium* (ITC, 23; see *C. ep. Parmeniani* 3.24).

Augustine and the *Sensus Fidei Fidelis*

If the *sensus fidei fidelis* is that "personal aptitude" of the individual believer to discern matters of faith truthfully and to apply them in the world, one

---

10. In addition to the ITC document, see William M. Thompson, "Sensus Fidelium and Infallibility," *American Ecclesiastical Review* 167 (1973) 450–86, at 452.

cannot doubt that such an "inner sense" constituted an important thread running through Augustine's thought from his early philosophical works, across his scriptural commentaries, to the anti-Pelagian writings of his later years, like the *De praedestinatione sanctorum*.

The early philosophical works—the *Soliloquies* and *De magistro*, for example—carefully explore the doctrine of illumination that underwrote the Platonists' "interior ascent," an ascent that moved from awareness of physical realities to an awareness of the reasoned judgments that the human mind makes about these realities and that, in asking what the origin of the power by which the mind can make these rational judgments might be, discovers the presence of divine reason, of the Logos, illuminating the mind (e.g., *mus.* 6.11.33). It was this ascent that led to Augustine's own conversion from skepticism to theism (see *conf.* 7.10.16). Augustine remained deeply committed to it: Given the opportunity while a bishop to preach about Christianity to a pagan crowd in the African countryside, Augustine guided them through this very ascent (*s.* 360b).[11] In his early works, Augustine speaks of ascent and illumination at length. In the *Soliloquies*, illumination entails the belief that the unlike the senses, which only perceive the passing things of this world (*sol.* 1.15.19) and are prone to error (*sol.* 2.3.3), the mind has a sort of interior eye of its own. Just as physical eyes require light to see, the eye of the mind sees by the light of Reason, of the Logos (*sol.* 1.13.23); just as physical eyes see the things of this world, the eye of the mind can see truth, even God (*sol.* 1.6.12). Any truth that is known is learned, not from the world, but from the contact of the mind with the Logos that illumines it, as he writes in On the Teacher (*mag.* 14.45). The doctrine of illumination shapes how Augustine appropriates Christ's injunction to "call no one teacher": Since truth is learned from the Logos that directly illumines each human mind, and since the Logos became a human being in Jesus Christ, Christ the Logos is the sole teacher, directly enlightening every mind with truth (*mag.* 14.46). Sometimes the physical eye can be overwhelmed by light; in a similar way, the eye of the mind does not have the strength to see the truth of God unless it turns away from attachment to physical goods—whether riches, honor, the marriage-bed, food—and turns towards God with a love that prefers God to all else; only the soul that prefers nothing to God will behold God with the mind's eye (*sol.* 1.9.16–1.10.17). Thus, to know God through divine illumination requires love of God, and when that love is had, the soul will see what it desires (*sol.* 1.14.24). Love is a condition of knowing God—but here it is not itself a means of knowing God (*sol.* 2.1.1)

---

11. WSA III/11 (1997).

In another early work, a dialogue with his friends and family, Augustine gives us the opportunity to see the power of this Inner Teacher, of Christ the Logos, working within the soul of the simple faithful through the beloved figure of his mother, Monica. The *De beata vita* is eager to present Monica as simultaneously uneducated (he remarks on her Latin vulgarisms) and yet instinctively able to resolve theological problems that baffle his educated friends. The premise of the work is Augustine's promise to celebrate his thirty-third birthday in the form of an intense, three-day discussion about the nature of happiness. Augustine professes not to know what direction the discussions will take, content simply that they will be guided by the One who, dwelling in the hearts of the participants, makes them happy (*b. vita* 17).

At each critical juncture of the dialogue, it is Monica who resolves the challenges Augustine puts to the group. When, at one point, she recreates *de novo* a position of Cicero, Augustine can only stammer: "I understood, as well as possible, from what source those words came and how divine was the source" (*b. vita* 10).[12] As the discussions continue, Monica leads the group to realize that having what one might desire cannot bring happiness, but only having the good; when Augustine draws out that "the good" must be neither mortal nor transient but, instead, must be God, Monica realizes that those who are made happy by material things are in fact made happy not by the material things themselves, but by the virtue that moderates their desires. And, as Augustine and his companions take up the important question happiness and the presence of God in the soul, Monica's role is again decisive. When the group concludes that happiness is the possession of the eternal good that is God, it struggles with what it means to possess God. Happiness is possessing God; but Christians seek God. Therefore, while the soul seeks God, it does not possess God and is, therefore, miserable. However: By seeking God, it also pleases God; therefore, in seeking God, the soul pleases God but is itself miserable. After taking a swipe at the craziness of philosophers, Monica resolves the dilemma: The good possess God in God's fullness and God's favor and, therefore, are happy; the evil possess God but not God's favor and so are miserable; those who seek God do not yet possess God in God's fullness, but God is not absent from them, and they possess God's favor (*b. vita* 21). Again, Monica is a living illustration of the ability of the simple faithful to understand the God to whom they are devoted and whom they love. But more than another example of Monica's knowing piety, the question of the manner in which the soul searching for God can be said to possess God is important in its own right. Once resolved, the manner in which those

12. FC 1 (1948).

who search for God can be said to possess God provides the foundation for Augustine's understanding of how the faithful come to this knowledge of God, a foundation upon which Augustine will build later in life.

As the group gathered for Augustine's birthday discussion grapples with the difference between God being "not absent" to a soul and a soul possessing God, Augustine inaugurates a very early version of a theme that will become a hallmark of his *De trinitate*. He suggests that the soul possesses God's fullness when it participates in the Trinitarian perfections of God. This fascinating attempt is early, before Augustine has clearly distinguished intellect and will within the soul; instead, he experiments with the "trinity" of wisdom, fullness, and measure (*b. vita* 32). But the dialog first shows how "wisdom" is a knowledge of God that comes from the experience of the full possession of God in charity and is not simply intellectual, and the dialog employs Monica to illustrate this idea that possessing God in fullness gives the soul an instinctive apprehension of truth. As Augustine remarks after Monica's simple piety again knocks the theological ball out of the park, "I myself was very excited and pleased because . . . [she] stated what I had learned with great trouble from the books of the philosophers . . . 'Do you all see,' I asked, 'that a great difference exists between [the soul that studies] many . . . doctrines and a soul wholly attentive to God?" (*b. vita* 27). Because Monica loves God, she has a sense of the truths of God that can equal or surpass the knowledge had by reasoned inquiry. This sense for the truth of the faith through the soul's possession of God is a different claim than the position that love of God is necessary for the knowledge of God, but additional Trinitarian reflection will be necessary before the means by which piety might give one a sense for the truth can be more fully identified.

De beata vita is an early attempt to explain that Wisdom means the possession of the trinitarian God in such a way that the entire person participates in the perfections of the Trinity, and the Trinity perfects the entire person. From this possession of God comes a kind of instinct for the faith. Augustine's later development of the psychological analogy for the Trinity—the manner in which the human soul mirrors the Trinity—allows him to fill out the "mechanics" of how this instinct for the faith might operate. Lewis Ayres has demonstrated how Augustine's gradual development of trinitarian theology grounded his view of the structure of the human soul. One of the first advances Augustine makes is to articulate, in an address given to a gathering of African bishops in 393 entitled *De fide et symbolo*, the place of the Holy Spirit within the Trinity: While theologians had long considered the relationship between God the Father and God the Son, Augustine laments that insufficient attention has been paid to the identity of the Holy Spirit and the Spirit's relationship to the Father and Son. He identifies the

Holy Spirit as the shared bond of divinity, and therefore the communion, between the Father and Son; as such, the Spirit can be considered the mutual love of the Father and Son, and Augustine can identify the Holy Spirit with love itself (see *f. et symb.* 9.18). The relationship of the Father and Son gives rise to the identity of the Holy Spirit as love, and this identity also reveals the role which the Holy Spirit plays in the drama of salvation: The Holy Spirit is the gift of God's charity to the human heart, uniting it to God (see Rom. 5:5).[13]

If this identification of the Holy Spirit with the love shared by the Father and Son and with the gift of love graciously given to the human heart is the first part of the intellectual architecture which underlies Augustine's understanding of how the devout have an instinctive understanding of the truth of God, his later development of the psychological analogy is the second. The psychological analogy, which claims that structure of the Trinity (Father, Son, and Spirit) parallels the structure of the human psyche (memory, intellect, and will), represents one of the most influential developments in Western thought. In a famous essay, Albrecht Dihle argued that, in developing the psychological analogy, Augustine effectively invented the concept of the will: While Greco-Roman philosophy had assumed that once one is properly educated in the truth, then one will behave accordingly, Augustine—influenced by the Apostle Paul—experiences and describes the will as a distinct step beyond cognition (or *knowing* the truth), in which one must be moved to love the truth enough to act upon it.[14] For Augustine, human nature marked by sin is unable to will the good, unable to love neighbor as self and God above all; therefore, the gracious gift of the Holy Spirit—of God's love—is necessary to move the will to love the good.[15] Knowledge of truth and the grace of love thus become separate moments in the quest for sanctification.

Separate, but deeply related—and here the mechanics of the devout soul's instinct for the truth of the faith lie. Augustine develops his psychological analogy of the Trinity most clearly in books nine and ten of his *De Trinitate*, where he delves into the relationship between the mind's act of knowing and of loving: "The same appetite with which one longs open-mouthed to know a thing becomes love of the thing known when it holds and embraces [knowledge of that thing], and joins it to its begetter [the mind]. And so you have a certain image of the trinity, the mind itself and

---

13. Lewis Ayres, *Augustine and the Trinity* (New York: Cambridge University Press, 2010) 86–89.

14. Albrecht Dihle, *The Theory of Will in Classical Antiquity* (Berkeley: University of California Press, 1982) 18–21, 46.

15. Ibid., 127.

its knowledge, which is its offspring and its word about itself, and love as the third element" (*trin.* 9.3.18).[16] Two important observations follow from this passage.

In the first place, nothing is known without the will's desire. Robert Cushman explains, "there is no having or knowing God without having Him in the will," a will that is moved by divine charity. "In the case of God, as in the instance of all other cognition, full knowledge waits upon desire"; no thought can be fully conceived without the cooperation of the will's desire, precisely because, while Aristotle believed that desire could only follow upon knowledge of the thing desired, Augustine saw that act of knowing itself involved "a movement of the will or consent."[17] Augustine's belief in illumination would seem to privilege God's movement of the intellect, but he actually held that human beings resist this divine illumination of their intellect until God, who continuously visits the mind, is embraced, possessed, and experienced first by divine charity.

The second observation is the transformation of desire to love, which occurs only when knowledge is present; while desire is needed to arrive at knowledge, knowledge is necessary for desire to become love. For this reason, the will's love mirrors the origin of the Holy Spirit in proceeding from the intellect's knowledge.[18] This logical priority of knowledge to love means that the "love of God poured out into our hearts through the Holy Spirit" (Rom. 5:5), precisely because it is love rather than desire, contains an implicit knowledge or a pre-apprehension of the truth about the divine Beloved. Love, then, has noetic implications: Possessing the Beloved in infused charity can itself be a source of knowledge about the Beloved—an inversion of the Scholastic presumption that one moves sequentially from the knowledge of faith through hope to agapic love. In a homily on the John's gospel, Augustine illustrates this understanding implicit in the gift of infused, gracious love when, after attempting to explain an intricate point of Trinitarian doctrine, he invites those members of his congregation who remain confused to turn toward God, "who opens the heart that he may

---

16. WSA I/5 (1991). Note: I have supplied the numbering found in this translation.

17. Robert Cushman, "Faith and Reason," in *A Companion to the Study of St. Augustine*, ed. Roy W. Battenhouse (New York: Oxford University Press, 1955) 300–303.

Cushman explains that the necessity of the will's cooperation in reaching the truth of God is related to the famous Augustinian dictum *credo ut intelligam*: The will which chooses to embrace God in faith will experience God and, from that experience, have the evidence needed to understand the faith.

18. The will's procession from and logical dependence upon the intellect was inadequately appreciated by Dihle, who wrongly attributes to Augustine the definition of will as "sheer volition," a position that suggests no relationship between goods willed and truths known (143–44).

pour in what he gives." The use of "pour" (*infudat*) echoes the "pouring out" (*diffusa*) of the love of the Holy Spirit (Rom 5:5), and indeed, Augustine concludes, it is through this pouring that is the Catholic faith "made firm by the Spirit of God," present "in its saints" (*Jo. ev. tr.* 20.3).[19]

Augustine can believe in the divine illumination of the minds of all; but the acceptance of that illumination is only by charity, and, through that charity, the particular experience of the Son illuminating the intellects of the faithful. The importance of gracious love or charity in moving the will to receive the illumination of Christ the inner Teacher is made clear in Augustine's later work *On the Predestination of the Saints*, whose refrain is "What do you have that you have not received" (1 Cor. 4:7) and whose purpose is to argue that every aspect of the Christian life, including the initial act of faith, is a gift of grace for which the human person cannot take credit. Noting that his opponents "remain in the dark concerning the question of predestination," Augustine writes that they nonetheless "have the source from which . . . God may reveal" what they do not understand (1.2). As already seen, Augustine believes that God the Father gives Christ as the inner Teacher to illumine the minds of all (8.14). Not all "will to believe," and the will to believe is a gift of God's grace; otherwise, Augustine wonders what sense it would make to pray for the conversion of the unwilling (8.15). However, those who hear and heed the Teacher receive that grace from the Father, and for these the Father "takes away the heart of stone and bestows a heart of flesh" (8.13)—an image of the Holy Spirit's infusion of charity that recalls a basic trope of his *On the Spirit and the Letter*: While once the law was written on stone tablets, now it is written again on the fleshly tablets of the heart by the finger of God, the Holy Spirit (see *spir. et litt.* 14.24; 16.28). The Holy Spirit must move the human heart to accept the faith as true, for the will is too cold or weak or self-centered to do so on its own (see *Jo ev tr.* 48.3).

Many more examples of Augustine referring and entrusting his congregation to the noetic implications of God's gracious charity or love can be brought forth to supplement the example briefly offered above. Commenting on the line "No one has ever seen God" (1 John 4:12), Augustine notes that God "must be sought not with the eye but with the heart," invoking the beatitudes: "Blessed are the clean of heart, for they shall see God" (Matt 5:8). If God is love, he asks in a sermon on 1 John, one might wonder what the face, hands, or feet of love look like; yet they look like hands stretched out to the poor and like the feet that walk to the church—and love has eyes, too, for whoever has charity "sees everything all at once with his understanding"

---

19. WSA III/12 (2009).

(*ep. Jo.* 7:10).[20] Augustine invokes this beatitude regularly in his sermons, consistently discussing the inner eye and the healing it requires, through sacraments and Scripture but always through Christ the Physician, to see God and to do good works in charity (*s.* 88.4-16; *s.* 53.6; *s.* 117.15-17). The employment of this beatitude reaches a crescendo, however, in one of its last uses. Augustine wants to encourage his people to open their hearts to Christ's wisdom, to join in Christ's own act of contemplating God, to "see with the Word's own act of seeing" (*s.* 126.15).[21] This type of vision is only possible, he continues, if one keeps the commandment of the Lord to "love one another" (see John 13:34). And so Augustine recommends that love by which a sort of infused knowledge of God shall come: "So let it be this charity, brothers and sisters, that we gulp from the abundance of the spring, this that we take hold of, on this that we are nourished ... Let charity bring you birth, charity rear you, charity perfect you, charity stiffen you, so that you may see the seeing of the Word." In possessing the fullness of God by charity, one may possess the very wisdom by which one knows God. Augustine acknowledges that this is "something which not everyone would be able to understand," but he expresses his confidence that the Lord will "ensure that some would in fact understand." This conviction is what grounds Augustine's consultations of the faithful as he preaches. In attempting to interpret a particularly awkward line of Psalm 120, Augustine says that he will offer what the Lord suggests to him, but he reminds his congregation that God "dwells in you too and will undoubtedly cause you to recognize the truth of what I say," so that he will not need to prove its truth to those gathered: "you will yourselves acknowledge the truth of it," because the Lord "who dwells in you will himself demonstrate it, insofar as you belong to the number of those who pray ..." (*en. Ps.* 120.7).[22] He goes on to make a request: "I want to put a few questions to your faith," precisely because "you are children of the Church, and have made progress in the Church" (*en. Ps* 120.8).

On the one hand, these invitations by Augustine for the members of his congregation to look for answers to his questions about the faith with the eyes of their hearts could be construed as a sort of *sensus fidei fidelium* that emerges from the corporate practice of the *sensus fidei fidelis*. On the other hand, the question of the precise meaning of *sensus fidei fidelium* arises again; the "mechanics" of the *sensus fidei fidelis* in these examples remain God's illumination of the soul through reason and charity, enabling the pure of heart to "see" God, deepening their knowledge of the beloved through

20. WSA III/14 (2008).
21. WSA III/4 (1992).
22. WSA III/19 (2003).

a rather deliberative process. On the other hand, the classic examples of a *sensus fidei fidelium* attributed to Augustine—the practice of infant baptism, of not rebaptizing heretics, of treating the Book of Wisdom as canonical—appears to function more by a collective witness to received tradition, but certainly not in a manner as self-reflective as this active deepening of the knowledge of God enabled by love.

The Augustinian Model of a *Sensus Fidei Fidelis* and Its Reception (or non-Reception)

The encyclical letter *Lumen Fidei*, released in 2013 by Pope Francis but largely drafted by his predecessor Benedict XVI, echoes these Augustinian themes. Faith, the popes explain, "knows because it is tied to love, because love itself brings enlightenment" (26).[23] Appealing to the twelfth-century theologian William of St.-Thierry, it invokes the image of faith-filled reason and love as two distinct "eyes," which "become one in rising to the contemplation of God" (27). Thus, it quotes Gregory the Great, "'love is itself a kind of knowledge' . . . possessed of its own logic." This insistence that love has noetic implications—that when something is loved, it is implicitly known—again depends upon the Trinitarian insight discovered by Augustine that love proceeds from truth, a bond that contemporary society too easily forgets (25). For *Lumen Fidei*, this bond between truth and love means that, while it is possible to first know and then to love what is known, love leads to a deeper knowledge because love brings about a deeper union with the beloved (27). Love itself becomes a "source of knowledge" about God (28).

The ITC's *Sensus Fidei in the Life of the Church* is divided into a historical overview interested in demonstrating the continuity of the *sensus fidei* with Catholic teaching and a three-part systematic appraisal of the *sensus fidei*. Perhaps regrettably, its appeals to Augustine are limited to the historical overview; Augustine's view of the "mechanics" by which this instinct for the faith functions are not represented in the systematic section of the document, which grounds its explanation of the functioning of the *sensus fidei fidelis* in a reading of the virtue theory of Thomas Aquinas (1225–1274). For Aquinas, every virtue "inclines the person who possesses it towards [a specific] object . . . [and] distances him or her from whatever is contrary to that object" (ITC 52). Thus, the virtue of prudence inclines someone *towards* effective practical reasoning and *away* from rash or foolish action; prudential reasoning becomes a sort of instinctive second nature. If faith

---

23. Francis, *Lumen Fidei*, June 29, 2013, 26. https.//w2.vatican.va/content/francesco/en/encyclicals/documents/papa-francesco_20130629_enciclica-lumen-fidei.html.

is the virtue that inclines the believer towards true belief in God and away from error, then the *habitus* (or virtue) of faith would make it second nature for the believer to incline, instinctively, towards patterns of thought which accord with his or her habituated beliefs of faith: "by the habit of faith the human mind is directed to assent to such things as are becoming to a right faith, and not to assent to others" (ITC 53). Thus, while the primary efficient cause of the *sensus fidei* remains the Holy Spirit insofar as the Spirit infuses the individual believer with the virtue of faith, the immediate efficient cause of the *sensus fidei* is that habit of faith formed within the intellect of thinking correctly about God, moving the believer to think in ways similar to those by which she is accustomed to think. Someone who has read many mystery novels by Agatha Christie might develop something of a sense for how she thinks and might therefore be able to anticipate the identity of a crime's culprit; in a similar way, a Christian, used to thinking as the church thinks, would be able to anticipate Christian teaching on some topic about which she or he is unfamiliar.

This approach of understanding the *sensus fidei* as a movement of the intellect by the believer's habit of faith reflects the generally scholastic belief that faith perfects the intellect rather than the will.[24] As is well-known, the biblical sense of faith is broader than assent to religious information by the intellect, though in the course of the development of medieval Scholasticism the biblical conception of faith becomes divided into the distinct virtues of faith, hope, and charity, with faith perfecting the "faculty" of the intellect and hope and charity perfecting the will—a fact the document recognizes (ITC 8–10).[25] Despite that acknowledgement, the commission's account of the mechanics of the *sensus fidei* restricts itself to the perfection of the intellect by faith, preserving the scholastic progression from the intellectual ascent of faith to the hope which that inspires and then, finally, the selfless charity that those who know and trust God may attain. This account of the *sensus fidei* thus presumes that the intellect moves the will but does not envision that the will should not move the intellect. Interestingly enough, while the document was released a year after *Lumen Fidei*, it never cites that encyclical, nor does it explore its emphasis on the noetic value of love.

---

24. This position is not universal in the Middle Ages; Hugh of St. Victor (1096–1141), for example, followed Augustine in seeing faith as a movement of the intellect and of the will.

25. "The understanding of faith in the New Testament is rooted in the Old Testament, and especially in the faith of Abraham, who trusted completely in God's promises (Gen 15:6; cf. Rom 4:11, 17)" (ITC, 8). Thus the biblical sense of faith "is not simply the conveying of religious information," not simply a matter of intellectual ascent, of *fides quae*, but also a movement of the will, of *fides qua* (see ITC, 9–10).

Caution prevents too quick a judgment as to whether Augustine's belief in the infallibility of the church's consensus is an adequate analogue to the contemporary articulation of the *sensus fidei fidelium*, with its active dimension by which the body of believers senses and applies the faith and that seems deeply connected to Newman's description of the development of doctrine. Little such caution is needed in the case of the *sensus fidei fidelis*: Augustine frequently repeats his conviction that the believer's sense for what is truly part of the faith, what the International Theological Commission called an "instinct" for the truth that "is not primarily the result of rational deliberation, but is rather a form of spontaneous and natural knowledge, a sort of perception" (ITC, 49). For Augustine, this instinctive pre-apprehension of the Beloved results from the will that loves moving the intellect to know what it loves, both because the will must be open to consenting to any act of knowledge and also because, in the Christian life, the loving will moves the intellect towards a sort of pre-apprehension of God rooted in the experience of possessing God through divine charity. To love is to know the Beloved at least implicitly. Although this Augustinian explanation of the mechanics of the *sensus fidei* prioritizes love rather than the intellect, it is a model that does not lapse into fideism; on the contrary, it requires love to be, in principle, so rooted in truth as to be at least implicitly present in every movement of infused charity. Love, in that sense, can be its own way of knowing, in the sense that when one receives divine charity, one receives with that grace at least a sort of pre-apprehension of charity's object.

2

St. Thomas Aquinas and the Foundations of the *Sensus fidelium*

Jonathan M. Kaltenbach

Although St. Thomas Aquinas does not use the phrase *sensus fidelium* in any of his works, he approaches the idea through his use of a particular verse from St. Paul: "The one who is spiritual judges all things" (1 Cor 2:15).[1] In the *Summa theologiae*, which is recognized as his mature work, Thomas relates this verse to the individual believer in the very first question, and this line of thought culminates in a discussion of the spiritual gift of wisdom within his treatment of charity as a human virtue. In the final part of the *Summa*, Thomas also applies the verse to Jesus Christ, who is preeminently the "spiritual human being" and, therefore, "judges all things." After Thomas's two different uses of this verse are examined in detail, both interpretations will be brought together. Through an analysis of the "spiritual sense" of the believer, the ecclesial and sacramental aspects of this idea in the *Summa* will show how this sense depends upon Christ and how it unites all other believers. As a result of these inquiries, the important foundations of the *"sensus fidelium"* that are present in Thomas's thought will be brought to light.

---

1. A comprehensive search for *"sensus fidelium"* in the *Index Thomisticus* yields no results. For the *Index* and the works of Thomas Aquinas cited below, I consulted the Latin texts online at http://www.corpusthomisticum.org. All translations from the Latin are my own, with occasional reference to the English Dominicans' translation of the *Summa theologiae* at http://www.newadvent.org/summa. The verse numbers of Thomas's scriptural citations have been added after consultation of *The Holy Bible*. Revised Standard Version, Catholic Edition (San Francisco: Ignatius, 1966).

The "Spiritual" Believer Who "Judges All Things"

At the beginning of the first part of the *Summa* (question 1, article 6), Thomas asks whether *sacra doctrina*, "sacred teaching or doctrine," is the same as wisdom. He argues in the affirmative, but the third objection of the article forces him to qualify his teaching. If wisdom is an infused gift of the Holy Spirit (which Thomas believes), how can *sacra doctrina* be wisdom when it does not require the grace of God but does demand an extended course of study?[2] In response, Thomas contends that, "because judgment pertains to one who is wise, according to a two-fold manner of judging, wisdom is taken in two ways."[3] The two kinds of judging that he has in mind are judging through virtuous inclination and judging through knowledge. When it comes to divine things, judgment through virtue "pertains to the wisdom which is set down as a gift of the Holy Spirit, according to 1 Cor 2:15: 'The spiritual human being judges all things,' etc."[4] Just as a virtuous person can judge rightly about moral acts without having received any formal education in ethics, Thomas is asserting that the person who has received the infused gift of wisdom can judge rightly concerning *sacra doctrina* even without a formal course of theological studies. On the other hand, judging through knowledge "pertains to this *doctrina*, because it is possessed through study."[5] So in this first question of the *Summa*, Thomas has argued that those who are "spiritual" are able to judge divine things through the Holy Spirit's gift of wisdom in the manner of a virtuous inclination that he distinguishes from the study of knowledge.

It is not surprising, therefore, that 1 Cor 2:15 reappears in a much later question in the *Summa theologiae* (II–II.45), which formally treats this gift of wisdom. For the most part, Thomas classifies the seven gifts of the Holy Spirit with the three theological and four cardinal virtues, and he pairs the gift of wisdom with charity, the greatest of the virtues. In the first article of the question, Thomas writes:

> The one who knows the highest cause simply, which is God, is called wise simply, insofar as, through divine rules (*regulas divinas*), he is able to judge and to order all things. A human being, moreover, obtains judgment of this kind through the Holy

---

2. See Thomas Aquinas, *Summa theologiae* (hereafter *ST*) I.1.6 obj. 3.

3. *ST* I.1.6 ad 3.

4. Ibid.

5. Ibid. Even intemperate or malicious persons, for example, can acquire this second kind of wisdom through the study of sacred teaching. Nevertheless, as Thomas concludes, its principles are still possessed only through revelation ("*ex revelatione*") and not through human reason.

Spirit, according to 1 Cor. 2:15: "The one who is spiritual judges all things;" because, as it is said in the same place (2:10), "The Spirit searches all things, even the deep things of God." Whence it is manifest that wisdom is a gift of the Holy Spirit.[6]

Thomas reiterates that right judgment in accordance with "divine rules" proceeds from the gift of wisdom, which those who are spiritual receive from the Holy Spirit. In the response to the second objection, Thomas also reminds us that this wisdom is not acquired through human study. He explains, "For faith assents to divine truth itself, but judgment which is according to divine truth pertains to the gift of wisdom. And, therefore, the gift of wisdom presupposes faith, because each one judges well the things which he knows, as it is said in the first book of the *Ethics*."[7] In this way, just as the virtue of charity itself presupposes faith, the gift of the Holy Spirit that Thomas joins to it depends on faith as well.

Up to this point, Thomas's use of 1 Cor 2:15 in the *Summa* refers to the individual believer who has received the infused gift of wisdom from the Holy Spirit and, therefore, is able to judge rightly. Briefly consulting Thomas's *Commentary on the First Epistle to the Corinthians* at this juncture, one can see that he discusses the verse in similar terms in this work as well. As a representative passage of his longer commentary on this verse, Thomas argues that "a human being who has an enlightened intellect and an ordered affection through the Holy Spirit possesses right judgment concerning those things which pertain to salvation."[8] Although he does not discuss the gift of wisdom in this passage, Thomas does mention the work of the Holy Spirit. In this context, furthermore, the possession of an "enlightened intellect" could certainly refer to the gift of wisdom, just as an "ordered affection" could refer to the virtue of charity which is connected to wisdom.

On the other hand, Thomas's relation of this human judgment to "those things which pertain to salvation" could be seen as a qualification of Paul's statement that those who are spiritual judge "all things." In the very first question of the *Summa*, however, Thomas did refer the two kinds of wisdom to "judging divine things."[9] In the later question on the gift of wisdom, furthermore, he noted that whoever knows God through this wisdom "is able to judge and to order all things."[10] If one is capable of judging divine

---

6. *ST* II-II.45.1c.

7. *ST* II-II.45.1 ad 2. The reference is to Aristotle's *Nicomachean Ethics*.

8. Thomas Aquinas, *Commentary on the First Epistle to the Corinthians*, chapter 2, lecture 3.

9. *ST* I.1.6 ad 3.

10. *ST* II-II.45.1c.

things, therefore, it would seem that one is capable of judging all things. Because Thomas relates 1 Cor 2:15 to all of these texts, he underscores that the ability to judge all things follows from the knowledge of divine things obtained through the gift of wisdom. As a consequence, the language of "things which pertain to salvation" or "divine things" rather than "all things" should not be understood as a qualification of Paul's statement but as Thomas's explanation of how the judgment of all things is possible for the individual believer.

Even if this power of judging on the part of the spiritual does extend to all things, what about this power itself? For Thomas, all of the virtues (including faith and charity) and all of the gifts of the Holy Spirit (including the gift of wisdom) are infused into those who receive the gift of God's grace.[11] The individual believer, therefore, needs habitual grace in order to exercise this kind of judgment. The necessity of grace, moreover, meshes nicely with Thomas's interpretation of the verse because the possession of grace can serve as a compact definition of what it means to be "spiritual" for the individual believer. Which Christian, however, is sufficiently full of grace as to have no doubts about the rectitude of his judgment? What if faithful Christians disagree concerning the judgment of divine things? Fortunately, there is someone to whom 1 Cor 2:15 can be applied absolutely, without reservation.

Christ as "Spiritual" Judge of "All Things"

After discussing the wisdom of the spiritual believer but also her uncertain possession of this wisdom for the purposes of judgment, how could 1 Cor 2:15 relate to Jesus Christ? If one reflects upon the status of Christ as the ultimate judge of the living and the dead, the applicability of the verse to Christ himself becomes apparent. For who could be more spiritual than the Word of God in his human nature? It makes eminent sense, furthermore, that his power of judging follows from the Incarnation and his perfect fullness of grace.[12]

In these and similar ways, one can see how this verse can be applied to Christ above all other creatures. Bolstering these claims, Thomas actually cites this verse in his discussion of Christ's judiciary power in the third part

---

11. See *ST* I–II.110.3 on grace and the virtues; see *ST* I–II.68.1 on the virtues and gifts.

12. At the beginning of the third part of the *Summa theologiae*, Thomas treats the union of the divine and human natures in Christ (question 2) and his fullness of grace (question 7) among many other topics.

of the *Summa theologiae* (question 59). This question stands at the end of Thomas's teaching on Jesus and immediately prior to his discussion of the sacraments, which takes up the remainder of his unfinished *Summa*. After acknowledging in the first article that such power of judging belongs to God principally and is attributed to the Son of God as the Truth and Wisdom of the Father, Thomas asserts that Christ also possesses judiciary power as a human being because he is the head of the church through grace. Thomas explains:

> Although the primary authority of judging remains with God, nevertheless, judiciary power is committed to human beings by God with respect to those who are subject to their jurisdiction . . . It was said above, moreover, that Christ, even in his human nature, is the head of the whole church (*caput totius Ecclesiae*) and that God has put (*subiecit*) all things under his feet. Whence it also pertains to him, even according to his human nature, to have judiciary power.[13]

By arguing that Christ's power of judging is dependent on his unique role as the "head of the whole church," Thomas is anchoring this power in the grace and holiness of Christ, which he discussed earlier in the third part of the *Summa*. In question 8, Thomas holds that the fullness of habitual grace that sanctifies the human soul of Christ is the same grace that enables Christ to be the head of the church and communicate grace to others.[14] This same headship, Thomas is now teaching, affords Christ the power of judging (and judging rightly) all things.

How do we know that Christ's judgments are right and just? As we have seen in the discussion of the gift of wisdom, truth is connected to holiness. Thomas explains again:

> Judgment pertains to truth as to a rule of judgment, but it pertains to a human being who is steeped (*imbutus*) in truth because he is, in some way, one with truth itself, as a kind of law and a kind of living justice (*iustitia animata*). Whence Augustine also introduced in the same place that which is said in 1 Cor. 2:15: "The one who is spiritual judges all things." The soul of Christ, moreover, before all other creatures, was more united to truth and more filled with it, according to Jn. 1:14: "We saw him, full of grace and truth." And according to this, it maximally pertains to the soul of Christ to judge all things.[15]

13. *ST* III.59.2c.
14. See *ST* III.8.5.
15. *ST* III.59.2 ad 1.

Because Christ as a human being, therefore, is perfectly holy and perfectly united to truth (above all to the Son of God who is Truth), he embodies this "living justice" in himself, and for this reason, he can always judge rightly. In this way, Thomas's teaching in this article has served as an extended commentary on 1 Cor. 2:15 and how it not only applies to Christ himself but does so "maximally."

In fact, Thomas makes similar use of this verse again in two other articles later on in the same question. Reiterating the same idea in the fourth article, he writes, "If 'the one who is spiritual judges all things,' as it is said in 1 Cor. 2:15, insofar as one's mind adheres to the Word of God, much more does the soul of Christ, which is full of the truth of the Word of God, hold judgment over all things."[16] The preeminence of Christ over other spiritual human beings can be more fully grasped by Thomas's treatment of the remainder of the verse. For in 1 Cor 2:15, Paul goes on to claim that the one who is spiritual "is judged by no one." Now, this obviously cannot hold in the same way if Christ truly "judges all things." In the sixth article, therefore, as he discusses how Christ even judges the angels, Thomas adopts Augustine's solution to this problem. He argues that, "as Augustine says in *On True Religion*, although the one who is spiritual judges all things, nevertheless, that one is judged by truth itself. And, therefore, although angels judge because they are spiritual, nevertheless, they are judged by Christ insofar as he is Truth."[17] Thus, Thomas again reminds us that truth is the rule of judgment and that all judgment proceeds from God through Christ, who fully embodies living justice.

So how does the judgment of the individual believer and the judgment of Christ more directly relate to the concept of the *sensus fidelium*? The ecclesial and sacramental aspects of spiritual judgment must now be explored in relation to the analysis of 1 Cor 2:15, and this investigation will reveal how the idea of the *sensus fidelium* can be approached in the *Summa*.

"Spiritual Sense" through Incorporation into Christ at Baptism

After charting Thomas's use of 1 Cor 2:15 in relation to the individual believer and especially in relation to Christ, it is probably unsurprising that his references to a "spiritual sense" (*sensus spiritualis*) in the *Summa* that might be akin to the *sensus fidelium* are found in two major places: his discussion of Christ as head of the church (question 8) and his description of the effects

16. ST III.59.4c
17. ST III.59.6 ad 2.

of baptism (question 69).[18] The first provides only a tangential reference, but the context of the question is certainly important. It has been seen how Thomas argues that Christ's power of judging proceeds from his fullness of grace and truth by which he is also head of the church and has jurisdiction over all creatures. In this earlier question, Thomas discusses the grace of Christ as head insofar as it can be poured out on others, who then become members of Christ's mystical body and are united to him through faith and charity. An objection in the second article describes it this way: "Christ is called the head of the church insofar as he pours (*influit*) a spiritual sense and a motion of grace into the church."[19] Thomas does not always accept the premises of the various objections that he makes, but in this case, his response affirms a "spiritual sense of grace" that pertains primarily to the soul but also to the body as the instrument of the soul.[20] Beyond broadly situating this "spiritual sense" in an ecclesial context, however, this passage does not really help one to grasp what Thomas means by this term.

Nevertheless, Thomas returns to the concept of "spiritual sense" in his treatment of the effects of baptism and provides us with a much fuller account that brings together many of the other themes that have been highlighted so far. After noting that properly disposed human beings who accept the sacrament of baptism receive grace and the virtues along with forgiveness of all sin and punishment, Thomas inquires in the fifth article about the "effects of the virtues which are conferred through baptism."[21] The objections highlight three such effects: incorporation into Christ, illumination, and fruitfulness (*incorporatio, illuminatio, fecundatio*).[22]

Thomas begins the *corpus* of the article by considering incorporation into Christ. He writes, "Through baptism, one is regenerated into spiritual life, which is proper to the faithful (*fidelium*) of Christ, just as the Apostle says (Gal. 2:20): 'Although I live now in the flesh, I live in faith of the Son of God.' There is not life, however, except in members united to a head, from which they receive sense and motion."[23] This passage immediately recalls the short discussion of question 8 not only for its allusion to Christ's headship but also for the juxtaposition of "sense" and "motion" in relation to it. Thomas continues, "And, therefore, it is necessary that, through baptism,

18. Thomas usually employs the term "spiritual sense" (as opposed to a literal sense) in discussions of the different senses of Scripture. See *ST* I.1.10.

19. *ST* III.8.2 obj. 1.

20. *ST* III.8.2 ad 1.

21. *ST* III.69 prol.

22. See *ST* III.69.5 obj. 1–3.

23. *ST* III.69.5c.

one is incorporated into Christ as a member of him."[24] This is also a further specification of Thomas's earlier teaching that the members of Christ's mystical body are most closely joined to him in this life through faith and charity. In this later question, then, Thomas shows how this incorporation is closely related to the sacrament of baptism.

The other effects that Thomas discusses here, illumination and fruitfulness, flow from this incorporation into Christ's body. Thomas explains:

> Just as sense and motion, moreover, are diverted to members by a natural head, thus, a spiritual sense, which consists in the knowledge of truth, and a spiritual motion, which is through the inspiration of grace, are diverted to his members by a spiritual head, which is Christ. Whence in Jn. 1:14, 16 it is said, "We saw him, full of grace and truth, and of his fullness we have all received." And, therefore, it follows that the baptized are illuminated by Christ concerning the knowledge of truth and are made fruitful by him in the fruitfulness of good works through the infusion of grace.[25]

In this passage, he describes in much greater detail that sense and motion that Christ's members receive from him as the head of the mystical body. "Spiritual sense," Thomas teaches, has to do with knowledge of the truth by which Christ's members are illuminated, while fruitfulness comes from the spiritual motion of grace. Thomas also cites John 1:14 in this regard to bring grace and truth even more closely together by anchoring them in Christ. In fact, Thomas uses this same verse to substantiate Christ's judiciary power in the earlier question discussed above. In this article, moreover, he goes on to cite John 1:16 as well: "And of his fullness we have all received." Would Thomas suggest, therefore, that those who are joined to Christ can participate in his judiciary power just as they can participate in his grace and truth?

An intriguing connection can be made here between this "spiritual sense" and the concept of right judgment. The spiritual sense that Thomas treats of here consists in true knowledge and the illumination of the baptized believer, and it can be related to judgment because truth is the rule of judgment and enables one to judge rightly. Thomas has already explained how Christ receives jurisdiction over all things as head of the church and is the truly spiritual one who judges rightly from his fullness of truth. Likewise, those who have been incorporated into his mystical body (especially

---

24. Ibid.
25. Ibid.

through baptism) can become spiritual through participation in him and judge rightly from the spiritual sense of truth that they receive from him.

After all that has been discussed, a final synthesis can be approached by recalling Thomas's teaching on the gift of wisdom. Thomas does not explicitly mention this gift in relation to the judgment of Christ or to the spiritual sense that the faithful receive from him, but there is certainly an implicit relationship between these concepts.[26] Thomas does teach that the perfect fullness of Christ's grace meant that he also fully possessed the gifts of the Holy Spirit (which includes the gift of wisdom).[27] If Christ judges rightly from his fullness of truth, it can also be said, therefore, that he judges rightly from the fullness of the gift of wisdom that he possesses. As a result, the spiritual sense that the faithful receive as members of Christ would be the gift of wisdom itself. In other words, the faithful would receive this gift of the Holy Spirit as a participation of Christ's fullness of wisdom by which he (and, therefore, all other spiritual believers) can judge all things.

Thomas's use of 1 Cor 2:15 has revealed how he approaches the *sensus fidelium* in his work without ever actually using the term. His first applications of the verse in the *Summa theologiae* as well as his treatment in the *Commentary on the First Epistle to the Corinthians* relate it to the gift of wisdom, which is given to the individual believer by the Holy Spirit, and the believer's subsequent capacity for judging divine things. Thomas is able to provide a fuller account of such judgment, however, by applying the verse preeminently to Jesus Christ, who is "maximally" judge of all things on account of his perfect possession of grace and truth and his consequent jurisdiction over the whole church as head of the mystical body. As a result, the "spiritual sense" that flows from Christ the head and illuminates his members (principally as an effect of baptism) can be correctly viewed as a rule of judgment that is the gift of wisdom itself. In order to be faithful to Thomas's writings, therefore, a teaching on the *sensus fidelium* would have to include reference not only to the grace and gifts of the Holy Spirit but also to Christ as head and judge of all, not only to a majority of the present faithful but to the whole mystical body of the living and the dead, and to the importance of baptism by which the faithful are sacramentally incorporated into Christ as his members. Although he makes no direct reference to the *sensus fidelium*, Thomas has provided us with its sure foundations nonetheless.

---

26. Thomas often leaves various connections implicit, possibly because he expects the reader to have covered all (!) of the preceding questions of the *Summa theologiae*.

27. See *ST* III.7.5.

3

Sensuous History

The Medieval Feast of Corpus Christi as an Expression of the Sensus Fidelium

THOMAS RYAN

Introduction

IN A 2007 ARTICLE in the *Journal of Social History*, Mark Smith writes, "It is a good moment to be a sensory historian. Sensory history—also referred to as a history of the senses, sensate history, and sensuous history—is booming among historians."[1] This paper represents a contribution to such a history as it addresses a particular instance of another sense, the *sensus fidelium*, whose importance has been affirmed by the International Theological Commission's 2014 document *Sensus Fidei in the Life of the Church*.[2] In particular, it explores the intersection of the study of materiality, a medieval instance of the *sensus fidelium* in the eucharistic Feast of Corpus Christi, and the paradox that the bodily senses other than taste and touch can be a means of encounter with the divine. In doing so, it gestures toward implications for spirituality and theology today.

---

1. Mark M. Smith, "Producing Sense, Consuming Sense, Making Sense: Perils and Prospects for Sensory History." *Journal of Social History* 40 (2007) 841.

2. The International Theological Commission's (abbreviated subsequently as ITC) *The Sensus Fidei in the Life of the Church* relates the *sensus fidei* to physical senses (54) and speaks of it as a kind of sixth sense (52–53).

Preliminaries

"*Sensus Fidei* in the Life of the Church" provides foundational resources for this project, in the first place by distinguishing between different permutations of this term. *Sensus fidei fidelis* (or just *sensus fidei*) refers "to the personal aptitude of the believer to make an accurate discernment in matters of faith, and *sensus fidei fidelium* [or simply *sensus fidelium*] . . . to the Church's own instinct of faith."[3] It also touches on the place of the *sensus fidelium* in history, the topic this essay will explore. With assistance primarily from Yves Congar and John Henry Newman, it reviews the role of the *sensus fidelium* in the development of doctrine from the patristic period to the present.[4] As evidence for the *sensus fidelium* in action, it cites Newman on ninth-century eucharistic controversies and the role the faithful played in supporting the more physical perspective on the Eucharist advanced by Paschasius Radbertus.[5]

In identifying history as a resource for the *sensus fidelium*, the ITC suggests that it has a retrospective character in that "believers rely on the Scriptures and on the continuing apostolic Tradition in their life of faith and in the exercise of the *sensus fidei*."[6] Yet, it is also prospective. It "gives an intuition as to the right way forward amid the uncertainties and ambiguities of history, and a capacity to listen discerningly to what human culture and the progress of the sciences are saying."[7] The ITC also presents an irenic view of the topic. It urges "patience and respect" among the "faithful at large, pastors and theologians" since it "can take a long time before this process of discernment comes to a conclusion."[8] It anticipates disagreement and uses the language of musical taste to articulate it. The faithful who detect disharmony between preaching, for example, and "authentic Christian faith . . . react as a music lover does to false notes in the performance of a piece of music. In such cases, believers interiorly resist the teachings or practices concerned and do not accept them or participate in them."[9] The history of the development of doctrine by means of the *sensus fidelium* is messier, as we will see. It is also retrospective in another way. Only in retrospect does

---

3. Ibid., 3. In keeping with the CTSA theme, I will use *sensus fidelium* as the generic term that includes the laity's aptitude to "make an accurate discernment in matters of faith."

4. Ibid., 22–46.

5. Ibid., 27, more on this below.

6. Ibid., 68.

7. Ibid., 70.

8. Ibid., 71.

9. Ibid., 62.

it become clear that a development in fact was representative of the *sensus fidelium* that participates in the faith of the church that does not err. At the time, in the moment, often in a conflictual moment, it is not always clear that a development represents the *sensus fidelium*.

Similarly, the ITC document expresses aims similar to some of the most recent trends in the study of history and its attempt to chronicle the ordinary and everyday. It mentions popular religiosity, that is, popular attempts to bridge the divide between divine and created, popular attempts at encounter with the divine through objects and practices. "As a principle or instinct and as a rich abundance of Christian practice, especially in the form of cultic activities, e.g. devotions, pilgrimages and processions, popular religiosity springs from and makes manifest the *sensus fidei*, and is to be respected and fostered."[10]

Before turning to a medieval instance of the *sensus fidelium* at work, it is worthwhile looking at Bernard Cooke's *The Distancing of God*. It offers effective language for making sense of the last two millennia of church history, which is, in many ways, the story of the increasing distance between laity and clergy and between laity and their access to God. Cooke locates the ideal in the church's first years. The "earliest Christian generation (or perhaps two) had a pervading sense of the immanence of a personal God. Just as Jesus had been in their midst as one of them and still dwelt with them in the mysterious presence of his risen existence, so the God who was his *Abba* was not off in some distant 'heaven.' Instead, this God lived with them in the communication of the Word and the Spirit."[11] For Cooke, the story of the next two millennia is not one of ceaseless distancing, but almost. Faith becomes less a life commitment and more a reflection on the divine, less ministry and more contemplation, less a way of life and more a religion.[12] Liturgy "became a 'text' to be interpreted instead of a mystery to be experienced."[13] The "eucharistic presence of Christ was clearly shifting from the community as the body of Christ to the consecrated elements."[14] In a summary piece, Cooke identifies three main modes of distancing.

> *Institutional mediation* is being crystallized in both imperial and ecclesiastical hierarchies; it is just a question of which one can lay more ultimate claim to being "vicar of Christ." The liturgy

10. Ibid., 108.

11. Bernard J. Cooke, *The Distancing of God: The Ambiguity of Symbol in History and Theology* (Minneapolis: Fortress, 1990), 10.

12. Ibid., 42, 56.

13. Ibid., 127.

14. Ibid., 141.

and everything surrounding it, as the church building, is firmly situated in a realm of *ritual sacrality*, carefully separated from the profane space and things of daily life; sacred personnel enjoy a higher level of sacred existence.... And the philosophical notion of participation has been thoroughly accepted as the way of understanding relationship to God. *Theosis* rather than personal relatedness is the basic effect of sacramental rituals. Terms like "filiation" are still used, but interpreted in terms of "participation in the divine nature."[15]

For Cooke, despite "certain countercurrents," laity were distanced from God institutionally, liturgically, and theologically.[16]

The Eucharist before the Feast of Corpus Christi

As the millennium approached and beyond, the laity did indeed grow increasingly distant from the ordained. One cause was linguistic.[17] Latin remained the church's official language, which the laity were less and less likely to speak. Its use served several ecclesiastical purposes, including, earlier on, associating Christianity in outlying areas with major cities like Rome and Milan and their elite while distancing itself from non-Latin-speaking and sometimes heterodox Christians elsewhere in the empire. Later, it directed the attention of a much more extensive church back to Rome.[18] By the millennium, other, related linguistic innovations—including the priests' uttering of private and inaudible prayers—served to distance the laity liturgically.[19]

15. Ibid. 108. Cooke's concern with *theosis* in contrast to filiation is that it is a kind of participation in the divine life worked from within the human by the action of the Incarnate Word apart from human instrumentality. It minimizes the role of community, the human Jesus, and people's relationship with him.

16. Ibid., 122.

17. G.J.C. Snoek, *Medieval Piety From Relics to the Eucharist: A Process of Mutual Interaction* (Leiden: Brill, 1995) 30. For literature on the distancing of the laity from the Eucharist in general, see the extensive notes in chapter 2, "The Process of Independence of the Eucharist." This chapter is also found in Thomas J. Fisch, ed., *Primary Readings on the Eucharist* (Collegeville: Liturgical, 2004). See also Nathan Mitchell, *Cult and Controversy: The Worship of the Eucharist Outside of Mass* (New York: Pueblo, 1982), 66–198.

18. Maura Lafferty, "Translating Faith from Greek to Latin: Romanitas and Christianitas in Late Fourth-Century Rome and Milan," Journal of Early Christian Studies 11 (2003) 21–62.

19. Snoek, *Medieval Piety*, 44.

An associated development was attention to the sacredness of the priestly body and, in particular, to the priests' hands, which differed dramatically in their power from other hands. For example, Pope Urban II was reputed to have said that the "priests' hands had the power 'to create the Creator of all things and offer him to God for the salvation and healing of the world.'"[20] Women, in particular, were increasingly distanced from the ordained, and this apart from their traditional association with Eve as temptress.[21] Reforms associated with the eleventh-century Pope Gregory VII made clerical marriage ever more difficult. To justify the blanket prohibition of such marriage, the extreme rhetoric of writers like Peter Damian elevated celibate priesthood at the expense of women. Damian, for example, compared clergy wives to prostitutes and worse.[22] Women religious were not unaffected. At the end of the thirteenth century, Pope Boniface VIII published his decretal *Periculoso* that demanded "strict enclosure of all nuns of every of order throughout Christendom."[23] Though its enforcement would be inconsistent, it held out as the ideal that all women religious, unlike their male counterparts, should remain cloistered.[24]

Medieval theological and liturgical uses of the Bible represented a source of distancing with regard to the Eucharist. Paul in 1 Corinthians 11 levels warnings against those who approach the Lord's Supper unworthily;

---

20. Ibid., 39.

21. The third-century Tertullian in *The Apparel of Women* writes of women, "You are the one who opened the door to the Devil, you are the one who first plucked the fruit from the forbidden tree, you are the first who deserted the divine law, you are the one who persuaded him whom the Devil was not strong enough to attack." See Tertullian, *The Apparel of Women*, trans., Edwin A. Quain, in *Disciplinary, Moral and Ascetical Works*, Fathers of the Church 40 (New York: Fathers of the Church, 1959).

22. Having criticized priests for taking wives, Peter Damian in Letter 112 turns to women. "And now, let me speak to you, you charmers of clerics, tasty tidbits of the devil, expulsion from paradise, venom of the mind, . . . source of sinning, and occasion of damnation. I am talking to you, female branch of the ancient enemy. . . . How dare you not be horrified at touching the hands of priests that were anointed with holy oil and chrism" (276, 278). See Dyan Elliott, *Fallen Bodies: Pollution, Sexuality, and Demonology in the Middle Ages* (Philadelphia: University of Pennsylvania Press, 1999), 81–106.

23. Elizabeth Makowski, *Canon Law and Cloistered Women: Periculoso and Its Commentators, 1298–1545* (Washington, DC: Catholic University of America Press, 1997), 11.

24. Pope Boniface VIII in *Periculoso* (in Makowski, *Canon Law*, 135) addressed "the dangerous and abominable situation of certain nuns, who, casting off the reins of respectability and impudently abandoning nunnish modesty and the natural bashfulness of their sex, sometimes rove outside of their monasteries. . . [He did so in order that nuns may] be able to serve God more freely, wholly separated from the public and worldly gaze and, occasions for lasciviousness having been removed, may most diligently safeguard their hearts and bodies in complete chastity."

doing so has dire consequences. He (from the Douay Rheims translation of the Vulgate) warns that those eating and drinking the eucharistic bread and wine unworthily "are guilty of the body and blood of the Lord" (11:27). Those eating and drinking without discerning the Lord's body, eat and drink judgment on themselves (11:29). Therefore, "there are many infirm and weak among you: and many sleep" (11:30). In general, medieval commentators take for granted the danger of unworthy reception and elaborate the different ways that one can receive unworthily. For example, ninth-century Haimo of Auxerre exemplifies medieval approaches when he distinguishes three different ways of receiving unworthily: not celebrating the Eucharist correctly, not believing in a difference between it and other food, and consuming it in great sin. All of these are sinful, in some cases, mortally. Haimo, however, goes further and underscores the danger of sacramental communion. "We ought to approach that terrible sacrament with fear and trembling."[25] While few go as far as Haimo, medieval commentators regularly draw out the hazards of unworthy reception.[26]

Similarly, lectionary choices would come to accentuate Paul's warnings. As a point of comparison, the second reading currently for the evening Holy Thursday mass as well as for the Corpus Christi mass (in Cycle C) is 1 Corinthians 11:23–26, the institution of the Eucharist. It begins with Paul indicating that he is handing on what he has received and concludes with "For as often as you eat this bread and drink the cup, you proclaim the death of the Lord until he comes." Though from a slightly later period than the one under consideration for this essay, it is telling that the *Missale Romanum*, issued at the direction of Pope Pius V in 1570, heightens liturgically the danger of unworthy reception. It sets as the second reading on Holy Thursday 1 Corinthians 11:18–32, a lengthy excerpt in which Paul narrates troubles in the church in Corinth, the institution of the Eucharist, and warnings about the mortal consequences of unworthy reception. One of the readings in the *Missale Romanum* for the Feast of Corpus Christi is 1 Corinthians 11:23–29, which includes the institution and some of Paul's warnings.[27]

---

25. Haimo of Auxerre, *Expositio in* Epistolis, 574B. The Latin for the quote is "Cum timore et tremore debemus accedere ad illud sacramentum terribile."

26. According to Fitzmyer, *First Corinthians*, 446, earlier manuscripts of 1 Corinthians include "unworthily" only in verse 27; later manuscripts, on which medieval translations were based, add this word to verse 29 and so sharpen the emphasis on unworthiness. See Joseph A. Fitzmyer, *First Corinthians: A New Translation with Introduction and Commentary*, Anchor Yale Bible (New Haven: Yale University Press, 2008).

27. See http://catholic-resources.org/Lectionary/Roman_Missal.htm for a list of readings from the *Missale Romanum*.

Developments in theologies of the Eucharist also played a role. Scholars have identified different emphases—some more spiritual or mystical and some more physical or realist—from the early middle ages on.[28] The more physical accounts—associated with the ninth-century Paschasius Radbertus and increasingly in the ascendancy from the turn of the millennium onward—emphasized the presence of Christ's very nature in the eucharistic elements. Only such a strong presence could account for the Eucharist's salvific effects.[29] In the ongoing and often bitter debate, the eleventh-century Berengar of Tours disagreed but eventually capitulated and was forced to utter an oath that held "the bread and wine . . . are after consecration . . . the true body and blood of our Lord Jesus Christ, and they are physically taken up and broken by the hands of the priest and crushed by the teeth of the faithful, not only sacramentally but in truth." This oath found its way into canon law collections and so continued to influence later generations with its extreme account of eucharistic presence. Berengar quickly disavowed this oath but was later forced to utter more moderate words.[30]

The language of transubstantiation, which describes the change from bread and wine to Body and Blood, also contributed to the distancing of the laity from the Eucharist. First used in the twelfth century, it was not established as the terminology characterizing eucharistic change until the Fourth Lateran Council under Pope Innocent III in 1215.[31] Even then, this term was not definitive in the sense that the council did not define exactly what it meant. Theologians at the time "fell roughly into three camps in regard to the eucharistic change. Some believed that bread and wine remained present along with the Body and Blood of the Lord; others felt that the sub-

28. Gary Macy, *The Theologies of the Eucharist in the Early Scholastic Period: A Study of the Salvific Function of the Sacrament According to the Theologians c. 1080–c. 1220* (Oxford: Clarendon, 1984) 5. See de Lubac's *Corpus Mysticum* for a careful study of the transition from more spiritual to more physical accounts of Christ's presence in the Eucharist. Coinciding with this development was a transition away from more communal theologies of church and Eucharist. There "is a noticeable tendency in the [early] tradition to preserve *corpus* [body] for designating the Church. Was there not another, equally Scriptural word: *caro* [flesh] for the Eucharist?" (42). Later medieval theologians no longer linked "body of Christ," in the first instance, with the church but associated this term more closely with the Eucharist, which individuals received or viewed. Henri de Lubac, *Corpus Mysticum: The Eucharist and the Church in the Middle Ages*, trans., Gemma Simmonds (Notre Dame: University of Notre Dame Press, 2006).

29. Macy, *The Theologies*, 27–28.

30. Ibid., 36–37.

31. Miri Rubin, *Corpus Christi: The Eucharist in Late Medieval Culture* (Cambridge: Cambridge University Press, 1991), 24; Gary Macy, "The 'Dogma of Transubstantiation.'" In *Treasures from the Storeroom: Medieval Religion and the Eucharist* (Collegeville: Liturgical, 1999), 81.

stance of the bread and wine were annihilated, the substance of the Body and Blood alone remaining. Finally a third group argued that the substance of bread and wine was changed into the substance of the Body and Blood at the words of consecration."[32] The third option is associated with Thomas Aquinas and what most people today understand by the term, but it was not the only orthodox option in the thirteenth through sixteenth centuries. By not defining transubstantiation, Lateran IV kept open the question of the manner of Christ's presence in the sacrament, and this helped to heighten awareness of that presence, which as Paul suggests, could be dangerous to the unworthy recipient.

In sum, Latin distanced linguistically, and chrismated hands did so physically. Women especially experienced this distancing. Paul's threats to unworthy recipients were amplified by increasingly physical and complex theologies of eucharistic presence. Alongside these, fasting and sexual abstinence grew in importance as prerequisites for worthy reception. Later medieval church architecture distanced congregations from altar and Eucharist by means of choir and screen.[33] And so, laity began to communicate less frequently and only under one species, the cup being gradually withdrawn from them. When they did communicate, they began to do so outside of mass and in the mouth, not in the hand.[34] For all these reasons, the laity were growing increasingly distant from the Eucharist in terms of taste and touch.

Yet, "distancing" on its own does not capture the complexity of the laity's relationship to the Eucharist. Laity were developing other senses for the encounter with Jesus. While physical communion represented a danger mostly to be avoided, ocular communion, gazing upon Jesus in the Eucharist, provided many of the benefits without the dangers.[35] Liturgical innovations assisted the laity in this visual encounter. The elevation of the eucharistic host took place after its consecration; squints or openings in screens and walls gave congregants visual access to the Eucharist; bells

32. Macy, "The 'Dogma,'" 82–83.

33. Eamon Duffy, *Stripping of the Altars: Traditional Religion in England, 1400–1580*. 2nd ed. (New Haven: Yale University Press, 2005), 110–113.

34. Jef Lamberts, "Liturgie et spiritualité de l'eucharistie au XIIIe siècle." In *Fête-Dieu (1246–1996): 1. Actes du colloque de Liège, 12–14 Septembre 1996*, ed., André Haquin (Louvain-la-Neuve: Institut d'études médiévales de l'Université catholique de Louvain, 1999), 84–90.

35. Charles Caspers, "The Western Church during the Late Middle Ages: *Augenkommunion* or Popular Mysticism." In *Bread of Heaven: Customs and Practices Surrounding Holy Communion, Essays in the History of Liturgy and Culture*, eds., Charles Caspers, Gerard Lukken, Gerard and Rouwhorst, Kampen (The Netherlands: Kok Pharos, 1995), 83–97.

called and candles permitted the congregation to see, if not consume the Eucharist. In larger churches, masses were celebrated on side altars that were not separated architecturally from the congregation so that it could see the entire liturgy, including the elevation.[36]

The Feast of Corpus Christi

Against this background, it is worth revisiting the familiar story of the development of the Feast of Corpus Christi, which represents what Cooke would call a notable "countercurrent" to the distancing of God and an instance of the *sensus fidelium* at work in the middle ages.[37] The first centuries of the new millennium in Liege in present-day Belgium saw an increase in economic activity, changing political fortunes, a diversity of urban populations, and a range of perspectives on the Eucharist.[38] Already in the twelfth century, Rupert of Deutz and Alger of Liege each penned responses to Berengar.[39] Juliana of Cornillon a thirteenth-century laywoman from Liege and frequent communicant was intensely private "and by no means the most famous [of medieval holy women]. Yet it is she who arguably had the most profound and lasting influence on the church, for her name is inseparably linked with the feast she devoted her life to promoting: the 'Feast of the Sacrament' or Corpus Christi, as it was later dubbed."[40] Her promotion of the feast was prompted by her commitment to the Eucharist, including frequent reception if possible.[41] She was an early witness to the reservation of the Eucharist in tabernacles, a practice that spread more widely with the establishment of transubstantiation by Lateran IV.[42] She also had persistent visions of the moon with a segment missing. She took the moon to symbolize the church,

36. Duffy, *Stripping of the Altars*, 96–98.

37. For "countercurrent," see Cooke, *The Distancing of God*, 122.

38. Barbara R. Walters et al., *The Feast of Corpus Christi* (University Park: Penn State Press, 2006),

36–43. For a shorter account of the development of the feast, see Miri Rubin, "Corpus Christi: Inventing a Feast." *History Today* 40 (July 1990) 15–21.

39. Macy, *The Theologies*, 66–67.

40. Barbara Newman, "Introduction," in *Living Saints of the Thirteenth Century: The Lives of Yvette, Anchoress of Huy; Juliana of Cornillon, author of the Corpus Christi Feast; and Margaret the Lame, Anchoress of Magdeburg*, ed., Anneke B. Mulder-Bakker (Turnhout: Brepols, 2011), 145.

41. Newman, "The Life of Juliana of Cornillon," in *Living Saints of the Thirteenth Century: The Lives of Yvette, Anchoress of Huy; Juliana of Cornillon, author of the Corpus Christi Feast; and Margaret the Lame, Anchoress of Magdeburg*, ed., Anneke B. Mulder-Bakker (Turnhout: Brepols, 2011), 195

42. Ibid., 210 and Newman, "Introduction," 168.

a not uncommon symbol even today.[43] Over time, she discerned that this segment represented an absence in the church, namely the absence of a feast devoted to the Eucharist. Reactions to her proposal included ridicule. The liturgical calendar already included a mass, on Holy Thursday, dedicated to the Eucharist's institution, and doesn't mass daily celebrate the Eucharist?[44]

The feast eventually earned the support of Bishop Robert of Liege and members of the young Order of Preachers, in particular, the Dominican Cardinal Hugh of St. Cher. It was instituted locally in 1246 on the Thursday following Trinity Sunday (which is itself preceded by Ascension Thursday and Pentecost Sunday) and served to counter dualist critiques of materiality in general and of sacraments in particular.[45] To counter the growing distance between the laity and the Eucharist, the proponents of this feast framed it and the Eucharist in joyful terms and encouraged the laity to receive communion on that day.[46] Indeed, Julian bemoaned the loss she experienced after Ascension Thursday observances; she felt "heavy sadness, as if she had been left a lonely orphan."[47] The Viennese visionary Agnes Blannbekin, Julian's near contemporary, "perceived Eastertide as the saddest time of the year, since it marked the beginning of Christ's absence."[48]

---

43. Newman, "The Life of Juliana of Cornillon," 234. Ambrose of Milan, for example, compared the church to the moon in his *Hexameron* 4.8.32, "Not from her own light does the Church gleam, but from the light of Christ. From the Sun of Justice has her brilliance been obtained, so that it is said: 'It is no longer I that live, but Christ lives in me.'" See Ambrose, *Hexameron, Paradise and Cain and Abel*, trans., John J. Savage, Fathers of the Church 42 (New York: Fathers of the Church, 1961), 156. Cardinal Bergoglio referenced the same imagery in his speech before the conclave that elected him. "Evangelizing pre-supposes a desire in the Church to come out of herself. The Church is called . . . to go to the peripheries, not only geographically, but also the existential peripheries: the mystery of sin, of pain, of injustice, of ignorance and indifference to religion, of intellectual currents, and of all misery. When the Church does not come out of herself to evangelize, she becomes self-referential and then gets sick. . . . When the Church is self-referential, inadvertently, she believes she has her own light; she ceases to be the *mysterium lunae* [mystery of the moon] and gives way to that very serious evil, spiritual worldliness (which according to De Lubac, is the worst evil that can befall the Church). It lives to give glory only to one another." From Vatican Radio, "Bergoglio's Intervention," http://www.news.va/en/news/bergoglios-intervention-a-diagnosis-of-the-problem.

44. Newman, "The Life of Juliana of Cornillon," 251.

45. Ibid. See also Rubin, *Corpus Christi*, 319–334.

46. Ibid. See also James T. O'Connor, The *Hidden Manna: A Theology of the Eucharist* (San Francisco: Ignatius, 2005), 192–197 for the English of Pope Urban IV's bull *Transiturus* establishing the feast church-wide.

47. Newman, "The Life of Juliana of Cornillon," 206.

48. Newman, "Introduction," 164 for this quote and her proposal about the placement of the feast after Trinity Sunday.

The dating of the feast represents, then, perhaps further evidence of Jesus' words at his ascension, "I am with you always,"[49] and one last celebration of Christ's presence before the start of ordinary time and the long wait for the anticipation and celebration of Jesus' birth in Advent and at Christmas.[50]

However, Bishop Robert soon died, forces opposed to the feast gained ascendancy, and so it was suppressed and Juliana driven from town—the feast was not immediately accepted as an instance of the *sensus fidelium* at work. However, an associate of Bishop Robert and former resident of Liege became Pope Urban IV in 1261. He commissioned the Dominican Thomas Aquinas to compose the feast's divine office and instituted the feast church-wide in 1264. He soon died, and it again languished. Pope Clement V also sought to promote it in 1311–1312, but, with his death in 1314, it again languished. Only in 1317 was the feast firmly established by Pope John XXII. This "most controversial" and "least populist" of late medieval popes, canonized Thomas Aquinas, condemned positions held by spiritual Franciscans, and criticized some prominent women religious.[51]

It took some years following Pope John XXII's promulgation for the Feast of Corpus Christi to gain widespread observance in Western Europe. Celebrations associated with it included the divine office and mass. It also spawned para-liturgical events such as pageants, carnivals, and dramas. The most prominent development associated with it was the proliferation of eucharistic processions with attendant adoration and benedictions. Corpus Christi processions gave birth to more frequent eucharistic processions beyond this feast so that that they became regular features of late medieval church life.[52] Indeed, in its thirteenth session that addressed the Eucharist, the Council of Trent treated first doctrinal issues such as real presence and transubstantiation. It then turned to the cult and veneration shown the sacrament and specifically mentioned the feast and its processions. Only then did it encourage frequent reception but only after warning about unworthy reception on the authority of Paul in 1 Corinthians 11.[53]

And so the Feast of Corpus Christi was an innovation. It started with a laywoman pondering for decades the meaning of a vision of a fragmentary moon, was promulgated for decades by bishops and popes subject to untimely deaths, and caused the proliferation of late medieval eucharistic

---

49. See Matt 28:20 and Newman, "The Life of Juliana of Cornillon," 206.

50. The quote from Matthew 28:20 also appears in Pope Urban IV's bull *Transiturus*.

51. Newman, "Introduction," 169 and Rubin, *Corpus Christi*, 185.

52. Rubin, *Corpus Christi*, 243–271

53. H.J. Schroeder, *Canons and Decrees of the Council of Trent. Original Text with English Translation* (St. Louis: Herder, 1941), 73.

processions, which privileged the sense of vision at the expense of touch and taste. As a result, the feast might be seen as distancing the faithful from encounter with God.

Yet, medievals did not draw such sharp distinctions among the senses. Fundamental to Thomas Aquinas's theory of vision, derived as it was from Aristotelian sources, is that the viewed affects the viewer. "For vision is made actual only when the thing seen is in a certain way in the seer."[54] Thomas adds later that, though we do see Christ's body in the Eucharist by the eyes of faith, we humans do not actually see it with our physical eyes, a claim that medieval visionary literature would dispute.[55] Thus, qualities of the thing seen, memories of it, and thoughts about it impress themselves on the viewer, touch the viewer. The same holds for the other senses. They function to impress sensations on the person who senses. That is, they transform in some way. This transformation was heightened when the thing seen was the body and blood of Christ and had moral consequences as suggested by Albert the Great in his discussion of whether those in the state of mortal sin ought to be allowed to see the Body of Christ. In support of his affirmative response, he states, "exposition of the good provokes to the good."[56] In sum, medieval visionary practice was transformative. Vision itself transformed the viewer.

Ann Astell in her book *Eating Beauty: The Eucharist and the Spiritual Arts of the Middle Ages*, cites Simone Weil on eucharistic vision as bridging the distance between human and divine and as building community with

---

54. Thomas Aquinas, *Summa theologica* I.12.2c. On vision and communion, see Caspers, "The Western Church." On the tactility of vision, see Ann W. Astell, *Eating Beauty: The Eucharist and the Spiritual Arts of the Middle Ages* (Ithaca: Cornell University Press, 2006), 3–4.

55. Thomas Aquinas, *Summa theologica* III.76.7. Medieval literature is replete with accounts of visionary women seeing the eucharistic elements transformed into Christ. For example, Hadewijch of Brabant, a contemporary of Julian's, in her striking Vision 7 describes her encounter with Christ on a Pentecost Sunday. "Then he came from the altar, showing himself as a child; and that Child was in the same form as he was in his first three years. He turned toward me, in his right hand took from the ciborium his body and in his left hand took a chalice . . . With that he came in the form and clothing of a Man, as he was on the day when he gave us his Body for the first time; looking like a Human Being and a Man, wonderful, and beautiful, and with glorious face, he came to me as humbly as anyone who wholly belongs to another." Hadewijch, *The Complete Works*, trans., Columba Hart (New York: Paulist, 1980), 281. See also Carolyn Walker Bynum, "Women Mystics and Eucharistic Devotion in the Thirteenth Century," in *Fragmentation and Redemption: Essays on Gender and the Human Body in Medieval Religion* (New York: Zone, 1992), 119–150.

56. Albert the Great, *Commentarii in IV Sententiarum*, 365. "Saepe vidimus, quod ostensio boni provocat ad bonum; ergo videtur, quod non debeant prohiberi videre peccatores" (Dist. 13, Art. 18 *sed contra* 1).

other people and with all creation. Never baptized a Catholic and never a communicant, Weil nonetheless cultivated a strong eucharistic spirituality based on her commitment to the material. Among her last written words are those on the importance of material creation. For us here below "in this world, sensible matter—that is to say, inert matter and flesh—is like a filter or sieve; it is the universal test of what is real in thought, and this applies to the entire domain of thought without exception. Matter is our infallible judge."[57] For her, seeing matter can be salvific. In particular, looking at the eucharistic bread was a gazing upon the absurd bridging of creator and created. It exemplifies docility; it is teach-able; it appears to be bread but obediently relinquishes its own reality to take on another reality and so in its simplicity is utter beauty.[58] The implications of this are anything but anti-social. Adoration de-centers the adorer; it invites us to see ourselves as we are, namely not as centers of the universe. "It, enables us to turn the 'face of [our] love' . . . toward other centers of attention: toward God, who is 'the true center' . . . ; toward our neighbor; and toward the epiphanic beauty of the world, which appears before us, and which we truly see, perhaps for the first time."[59]

And so vision for Aquinas and other medievals was as if tactile and so impacted viewers physically. Weil concurred. For her, eucharistic vision was not an escape from the material but an immersion into it and was, at the same time, a spur to solidarity with the rest of creation. In light of all this, the worship of the Eucharist outside of mass in late medieval Corpus Christi practices could be seen as tactile in a different way and was anything but anti-social. It assembled on streets and for dramas; it did not isolate.

Conclusion

The establishment of the Feast of Corpus Christi exemplifies the power of the *sensus fidelium*; it is the story of a laywoman's initial resistance but eventual assent to persist in the promotion of the feast. But only in retrospect is it clear that this was the *sensus fidelium* at work. In the moment, ridiculed for proposing a redundant feast, caught up in political machinations, sent into exile, dying before its initial promulgation in Rome and almost a half a century before John XXII re-promulgated it, Juliana of Cornillon would not live to see its wide popularity and the range of popular practices it

---

57. Simone Weil, *First and Last Notebooks*, trans. Richard Rees (London: Oxford University Press, 1970), 364. Cited in part in Astell, *Eating Beauty*, 247.

58. Astell, *Eating Beauty*, 228–31.

59. Ibid., 246; see also 5, 252.

generated. The ITC's "*Sensus Fidei* in the Life of the Church" does not seem to do justice to the provisional, complex, and retrospective character of this instance of the *sensus fidelium*.

The ITC document does, as noted above, recognize the link between popular religiosity and the *sensus fidelium*. As ordinary and everyday phenomena, popular religious practices in history tend not to be the subject of intentional reflection, tend not to be treated in magisterial works. As scholars like Bynum, Duffy, and Rubin point out, the main access to them and so to parts of the *sensus fidelium* in history is through practices as they appear in works of art, parish and municipal records, and material objects. As a result, theologians interested in the *sensus fidelium* can learn and have learned from the most recent trends in academic history.[60]

Let me conclude by following this thread just a bit farther. Carolyn Walker Bynum begins her 2011 book *Christian Materiality* with an epigraph from the introduction to *Things that Talk* by Lorraine Daston, "Talkative things instantiate novel, previously unthinkable combinations. Their thingness lends vivacity and reality to new constellations of experience that break the old molds . . . . As in the case of constellations of stars, the trick is to connect the dots into a plausible whole, a thing. Once circumscribed and concretized, the new thing becomes a magnet for intense interest, a paradox incarnate. It is richly evocative; it is eloquent. Only when the paradox becomes prosaic do things that talk subside into speechlessness."[61] In her conclusion, Bynum writes, "To moderns, the problem is to explain how things talk; to medievals, it was to get them to shut up." In naming the significance of materiality, she continues, "Paradox is inexplicable. Rude, other-denying facts such as identity and annihilation, or the haunting presence and yet utter beyondness of ultimate meaning cannot be spoken together. Yet together is how they must be lived. Their simultaneity cannot be stated; it can only be evoked [by material objects] and even this only inadequately."[62]

Our access to the *sensus fidelium* in history depends not always on texts but also on objects, and scholars of material culture can sharpen our senses when it comes to what such objects have to say about those who

---

60. On the importance of the ordinary and everyday in current Latino/a theology, see Carmen Nanko-Fernández, "Lo Cotidiano As Locus Theologicus," in *The Wiley Blackwell Companion to Latino/a Theology*, ed. Orlando O. Espin (Malden, MA: Wiley, 2015) 15–33.

61. Lorraine Daston, "Things that Talk" in *Things that Talk*, Daston, Lorraine, ed., *Things that Talk: Object Lessons from Art and Science* (New York: Zone Books, 2004), 24.

62. Carolyn Walker Bynum, *Christian Materiality: An Essay on Religion in Late Medieval Europe* (New York: Zone Books, 2011), 284, 286.

made and used them. In his most recent encyclical *Laudato Si'* and with biblical support, Pope Francis further de-centers humanity by extending the notion of objects' eloquence to include not just those made by human hands but all creation. He writes, It "is not enough to think of different species merely as potential 'resources' to be exploited, while overlooking the fact that they have value in themselves. . . . Because of us [and our contribution to extinctions], thousands of species will no longer give glory to God by their very existence, nor convey their message to us."[63] The ITC invites readers to a broader understanding of the *sensus fidelium*, and church history from the beginning to Pope Francis suggests a more sensuous *sensus fidelium*, a sixth sense sharpened to detect God's presence and action in otherwise unexpected places.

---

63. Pope Francis, *Laudato Si'. On Care for Our Common Home* (Vatican City: Libreria Editrice Vaticana, 2015) par. 33.

4

John Henry Newman on Consulting the Faithful

An Idea in Need of Development

Ryan Marr

Few experiences in John Henry Newman's theological career were more traumatic than the blowback from his 1859 article "On Consulting the Faithful." John Coulson has described Newman's "publication of this essay" as "an act of political suicide from which his career within the Church was never fully to recover."[1] The starting point of Newman's reflection was the idea that the "body of the faithful" serves as "one of the witnesses to the fact of the tradition of revealed doctrine."[2] Building on this conviction, Newman urged the hierarchy to engage in more regular consultation of the faithful, especially on matters in which the laity were likely to possess greater expertise. In defense of his position, Newman appealed to the active contribution of the faithful throughout Christian history. He pointed, for example, to the Arian controversy, in which the episcopate, in Newman's words, "failed in their confession of faith," while "the body of the laity was faithful to its baptism."[3] In this and other historical instances, "to know the tradition of the Apostles," Newman asserted, "we must have recourse to the [witness of the] faithful."[4]

1. Coulson, "Introduction" to *On Consulting the Faithful*, 2, continuing: ". . . at one stroke he, whose reputation as the one honest broker between the extremes of English Catholic opinion had hitherto stood untarnished, gained the Pope's personal displeasure, the reputation at Rome of being the most dangerous man in England, and a formal accusation of heresy proffered against him by the Bishop of Newport."

2. Newman, *On Consulting the Faithful in Matters of Doctrine*, 63. [hereafter *OCTF*]

3. Ibid., 76–77.

4. Ibid., 76.

From our vantage point, looking back on the debates surrounding Newman's essay, the controversy appears overblown. Newman supported his thesis with various appeals to historical data, and his overall conclusions could hardly be described as radical. Today, standing in the shadow of Vatican II, we take for granted the idea that the people of God share in Christ's prophetic office,[5] and thus have an active role to play in the reception and transmission of doctrine. Similarly, we assume as a theological starting point that "the entire body of the faithful . . . cannot err in matters of belief" when they achieve a consensus in their discernment of faith.[6] In fact, standing some 155 years removed from the publication of Newman's essay, certain facets of his approach appear in need of updating. When Newman encountered challenges to his proposal, he retreated somewhat from his original stance, indicating that he had used the language of consultation not in the technical sense of "taking counsel from," but in the popular sense of the term, meaning to inquire into a matter of *fact*—much like we talk about "consulting our barometer" about the weather.[7] Here and in other places Newman described the sense of the faithful in primarily passive terms, leaving the impression that the laity merely reflect what might be called the "sense of the hierarchy." Since Newman's time, theologians have developed a more robust understanding of the role of the faithful as active contributors in doctrinal discussions.[8] In a certain sense, Newman planted the seeds for this idea, which theologians after him have watered and tended to, enabling a growth that has exceeded Newman's original intentions.

As a way of tracing out the development that has taken place from Newman's time to our own, in what follows I will compare the substance of Newman's argument with the 2014 document issued by the International Theological Commission (ITC), "*Sensus Fidei* in the Life of the Church."[9] In years to come, this 2014 document will serve as a touchstone for theological reflection on the *sensus fidelium*. Not only does it provide a systematic overview of the topic, but it also presents one of the strongest official statements in support of the idea that the faithful have an active role to play in "the articulation and development of the faith" (67). With this document, we have moved far beyond the *de facto* assumption of some older ecclesiolo-

---

5. See *Lumen Gentium*, 12.
6. Ibid.
7. *OCTF*, 54.
8. Cf. Vorgrimler, "From Sensus Fidei to Consensus Fidelium," 3–11; Dulles, "Sensus Fidelium," 240–42; Nichols, *The Shape of Catholic Theology*, 221–31; Gaillardetz, "The Reception of Doctrine," 95–114; Pope Francis, *Evangelii Gaudium*, 199.

9. All quotations of the ITC document will be cited by parenthetical reference to the relevant paragraph.

gies that the main duties of the faithful are to pray, pay, and obey.[10] In this respect, "*Sensus Fidei* in the Life of the Church" stands in continuity both with Newman's theology of the laity and also with the communion ecclesiology articulated by the council fathers at Vatican II.[11] Of course, as with any document issued by the church, the Theological Commission's treatment represents not an end point to the discussion, but one step in an ongoing journey of theological reflection. Thus, after comparing Newman's position to that of the 2014 document, my conclusion will briefly examine persistent matters of debate related to this topic and also offer a constructive word on navigating these tensions.

Newman's Vision of the *Sensus Fidelium*

Although Newman popularized his ideas regarding the sense of the faithful during the Roman Catholic years of his life, the roots of his perspective can be traced back to his writings as an Anglican. As mentioned above, one of the key planks in Newman's essay "On Consulting the Faithful" was the laity's role in maintaining orthodoxy during the Arian controversy, which had been the topic of Newman's first major theological treatise, published in 1833. In 1859, looking back upon his earlier work, Newman pointed out that the defeat of Arianism would not have been possible without the struggles of the faithful in defense of the Nicene position. In fact, in this particular historical instance, the body of the laity arguably did more to secure the orthodox position than did the episcopate. In Newman's words:

> It is not a little remarkable, that, though, historically speaking, the fourth century is the age of doctors . . . nevertheless in that very day the divine tradition committed to the infallible Church was proclaimed and maintained far more by the faithful than by the Episcopate . . . that in that time of immense confusion the divine dogma of our Lord's divinity was proclaimed, enforced, maintained, and (humanly speaking) preserved, far more by the "Ecclesia docta" than by the "Ecclesia docens;" that the body of

---

10. In the nineteenth century, Newman's sometimes enemy, Monsignor George Talbot, bluntly communicated a similar outlook, writing to Cardinal Manning, "What is the province of the laity? To hunt, to shoot, to entertain. These matters they understand, but to meddle with ecclesiastical matters they have no right at all." Quoted in Coulson, "Introduction," 41.

11. For an overview of this topic, see Doyle, *Communion Ecclesiology*, 11–22 and 168–80.

the episcopate was unfaithful to its commission, while the body of the laity was faithful to its baptism . . .[12]

In response to criticisms leveled against his article, Newman nuanced certain facets of his original position,[13] but he refused to back down from his basic historical claim. From his perspective, the laity's historical track record of upholding orthodoxy should serve as an impetus for bishops to consult the faithful on a regular basis.

The keystone of Newman's perspective on this matter was his firm conviction that the church, when healthy, operates not according to the guidance of the clergy alone, but also takes into account the outlook and opinions of all the faithful. As Edward Jeremy Miller sums up the matter,

> Just as Newman insists that the whole person thinks—not only one's intellect but also one's feelings, memories, etc.—he also insists that the whole ecclesial body is involved in discerning and living out the revealed truth. The laity have their rightful role in church affairs just as the clergy do, and the process by which religious doctrines come to expression involves theologians as importantly as it involves episcopal authorities.[14]

When the clergy forget this truth, they fall into the error that Saint Paul condemns in 1 Corinthians 12, assuming that as the "head" they have no need for other parts of the body. To the contrary, the body of Christ is at its strongest when its various parts are working together and towards the same ends.[15]

As we have seen, Newman pointed to the past to confirm his thesis, outlining various historical instances in which the faithful have contributed to the guardianship and transmission of doctrine. The preeminent example

---

12. *OCTF*, 75–6.

13. For example, in response to criticisms leveled against his statement that "the *body* of Bishops failed in their confession of the faith," Newman wrote that his use of the word "body" here was not in the sense of the Latin "corpus," as one might find it used in a technical theological treatise, but in the sense of "'the great preponderance,' or, 'the mass' of Bishops, viewing them in the main or the gross, as a *cumulus* of individuals." See ibid., 116.

14. Miller, *John Henry Newman on the Idea of Church*, 59.

15. Newman expounded upon this and other key passages related to ecclesiology in a sermon from his Anglican Period, "The Unity of the Church," in *Parochial and Plain Sermons*, 1550–57. In the multivolume edition of the *Parochial and Plain Sermons*, this piece is sermon 17 of volume 7. For another example of Newman's exegesis of 1 Corinthians 12, see his sermon from 21 January 1827, "Almsgiving on Christian Principles—(for Distressed Manufacturers)," sermon 83, no. 159, in *John Henry Newman Sermons 1824–1843, Vol. 5*, 411–21.

of this contribution was the laity's defense of Nicene Christology during the Arian controversy, but, lest one think this kind of activity was merely a relic of the past, one could look more recently to Pius IX's consultation of the faithful before declaring the Immaculate Conception a dogma of the church.[16] On the foundation of this historical testimony, Newman constructed a fairly elaborate vision of the role of the faithful in the life of the church, driving home the point that in certain instances—namely, those in which the laity are likely to possess greater expertise than bishops—it only makes sense that the hierarchy would consult the faithful for their input.

All that being said, ultimately Newman maintained a moderately conservative position on how this process works. Although the laity ought to be consulted during the process of doctrinal discernment, the "power and prerogative" of defining doctrine belongs exclusively to the pope and college of bishops.[17] Moreover, as mentioned earlier, Newman employed images for the faithful's relationship to the hierarchy that were primarily passive in orientation: for example, an individual consulting a barometer to learn about present weather conditions, the imprint of a seal on wax,[18] and a physician checking the pulse of her patient. Nevertheless, Newman clearly believed that something is substantively gained when the hierarchy does consult the faithful, and stated so explicitly near the end of his essay: "Though the laity be but the reflection or echo of the clergy in matters of faith, yet there is something in the 'pastorum et fidelium *conspiratio* [pastors and faithful *thinking together*],' which is not in the pastors alone."[19] Thus, Newman could become impatient when the idea of the laity's *passive* infallibility was used to downplay the episcopate's responsibility to consult them. Commenting on Bishop Ullathorne's remark that the pious belief of the laity is the "faithful reflection of the pastoral teaching," for example, Newman exasperatingly remarked, "[His Excellency talks about] Reflection; that is, the people are a *mirror*, in which the Bishops see themselves. Well, I suppose a person may *consult* his glass, and in that way may know things about himself in which he can learn in no other way."[20]

These insights constitute the fundamental achievement of Newman's essay. Through his tireless efforts, underappreciated in his own day, Newman commenced a theological discussion about the role of the faithful in the

---

16. *OCTF*, 70–71.

17. See Newman's letter to Gillow from 25 May 1859, *The Letters and Diaries of John Henry Newman*, 19:145 [hereafter *LD*]. For more on this matter, see Dulles, "Authority in the Church," 182.

18. *LD* 19:136.

19. *OCTF*, 104.

20. Ibid., 72.

life of the church that would eventually culminate in *Lumen Gentium*'s firm affirmations that "the holy people of God shares also in Christ's prophetic office," and that "the *entire* body of the faithful, anointed as they are by the holy one, cannot err in matters of belief."[21] The International Theological Commission's 2014 document, "*Sensus Fidei* in the Life of the Church," utilizes both Newman's work and *Lumen Gentium* as essential reference points for a proper understanding of the sense of the faithful. Notably, "*Sensus Fidei*" does not merely repeat the insights of these past treatments, but advances the conversation in significant ways, setting the stage, one hopes, for a renewed engagement with this crucial theological concept.

Sensus Fidei in the Life of the Church

Since space constraints prevent me from providing a detailed analysis of the entirety of "*Sensus Fidei*," in what follows I will limit myself to highlighting what I see as some of its primary strengths. First, the document seeks to overcome the sharp demarcation between the "teaching church" (*Ecclesia docens*) and the "learning church" (*Ecclesia discens*) that arose after the Council of Trent. After praising the theologies of Melchior Cano and Robert Bellarmine for maintaining a proper emphasis on the active contribution of the faithful, the document then goes on to note that, "Other theologians of the post-Tridentine era continued to affirm the infallibility of the *Ecclesia*, but began to distinguish the roles of the 'teaching Church' and the 'learning Church' rather sharply. The earlier emphasis on the 'active' infallibility of the *Ecclesia in credendo* was gradually replaced by an emphasis on the active role of the *Ecclesia docens*. It became common to say that the *Ecclesia discens* had only a "passive infallibility" (33). The authors of "*Sensus Fidei*" clearly view this particular framework as inadequate, and credit the contributions of such nineteenth century luminaries as Newman, Johann Adam Möhler (1796–1838), and Giovanni Perrone (1794–1876), with helping to loosen its grip on Catholic theology. But it was in the twentieth century, the document asserts, that noticeable strides were made: "Catholic theologians in the 20th century . . . emphasized that 'the Church' is not identical with her pastors: that the whole Church, by the action of the Holy Spirit, is the subject or 'organ' of Tradition; and that lay people have an active role in the transmission of the apostolic faith" (41). Pius XII's consultation of the faithful prior to the definition of the Assumption of the Blessed Virgin Mary manifested the active role of the faithful in practice, while Vatican II provided official confirmation of the doctrine of the *sensus fidelium*. Both helped to banish

21. *Lumen Gentium*, 12.

the notion that the *Ecclesia discens*, or learning church, possesses only a passive infallibility.

As an antidote to ecclesiological paradigms that draw a strong demarcation between the teaching church and the learning church, "*Sensus Fidei*" prefers to emphasize the organic unity of pastors and faithful. This emphasis, rooted in a communion ecclesiology, constitutes the second strength of the document. In elaborating upon this concept, "*Sensus Fidei*" quotes Yves Congar, who described the *sensus fidelium* as a gift of the Holy Spirit "given to the hierarchy and the whole body of the faithful together."[22] As "*Sensus Fidei*" observes, "Where earlier authors had underlined the distinction between the *Ecclesia docens* and the *Ecclesia discens*, Congar was concerned to show their organic unity. [In Congar's words:] 'The Church loving and believing, that is, the body of the faithful, is infallible in the living possession of the faith, not in a particular act of judgment'" (43). In this light, it would be wrong to construe revelation as passing from God to the pope and bishops, with the faithful passively waiting for instruction from "on high." The episcopate does not tower above the rest of the body of Christ, but is ordered to the service of it. In the phrasing of "*Sensus Fidei*", "The teaching of the hierarchy is at the service of communion" (43). Furthermore, the Holy Spirit animates the entire body, both pastors and faithful, which is why "the *consensus fidelium* is a *sure* criterion for determining whether a particular doctrine or practice belongs to the apostolic faith" (3; emphasis mine). On such occasions, the shared sense of how the Holy Spirit is moving provides a certainty that may be lacking in reflections on the faith that are derived from only one segment of the church.

Finally, the third strength of the document is its willingness to broach the topic of how to discern authentic manifestations of the *sensus fidei fidelium*. In my view, this is the most pressing issue in contemporary discussions of the sense of the faithful.[23] On account of the strident debates

22. Congar, *Jalons pour une théologie du laïcat*, 399; ET: *Lay People in the Church*, 289.

23. Now, one might take issue with the criteria set forth by "*Sensus Fidei*." In a soon-to-be-published article, for example, Kenneth Parker and Stephen Lawson express concern that by creating criteria for whose voice counts as an authentic expression of the *sensus fidelium*, the document marginalizes the experience of a vast proportion of the baptized. In their view, this move represents a "failure of nerve, a reluctance to trust the Holy Spirit at work in the lives of all the baptized" ("Sense of the Faith," 2). For Parker and Lawson, "There should be no criteriology for the authentic *sensus fidei fidelium* beyond baptism" (ibid., 21). From their vantage point, by setting forth such criteria as "participation in the life of the Church" and "adherence to the magisterium" as necessary "dispositions ... for authentic participation in the *sensus fidei*," the ITC's document risks silencing the voices of baptized Christians who might have an important contribution to make to the Church's ongoing discernment on moral and theological matters.

of the postconciliar era, Catholics today are more aware than ever that the *sensus fidelium* is not always easily discernible. Life in the church is simpler when pastors and faithful manifest a convergence of belief on a particular theological issue—say, with regard to the Immaculate Conception. Things become much more difficult when different segments of the church disagree on a question of faith or morals. In recent years, one of the most persistent areas of disagreement is in the realm of sexual morality—on a number of different questions, for sure, but particularly with regard to the question of whether it is licit for married couples to space births through the use of artificial contraception. While the bishops, in line with the stated teaching of Paul VI's encyclical, *Humanae Vitae*, have continued to insist that it is immoral to do so, the vast majority of Catholics—at least those residing in North America and Western Europe—have reached the opposite conclusion.[24] What are we to make of this disparity in belief? Does the position of a large portion of the faithful on this matter represent an authentic manifestation of the *sensus fidelium* over and against the witness of the bishops, along the lines of what took place during the Arian controversy? Or, is it a case of persisting and lamentable dissent? Finally, what means should the church use for adjudicating this dispute as she moves forward into the future?

While "*Sensus Fidei*" does not specifically treat this moral issue, it does suggest some criteria for determining when a stated conviction represents an authentic manifestation of the *sensus fidei [fidelium]*. Concretely, the document identifies six dispositions needed for authentic participation in the *sensus fidei*: (1) regular participation in the life of the church, (2) listening to the word of God, (3) openness to reason, (4) adherence to the magisterium, (5) holiness, and (6) seeking the edification of the church. Of this list, number 4 is likely to spark the most debate, as it could be taken to imply that the sense of the faith on the part of the faithful merely reflects the stated teaching of the *Ecclesia docens*. If this were true, however, we would find ourselves back to the post-Tridentine demarcation between the active infallibility of the teaching church and the passive infallibility of the learning church—a position criticized by the authors earlier in the document. Something could have been said, perhaps, about whether there are ever legitimate instances for the faithful to dissent from presently held magisterial teachings that have not been infallibly defined. Unfortunately, for guidance

---

See Parker Lawson, "'Sense of the Faith' in the Life of the Church" (unpublished article).

24. See, e.g., Küng, *Infallible?: An Unresolved Inquiry*, 27–52; cf. Curran, "Ten Years Later: Reflections on the Anniversary of *Humanae Vitae*," 425–30. For a defense of Paul VI's teaching, Ford and Grisez, eds., *The Teaching of Humanae Vitae: A Defense*; cf. Smith, ed., *Why Humanae Vitae Was Right: A Reader*.

on this question, the document through its silence asks its readership to look elsewhere.[25]

Conclusion

Undoubtedly, the ITC's 2014 document represents an advance from Newman's thoughts on the *sensus fidelium*, as articulated in his 1859 essay "On Consulting the Faithful." While Newman's approach was controversial in its day—standing out for its strong affirmation that the lay faithful have a substantive contribution to make to the process of doctrinal discernment—it still leaned in the direction of viewing the laity in primarily passive terms. This tendency shows up distinctly in the metaphors that Newman employed for describing the faithful's relationship to the hierarchy (e.g., imprint on wax, reflection in a mirror, barometer, etc.). "*Sensus Fidei* in the Life of the Church," on the other hand, leaves no doubt that the lay faithful have an active role to play in the reception and transmission of doctrine. Appealing to the teaching of Vatican II, the document explicitly teaches that "the faithful are not merely passive recipients of what the hierarchy teaches and theologians explain; rather, they are living and active subjects within the Church" (67). As the document notes, "It can take a long time before this process comes to a conclusion. In the face of new circumstances, the faithful at large, pastors, and theologians all have their respective roles to play, and patience and respect are needed in their mutual interactions if the *sensus fidei* is to be clarified and a true *consensus fidelium*, a *conspiratio pastorum et fidelium*, is to be achieved" (71). As a positive sign, the document points to Pope Francis's initiative in calling for bishops and pastors around the world to query the faithful on issues of marriage and family life in the lead up to the 2014 extraordinary synod on the family.[26] This is a positive sign, but the question that arises in the wake of this initiative is, what use, if any, will be made of the responses submitted by the faithful? In other words, how will the bishops incorporate the responses to the questionnaire in their discernment process at the synod?[27] Furthermore, getting back to the issue of tensions within the body of Christ, what import should we give to any divergence

---

25. The CDF's 1990 Instruction *Donum Veritatis: On the Ecclesial Vocation of the Theologian* provides detailed guidance for theologians who find themselves in disagreement with a teaching authoritatively taught by the magisterium. See *Donum Veritatis*, 32–41.

26. "Vatican Seeks 'Widespread' Input on Marriage and Family Life," *America* 209.15 (Nov. 18, 2013) 8–9.

27. It seems to me that this approach could prove counterproductive if the sense of the faithful is discerned, but not explicitly addressed in the deliberations at the synod.

of opinions on these matters, particularly if they remain unresolved at the conclusion of the synod?

On these questions, Michael Slusser's 1993 article, "Does Newman's 'On Consulting the Faithful in Matters of Doctrine' Rest Upon a Mistake?," has some wisdom to offer us.[28] In brief, Slusser asserts that the historical evidence does not support Newman's claim that, during the Arian controversy, the Christian faith was upheld more consistently by the ordinary faithful than by their pastors. Within the article, Slusser does not judge one group's witness—either the laity's or the pastors'—as more faithful than the other's. His goal, rather, is to show that the situation on the ground was more complex than Newman's construal of events suggests: in some places, a large portion of the faithful opposed Arianizing currents, in others the orthodox contingent was clearly a minority. In certain other contexts, the evidence is simply not as clear-cut as Newman made it out to be. For our purposes, the point of interest is not Slusser's historical analysis, but the concluding section of the article, in which he speaks more directly to the significance of these historic disputes for our present situation. Pointing to the example of bishops who sought to maintain the unity of disputing factions, Slusser writes:

> The saving grace in times of doctrinal dispute and disunion may not be disclosed either in the witness of the laity or in that of the bishops, seen as distinct voices in the church, but in those local churches where the faithful, including the bishops, live the Christian life intensely without succumbing to envy, anger, or partisan spirit. The real mistake in Newman's proposal may lie less in the weakness of his historical evidence than in his and our overestimation of the importance of verbal formulations, and our willingness to see those who disagree with us as tools of the Adversary. If the *sensus fidelium* becomes just another weapon for use in doctrinal combat, we shall surely have failed to learn the lesson of the Arian controversy.[29]

This remark by Slusser draws attention to a concrete example of "the patience and respect" that "*Sensus Fidei*" describes as indispensable in the mutual interactions among the faithful at large, pastors, and theologians. The foundation of a healthy relationship among the constituent parts of the Church is patient listening grounded in charity. This call to patient listening is a challenge to all the members of the body. On the hierarchy's part,

---

28. Slusser, "Does Newman's 'On Consulting the Faithful in Matters of Doctrine' Rest Upon a Mistake?," 234–40.

29. Ibid., 240.

adequate structures have to be put into place by these leaders to create a context in which all voices in the Church can be heard. As for the laity, we must make every effort to listen intently to the voice of the magisterium, and to engage our shepherds charitably, even when we find it difficult to accept particular teachings that they espouse.

Looking back over the church's journey through history, one finds that quite often the sense of the faithful proved difficult to discern in the historical moment, that is to say, while theological dispute around a particular question still raged. To return to the Arian controversy, from our historical vantage point, the *consensus fidelium* in support of orthodoxy might seem easily discernible among the prevailing christologies of the time, but imagine how disorienting it must have been for some Christians living in the midst of the debates? I point this out not to sound a note of sophistry within the context of presently raging intra-ecclesial disputes, but so as to reiterate the call of "*Sensus Fidei*" for patience and respect on the part of all parties involved in them. In many (most?) cases, authentic manifestations of the *sensus fidelium* can only be identified retrospectively. For now, we do our part by faithfully transmitting the tradition that has been handed down to us while at the same time carefully discerning the signs of the times. As both Newman and "*Sensus Fidei*" make clear, all the members of the church, whatever their station in life, have a vital contribution to make to this process.

5

Supremacy in the Sense of the Faithful

Theological Anthropology and the "Various Ranks" (Lumen Gentium 13)

Jeannine Hill Fletcher

Sensus fidelium: Theological Democracy or the Holy Spirit's Conspiracy?

SENSUS FIDELIUM APPEARS TO function as an equalizing concept, drawing all believers into the truth of the Catholic faith. Optimistically, this line of thought provides room for dissent and diversity: if the magisterium proposes one way of accounting for faith and practice, but the laity diverges, *sensus fidelium* serves as a mechanism by which this dissent is not eliminated merely on the basis of episcopal power. This seems like a democratic concept. In the explanation of the International Theological Commission, in their 2014 statement, "*Sensus Fidei* in the Life of the Church," the concept of "sensus fidelium" proposes that truth is embedded in the consensus that emerges over time and the faithful play an active role in Christian belief.[1] While readers may be lured by the magnetism of inclusion of *all* in the life of the faith, this democratic opening is both disingenuous and dangerous. Focusing on the most extended articulation of the life of the Church at Vatican II, The Dogmatic Constitution on the Church, *Lumen Gentium*, we can see more clearly that the equalizing appeal of *sensus fidelium* is disingenuous insofar as this concept is not actually democratic, and dangerous in the promise of certainty that it holds.

---

1. International Theological Commission, "*Sensus Fidei* in the Life of the Church" (2014) 72, http://www.vatican.va/roman_curia/congregations/cfaith/cti_documents/rc_cti_20140610_sensus-fidei_en.html.

The disingenuousness of *sensus fidelium* is felt acutely when situating *Lumen Gentium* in its historical context and imagining its reception by U.S. Catholics in 1964. Anticipating the way Church teaching might function in the minds and practices of actual Catholics in the real world invites us to ask questions about the sufficiency of *sensus fidelium* as a theological concept. For in the real world of North America in the 1960s, democratic equality was an ideal that gave rise to movements among the dispossessed in the groundswell for rights for African Americans, for women, and for First Nations peoples. In assessing the resonance of *sensus fidelium* with wider movements for human wellbeing, its disingenuousness comes into view. Its dangerousness can be seen when considering the theological claims it is making in light of the multireligious landscape emerging in the U.S. at the time. For in 1964, the U.S. was nearing the end of more than forty years of racist immigration policies that all but excluded non-White peoples from non-Christian lands to enter as citizens. Conceptualizing this historic landscape invites us to investigate closely the conceptual building blocks of *sensus fidelium* to ask what might have been its practical efficacy for Catholics in the church and for Catholics in the wider world. It's with a close look at the theological anthropology that grounds the *sensus fidelium* that we can uncover a distinct sense of supremacy rather than democratic equality.

The Building Blocks of *Sensus Fidelium*: Theological Anthropology and the "Various Ranks"

To begin, it's obvious that the expression *sensus fidelium* within *Lumen Gentium* certainly does have elements that lend themselves to an equalizing interpretation. These are rooted in a theological anthropology and doctrine of God that assert universality. An egalitarian reading of *sensus fidelium* draws its strength from the fundamental affirmation that God is creator of the whole world (LG, 2) and a basic equality pervades humanity when "in the beginning God made human nature one" (LG, 13).[2] This theological foundation supports a mission for the Church, and *Lumen Gentium* plans to be a reflection on the Church and Christ as sign and instrument of "the unity of the whole human race" (LG, 1). Unity and oneness are key themes explicit in the text, with an implicit vision of Genesis 1 and the creation of all humanity in the image of God. Such a theological anthropology would

---

2. All citations of *Lumen Gentium* come from http://www.vatican.va/archive/hist_councils/ii_vatican_council/documents/vat-ii_const_19641121_lumen-gentium_en.html. The document will be referenced throughout this essay with internal citations (LG) subsequently indicating the section number within the document (e.g., LG, 13).

appear to guarantee the equality of all believers (indeed, the equality of all persons), which lends *sensus fidelium* its democratic tone. As far as a practical theological trajectory in the idea of *sensus fidelium*, we are off to a good start toward grounding racial, gendered, and religious diversity as a reflection of the God who created all. One can imagine this basic affirmation of common humanity as a positive resource in the various movements for equal dignity that were widespread as *Lumen Gentium* was published. God created with a singular human nature, men and women, Black, White, and Native American, all the diverse peoples of the world, and God intended a unity from out of this diversity that would be the unity of the whole human race. The Church's role, *Lumen Gentium* proclaims, is to be a part of that unifying project.

But the theological anthropology exhibited in *Lumen Gentium* is a qualified equality, one that is comfortable with the idea of persons being of various "ranks." (A term used in the Vatican's own translation of *Lumen Gentium* in paragraphs 11, 12, 13, 29, 40, 41.) In this theological anthropology, the three persons of the Trinity appear to have different roles in transforming God's community of equals into a hierarchy of persons among the faithful. While God the Creator may have created all in God's image, the Holy Spirit bestows "His" gifts in different ways "among the faithful of every rank" (LG, 13). Some of these gifts are "outstanding" and "extraordinary," others "more simple" (LG, 13). In the words of *Lumen Gentium* paragraph 12:

> It is not only through the sacraments and the ministries of the Church that the Holy Spirit sanctifies and leads the people of God and enriches it with virtues, but, "allotting his gifts to everyone according as He wills" (1 Cor 12:11), He distributes special graces *among the faithful of every rank.*[3]

If God the Father has created all in God's own image, it appears that it is the Holy Spirit who has the special ability to discern and distribute "according as He wills" and the variety of gifts that are bestowed creates the people of God of various ranks.

The second person of the Trinity has his part to play in creating a theological anthropology of the various ranks as well. The One who walked this earth gathering to him a discipleship of equals appears to have chosen to employ the discerning power of the Holy Spirit in order to leave behind a ranked discipleship. In the words of *Lumen Gentium,*

---

3. In this, and other subsequent citations, all italicized words in quotes from *Lumen Gentium* indicate my emphasis.

> The apostles were *enriched* by Christ with a *special outpouring of the Holy Spirit* coming upon them, and they passed on this spiritual gift to their helpers by the imposition of hands and it has been transmitted down to us in Episcopal consecration. (LG, 21)

The distinguishing Holy Spirit is channeled by the One who proposed that the last shall be first (as remembered in Matthew 20:16) in order to guarantee the "primacy" (LG,13) of the Chair of Peter, "*over* the apostles" (18), the apostles then "appointed as *rulers*" (LG, 20) such that "the *chief place* belongs to the office of those who . . . are passers-on of the apostolic seed" (LG, 20). The Holy Spirit's special gifts, channeled through Jesus, establishes the Father's surrogates in the world with the bishops "*presiding in place of God* over the flock" (LG, 20). If there was any question as to whether this was ecclesiology or anthropology we were discussing, Appendix note #2 clearly states that there is an "ontological participation" in the power of primacy. "Ontology" points to the level of human *being* that is anthropology, not the level of human organizing that is ecclesiology.

The result is an ecclesiology that betrays a theological anthropology of various ranks. There are ministers of "*lesser* rank" (LG, 41) and "*lower* levels" (LG, 29); and others with "*supreme* power" (LG, 22) and "*primacy*" (LG, 13) "*over*" others (LG,18). As Paul Lakeland describes, despite the inclusion of the laity in the understanding of the People of God and a broad sense of "the faithful," the text's "rooting of hierarchy in apostolic authority cannot but make us see lay people as subordinate if not second-class members of the community of faith."[4] Thus, returning to the seemingly positive expression of *sensus fidelium*, we notice the ranking embedded within the concept when it is described as a "special property by means of the whole peoples' supernatural discernment in matters of faith when 'from the Bishops down to the last of the lay faithful' they show a universal consensus in matters of faith and morals" (LG, 12). The directional "down to" subtly reflects back to us the ordering of persons within their ranks. *Sensus fidelium* ensures that "all the faithful of Christ, of whatever rank or status" (LG, 40) *have* a rank or status. Stated explicitly in *Lumen Gentium* 13: "Not only, then, is the people of God made up of different peoples but in its inner structure also it is composed of various ranks" (LG, 13).

A theological anthropology and ecclesiology comfortable with conceptualizing persons with "rank or status" not only seems to invert the priorities expressed in Gospel passages where the first shall be last, but also has

---

4. Lakeland, *A Council that will Never End*: Lumen Gentium *and the Church Today* (Collegeville, MN: Liturgical, 2013) 63.

practical outcomes that contribute to the disingenuousness and dangerousness of *sensus fidelium*. For while all within the church contribute to the truth of the faith, some boast a more elevated status in this project. More specifically, while the ranking may express priority of teaching authority, the ranked positions of status (*over* others, with *supreme* power, *presiding in the place of God*) are ranked positions of status reserved for men. From the perspective of gender justice, the disingenuous opening of *sensus fidelium* masks the reality that males are ranked in the elevated positions of status among the faithful. It would be hard to square the gendered elevation of certain members among the faithful with the movement for women's rights in the 1960s, just as it is today. As a lay, female, Catholic theologian, this hierarchical ordering should come as no surprise to me (although I'm astounded by it every time); the democratic opening of *sensus fidelium* is disingenuous in ultimately being situated in a hierarchical theological anthropology and the gendered reality of the church.

But my particular interest in critically engaging this concept rests less in that it is disingenuous to me and more in its dangerous potential for my Others. As a White Catholic theologian, I must attend to those places where Catholic theological anthropology—like those embedded in *Lumen Gentium's* sense of the faithful—serve to elevate *me* at the expense of my Others. In addition to the problematic expression of "various ranks" from the perspective of gender justice, the practical outcome in relation to racial justice and religious pluralism are equally troubling. It is difficult to see how *sensus fidelium* would have positively informed these movements in the Vatican II era, but not difficult to see the importance of unmasking the pretensions to equality for those of us working with this concept today.

Supremacy of the Faithful

The root of *sensus fidelium's* dangerous ideology lies in the guarantee to truth that it proclaims—an instinctual sense of certainty that elevates me above others. For the *sensus fidelium* guarantees *my* lay, female place in the hierarchy within the church ("simple" though it may be), as the Holy Spirit in His wisdom apparently guarantees *my* truth above my Others. So, I have my lowly part to play when "the body of the faithful as a whole, anointed as they are by the Holy One, cannot err in matters of belief" (LG, 12).

In the logic of *sensus fidelium,* the Trinitarian life of God has endowed me and my fellow Catholics with a natural "instinct" that guarantees our truth as "the word of God." In the description of the ITC, "as its name (*sensus*) indicates, it is akin rather to a natural, immediate and spontaneous reaction, and comparable to a vital instinct or a sort of 'flair' by which the believer clings spontaneously to what conforms to the truth of faith and shuns what is contrary to it. The *sensus fidei fideili* is infallible in itself with regard to its object: "the true faith" (ITC, 54). *Sensus fidelium* guarantees that my place, in my rank—however lowly within the Church—is exalted and ranks above those outside the church. Although with a caveat *Lumen Gentium* insists: "All the Church's children should remember that their exalted status is to be attributed not to their own merits but to the special grace of Christ" (LG 14).

It is too easy to recount—but apparently also quite easy to forget—the dangerous memory of how claims to the one true faith and the elevation by Christ have functioned. This dangerous theological superiority propelled European Christian destructions of the world, and enslaved Africans on the basis of how being claimed by the Christian faith might elevate them. As Willie James Jennings describes, in the encounter of the so-called New World, "Theology [becomes] the trigger for the classificatory subjection of all nonwhite, non-Western peoples."[5] In the colonial moment, God as the creator of all provided the Christian truth as the lens through which to view, assess, and hierarchically arrange the peoples of the world.[6]

The non-Christian deficiency of native Africans was a key theme in defending slavery on religious grounds even as late as the 1850s when Bishop August Martin of Louisiana identified: "slavery as an eminently Christian work . . . [which saw] the redemption of millions of human beings who would pass in such a way from the darkest intellectual night to the sweet . . . light of the Gospel."[7] The hierarchy of rank functioned here as well:

> snatch[ed] from the barbarity of their ferocious customs thousands of children of the race of Canaan, upon whom the curse of an outraged Father continues to weigh heavily, almost everywhere. He commits them to the care of the privileged ones of the great human family for His own purposes and these people must be their shepherds and their fathers rather than their masters.[8]

Arguments for Christian supremacy over non-White, non-Christian Others were not limited to the conditions of enslaved Africans and their

---

5. Jennings, *The Christian Imagination: Theology and the Origins of Race* (New Haven, CT: Yale University Press, 2010) 87.

6. Ibid., 105.

7. Martin, quoted in Cyprian Davis, "God of our Weary Years: Black Catholics in American Catholic History," in Diana Hayes and Cyprian Davis, eds., *Taking Down Our Harps: Black Catholics in the United States* (Maryknoll, NY: Orbis, 1998) 25.

8. Martin, "The Defense of Slavery," 35.

descendants. The non-Christian deficiency of First Nations peoples was the root of papal Bulls in the fifteenth century that established the 'doctrine of discovery,' by which European Christians claimed the "right" to the land.[9] This foundational ideology served as a precedent written into U.S. law, functioning to dispossess Native Americans for generations to come. When First Nations would present challenges to their dispossession, the U.S. government would debate in the same language of non-Christian deficiencies the rights of expansion in the nineteenth century, seeing the divine command of the land given to "the White race alone."[10]

In the late nineteenth century, a Catholic ideology of theological supremacy entered the debate over Chinese immigration and citizenship in San Francisco when the Jesuit Father Buchard publicly proclaimed the Chinese as "pagans . . . vicious . . . immoral creatures, that are incapable of rising to the virtue that is inculcated by the religion of Jesus Christ, the World's Redeemer."[11] On the basis of his elevated position, Fr. Buchard could see that the "Chinese are an inferior race, not capable of becoming Christians."[12] Considering their non-Christian deficiency, Senator A.A. Sargent argued to Congress that the Chinese be barred from U.S. citizenship. In his words:

> The command of the Scripture is: "Go ye into all the world, and preach the gospel to every creature;" not overwhelm your own family, your own neighborhood, your own nation with the bigots and effects of heathenism. Let the missionary go to China and convert these men from their heathenish practices, wash their robes and make them white in the blood of the Lamb, and then, being fit for American citizenship and to become an integral part of our society, to be cemented into our political and moral structures, then let them come as immigrants. Until then, they deteriorate our body-politic and destroy our civilization.[13]

---

9. Steven Newcomb, *Pagans in the Promised Land* (Golden, CO: Fulcrum, 2008).

10. Thomas Hart Benton, "Address to Congress," *Congressional Globe* 29:1 (1846), 917.

11. Rev. O. [Otis] Gibson, *Chinaman or White Man, Which?: A Reply to Father Buchard, Delivered in Platt's Hall, San Francisco, Friday Evening, March 14, 1873* (San Francisco: Alta California Printing House, 1873) 19, http://sunsite.berkeley.edu/cgi-bin/flipomatic/cic/brk7190.

12. Ibid., 20–21.

13. Aaron Augustus Sargent, "Chinese Immigration: Speech of Hon. A.A. Sargent of California, in the Senate of the United States, March 7, 1878." Washington, 1878, 23, http://sunsite.berkeley.edu/cgi-bin/flipomatic/cic/brk6526.

History suggests that supremacy in the sense of the faithful is a dangerous thing. But this sense of supremacy has not gone away. *Lumen Gentium*, the theology of Vatican II, and *Dominus Iesus* maintain the necessity of the Catholic Church for salvation in such a way that Christian truth remains in a state of supremacy vis-à-vis our religious Others and this supremacy remains the teaching of the Church. My friends of other faiths remind me of the hubris involved in my church's sense of the faithful; but this hubris is not inconsequential speculation. The "doctrine of discovery" that privileged Christian truth and gave Christian nations the right to ownership of lands they might discover, except those "in the actual possession of any Christian king or prince"[14] was written into U.S. law and *continues* to impact First Nations peoples in their struggle for sovereignty and land rights.[15] A sense of supremacy of the Christian faith indirectly sponsors immigration laws designed to restrict access from majority Muslim nations, when majority Christians do nothing to address this practice.[16] And a sense of the supremacy of the Christian faith continues to have deadly consequences for our neighbors of other faiths when military actions and demonstrations of hate are propelled by the Christian ideologies in our time. The "conspiratio" of which the ITC speaks when discussing *sensus fidelium* as "unanimous consent, or *conspiratio*, of the faithful and their pastors" (ITC, 37), begins to feel more like conspiracy grounded in a sinister spirit than concord among God's faithful.[17]

In light of the particular movements for human wellbeing at the time *Lumen Gentium* was released, this conspiracy of supremacy might have influence relevant to the struggles for justice among First Nations peoples in the U.S. It could have influence in Catholic attitudes toward non-Christian peoples who would enter the country in much larger numbers following the passage of the Hart Cellar Act in 1965. As we've seen, it would have

---

14. Pope Alexander VI, *Inter Caetera* (1493) http://www.nativeweb.org/pages/legal/indig-inter-caetera.html.

15. As recently at 2005, this logic of Christian supremacy was cited in 2005 by Supreme Court Justice Ruth Bader Ginsburg "in a land-claim ruling against the Oneidas, one of the six nations of the Haudenosaunee." See Renee Gadoua (Religion News Service), "Nuns Blast Catholic Church's 'Doctrine of Discovery' That Justifies Indigenous Oppression," *Huffington Post* (September 10, 2014), http://www.huffingtonpost.com/2014/09/10/catholic-church-doctrine-of-discovery_n_5793840.html.

16. See Liav Orgad and Theodore Ruthizer, "Race, Religion and Nationality in Immigration Selection: 120 Years After the Chinese Exclusion Case," in *Constitutional Commentary* 26:237 (2010) 237–96.

17. cōnspīrātiō *f* (*genitive* cōnspīrātiōnis); *third declension* 1. Union, unanimity, concord, harmony 2. Plot, mutiny, conspiracy (http://en.wiktionary.org/wiki/conspiratio).

consequences relevant to the struggles for women's rights. And its deadly consequences would be in evidence in Catholic responses to the movement for civil rights for African Americans.

Supremacy among the Faithful

Supremacy in the sense of the faithful is not only a theological supremacy guaranteed by the instinct of the church that elevates Christians above persons of other faiths and convictions, it is also a cultural supremacy that becomes a racialized supremacy when enacted. In the logic of *Lumen Gentium,* the function of the church (through the workings of the Trinitarian God) is to draw all people into the hierarchically ordered People of God, and so to make them fully human. Section 7 speaks of redeeming man and remolding him into a new creation. In this process of recreating humanity, the church is able to weed out what is less than human in the world and make it fully human. As expressed in section 13, the church takes to itself the "ability, riches and customs in which the genius of each people expresses itself. Taking them to itself, it purifies, strengthens, elevates and ennobles them" (LG, 13). Coupled with the cultural supremacy of Greco-Latin heritage as affirmed in the much later *Fides et Ratio* as "the providential plan of God" (John Paul II, *Fides et Ratio* (1998), 72)[18] one cannot help but have a sense that the "sense of the faithful" within a global faith has been filtered through Western power structures of the Eurocentric Church.

This is most troubling in light of the historical context of the Civil Rights movement, and the way that theological and cultural supremacy created the conditions for racial supremacy to develop *as* the sense of the faithful in a White Catholic Church. In this country examples stretch back before the founding of the United States in ecclesiastical and civil records from Catholic Louisiana (in 1724), which forbid the marriage of "white subjects" to "black," and forbid pastors, priests, and missionaries to marry them.[19] In 1784 Spanish Catholic Florida's sacramental registers were kept

---

18. "In engaging great cultures for the first time, the Church cannot abandon what she has gained from her inculturation in the world of Greco-Latin thought. To reject this heritage would be to deny the providential plan of God who guides his Church down the paths of time and history. This criterion is valid for the Church in every age, even for the Church of the future, who will judge herself enriched by all that comes from today's engagement with Eastern cultures and will find in this inheritance fresh cues for fruitful dialogue with the cultures which will emerge as humanity moves into the future." See John Paul II, Encyclical Letter, *Fides et Ratio: On the Relationship Between Faith and Reason* (1998) 72.

19. "Civil and Ecclesiastical Records of Louisiana: The Code Noir, 1724," in Cyprian

separately for blacks and whites.[20] Extend from here to the long history of White Catholic slaveholding at every rank of the faithful: bishops, seminaries, priests, religious congregations and laity who possessed other human beings—even other Catholics.[21] These examples demonstrate clearly how the authorized ranking of human beings might have deadly consequences.

Recognizing that the sense of the faithful had emerged to embody a racialized practice of discrimination at odds with the church's universal mission, in 1853 Harriet Thompson, a black Catholic woman, wrote to Pope Piux IX challenging the Catholic Church to see its own contradictions: "It is a great mistake to say that the church watched with equal care over every race and color," she wrote, "for how can it be said they teach all nations when they will not let the black race mix with the white."[22] Describing the conditions of education for black Catholic children, Thompson continued,

> If your Holiness's Nuncio were to condescend while he is here to inquire about the colored people, he would find many families with parents Catholics and the children Protestants, overwhelmed with the belief that the name of Catholic amongst the black race will in a few years fall away.[23]

While Thompson's 1853 letter helps us to mark a historical moment of black and white Catholics "of different ranks," her invitation for the Nuncio to "condescend . . . to inquire about the colored people" witnesses further the analogs in the People of God in various ranks and the races of God's People in various ranks. We do not know whether she meant the former (that the nuncio would condescend to the lowly of the ecclesial ranks) or the latter (that the colored races were counted among the lowly), but in its context the sense of these as parallel hierarchies rings in her words, especially given the refusal of the White Catholic Church to ordain black Catholics. The sense of White Supremacy among the Catholic faithful was little diminished after the abolition of slavery, where Reconstruction maintained separate Catholic spaces for the emancipated—a practice widely held long into the twentieth century—and clerics continued to argue against the ordination of black

---

Davis and Jamie Phelps, eds., *Stamped with the Image of God: African Americans as God's Image in Black* (Maryknoll, NY: Orbis, 2003) 9.

20. "Ecclesiastical Records of St. Augustine Parish in Florida, 1796, 1812," in *Stamped with the Image of God*, 5.

21. Badin, "Portrait of a Saintly Slave, 1806," in *Stamped with the Image of God*, 18. See also Davis, "God of our Weary Years."

22. Thompson, "A Black Woman's Letter to Pope Pius IX," in *Stamped With the Image of God*, 31.

23. Ibid.

Catholics on the logic that their status was "irregular because they are held in contempt by white people."[24]

The point of exploring this historically is to demonstrate how White supremacy emerged *as* the sense of the faithful in the North American context. So that by the time of *Lumen Gentium* an ideology of White Supremacy was embedded in the life of the Catholic faithful, as John McGreevy's study of White Catholic resistance to integration throughout the twentieth century demonstrates with great clarity. In the 1930s, Monsignor John Belford of Brooklyn argued, "Our people do not want the Negroes in the church, in their homes, or their neighborhood."[25] It is not surprising that a leading African-American Catholic would write that "the larger part of the colored population regards the Catholic Church as its bitter enemy, and looks upon Catholics as perhaps the most prejudiced group in the United States."[26] In the 1940s, the pastor at Chicago's Holy Angels, "had routinely requested his few African-American parishioners to sit in six back pews on the right side and 'let the white people who built this church sit in the center.'"[27] As war efforts increased factory work and economic opportunities in the North, and Southern African-Americans sought relocation in large numbers, it was Catholics and their priest-pastors who often lobbied against new government housing for the new Black population, in order to maintain the position achieved by the White parish.[28] It was in a majority Catholic neighborhood outside Chicago in 1951 that Henry Clark rented an apartment for his family, and was met with crowds of 5,000–6,000 angry Whites who protested his act of racial integration until they were dispersed by the National Guard (the material culture of young women's crosses and young men's letterman jackets from Catholic high schools indicating Catholic resistance).[29]

By the time of *Lumen Gentium*, the White Catholic Church sat uneasily in the broader movements for racial justice of the day. For example, White Catholic Sisters may have ministered to Black Catholics in the Jim Crow South as a way of responding to social inequalities, but they did so *within* segregated parishes, hospitals, and schools that at times reinscribed social segregation even while attempting to mitigate its impact. The White Catholic Sisters of Saint Joseph lived next door to the historic Tabernacle

24. Anciaux, "A Report to the Holy See" in *Stamped With the Image of God*, 88.

25. John McGreevy, *Parish Boundaries: The Catholic Encounter with Race in the Twentieth-Century Urban North* (Chicago: University of Chicago Press, 1996) 55–56.

26. Ibid., 61.

27. Ibid., 57.

28. Ibid., 72–74.

29. Ibid., 97.

Baptist Church, where voter registration was being mobilized in Selma, but when White Catholic Sisters from the North came for the historic marches, Selma's own Sisters could not join them because their Archbishop (Thomas Joseph Toolan) would not allow them to march.[30] While many women religious, priests, and lay Catholics did commit themselves to the cause of racial justice, many more refused to see Catholic concern beyond White protectionism. In Northern cities, numerous priests in leadership positions mounted opposition to integration and enacted discrimination and harassment of African-Americans, often on the basis of protecting the White Catholic parish boundaries. In the 1960s, when Northern cities experienced significant increases in the African-American population, they were not necessarily welcomed by White Catholics. White Catholic participation in Civil Rights councils and demonstrations did not represent the whole of the White Catholic community, and at the height of the Civil Rights movement, when Martin Luther King marched through Chicago, Catholic presence in the counter-demonstrations *against* King was evident. One eyewitness recounted seeing "people I went to church with, screaming 'Nigger!' and throwing rocks and dirt at King—these nice people I knew all my life. I couldn't believe it."[31]

The historian's view can demonstrate that a sense of supremacy among the White Catholic Church in America was not reflected in isolated incidents, but formed a broad pattern of practice, nearing consensus. At times, this White racial supremacy may have been underwritten by Catholic theological supremacy as African-Americans migrating from the South were largely Protestant. But, the frightening instinct of White Catholics regarding their own racial supremacy is evidenced in McGreevy's history when interracial cooperation is prioritized by hierarchy of the church, but the instinctual sense of the faithful at large resists and mobilizes against black families moving in, even black *Catholic* families. In Chicago's Trumbull Park, "at St. Kevin's [Catholic parish] three African-American Catholic women who dared attend Sunday mass found parishioners moving themselves away from the pews in which the women were seated . . . . Following one mass, crowds lining both sides of the steps leading to the church 'hissed at . . . hooted at and assaulted' the terrified women as they walked to the rectory to pick up their church envelopes."[32] The women recount being called names,

---

30. Amy Koehlinger, *The New Nuns: Racial Justice and Religious Reform in the 1960s* (Cambridge: Harvard University Press, 2007) 172.

31. McGreevy, *Parish Boundaries*, 190.

32. Ibid., 98.

"even during Mass . . . when we went to the communion rail there were comments."[33]

In its 2014 document, the International Theological Commission defined the *sensus fidei* as:

> reflected in the convergence of the baptized in a lived adhesion to a doctrine of faith or to an element of Christian *praxis*. This convergence (*consensus*) plays a vital role in the Church: the *consensus fidelium* is a sure criterion for determining whether a particular doctrine or practice belongs to the apostolic faith.[34]

The overwhelming evidence that Catholics in America acted on the instinct of White supremacy and abided by the ITC criteria of participation in life of the Church and liturgy, makes it difficult to read the 1964 theological anthropology of "various ranks" and the 2014 ITC explanation of *sensus fidelium* guaranteed by "instinct" and not imagine a correlation between the anthropology of White supremacy and the anthropology of various ranks. What does it mean if the instinct of the Catholic Church in America was as a White racist institution—where racism was not an isolated anomaly but a praxis of most Catholic Christians, as was challenged by the Black Catholic Clergy Caucus in 1968?[35] The instinctual guarantee of Christian truth in Christian praxis seems like a dangerous proposal. If it nears consensus, what in the theology of the *sensus fidelium* is sufficient to disrupt the certainties for some that White supremacy is an instinctual expression "conforming to the truth" (ITC, 54). What sorts of lingering instincts of White Supremacy inform interracial parishes as Catholicism in the U.S. increasingly becomes non-White?

Dissent from the Sense of the Faithful

A theological anthropology that allows for human beings to be "ranked" is dangerous for a church and for the world. But it's there, in *Lumen Gentium's* sense of the faithful, and its damage is being done. The kind of theological anthropology that's required instead is one that admits of no ranks. One that does not allow itself to be lured into the conspiracy of the Spirit in producing ranks and distinctions, and guaranteeing the elevation of some over

---

33. Ibid., 100.

34. International Theological Commission, "*Sensus fidei* in the Life of the Church," sec. 3.

35. Black Catholic Clergy Caucus, "Statement," in *Stamped with the Image of God*, 111.

others. Such a theological anthropology might admit that the commitment to the faith and to the tradition are not on the basis of its guaranteed truth or an inability to err. As a human institution, of course it errs in matters of both doctrine and practice, as is evidenced by the consensus of White cultural and racial supremacy that has been death-dealing, both to Christians and to peoples of other faiths.

The theological anthropology necessary as a first step to undo the racist and theologically supremacist ideologies of the Catholic faith tradition must not speculate in the working of the ineffable Spirit who blows where he wills, nor in the incomprehensible mystery that is God. The only place to root a Christian *theological anthropology* is in the person of Jesus Christ—elevated above others only insofar as his body is tortured, broken, crucified, and raised in spectacle. To undo the damage of a theological anthropology of the various ranks, the only first step is that the "last" be made first.

Perhaps if I have a part in guaranteeing the truth of the Catholic faith—its inability to err in matters that "show a universal consensus" (LG, 12), perhaps dissent is essential in a new way. For while the instinct of White Christians has been to theological, cultural, and racial supremacy, there have always been counter-indications among the faithful that this sense of supremacy is *not* consensus. And as long as we can show that there *is no universal consensus (ever!)* the Catholic Church's ability to claim a truth guaranteed by the Holy Spirit is fundamentally undercut. Perhaps then, *all* Catholics—lay and ordained—would embrace the fallibility of our faith, that we, like all people, have no guarantees to truth and certainty, but put our faith in the crucified One, willing to be in those places where rank and superiority have made claims to truths by which "the lesser" and "simple" have been tortured, crucified, and continue to be put to death. Our theological anthropology need not be guaranteed by the Holy Spirit (functionary of rank) but ought to be fashioned on the One who rejected the hierarchical ordering of the world and assumed his place first among those who ranked as "lowly" in the hopes of calling forth a discipleship of equals.

Part 2

Disputed Questions on the Use of Social Sciences

6

Sensus Fidelium and the International Theological Commission

Has Anything Changed between 2012 and 2014?

GERARD MANNION

THIS CHAPTER BRIEFLY EXAMINES, in a comparative fashion, the understanding of *sensus fidelium* and related concepts (particularly that of *sensus fidei*) in two documents issued by the International Theological Commission (henceforth ITC). The first, issued in 2012, was titled *Theology Today: Perspectives, Principles and Criteria* (completed in November 2011 but published March 8, 2012). The second, issued in June 2014 was *Sensus Fidei in the Life of the Church*.

What degree of consistency between the two ITC documents are we entitled to expect? And what do we actually find? Are there significant developments in the ITC's treatment of these concepts between the two documents? Given that the same group of personnel were responsible for producing the final form of both documents, this paper seeks to explore and analyze whatever developments, changes, and even contradictions may exist between the two documents.

Such a comparative analysis requires attention to the finer nuances of each document. So, following a brief summary of both, I compare and contrast the texts to discern what similarities and differences can be perceived in their respective treatments of the *sensus fidelium* and *sensus fidei* as ecclesial concepts themselves. Second, I consider their treatments of the authority of the wider people of God in discerning, interpreting, and communicating the faith. Third, I explore what they both say about theology and the role of the theologian today. Fourth, I treat the respective understandings of magisterium, particularly as exercised by the hierarchy and specifically vis-à-vis the role of the Catholic theologian and in relation to the *sensus fidelium* itself (and related concepts by implication).[1]

I hope to illustrate that both ITC documents repeat with some consistency a number of interpretative points on the core issues in hand. And both documents appear to contain some ambivalent sections on key issues. But there are also important differences, developments, and even some possible contradictions between the texts. These may ultimately offer grounds for positive hope for future studies and debates on the role of *sensus fidelium* in the church as well as other important considerations with regard to participation and co-responsibility in the practice of magisterium.

Conceptual Background

Traditions in the church's story referring to the collective undertaking to draw together, articulate, and explicate the "sense of the faith" (*sensus fidei*) would be understood as leading to the *sensus fidelium* (the sense of the faithful). Although this actual phrase only began to appear explicitly and more commonly in ecclesial discourse from the nineteenth century onwards, it had featured in discourse in the preceding centuries since the Council of Trent, and *what* it actually refers to was expressed in various ways at least from the times of the early church fathers. Vatican II's *Lumen Gentium*, for example, cites St. Augustine to explicate the notion.[2] As the ecclesiological thinking in relation to this reality became more systematized (in many ways mirroring the evolution of systematic discourse on the notion of magisterium itself, not least of all because many of the same theologians would be involved in the nineteenth-century theological articulations of both terms), the notion of a *consensus* of the faithful concerning a particular aspect of the faith, be this concerning Christian belief or practice, or teaching/doctrine relating to the faith, would be referred to in accordance with the term *consensus fidelium* (consensus of the faithful).

There have been differing understandings within the church of all three of these ecclesiological concepts at different points of history. Although they have often been and continue to be conflated in recent times, Francis A. Sullivan has illustrated how the terms actually concern distinct ecclesial

---

1. Here I focus on *sensus fidelium* as the main focal point because it helps draw together attention given to related concepts and other related debates.

2. C.f. John J. Burkhard, "The *Sensus Fidelium*" in Gerard Mannion and Lewis S. Mudge, ed., *Routledge Companion to the Christian Church* (London: Routledge, 2007) 565–66.

experiences.³ While *sensus fidei* refers to the believer, *sensus fidelium* refers to what is believed and so has an objective dimension, whereas *consensus fidelium* adds the notion of "universal agreement" to the latter concept. *Sensus fidelium* is often equated with the notion of *sensus Ecclesiae* (i.e., the sense or mind of the church) on a given matter (e.g. in the documents of the sixteenth century Council of Trent).⁴

I would add that, in the hermeneutical and existential processes necessary for the emergence of the *sensus fidelium*, complete objectivity remains elusive—for subjective elements must always be involved by necessity.

Much of the discourse over these concepts in recent years has been set against the backdrop of the reception and interpretation of the documents of Vatican II. For example and in particular, consider *Lumen Gentium*, 9–10, 12, 35 and *Dei Verbum*, 7, 8, and 10. As Sullivan further states, the latter document makes clear that the entire church receives the word of God, is apostolic in nature, and hands the faith on.⁵ Sullivan therefore helps demonstrate that bearing witness to the faith is the task of the wider church and that the deposit of faith is given to all within it, as well as pointing toward how these concepts are vitally important to the very formation, reception, and interpretation of tradition and doctrine.

The ITC Document *Theology Today*

The ITC document *Theology Today: Perspectives, Principles and Criteria*⁶ bears all the signs of the manner in which it was composed: by a subcommission, albeit one comprising differing people at different times across

---

3. Francis Sullivan, "The Sense of Faith: the Sense/Consensus of the Faithful" in Bernard Hoose. ed., *Authority and Roman Catholicism* (Aldershot, UK: Ashgate, 2001) 85–94. For further background, see also, John J. Burkhard, "*Sensus fidei*: Meaning, Role and Future of a Teaching of Vatican II," *Louvain Studies* 17 (1992) 18–34; Ormond Rush, "*Sensus Fidei*: Faith 'Making Sense of Revelation,'" *Theological Studies* 62 (2001) 231–261; finally, Jan Kerkhofs, ed., "The *Sensus Fidelium* and Reception of Teaching," Part Five of Gerard Mannion, Richard R. Gaillardetz, Jan Kerkhofs and Kenneth Wilson, ed., *Readings in Church Authority* (Aldershot, UK: Ashgate, 2003) 149–218.

4. E.g. in the documents of the sixteenth-century Council of Trent, Francis A. Sullivan, *Magisterium* (Dublin: Gill & Macmillan, 1983) 23.

5. *Magisterium*, 11. See, also, 21–23, on *Lumen Gentium* 12 and the "supernatural" sense of the faith that "is aroused and sustained by the Spirit of truth" and the two related concepts.

6. International Theological Commission, "Theology Today: Perspectives, Principles and Criteria" (March 2012), http://www.vatican.va/roman_curia/congregations/cfaith/cti_documents/rc_cti_doc_20111129_teologia-oggi_en.html, see, esp. 33–36, 37–44, 55.

several years—i.e. the personnel involved changed at differing stages of its evolution. It is fair to say that, in many vital respects, despite the best efforts of those who *completed* the document, it therefore lacks overall coherence and consistency.[7] *What is most significant, however, is that the final list of ten people responsible for the finished text would be the very same ten who produced the 2014 document.*

Theology Today consists of three chapters. Each is divided into subsections each of which in turn works toward a summary criterion of what Catholic theology is and should be about and/or concerned with. The first, titled "Listening to the Word of God" revisits the nature and primary source and inspiration for theology.[8] It explores the primacy of God's word, the nature of faith as response to this word, and theology's role in helping to understand the faith.

The second chapter, "Abiding in the Communion of the Church" examines the foundational importance of Scripture for theology, the need for fidelity to the apostolic tradition, the need for "responsible adherence to the ecclesiastical magisterium," the role and work of theologians, and the necessity of engaging with the wider world. Midway through this chapter, the document discusses the *sensus fidelium*, a section to which we shall return.

The third and final chapter looks at the task of "Giving an Account of the Truth of God" and features sections on God's truth vis-à-vis the rationality of theology, theology's unity despite the existence of a plurality of methods and disciplines in theology, and a final section that is titled "Science and Wisdom" but is part meditation on the mystical aspects of engaging and making sense of the faith, part reflection on the relationship between human reason and divine knowledge, and part commentary on the Wisdom tradition in the Hebrew Bible and its impact in Christian theology.

The document ends, rather neatly, at its one hundredth paragraph with a conclusion that, it must be said, does not state anything particularly new—neither with regard to offering a novel interpretation of aspects of Catholic theology through its own assertions nor with regard to the synthesis of other interpretations and understandings of the nature and task of theology.

---

7. See the "Preliminary Note," which lists how the work was completed by "a new subcommission" led by Mgr Paul McPartlan and comprising "Most Reverend Jan Liesen, Reverends Serge Thomas Bonino, OP, Antonio Castellano, SDB, Adelbert Denaux, Tomislav Ivančić, Leonard Santedi Kinkupu, Jerzy Szymik, Sister Sara Butler, MSBT, and Doctor Thomas Söding."

8. The first chapter therefore contains three sections that each end in three respective criteria for Catholic theology at 9, "recognition of the primacy of the Word of God"; 15, "that it takes the faith of the Church as its source, context and norm," and 19, "that, precisely as the science of faith, 'faith seeking understanding' . . . it has a rational dimension."

Throughout, the document contains multiple positive and encouraging messages for theology and yet, by and large, the most positive statements are also qualified, held in check, or even contradicted by more restrictive statements that appear to challenge the very vibrancy of the theological enterprise the document seeks to affirm and elucidate. The document, of course, was a creature of the atmosphere and mindsets prevailing in Rome and other ecclesial quarters during its formative time. It is also prone to that long-held Vatican habit of self-referring to other documents generated either by the same office or additional curial dicasteries. So we see numerous self-references to other documents from the ITC alongside various CDF documents. In the process of so doing it manages to offer rather contestable interpretations of more important church teaching documents as well as of other concepts and traditions of vital importance to ecclesiology in particular and theology in general. Again, such is not a surprising modus operandi to find in a document stamped with the approval of the CDF in recent decades.

For the purposes of this essay, the third section of the second chapter, 33–36 is of especial importance. It outlines an *interpretation* of what Vatican II, specifically *Lumen Gentium,* said about the *sensus fidelium*, albeit with a distinctive tone more resonant with the interpretation of the nature and scope of magisterium and theology in-keeping with that which prevailed in Rome during the 1980s and beyond, down through the pontificate of Benedict XVI.

Twice it underlines, on the one hand, that Vatican II affirmed that the whole people of God are charged with making sense of and bearing witness to the faith, but also that the pope and episcopal hierarchy are responsible for authentically (i.e. authoritatively) interpreting the faith. Such a tension, indeed even ambiguity is, of course, there in the Vatican II documents themselves. Thus 33.

Among the most significant passage for our considerations is 34, and so I quote it in full. This also maintains the ambivalence of the earlier passage, as of the council itself,

> The nature and location of the *sensus fidei* or *sensus fidelium must be properly understood.* **The sensus fidelium does not simply mean the majority opinion in a given time or culture, nor is it only a secondary affirmation of what is first taught by the magisterium.** The *sensus fidelium* is the *sensus fidei* of the people of God as a whole who are obedient to the Word of God and are led in the ways of faith by their pastors. So the *sensus fidelium* is the sense of the faith that is deeply rooted in the people of

God who receive, understand, and live the Word of God in the Church.

This paragraph is important because it reflects the somewhat conflicting notions of what the *sensus fidelium* actually is in a most succinct fashion (especially in the second sentence).

Paragraph 35 goes on to state that the *sensus fidelium* serves as a base and locus for the work of theologians, who should themselves maintain a life within the church itself, while

> On the other hand, part of the particular service of theologians within the body of Christ is precisely to explicate the Church's faith as it is found in the Scriptures, the liturgy, creeds, dogmas, catechisms, and in the *sensus fidelium* itself. Theologians help to clarify and articulate the content of the *sensus fidelium*, recognising and demonstrating that issues relating to the truth of faith can be complex, and that investigation of them must be precise.

So also, it states, should theologians scrutinize forms of "popular piety, new currents of thought and movements within the Church, in the name of fidelity to the Apostolic Tradition" in a constructive and humble fashion. The section ends with the criterion thereby identified that "Theology should strive to discover and articulate accurately what the Catholic faithful actually believe."[9]

Now in one sense these sections do not actually tell us a great deal about the precise understanding of *sensus fidelium* that the ITC was working with in the composition of this document. Rather it suggests that diverse opinions among their number mirrored the differing understandings and interpretations of the same that have been prevalent in the church since even before Vatican II. Yet we gain some insight into the finer nuances of what the prevailing attitudes may have been when we move onto the next section of the document, which discusses "Responsible adherence to the ecclesiastical magisterium."[10]

---

9. 36.

10. 37 illustrates the contradictory nature of some of the positions juxtaposed in the document further, e.g., "Bishops and theologians have distinct callings, and must respect one another's particular competence, lest the magisterium reduce theology to a mere repetitive science or theologians presume to substitute the teaching office of the Church's pastors." The positive final sentence is negated by the foregoing in the preceding sentences and indeed sections of the document as a whole. In 38 this is underlined—theologians do "work," while bishops exercise "magisterium." While 39 speaks of many ways in which the magisterium of bishops and work of theologians can complement one another, it also goes on to make clear that the relationship is ultimately

And despite some tentative hints to the contrary, as well as a very qualified acknowledgment of plurality in theology, in the final analysis, it would appear that the 2012 document—by and large—does not perceive theologians to be practitioners of magisterium (except in a very limited and heavily qualified sense) nor are they able legitimately to scrutinize the teaching that comes from the hierarchy or curia in a thoroughgoing fashion.[11]

Another way of looking at the significance of this 2012 document is to suggest that what ultimately prevails in the text risks being a topsy-turvy, even self-contradictory account of the processes of making sense of and bearing witness to the faith. Although the whole people of God are rightly acknowledged as the subject of faith, the document clearly does not acknowledge either theologians or, indeed, the wider faithful as being subjects in the practice of magisterium and yet the history of the church demonstrates clearly that they have always and must continue to be so. Rather the document encapsulates the post-Vatican II version of that narrower sense of magisterium that identifies a function with a very particular and limited set of functionaries, *viz.* the hierarchy and by implication Roman curia.

Furthermore, the *sensus fidelium* appears ultimately prevented from being precisely the activity that it was traditionally understood to be, and this despite the fact that the ITC also acknowledges with Vatican II that the faithful all share in the entire threefold office of Christ, which therefore logically includes participation in ecclesial activities and processes that the rest of the document seeks to reserve for a smaller body within the faithful. Instead the roles of both theologians and the faithful who express the *sensus fidelium* are subordinated to the authority of 'the' hierarchical magisterium.

The outcome is a unidirectional sense of who has the authority to discern what is authentically part of the faith, what are valid interpretations of it and what are not. The direction is from the center outwards and top-down. And yet the notion of the *sensus fidelium* is actually more an affirmation of processes that work the other way around. It is also intended to acknowledge what is, logically speaking, authentically part of the faith.

Finally, both the understanding of *sensus fidelium* and of the role of Catholic theology and of theologians in the 2012 document are framed both implicitly and in parts explicitly within an ecclesiology of communion (e.g. 38) that appears to privilege an understanding of communion that is dependent upon conformity with centrally defined and interpreted criteria.

All in all the document from 2014 does not settle or especially elucidate any of the divisive questions over *sensus fidelium* and related concepts

---

one of subordinate ecclesial function to superior ecclesial authority.

11. See 37–38.

that have been present in the postconciliar church, particularly since the 1980s. Rather it reflects them back at the church and therefore serves less as an important resource in and of its own right and more as an example of some of the ecclesiological problems that not so long ago appeared almost insurmountable to many in the church. This restrictive sense owes more to the vision of, for example, the CDF's 1990 document *Donum veritatis,* which both reflected and exacerbated deep divisions throughout the church in relation to who can and should seek to bear witness to the faith and interpret and explicate authentic doctrine.[12]

"*Sensus Fidei* in the Life of the Church"[13]

The June 2014 ITC document on "*Sensus Fidei* in the Life of the Church" comprises four chapters—the first exploring the notion of *sensus fidei* in Scripture and tradition before discussing the concept in relation to the individual believer's personal life. Chapter 3 is focused on the notion in ecclesial life, first in relation to doctrine and Christian practice, including the contribution of the laity to the *sensus fidei* itself, before turning to consider the concept in relation to "the" magisterium and then in relation to theology, with the fourth and final section being a welcome section on ecumenical considerations in relation to the topic in question.

The fourth and final chapter bears the tantalizing title "How to discern authentic manifestations of the *sensus fidei,*" which discusses dispositions that function as pre-requisites for the apparently "authentic" participation in the *sensus fidei* (it may have been preferable here to say something like "participation in shaping/discerning the *sensus fidelium*"). These are, namely, a) Participation in the life of the Church; b) Listening to the word of God; c) Openness to reason; d) Adherence to the magisterium; e) Holiness—humility, freedom, and joy and, finally, f) Seeking the edification of the Church. The final section explores applications for the charism, specifically vis-à-vis

---

12. Congregation for the Doctrine of the Faith, *Donum Veritatis* (Instruction on the Ecclesial Vocation of the Theologian (May 24, 1990), http://www.vatican.va/roman_curia/congregations/cfaith/documents/rc_con_cfaith_doc_19900524_theologian-vocation_en.html. In the latter document, *Sensus Fidei* is first mentioned in §4, but there it is a direct citation from *Lumen Gentium* 12's articulation of the "supernatural sense of the faith" (the latter also being mentioned in 8 and 13, although, all in all, the council's own understanding appears significantly altered in and by *Donum Veritatis*. The discussion of *Sensus Fidei* that further subordinates the notion to official teachings and opinions comes in 35.

13. International Theological Commission, *Sensus Fidei* in the Life of the Church (June 2014), http://www.vatican.va/roman_curia/congregations/cfaith/cti_documents/rc_cti_20140610_sensus-fidei_en.html#_ftnref5.

popular religiosity, public opinion, and a section on "ways of consulting the faithful."

One of the first things that strikes the reader of this text, in contrast with much of the earlier 2012 ITC document, is the more direct and less ambivalent nature of its assertions. For example, at the outset the document declares that "the faithful have an instinct for the truth of the Gospel, which enables them to recognise and endorse authentic Christian doctrine and practice, and to reject what is false. That supernatural instinct, intrinsically linked to the gift of faith received in the communion of the Church, is called the *sensus fidei*, and it enables Christians to fulfil their prophetic calling . . . It is clear, therefore, that the *sensus fidei* is a vital resource for the new evangelisation to which the Church is strongly committed in our time."[14] In relation to the last sentence, they cite Pope Francis' Apostolic Exhortation, *Evangelii Gaudium*.[15]

The ITC in 2014 distinguishes between the implications of the concept of *sensus fidei* with reference to the individual Christian and its wider ecclesial and consensual application.[16] It may be significant both that there is such a balance and that the individual Christian's experience of *sensus fidei* is not prioritized, as well as the fact that its treatment of the ecclesial and collective unpacking of the *sensus fidelium* is much broader in range and focus, allowing for a multitude of perspectives and voices in comparison with the narrower ecclesiological focus in 2012.

As an illustration of both this more direct language and the wider ecclesiological focus of the 2014 text consider 4,

> The importance of the *sensus fidei* in the life of the Church was strongly emphasized by the Second Vatican Council. Banishing the caricature of an active hierarchy and a passive laity, and in particular the notion of a strict separation between the teaching Church (*Ecclesia docens*) and the learning Church (*Ecclesia discens*), the council taught that all the baptised participate in their own proper way in the three offices of Christ as prophet, priest, and king. In particular, it taught that Christ fulfills his prophetic office not only by means of the hierarchy but also via the laity.[17]

14. 2.

15. 119–20.

16. "In the present document, we use the term, *sensus fidei fidelis*, to refer to the personal aptitude of the believer to make an accurate discernment in matters of faith, and *sensus fidei fidelium* to refer to the Church's own instinct of faith. According to the context, *sensus fidei* refers to either the former or the latter, and in the latter case the term, *sensus fidelium*, is also used," 3.

17. 4. Note that the 2012 document pays lip service to such a position but only

The 2014 document is also refreshing in not only openly acknowledging that there is a variety of opinions and important questions in relation to the concepts in hand but also in how it seeks to begin to offer resources for those seeking to address some of the more pressing controversies among them. So 5 admits, "In the reception and application of the council's teaching on this topic, however, many questions arise, especially in relation to controversies regarding various doctrinal or moral issues. What exactly is the *sensus fidei* and how can it be identified? What are the biblical sources for this idea and how does the *sensus fidei* function in the tradition of the faith? How does the *sensus fidei* relate to the ecclesiastical magisterium of the pope and the bishops, and to theology? What are the conditions for an authentic exercise of the *sensus fidei*? Is the *sensus fidei* something different from the majority opinion of the faithful in a given time or place, and if so how does it differ from the latter?"[18]

This stands in contrast to the manner in which the 2012 document appeared to infer or even explicitly state closure on many such questions, such closure being even more forthright in Benedict XVI's December 2012 address to the ITC.

But the 2014 document does, however, limit itself to modest objectives as opposed to resolving these thorny doctrinal conundrums and disagreements,

> The purpose of the present text is not to give an exhaustive account of the *sensus fidei*, but simply to clarify and deepen some important aspects of this vital notion in order to respond to certain issues, particularly regarding how to identify the authentic *sensus fidei* in situations of controversy, when for example there are tensions between the teaching of the magisterium and views claiming to express the *sensus fidei*.[19]

The ITC 2014 document also acknowledges a variety of differing ways of expressing the same truth that the notion of *sensus fidei* seeks to communicate, including those found in other churches. Indeed its section on ecumenical considerations is one of the more refreshing parts of the document

---

through citing *Gaudium et Spes* 44 and in a much less forthright fashion than how it is expressed in 2014. So, for 2012 c.f. 51–58, "In Dialogue with the World," one of the more positive and open sections of this document.

18. 5. Here the ITC references itself and its earlier document, *Theology Today*, see 5n.5.

19. 6.

in its entirety, albeit with some limited qualifying statements accompanying it also.[20]

Some 128 paragraphs long, the 2014 document ends with the following upbeat conclusion, speaking of Vatican II as a "new pentecost" and of the council's positive "renewed emphasis" on the *sensus fidei*, which "constitutes a most important resource for the new evangelisation." It continues, "By means of the *sensus fidei*, the faithful are able not only to recognise what is in accordance with the Gospel and to reject what is contrary to it, but also to sense what Pope Francis has called "new ways for the journey in faith of the whole pilgrim people."[21]

With the limits of space here, I will offer some reflections on just a few specific sections of this document that appear to be especially important for our considerations today. Among the more significant passages are 72 and 73. There we hear that,

> From the beginning of Christianity, all the faithful played an active role in the development of Christian belief. The whole community bore witness to the apostolic faith, and history shows that, when decisions about the faith needed to be taken, the witness of the laity was taken into consideration by the pastors ... [T]here is evidence that the laity played a major role in the coming into existence of various doctrinal definitions. Sometimes the people of God, and in particular the laity, intuitively felt in which direction the development of doctrine would go, even when theologians and bishops were divided on the issue. Sometimes there was a clear *conspiratio pastorum et fidelium*.[22]

It continues in 73:

> What is less well known, and generally receives less attention, is the role played by the laity with regard to the development of the moral teaching of the Church. It is therefore important

20. It also states, in note 56 (following an affirmation that Christians in other churches contribute to the *sensus fidelium* in the main text), how "In several other places, the council refers to the 'sense' of believers or of the Church in a way analogous to the *sensus fidei* of LG 12. It refers to the *sensus Ecclesiae* (DV 23), *sensus apostolicus* (AA 25), *sensus catholicus* (AA 30), *sensus Christi et Ecclesiae* and *sensus communionis cum Ecclesia* (AG 19), *sensus christianus fidelium* (GS 52), and to an *integer christianus sensus* (GS 62)."

21. The final paragraph declares, "The *sensus fidei* is closely related to the '*infallibilitas in credendo*' that the Church as a whole has as a believing 'subject' making its pilgrim way in history."

22. Furthermore, "Sometimes, when the Church came to a definition, the *Ecclesia docens* had clearly 'consulted' the faithful, and it pointed to the *consensus fidelium* as one of the arguments which legitimated the definition," 72.

to reflect also on the function played by the laity in discerning the Christian understanding of appropriate human behaviour in accordance with the Gospel. In certain areas, the teaching of the Church has developed as a result of lay people discovering the imperatives arising from new situations. The reflection of theologians, and then the judgment of the episcopal magisterium, was based on the Christian experience already clarified by the faithful intuition of lay people.

The frank and refreshingly unqualified nature of this acknowledgment cuts through a swath of more controversial and tentative exchanges throughout the church on such issues in recent decades. Further key sections of the document come in the following section, on "the *sensus fidei* and the magisterium" where the document acknowledges not only that "magisterium listens to the *sensus fidelium*" as a statement of fact, but also asserts that because "in matters of faith the baptised cannot be passive," and, *therefore* the (hierarchical) magisterium[23]

> **has to be** attentive to the *sensus fidelium*, the living voice of the people of God. Not only do they have the right to be heard, but their reaction to what is proposed as belonging to the faith of the Apostles must be taken very seriously, because it is by the Church as a whole that the apostolic faith is borne in the power of the Spirit. The magisterium does not have sole responsibility for it. The magisterium should therefore refer to the sense of faith of the Church as a whole. The *sensus fidelium* can be an important factor in the development of doctrine, and it follows that the magisterium needs means by which to consult the faithful (74).

This brings to the fore a very different overall understanding of magisterium, of the place and role of the laity in contributing to it and returns the focus to the intentions of many Vatican fathers and *periti*, especially Yves Congar who is especially singled out for his visionary work on these concepts by the 2014 text itself. I suggest that one line, "The magisterium does not have sole responsibility for [the faith]. The magisterium should therefore refer to the sense of faith of the Church as a whole" offers something of a hermeneutical key to discerning the differences between the 2012 and 2014 documents as we shall see.

However, lest we believe that there is a new genre of ecclesial document being rolled out in the 2014 text, in the following sections, the document

---

23. Both documents make the familiar category mistake of identifying magisterium with a select hierarchical group of its practitioners rather than primarily seeing the term as referring to an activity that involves multiple processes and practitioners alike.

returns to 'Roman type' more familiar prior to 2013 and in effect brings in heavy qualifications of everything positive it has just said. So, in 76 we are told "the magisterium nurtures, discerns and judges the *sensus fidelium*," while somewhat contradictorily stating that popes and bishops, who seem now, once more, to be affirmed as the only people who exercise magisterium, are nonetheless also part of the people of God themselves and so participate in (shaping/discernment of) the broader *sensus fidelium*. While 77 leaves us in no doubt that those earlier positive statements about the role of the wider faithful have most definite restrictions, because the

> magisterium also judges with authority whether opinions which are present among the people of God, and which may seem to be the *sensus fidelium*, actually correspond to the truth of the Tradition received from the Apostles . . . .[24] **Thus, judgment regarding the authenticity of the *sensus fidelium* belongs ultimately not to the faithful themselves nor to theology but to the magisterium.**[25]

Hence the document offers much promise albeit with a continued qualification that reserves particular privileges for "the" official magisterium. So the fluctuations and ambivalence on such issues, present with the church since before Vatican II but accentuated by the compromises in the final conciliar texts and both a symptom and cause of postconciliar ecclesiological and indeed ecclesial divisions, are far from absent in this document. Indeed the ambivalence is further entrenched in some respects when the document reaches its later sections on guidelines for consulting the faithful, something it commends the hierarchy to do. So in 121 we hear that "The word 'consult' includes the idea of seeking a judgment or advice as well as inquiring into a matter of fact. On the one hand, in matters of governance and pastoral issues, the pastors of the Church can and should consult the faithful in certain cases in the sense of asking for their advice or their judgment. On the other hand, when the magisterium is defining a doctrine, it is appropriate to consult the faithful in the sense of inquiring into a matter of fact."

This further compounds the sense of ambivalence and betrays fluctuating ecclesiological thinking at work behind the formation of the document.

---

24. Here it even undoes another earlier statement, namely its affirmation of Vatican II's seeking to transcend the teaching/learning church dichotomy by stating, "As Newman said: 'the gift of discerning, discriminating, defining, promulgating, and enforcing any portion of that tradition resides solely in the *Ecclesia docens*.'"

25. To further muddy the ambivalent waters thus stirred, it continues, "it is always within the communion life of the Church that the magisterium exercises its essential ministry of oversight."

This is also true of 123, which is another refreshingly honest acknowledgment of the tensions that surround all the issues in hand, because it recognizes the challenges posed when a majority of the faithful are indifferent to or even reject particular official doctrines, yet it also acknowledges the fault for such occurrences can have two distinct origins,

> This lack of reception may indicate a weakness or a lack of faith on the part of the people of God, caused by an insufficiently critical embrace of contemporary culture. *But in some cases it may indicate that certain decisions have been taken by those in authority without due consideration of the experience and the sensus fidei of the faithful, or without sufficient consultation of the faithful by the magisterium.*

Comparing the Two Texts: Did Anything Change between 2012 and 2014?

We are not strictly comparing like with like. The 2012 document had a much broader focus than *sensus fidelium* of course and the 2014 document deals first and foremost with *sensus fidei*, although it then moves onto explore the *sensus fidelium*, which it understands as the collective ecclesial form of the former. Despite these caveats we can and should compare the texts because they are closely related in so many ways, not simply in focus but also in terms of origin, composition, and even in terms of aims and objectives.

While the focus of each document is somewhat different, one could say, as both texts themselves imply throughout, the respective primary focal points of both are inseparably linked in the church's tradition and how it is formed, shaped, discerned and disseminated.

First what they share in common. Both ITC documents repeat with some consistency a number of interpretative points on the core issues in hand. But, as noted, both documents also appear to contain some ambivalent sections. Perhaps the most significant area where these documents appear to exhibit such ambivalence is with regard to the subordination of the voice of the faithful and so of the faithful's discernment of the faith to the practice of magisterium by the episcopal hierarchy.

In relation to this issue, the 2012 document certainly appears to owe more to its understanding of these concepts to the perspectives offered in documents such as the CDF's *Donum Veritatis* (1990). The 2012 document is clearly operating on a more subordinationist understanding of *sensus fidelium* and related concepts.

One key distinction between the two documents is that, despite many positive sections, including statements on theological pluralism, the 2012 document maintains a more *uniformly* hierarchical and subordinationist understanding of magisterium and of the role of the people of God in general and of Catholic theologians in particular with regard to discerning, interpreting, and communicating the faith, whereas the 2014 version—in many sections—is more consistently open to a dialogical and participatory understanding of the same.

That having been said, even in the 2014 document there is ultimately an ambiguity reminiscent of some of the tensions on key issues that were left unresolved also in the documents of Vatican II, particularly pertaining to questions of magisterium, collegiality, and the role of the faithful, among other issues.

But, these ambivalences notwithstanding, while some headlines announced the launch of the 2014 text with an agenda aimed firmly at underlining a hermeneutics of continuity, essentially with the line of predominant thinking of the 2012 document and therefore effectively of *Donum Vertitatis*,[26] this document from 2014 actually has very real and significant differences to the predominant line taken in both those earlier texts. Overall, the 2014 text contains fewer "neutralizing" qualifications in relation to its positive assertions. It thereby not only contains a lesser degree of ambivalence than the 2012 text but also—at least potentially speaking—allows for the possibility of a different and more nuanced understanding of both the *sensus fidei* and therefore of the *sensus fidelium*, as well as of the role of theologians and, overall, of magisterium in general. There are also further important differences, developments, and even some possible contradictions between the texts. All in all, one can say that the 2014 document is charged throughout with a recognition of a much more active and *creative* role of the *sensus fidei* by the same ITC that is less articulated—if genuinely present at all—in the document from 2012.

The 2014 document's default recognition of this more active and creative role of the *sensus fidei* could, in theory, lend itself to very positive and potentially innovative applications. So, two further key differences between the 2012 and 2014 documents are, first, in relation to their different ecclesiological tone and even mood—one is more cautious, guarded, and limited in optimism. The other more hope-filled and creatively energetic in most sections, albeit with limiting qualifications along the way. Second, and related, the respective documents reflect different nuances and emphases

---

26. E.g., the UK *Catholic Herald* announced the 2014 text under the banner "Vatican theologians: don't confuse *sensus fidelium* with majority opinion."

on core issues. Both of these characteristics lead to markedly different treatments of certain aspects of the main issues.

So, while the 2014 document retains a subordinating sense in parts, alongside ambivalence on key issues, it undoubtedly is more expansive and positive in other sections with regard to the scope of the role of the faithful and theologians in particular in identifying and interpreting the *sensus fidelium*. The document also devotes substantive sections to topics such as participation in the *sensus fidelium* and on encouraging a wider consultation of the faithful on the part of hierarchical practitioners of magisterium. An affirmation of the ecumenical implications of these ecclesiological concepts also receives positive treatment. As we have seen, there are some truly refreshing and potentially ecclesially transformative aspects to the text. But do the remaining ambivalences and ecclesiological fluctuations thwart the potential of those creative and constructive sections?

Why Was There Change?

In seeking to account for any differences between the two documents, what conclusions might we draw? Let us address the glaringly obvious difference in the church between 2012 and 2014—regime change. Clearly the change in papacy, in March 2013, has impacted the ITC, just as it is bringing about changes in the church in general.

Second, quite obviously members of the ITC may have felt inspired and/or less inhibited in going about their work and so will have felt more freedom to develop their collective discernment on these matters. Perhaps the debate around the sub-commission's table became more helpfully robust, even while the ambivalences that remain in the document also reflect tensions and ambivalences that remained in the final documents of Vatican II and that were subsequently exploited to privilege a more hierarchical and subordinationist understanding of *Sensus Fidei* and *Sensus Fidelium* and the role of the Catholic theologian in subsequent decades.

But one of the key explanations for the differences between the documents is that by 2014 the ITC had time already to reflect upon the fact that Pope Francis has clearly rehabilitated the sense of the church understood as the People of God and likewise sought to reemphasize and encourage other key aspects of Vatican II in a new fashion for these times, including a participatory sense of magisterium in the church, collegiality, and co-responsibility in the church. Francis has also publicly reiterated Vatican II's affirmation of the infallibility of the people of God, i.e., the church, as a whole,[27] later going so far as to declare at in his closing remarks to the 2015 synod that it was a "wonderful phrase."

Francis has also made it clear, particularly in his apostolic exhortation *Evangelii Gaudium* that he does not prioritise rigid doctrinal formulae and definitions nor ecclesial structures first and foremost, rather he priorities the faith, the putting into practice of the gospel, and prefers to emphasize themes such as unity in diversity, pluralism, the importance and validity of context and inculturation, the freedom of theological and biblical enquiry.

In all, we see Pope Francis is clearly affirming *Sensus Fidelium* and *Sensus Fidei* in an especially positive fashion and in multiple ways. For Francis, *all the faithful are agents of evangelization.* The "people of God" are not, he tells us, to be considered "passive recipients" of some special insights from a "professional class."[28] Francis states,

> In all the baptized, from first to last, the sanctifying power of the Spirit is at work, impelling us to evangelization. The people of God is holy thanks to this anointing, which makes it infallible *in credendo.* This means that it does not err in faith, even though it may not find words to explain that faith. The Spirit guides it in truth and leads it to salvation. As part of his mysterious love for humanity, God furnishes the totality of the faithful with an instinct of faith—*sensus fidei*—which helps them to discern what is truly of God. The presence of the Spirit gives Christians a certain connaturality with divine realities, and a wisdom which enables them to grasp those realities intuitively, even when they lack the wherewithal to give them precise expression.

He goes on to underline (198) how the poor, in particular, share in the *sensus fidei.*

The understanding of the *sensus fidelium* and of Catholic theology and ultimately of magisterium displayed thus far in the teachings, statements, and actions of Pope Francis appear to be something quite different to what prevailed for several decades prior to his election.

In EG section 139, Francis employs an evocative motif that John XXIII was fond of—the church understood as a mother. Here it would seem that the image is directly employed to help transform the understanding of magisterium, "a good mother can recognize everything that God is bringing about in her children, she listens to their concerns and learns from them." Both mother and child teach and learn from each other.

---

27. Cf. *Lumen Gentium*, 9–10, *Dei Verbum*, 7, 8 and 10; see Sullivan above, *Magisterium*, 11

28. *Evangelii Gaudium*, 120.

In his statements pertaining to *sensus fidei* and magisterium in general, Francis also wishes to transcend the outdated distinction between a hierarchical teaching church and the faithful understood as the learning church. And he has sought to practice what he has been preaching. Consider how he personally requested that nuncios, bishops, and episcopal conferences around the world elicit responses about questions concerning, divorce, remarriage, human relationships, and family life ahead of both the 2014 and the 2015 meetings of the Extraordinary Synod of Bishops on the Family, thereby at once helping to try and make the process more truly synodal than has been the case hitherto and to genuinely seek to take soundings from among the global participants in the *sensus fidelium* as fully as possible. His 2015 addresses to the synod firmly confirmed this.

Therefore it seems probable that the 2014 document, in part at least, attempted to try and incorporate some aspects of the ecclesiological vision and understanding of Pope Francis, albeit alongside those earlier already ambivalent notions of the core concepts under discussion present in earlier drafts of the 2014 text. Ambivalent because their sources were ambivalent and ambivalent because the conversation partners involved on the ITC would no doubt equally have had differences of opinion. And, finally, ambivalent because of that continued state of ecclesial liminality, the betwixt and between world of being caught between two radically different papacies with what could be perceived as even directly opposing ecclesiological visions in relation to many vital questions concerning the very subject of *sensus fidelium* and related concepts.

Regime change alone is not sufficient to explain the different perspectives in the documents, although it is a hugely important factor to consider. But other questions need to be explored also. Not least of all, when were the most frank and honest parts of the 2014 document composed? When did the new tone and focus get introduced and, above all else, when did the shift in ecclesiological focus start to take place in the work of the subcommission and what motivated this?

Concluding Remarks

The key difference between the ITC's 2012 and 2014 documents is their ecclesiological backdrop—one leans heavily toward a centralizing set of ecclesiological priorities, the other takes the first tentative steps toward embracing a more decentralizing ecclesiology with all the implications for the understanding and practice of magisterium such entails.

Yet, in the final analysis the 2014 document should be also judged to retain ambivalences and to maintain contradictions that it does not resolve (again some reflective of faults remaining in Vatican II documents), others of the ecclesial tensions exacerbated by official documents and activities in more recent decades). On these issues, at least, Pope Francis has thus far proved less ambivalent, quite the contrary.

The church's authorities have an even greater responsibility than that responsibility that 2012's *Theology Today* said belonged to theologians in stating that "Attention to the *sensus fidelium* is a criterion for Catholic theology. Theology should strive to discover and articulate accurately what the Catholic faithful actually believe. It must speak the truth in love, so that the faithful may mature in faith, and not be 'tossed to and fro and blown about by every wind of doctrine' (Eph 4:14–15)."[29] The great irony here is that the 2012 document to a large extent, and even the 2014 contributions to a significant degree, actually served to toss the faithful to and fro and blow them about on every wind of doctrine in the same fashion that much of the aggressive authoritarian stance of church authorities in the past decades have polarized, alienated, and driven away Catholics in equal measure. Pope Francis appears to understand this and hence has taken a different approach.

Another conclusion one could draw here is further support for the oft-stated call that the ITC itself needs radical reform (if not outright abolition—in the technological age we live in, for example, is it truly necessary if its only functions are those that it currently performs?). When one looks at the composition and remit of the ITC from its foundation until the mid-1970s it was clearly a gathering of some of the leading and most creative Catholic theological minds from around the globe. Not even its greatest supporters would seek to argue that it could be so described in recent decades, with some notable exceptions, because everybody knows that docility to the official position of Rome under the previous two pontiffs became the leading criterion for appointment to the commission and its remit became affirming positions already determined by other curial departments.

These issues require a much greater, explicit, and practical commitment to a dialogical and participatory understanding of magisterium, theological pluralism, and of *sensus fidelium* in order to become more consistent.

Perhaps a way forward, then, might be for a collaborative study of *sensus fidelium* that is independent of the need to be approved by the CDF and that might therefore rather genuinely start out from the notion of the people of God who live out and must therefore also make sense of and bear witness to the faith in the gracious self-communication of the threefold God. With

---

29. *Theology Today*, 36.

priorities duly ordered in such a fitting way, there might then be other opportunities for reflection upon the longstanding role of the teachers in the church who became known as theologians, and indeed also of those teachers who also exercised other ministries of oversight who became known as bishops.

The 2014 document text concludes, "It is only natural that there should be a constant communication and regular dialogue on practical issues and matters of faith and morals between members of the Church" (124). With a more consistent, holistic, and wide-reaching ecclesiological vision as the guiding principle, an understanding of magisterium as a collective process involving multiple sets of actors with differing and often truly complementary charisms (albeit sometimes also conflicting perspectives) might emerge.

7

Sensus fidei and Sociology

How Do We Find the Normative
in the Empirical?

 Neil Ormerod

WHILE THE NOTION OF the *sensus fidei* made its first appearance in a magisterial document in *Lumen Gentium*, the Dogmatic Constitution of the Church at Vatican II, its antecedents can be traced back to the New Testament and patristic conceptions of the Church.[1] However, its more prominent and proximate source was a relatively slight, highly influential but at the time significantly controversial work by John Henry Newman, "On consulting the faithful in matters of doctrine."[2] Published in 1869, the essay outlined Newman's argument on the role of the faithful during the Arian crisis in maintaining fidelity to Church belief, even at a time when those charged with the official teaching office had failed to do so. The work remained out of print in English until the eve of the Council, though it was available in German translation and undoubtedly influenced the debates of the Council fathers.[3]

Newman's argumentative essay, brief as it is, is rather more fulsome in its handling of the matter than the perfunctory statement to be found

---

1. The document "*Sensus Fidei* in the Life of the Church" [henceforth SFLC] by the International Theological Commission notes various NT texts, including John 15:26, Rev 3:14, and 1 John 2:20, 27, as well as various patristic sources including the dictum of Vincent of Lerins concerning what was "held everywhere, always and by everyone" (SFLC n. 23).

2. John Henry Newman, *On Consulting the Faithful in Matters of Doctrine* (London: Chapman, 1961). Interestingly the ITC document passes over the controversy around Newman's proposal in silence.

3. SFLC nn. 34–35 also highlights the contribution of Johann Adam Möhler prior to Newman, in reviving the notion of the *sensus fidei*.

in *Lumen Gentium* n.12. While I shall consider the text of this document later in this chapter, in a fashion fairly typical of Church documents it asserts certain notions with little or no concern (or desire) to specify its exact meaning.[4] While we may presume that Newman is the proximate source of the notion, we cannot infer that the document means exactly what Newman meant in relation to the *sensus fidei*, or even that the council Fathers had any precise meaning other than the fairly vague assertions made in the text itself.[5] As is often the case with the use of such notions in Church documents, it is left up to theologians to try to make sense of what it might all mean.

My first task then is to attempt to understand what this notion might mean. Various theologians have made significant contributions to this task in terms of unpacking the religious significance of the *sensus fidei* and its associated terms.[6] While of value, I shall adopt a different approach that seeks to understand the reality of the *sensus fidei* drawing on categories more commonly found in sociological writings. In part this approach will be in dialogue with the contribution of social scientist Jerome Baggett's work to the field.[7] The approach is motivated by the more general concern that ecclesiology requires engagement with the social sciences in order to properly understand the ecclesial object.[8] My second task will be to examine the ways in which theologians and church authorities utilize the notion of the *sensus fidei* to see whether it can stand the weight that is placed upon it.

---

4. For example, classical Trinitarian and Christological doctrines speak of persons, hypostases, natures, and so on without ever defining the terms.

5. Council teaching on the *sensus fidei* extends beyond the contribution of LG n.12. Though the term is not used elsewhere, the reality it intends is evident in other documents and other sections of LG. See SFLC nn. 45–46.

6. See for example the recent work of Ormond Rush, "Sensus fidei: Faith 'making sense' of revelation," *Theological Studies* 62 (2001) 231–61; *The Eyes of Faith: The Sense of the Faithful and the Church's Reception of Revelation* (Washington, D.C.: Catholic University of America Press, 2009); John J. Burkhard, "'Sensus fidei': Recent Theological Reflection (1990–2001), part I," *Heythrop Journal* 46 (2005) 450–75, and "'Sensus fidei': Recent Theological Reflection (1990–2001), part II," *Heythrop Journal* 47 (2006) 38–54, provided a thorough account of the literature up to 2001.

7. See Jerome P. Baggett, *Sense of the Faithful: How American Catholics Live Their Faith* (New York: Oxford University Press, 2009). Also his essay in the *Proceedings of the Catholic Theological Society of America* 70 (2015) 1–26; http://ejournals.bc.edu/ojs/index.php/ctsa/article/view/8750/7968.

8. A position long promoted by the noted ecclesiologist Joseph Komonchak. Also see Neil Ormerod, *Re-Visioning the Church: An Experiment in Systematic-Historical Ecclesiology* (Minneapolis: Fortress, 2014). This issue is simply not pursued in SFLC. Apart from a couple of mentions of sociological approaches in nn. 47, 113, which are largely cautions, no real engagement with or insights from the social sciences contributes to the discussion.

I begin with a more general discussion on the relationship between theology and the social sciences. It raises important questions about the relationship between empirical and normative stances, an issue of particular significance to any discussion of the *sensus fidei*. I then consider how the notion of the *sensus fidei* would look from the perspective of the social sciences. The advantage of this is that it places the *sensus fidei* into a more concrete context and hopefully provides a better grounding for studying its meaning and implications. I conclude with some comments in relation to the ways in which the *sensus fidei* is evoked to examine the extent to which such appeals may or may not be legitimate.

Empirical and Normative Stances

One of the better known of Bernard Lonergan's distinctions is that between the classicist and empirical notions of culture. The classicist notion of culture looks to the great achievements of the past and finds in them a normative guide to the present. The empirical notion of culture defines culture concretely as the meanings and values that inform a way of life.[9] With regard to empirical approaches to the question of the *sensus fidei*, what Jerome Baggett's book *Sense of the Faithful* has done is demonstrate the complexities involved once we take the empirical notion of culture seriously when applied to the Church.[10] We must always keep in mind that culture embraces a multilayered reality. There are dominant elements and subversive elements; indeed there may be relatively coherent subcultures which may be quite distinct from and opposed to the dominant culture; and even within a dominant culture there can be inconsistencies and contradictions where, for example, two relatively contradictory values might both be held up for appreciation. This is no more or less true whether we are investigating the culture of a nation or the culture of the Church. In both cases the empirical data can present us with a kaleidoscope of diversity.

Of course some have read Lonergan's distinction as promoting a cultural relativism, as denying the possibility of finding cultural or theological norms.[11] However, this is not the case. Lonergan advocated an empirical ap-

---

9. Bernard J. F. Lonergan, *Method in Theology* (London: Darton, Longman & Todd, 1972). Kathryn Tanner usefully outlines the historical shift within cultural anthropology from a more normative to an empirical notion of culture. See Kathryn Tanner, *Theories of Culture: A New Agenda for Theology* (Minneapolis: Fortress, 1997).

10. Baggett, *Sense of the Faithful*.

11. Many more popular presentations of Lonergan's position head in this direction. More seriously John Finnis has criticized Lonergan's whole methodology as promoting relativism. See John Finnis, *Fundamentals of Ethics* (Oxford: Clarendon, 1983)

proach to culture, but not an empiricist account. He had a strong conviction that the previous classicist culture did contain permanent achievements, but he located the normative elements of those achievements not in the products of culture so much as in the fundamental drive to meaning, truth, and goodness that led to their production.[12] For Lonergan the normative components of culture reside in our fidelity to the transcendental precepts: be attentive, be intelligent, be reasonable, be responsible, and be in love; and in religious, moral, and intellectual conversion that strengthen and protect that fidelity. Within this framework, the authenticity of the subject is never a permanent achievement but ever a withdrawal from inauthenticity, a precarious and fragile position that can never be taken for granted.[13]

None of this alleviates the problem of finding a normative stance in relation to the data provided by cultural anthropology. We can still ask: what does it mean to be a citizen of my nation? What does it mean to be Catholic? Implicit in such questions is the quest for a norm: what does it mean to be a *good* citizen or *good* Catholic? Again this is not a new question or concern. If we were to take the Aristotelian definition of a human being as a "rational animal" and compare it with the empirical data, we could easily find no shortage of irrational human behavior on display. The definition *is* the norm; we are meant to be creatures who are guided by the use of reason, even though we may fail to do so.[14] The multiple examples of failure to be rational do not undermine or negate the definition, and so amassing empirical evidence either way is beside the point. Rather the question we must address concerns the genesis of the norm. Why do we hold onto the definition, with its inherently normative elements, in the face of contrary empirical evidence?

In relation to the Church Baggett frames this same issue in terms of the question, "what does it mean to identify with an authoritative religious tradition?" How exactly can the claims of such an authoritative religious tradition be married to an understanding of faith which is now consistently framed in terms of a quest for personal authenticity, where faith is identified as valid "for me"? As he states it, "what does it mean to live in accordance

---

42–44. For a response see Frederick G. Lawrence, "Finnis on Lonergan: A Reflection," *Villanova Law Review* 57 (2012) 849–71.

12. In fact, Lonergan's discussion of meaning, particularly the functions, realms, and stages of meaning provide a good tool kit for cultural analysis and evaluation rather than just descriptive accounts. See Lonergan, *Method*, particularly chapter 3.

13. Ibid., 110.

14. See also Alasdair MacIntyre, *After Virtue: A Study in Moral Theory*, 2nd ed. (Notre Dame: University of Notre Dame Press, 1984) 51–61, on the issue of how an "is" can be an "ought."

with an authoritative religious tradition when the triumphant Subject reigns supreme?"[15] Or in more biblical terms, what is meant by the obedience of faith (Rom 1:5; 16:26)?

Theology and the Social Sciences

The problem we are dealing with is the gap between empirical and normative stances, a gap that is inescapable when we move into the human sciences, as well as the disciplines of philosophy and theology.[16] This is a distinguishing characteristic of the human sciences that differentiates them from the physical sciences.[17] In the physical sciences, if the data do not match the hypothesis to be tested, then the hypothesis does not stand. It needs revision, adjustment, or might simply need to be ditched. In the human sciences, if the data do not match the hypothesis, now acting as a *de facto* norm, then the problem may lie in the data, not the hypothesis. Just as the empirical fact of irrational behavior in human beings does not negate the normative stance that humans are rational animals, so too empirical data on their own in the social sciences cannot simply be used as evidence for or against any particular hypothesis. The relation between data- and norm-driven theory is much more complex than in the physical sciences.

Such insights into the inherent difficulties of the human sciences are not unknown in the discipline. Roy Bhaskar, in a school of social sciences known as "critical realism," acknowledges the possibility that "the phenomena themselves may be false,"[18] while Alasdair MacIntyre concisely argues:

> Unintelligible actions are failed candidates for the status of intelligible action; and to lump unintelligible actions and intelligible actions together in a single class of actions and then characterize actions in terms of what items of both sets have in common is to make the mistake of ignoring this.[19]

---

15. Quotes taken from the text of his paper presented to the CTSA.

16. Illustrative of this gap: "This is an appropriate reminder simply because there exists no one thing called American Catholicism." Baggett, *Sense of the Faithful*, 57.

17. Of course there are approaches to the human sciences that attempt to mimic the physical sciences, by eliminating what is most human about those sciences, such as questions of meaning and value. Such positivist approaches have little to offer to the questions we are considering. They are not only empirical, but empiricist.

18. Roy Bhaskar, "Societies," in Margaret Archer, et al., eds., *Critical Realism: Essential Readings* (London: Routledge, 1998) 231. For a recent work taking up Bhaskar's approach see Christian Smith, *What Is a Person? Rethinking Humanity, Social Life, and the Moral Good from the Person Up* (Chicago: University of Chicago Press, 2010).

19. MacIntyre, *After Virtue*, 209.

The idea that data may be false or unintelligible is also captured by Lonergan in his notion of the social surd.[20] The social and cultural orders may be so infected by the problem of evil, through institutional sinfulness and ideological distortions that they suffer from a major deficit in intelligibility; aspects of these orders resist our understanding and hence resist proper theoretical exposition.[21] A good example of such distortion was the nation of South Africa under the era of apartheid, where distinctions were drawn between people on the basis of their skin color. People in the same family would receive differing classification as "white," "colored," or "black" depending only on their skin color. This distortion created a massive unintelligibility or surd within the social order, as people's social, economic, and political future was subject to such arbitrary determinations. As with MacIntyre, Lonergan warns of the dangers of capitulating to such a social surd, of treating it as if it were intelligible and then conforming one's theories to fit such distorted "facts."[22] The outcome of such an error is simply to amplify the social surd leading to long term and perhaps terminal decline.[23]

These observations raise significant questions in relation to the social sciences, the problem of the fact-value split, the need to reorient the social sciences as they are presently constituted and so on. I have taken up these questions elsewhere.[24] It suffices to say here that these problems are not lessened in any way once we turn our attention to the application of these methods in relation to the church.

The *Sensus Fidei* in the Church and Socialization

We can now turn our attention to the notion of the *sensus fidei* in relation to the Church. It finds doctrinal expression in *Lumen Gentium* n.12 as follows:

---

20. Bernard J. F. Lonergan, *Insight: A Study of Human Understanding*, ed. Crowe Frederick E. and Robert M. Doran, Collected works of Bernard Lonergan 3 (Toronto: University of Toronto Press, 1992) 254–57.

21. As Bhaskar and Collier note, this approach parallels an Augustinian account of evil as privation. Roy Bhaskar and Andrew Collier, "Introduction: Explanatory critiques," in Margaret Archer et al., eds., *Critical Realism: Essential Readings* (London: Routledge, 1998) 389.

22. Lonergan, *Insight*, 255–56. I should note that this issue is very evident in the sociology of religion, which steadfastly holds to an empirical account of religion, bringing together intelligible and unintelligible elements into its understanding of the nature of religion.

23. As Lonergan notes, "A civilization in decline digs its own grave with a relentless consistency," *Method*, 55.

24. See Ormerod, *Re-Visioning the Church*, chapters 3 and 4.

> The entire body of the faithful, anointed as they are by the Holy One, cannot err in matters of belief. They manifest this special property by means of the whole peoples' supernatural discernment in matters of faith [*supernaturali sensu fidei*] when "from the Bishops down to the last of the lay faithful" they show universal agreement in matters of faith and morals. That discernment in matters of faith is aroused and sustained by the Spirit of truth.

Despite its brevity, much has been written by theologians on this statement and its theological antecedents and warrants in the tradition, and the nuances of its meaning. However, before we become overly theological about addressing this claim, it is worth attending to what a social scientist might make of it.[25]

Sociologists are well familiar with the notion of socialization. Children are socialized into the social and cultural meanings and values of their community through their family experiences, their education, and their initiation into the workforce and the body politic. This more or less successful process ensures that they can function properly in social situations and participate in the economy, the polity, and the culture they live in. Through this process, as Baggett puts it, people develop "a feel for this particular game, it means they have attained the requisite cultural competence."[26] With socialization we become socially and culturally adept. Without socialization, social and cultural identity would be dissipated or even lost altogether.

Viewed through the light of the scholastic axiom that "grace completes and perfects nature," the claim to the existence of the *sensus fidei* is a graced version of the natural process of socialization. Since the object of the *sensus fidei* includes revealed truth—"cannot err in matters of belief"—it must involve a supernatural component in the believer—it is a "supernatural discernment"—and so is the work of the Holy Spirit, the Spirit of Truth. However, this work of the Spirit can only build upon, and not replace, the natural processes whereby the believer is socialized into the world of faith by their parents, their schooling in the faith, their participation in prayer, liturgy, and sacraments, and the whole life of the church.[27] It may be supernatural,

---

25. Vatican I taught that one task of theology was to understand the mysteries of faith through analogies with what is naturally known. This can be read as one way to do just that.

26. As another social theorist puts it, socialization is "the means by which social and cultural continuity are attained." John A. Clausen, ed., *Socialization and Society* (Boston: Little Brown, 1968) 5.

27. Hence the insistence of SFLC n. 89: "The first and most fundamental disposition is active participation in the life of the Church. Formal membership of the Church

but it is not magic. These processes do not guarantee successful socialization into the *sensus fidei* any more than natural processes of socialization in society at large are guaranteed to produce sound citizens. They simply shift the probabilities towards a more successful outcome. The activity of the Spirit cannot be evoked to make up for deficits in the overall process.

We can identify some of this sense of historical realism in Newman's own account of the operation of the *sensus fidei*. In his essay "On Consulting the Faithful" he presents what I might call a realistically diffuse statement of its operation in relation to maintaining the faith of the Church:

> the body of the faithful is one of the witnesses to the fact of the tradition of revealed doctrine, and . . . their *consensus* through Christendom is the voice of the Infallible Church.
>
> I think I am right in saying that the tradition of the Apostles, committed to the whole Church in its various constituents and functions *per modum unius*, manifests itself variously at various times: sometimes by the mouth of the episcopacy, sometimes by the doctors [i.e. theologians], sometimes by the people, sometimes by liturgies, rites, ceremonies, and customs, by events, disputes, movements, and all other phenomena which are comprised under the name of history. It follows that none of these great channels of tradition may be treated with disrespect; granting at the same time fully, that the gift of discerning, discriminating, defining, promulgating, and enforcing any portion of that tradition resides solely in the *Ecclesia docens*.[28]

This is a beautifully balanced statement taking into account the various "channels" through which the tradition flows. The body of the faithful is "one of the witnesses," which itself must be placed in relation to a much larger "cloud of witness," so that "none of these great channels of tradition may be treated with disrespect" and due deference is given to the *ecclesia docens*, the magisterial office of the Church.

What then are we to make of claim of *Lumen Gentium* to the effect that "The *entire* body of the faithful . . . show *universal* agreement in matters of faith and morals"? Clearly there is a good deal of idealization present

---

is not enough. Participation in the life of the Church means constant prayer (cf. 1 Thess 5:17), active participation in the liturgy, especially the Eucharist, regular reception of the sacrament of reconciliation, discernment, and exercise of gifts and charisms received from the Holy Spirit, and active engagement in the Church's mission and in her *diakonia*. It presumes an acceptance of the Church's teaching on matters of faith and morals, a willingness to follow the commands of God, and courage both to correct one's brothers and sisters, and also to accept correction oneself."

28. John Henry Newman, *On Consulting the Faithful in Matters of Doctrine* (London: Collins, 1961) 63.

here. Historically we know that such unanimity is virtually unheard of. It is difficult to think of a single major dogmatic judgment that was met with "*universal* agreement" even among the episcopacy.[29] In general I think we could agree that ecclesial statements such as these are very good at specifying ideals, but very poor in clarifying what to do when the ideal is not manifest, or on how to read possible disagreement.[30]

Sensus Fidei and Sociology

This then brings us back to our initial observations. Baggett's book has illuminated the rich variety of positions held by various Catholic communities in the Bay region of San Francisco. While there are some underlying commonalities, there are also some quite fundamental disagreements and divergences in the meanings and values of these communities. While each represents a relatively cohesive subculture within the church, there are many ways in which they could be said to diverge from the "norm" of Catholic identity, however that norm might be understood or identified.[31] Of course the question we can ask is, does this diversity simply reflect the rich pluriformity possible within the Catholic Church, or does it represent a major breakdown in the processes of socialization within the Church that is thus in danger of losing its social and cultural identity?

These are complex issues of course, but what should be clear is that the data taken in isolation cannot and does not resolve them.[32] The data is a mix, as MacIntyre notes, of the intelligible and the unintelligible, and in the absence of a clearly identified normative frame, no resolution is possible. The development of such a normative frame is beyond the scope of this present essay, but Lonergan does provide some direction with his insistence on conversion, as religious, moral, and intellectual; the demands of

---

29. From Nicaea (325 CE) to Vatican I (1869–70) there has always been a small rump of disagreement among the bishops with every dogmatic definition issued by a Church council.

30. Similar observations could be made in relation to statements in *Lumen Gentium* on the relationship between the papacy and the college of bishops. They state the ideal case where no conflict arises, but say nothing about how to resolve matters when conflict is present.

31. This also raises questions about the relationship between the local and the universal Church and the scope of legitimate plurality within the Church, each of which is beyond the scope of this present essay.

32. Hence SFLC repeatedly states that the *sensus fidei* cannot simply be read from or identified with public opinion. See SFLC, nn. 5, 47, 55, 77, 83, 87, 106, 113, 114, 118, 119. The frequency of these references is a good indication of the depth of concern, not to say, anxiety, about such a confusion.

the transcendental precepts (be attentive, be intelligent, be reasonable, be responsible, and be in love); and his grounding of objectivity in authentic subjectivity.[33] Pertaining to this issues, I shall make three observations.

The first is that Baggett's work gives flesh to the bones observed by Karl Rahner in the 1970s in his essay "The Faith of the Christian and the Doctrine of the Church."[34] Rahner noted there the disparity between the faith of ordinary believers and the official position of the Church on various issues, and sought to argue that nonetheless one can remain a Catholic in good faith despite such disparity. Even apart from Rahner's context in relation to the upheavals of Vatican II, this is not a new situation. Working empirically, historians of the early Church now highlight the difficulty of discerning the normative component in Christianity amidst the pluriformity evident within the church at the time.[35] In other words, the problem is not entirely new. The tension between the empirical constitution of Christian identity and of its normative meaning is a constant element in the life of the Church. Current debates about the significance of the *sensus fidei* are just the latest manifestation of this tension.

Second, Lonergan has argued that the then-current "crisis" (he was writing in the '60s) in the Church was not a crisis of faith but of culture.[36] It is true that we have witnessed massive cultural shifts in the twentieth century, and that these shifts have had a major impact on the effectiveness of the previous forms of socialization present in the church. And it is not clear that the new forms of socialization (modern catechesis, RCIA programs, parish life, the new evangelization, etc.) are adequate to the task or what exactly the new task may be.[37] However, *pace* Lonergan, I would contend that where a crisis of culture is extended, it can produce a crisis of faith, or at least create a

---

33. All these concerns are evident in Lonergan, *Method*.

34. Karl Rahner, "The Faith of the Christian and the Doctrine of the Church," in *Theological Investigations* (London: Darton, Longman and Todd, 1976) 14:24–46.

35. See for example the comments of Peter Brown: "I never cease to wonder at the confidence with which scholars, Christian and non-Christian alike, declare that they somehow know for certain that such and such a feature of the Christian church is now a manifestation of 'true' Christianity." Peter Brown, *The Rise of Western Christendom: Triumph and Diversity, A.D. 200-1000*, 2nd ed. (Malden, MA: Blackwell, 2003) 18. He goes on to describe this as a reflection of a "pristine myth of the Primitive Church."

36. Bernard J. F. Lonergan, "Dimensions of Meaning," in Robert M. Doran and Frederick E. Crowe, eds., *Collection: Collected Works of Bernard Lonergan* (Toronto: University of Toronto Press, 1988) 244.

37. While it is often said that Vatican II did not define any new dogmas, it clearly shifted the Church's self-understanding in terms of its relationships to other Christian communities, other religions, and to the world at large (the rejection of Constantinianism). These shifts need to be reflected in new forms of socialization beyond the more sectarian forms present prior to the Council.

significant erosion of faith's credibility or even relevance. Indeed some sociologists of religion have suggested that what drives increasing secularization is not *hostility* to religion but a sense that it is just not *relevant* to people's lives.[38] Others have argued that the most potent cause of secularization and the diminishing relevance of religious beliefs and life is simply one's sense of existential security—the more one feels secure economically, socially, and politically in a stable society, the less interest one has in religious matters.[39] The less people engage with this religious tradition for whatever reason, the less successful any form of socialization will be. People will no longer grasp anything like the depths of their religious tradition.

Third, I would note that Joseph Komonchak in his 1987 essay "Authority and Magisterium" has already provided a sharp analysis of the difficulties that arise when there is a breakdown in the authority of the teaching office of the Church.[40] As Komonchak notes, teaching authority is a reciprocal relationship of trust, and that trust can break down in multiple ways. Drawing on the political thought of Hannah Arendt, Komonchak analyzes authority as a social relationship. Authority resides in the "mutual knowledge and expectations of . . . two parties."[41] He adapts Max Weber's sociological definition of authority as "legitimate power, power, that is, that is based on some grounds other than force, threat or promised reward."[42] What grounds legitimacy for Komonchak is the trustworthiness of the authority. "Authority is trustworthy power."[43] The authority of an office, as distinct from that of a person, resides in the antecedent expectation that "persons who can be trusted to provide the direction society needs" are in fact placed in the office.[44] When the expectation is not met, when persons who are not trustworthy are repeatedly placed in offices of authority, the offices themselves

---

38. Lack of relevance is one factor identified for the decline in religion in Steve Bruce, *God Is Dead: Secularization in the West* (Oxford: Blackwell, 2002).

39. See Pippa Norris and Ronald Inglehart, *Sacred and Secular: Religion and Politics Worldwide*, 2nd ed, Cambridge studies in social theory, religion and politics (Cambridge: Cambridge University Press, 2011).

40. Joseph Komonchak, "Authority and Magisterium," in W. May, ed., *Vatican Authority and American Catholic Dissent* (New York: Crossroad, 1987).

41. Ibid., 103.

42. Ibid. Komonchak's position is an adaptation, not an uncritical adoption. Weber's notion of authority lacks a normative frame and so is subject to distortions. Komonchak is here broadly following Bernard J. F. Lonergan, "The Dialectic of Authority," in F. Crowe, ed., *A Third Collection* (New York: Paulist, 1985) 5–12. Also see Neil Ormerod, "Power and authority—A response to Bishop Cullinane," *Australasian Catholic Record* 82 (2005) 154–62.

43. Komonchak, "Authority and Magisterium," 107.

44. Ibid., 105.

lose authority. However this is only one side of the ledger. There is a dialectic not only in terms of the trustworthiness or otherwise of those in authority, but also in those who accept or do not accept that authority. The acceptance or rejection of authority by the people is also a product of their authenticity. Authentic subjects of authority may reject inauthentic exercises of authority, while inauthentic subjects may accept inauthentic exercises while rejecting authentic exercises of authority. The authenticity of either teachers or learners cannot be presumed, but must be established on a case-by-case basis.

These three observations should sound a note of caution in relation to any empirical appeal to the *sensus fidei* as a means of settling doctrinal or moral issues in the life of the Church. The existence of dissonance between official Church teaching and what the body of Catholics largely believes raises questions about both, but it does not settle the answers.

Evoking the *Sensus Fidei*

It is perhaps instructive to consider an example of the way in which theologians and others evoke the notion of *sensus fidei* in relation to doctrinal and moral considerations. By all accounts the teaching of *Humanae Vitae* concerning the inseparability of the unitive and procreative aspects of sexual intercourse has not been "received" by the mass of Catholic laity. I use the term "received" in its common theological usage, meaning that most laity simply have not given their assent to this teaching, as evidenced in their actions. The statistical information available would indicate that Catholic couples use "artificial" contraception at about the same rate as the rest of the population. This non-reception of teaching has had various spill-over effects. First, it has led to a far more widespread questioning of Church authority on various matters, notably but not only in areas of sexual morality, where that authority has been further undermined by continued revelations of sexual abuse by clergy. Second, and more specifically, the acceptance of a spilt between the unitive and procreative aspects of sexual intercourse has generated a much higher level of acceptance of homosexual activity among Catholics than might have otherwise been the case. In both these areas, of contraception and homosexuality, the laity is significantly out of step with the Church's official teaching.

What can be read in terms of this dissonance between what the Church teaches and its lack of reception by the laity? I would suggest, following the line of argument given by Komonchak, very little of theological significance. There is a dialectic of authenticity and inauthenticity to be attended to in both the *ecclesia docens* and the *ecclesia discens*.[45] Did the teaching of Paul VI emerge from an act of authenticity, grasping the deep meaning of human sexuality, as suggested by those who promote the encyclical? Or was it driven by anxiety over the impact that changing previous Church teaching would have on papal authority, as is often suggested by those who reject its conclusions?[46] Have the laity largely ignored the teaching on contraception because their *sensus fidei* does not sit comfortably with the absolute inseparability of the unitive and procreative ends of marriage in each and every act of intercourse; or in our hypersexualized culture, they are simply not able to live up to the heroic demands of the teaching?[47] All that we can objectively say is that the situation demands further exploration; it raises questions about the teaching and the state of the laity, but it provides no answers as such.

Without mentioning *Humanae Vitae*, though I would suggest with this encyclical firmly in mind, SFLC comes to basically the same conclusion:

> Problems arise when the majority of the faithful remain indifferent to doctrinal or moral decisions taken by the magisterium or when they positively reject them. This lack of reception may indicate a weakness or a lack of faith on the part of the people of God, caused by an insufficiently critical embrace of contemporary culture. But in some cases it may indicate that certain decisions have been taken by those in authority without due consideration of the experience and the *sensus fidei* of the

---

45. It should also be kept in mind that this distinction is not a separation into two classes, but a functional distinction. Everyone belongs to the *ecclesia discens*, while some have a special role as authorized teachers. The best teachers are those who have listened most attentively to the tradition and continue to do so.

46. According to the minority report that rejected any change in teaching: "It should likewise have to be admitted that for a half a century the Spirit failed to protect Pius XI, Pius XII, and a large part of the Catholic hierarchy from a very serious error. This would mean that the leaders of the Church, acting with extreme imprudence, had condemned thousands of innocent human acts, forbidding, under pain of eternal damnation, a practice which would now be sanctioned. The fact can neither be denied nor ignored that these same acts would now be declared licit on the grounds of principles cited by the Protestants, which Popes and Bishops have either condemned, or at least not approved." August Bernhard Hasler, *How the Pope Became Infallible: Pius IX and the Politics of Persuasion* (New York: Doubleday, 1981) 170.

47. See for example the analysis of Avery Dulles, "Sensus Fidelium," *America* 155 (1986). Komonchak also has helpful insights into the role of the *sensus fidei* in relation to *Humanae Vitae*, Joseph A. Komonchak, "Humanae vitae and Its Reception: Ecclesiological Reflections," *Theological Studies* 39 (1978) 221–57.

faithful, or without sufficient consultation of the faithful by the magisterium.[48]

In the face of such equivocation it is just as illegitimate to claim that only those who follow the Church's teaching in this matter are truly representative of the *sensus fidei*, as it is to suggest that it is the majority of Catholic couples not following this teaching who represent the *sensus fidei*. To move beyond such a non-conclusion would require a far more profound entry into questions of human sexuality, its meanings and purposes, into the meanings and purposes of marriage, and the ways in which married couples live out their married vocation in a sense of Christian discipleship. In Lonergan's terms we would need to attend to matters of religious and moral conversion within their lives and their intentions to live authentic Christian and moral lives; and I would also suggest we would need to attend to questions of intellectual conversion in the ways in which teaching in the past has been formulated.

Conclusion

While this present essay has focused on the issue of the ways in which the social sciences might assist in a better understanding of the *sensus fidei*, the underlying issue remains the larger question of the relationship between ecclesiology and the social sciences overall. As I have noted elsewhere, "engagement with the social sciences by ecclesiologists has been eclectic, sporadic, intermittent, and secondary to what they view as their primary task."[49] On the other hand as Komonchak has repeatedly and forcefully argued, unless ecclesiologists engage with the social sciences in a more systematic fashion, their ecclesiologies will never move beyond the descriptive and into a truly explanatory account of the church.[50] Clearly, then, naïve appeals to sociological data on what Catholics actually believe will leave us none the wiser without such preliminary engagements; on the other hand, the use of sociological categories such as socialization can provide helpful and instructive analogies that can demystify theological language that fails to ground itself in more basic and common human experiences.

48. SFLC n. 123.

49. Ormerod, *Re-Visioning the Church*, 32.

50. See Joseph Komonchak, *Foundations in Ecclesiology*, ed. Fred Lawrence, vol. 11, Lonergan Workshop Journal, Supplementary Issue (Boston: Boston College Press, 1995), where he spells out his argument for this position.

8

The Use of Sociology in the Study of the *Sensus Fidelium*

An Evaluation of the Contribution of Jerome Baggett

ROBERT CORTEGIANO

JEROME BAGGETT IN HIS book, *Sense of the Faithful: How American Catholics Live Their Faith*, uses an ethnographic approach to the study of six Catholic parishes in the San Francisco Bay Area. This method is based on the use of interviews, surveys, and participant observation that is designed to provide a more nuanced exploration of the variegated religious lives and identities of American Catholics.[1] Baggett's methodology focuses on lived religion in which the researcher's primary concern is fostering a deep attentiveness to people's religious worlds and everyday lives, particularly through meaningful conversations.[2] In taking this approach, his goal is to bring to the surface the complex and multilayered aspects of local or grassroots Catholicism, thereby mitigating the dangers and pitfalls of a more data-driven or theory-driven method, that all too often produces distant observations and generalizations about the religious worlds of American Catholics.[3] As a participant-observer engaged in critical conversations with parishioners, Baggett wants to avoid creating neatly categorized blueprints of the religious lives of his informants that do not accurately reflect the complexity of on-the-ground realities in the Catholic parishes where he is conducting his research.[4]

---

1. Jerome P. Baggett, *Sense of the Faithful: How American Catholics Live Their Faith* (New York: Oxford University Press, 2009) 24.
2. Ibid., 24–25.
3. Ibid., 25.
4. Ibid.

Baggett maintains that he is providing a micro-view, a closer analysis, of the lived religion of American Catholics by relying heavily on the reporting of his informants through interviews and a subsequent analysis of their responses. In this essay I will argue that this research move by Baggett, and the underlying methodologies it employs, ultimately constrains his larger claims and risks sometimes losing the forest for the trees. I will offer a critique of Baggett's method, and his particular use of the sociological theory of Pierre Bourdieu, which does not go far enough in employing Bourdieu's categories of "habitus" and "field" as well as his treatment of language as a form of power that cannot be understood apart from the embodied power-struggles that are operative in a given field. The religious field of the American Catholic Church cannot be fully understood apart from the dynamics of the exercise of religious authority in interpreting and practicing the tradition, or what Bourdieu calls the "mobiliz[ation] of religious capital in the competition for the monopoly over the administration of the goods of salvation and over the legitimate exercise of religious power."[5] I argue that Baggett's use of Bourdieu's work is effective in situating the cultural negotiations of the parishioners in his study as members of a "deliberative Church" who have a "feel for the game" of religious meaning-making and identity construction in Catholicism, but it loses sight of a fuller and more realistic macro-view of American Catholicism as a polarized field marked by ongoing power struggles, particularly between the laity and Church hierarchy, for structural and doctrinal reform.[6]

The Sense of the Faithful and Interpretive Authority

Baggett uses Bourdieu's terminology to identify the "sense of the faithful," or the "intuitive sense," for negotiating with and innovating within a religious tradition that Catholics in his study displayed. As Bagget explains, "Through [Catholic parishioners'] relationships with others they acquire what social theorist Pierre Bourdieu calls a 'feel for the game,' a sense of how culture—in this case, Catholic culture—can be accessed, deployed, and improvised amid changing circumstances."[7] One difficulty is that Baggett does not sufficiently account for the fact that this "sense of the faithful" is an important theological category that has been developed and debated

---

5. Pierre Bourdieu, "Genesis and Structure of the Religious Field," *Comparative Social Research* 13 (1991) 22 [1–44].

6. Baggett, *Sense of the Faithful*, 66.

7. Ibid.

in post-Vatican II Catholic theology.[8] He uses this technical term more generally to mean how Catholics understand, talk about, and live their faith in daily life. Moreover, he fails to bring into focus how this term emerges in the landscape of U.S. Catholicism, where the authenticity of sources of "interpretive authority" and the validity of claims based on that authority are often contested, especially in conflicts between the laity and the institutional hierarchy, which compose the battlefield of ongoing struggles in the Catholic Church.[9]

According to Baggett, "the locus of religious authority [for American Catholics] has . . . shifted away from the institution and, consonant with the growing sense of their 'interpretive authority,' toward the individual."[10] He goes on to account for the various ways this shift is reflected in the lives of Catholics, saying:

> More than three-quarters say that both the sacraments and "spiritual and personal growth" are very important to them, whereas less than half of all Catholics say this about "the teaching authority claimed by the Vatican" . . . This [shift] is [also] reflected in the majority of American Catholics who agree that there should be more democratic decision making in Church affairs. It also becomes evident when they agree that one can be a "good Catholic" without doing things such as obeying Church teaching on abortion (58 percent) . . . and having their marriages approved by the church (67 percent).[11]

Similarly, large majorities of American Catholics also claim fearlessness in expressing "dissenting views" on other official teachings, showing their support for allowing women and married men to become priests and "disagree[ing] with the Church's prohibition of artificial contraception."[12] However, as Baggett points out, rather than "voting with their feet" they are "'defecting in place' when it comes to whatever doctrines they disagree about."[13] In his view, instead of being forced into silent defection, Catholics are freely choosing it, empowered as fully authorized religious meaning-

8. Ormond Rush, *The Eyes of Faith: The Sense of the Faithful and the Church's Reception of Revelation* (Washington, DC: Catholic University of America Press, 2009); John Burkhard, "*Sensus Fidei*: Recent Theological Reflection (1990–2001) Part I," *Heythrop Journal* 46 (2005) 450–75, John Burkhard, "*Sensus Fidei*: Recent Theological Reflection (1990–2001) Part II," *Heythrop Journal* 47 (2006) 38–54.

9. Ibid., x.
10. Ibid., 21.
11. Ibid.
12. Ibid.
13. Ibid.

makers. Here he is drawing on the work of Michele Dillon who argues that after the Second Vatican Council, there was a "decentering of interpretive authority in the church" that foregrounded the "agency" and "equality" of all Catholics who can have a voice in and take a hands-on approach to shaping the tradition apart from the "unilateral authority of church officials."[14] Nevertheless, Baggett maintains that when it comes to facing the challenge of striving to become "the deliberative church that so many seem to desire . . . [Catholics have] little incentive to engage in the difficult work of bringing about institutional change."[15] In other words, American Catholics are opinionated about the church they love, but apathetic when it comes to standing up, speaking out, and bringing the future Church they dream of to life.

A Sociological and Theological Evaluation of *Sense of the Faithful*

Contrary to this argument, I am suggesting that what seems like a failure of collective will, is more so the active repression of "communal agency" and the open denial of "interpretive equality" on the part of church officials whose power and authority remain uncontested and legitimated through the resulting silence and inaction of lay Catholics.[16] I am arguing that a more explicit grounding in Bourdieu's theorizing on social conflict, symbolic power, and the role of "misrecognition" in upholding religious authority—that is, the legitimizing of the "monopolization of a power and a competence in principle accessible to anyone"—would help Baggett to better account for this internalized but not always vocalized dissent among the people in the pews.[17] Furthermore, I am arguing that a more theologically grounded account of the implications of the church's teaching on the "sense of the faithful" would help Baggett to explain this interiorized but not always externalized prophetic discourse. Such theological grounding would enable him to re-evaluate the notion that Catholics, by remaining silent, are simply protecting the sacred spaces and safe havens of their parish communities from polarizing disputes. Instead, it would shift his focus towards giving more serious consideration to the reality of the systematic silencing of the laity by church officials who want to avert the threat of public scandal, protests, and the danger of unrest in the pews. In other words, if Bagget treated

14. Michele Dillon, "Pierre Bourdieu, Religion, and Cultural Production," *Cultural Studies, Critical Methodologies*, 1 (2001) 411–29, at 418.
15. Baggett, *Sense of the Faithful*, 123.
16. Dillon, "Pierre Bourdieu, Religion, and Cultural Production," 418.
17. Bourdieu, "Genesis and Structure of the Religious Field," 25.

"*sensus fidelium*" more rigorously as a theological category, his analysis would have to go beyond recognizing the democratizing tendency in the "sense of the faithful"—an impulse that surfaces the autonomy, agency, and interpretive authority of all the baptized—and present a deeper analysis of how the "sense of the faithful" is tempered by a persistent authoritarianism in the functioning of magisterial and clerical power.

Bourdieu characterizes this type of religious power struggle as the battle for interpretive authority between "the church and the prophet." He says, "prophet[s] . . . contest the very existence of the church" by questioning its monopoly on interpretive authority or what he calls the "instructional or sacramental capital of grace."[18] If Bourdieu is right in saying that Church authority is premised on a "misrecognition" of its power (symbolic, interpretive, political, etc.) as arbitrary, then Church leaders and their faithful flock will often tend towards upholding the conditions (doctrines and structures) that facilitate this misrecognition. In a post-Vatican II ecclesiology that privileges a more egalitarian and integrative construction of the "sense of the faithful," there is, however, a very open and active possibility for a "[collective recognition] that contributes to empowering Catholics to challenge the doctrines and practices put forward by the church hierarchy . . . [and] unveil the logic they believe church officials are masking."[19] According to the informants and interviewees in Baggett's study of Bay Area parishes, many active Catholic parishioners do feel empowered to dissent from church teaching and freely affirm this when asked to report about their own "sense of the faith." Still, there is an important distinction to be made, one that Baggett does not account for, between "withholding internal assent as a matter of individual conscience" and "public dissent from a teaching" as form of prophetic witness, the former being a more personal negotiation and the latter a potential political tactic intended to disrupt the institutional status quo.[20]

18. Ibid.

19. Dillon, "Pierre Bourdieu, Religion, and Cultural Production," 422–23.

20. This distinction is made by Richard R. Gaillardetz in his book, *By What Authority: A Primer on Scripture, the Magisterium, and the Sense of the Faithful* (Collegeville, MN: Liturgical, 2003) 132–33. Gaillardetz goes on to describe church officials' mixed response to the notion of public dissent, saying that "current ecclesiastical documents" tend to prefer private withdrawal of assent to official teaching as opposed to public statements or acts of dissent that "discredit the teaching office of the Church." This supports my view that is developed in this paper that church officials are not in the business of propping up prophetic disruptions and challenges from an empowered laity, but instead rely on tactics of silencing that more often than not guarantee an internalization of the "sense of faith" exercised by lay Catholics who fear ecclesiastical repercussions such as censure, restriction from the sacraments, loss of volunteer leadership positions

"Tacit Discursive Rules" and the Performance of Parish Life

It is important to understand this distinction and how it functions in the theological category of the "sense of the faithful." This is especially the case when considering one of the key interviews that Baggett focuses on—an interview with a young man in his mid-thirties named Jason who experienced a gradual de-conversion from Catholicism to atheism.[21] The interview describes how throughout Jason's religious formation in Catholic parishes, and in various encounters with laity and clergy, he heard the same response to all of his grappling with church teaching and practice: "Don't think too much or ask too many questions." In other words, just accept the established structures and doctrines of the Church as they are handed on from trustworthy and expert authorities. As a young person journeying to adulthood, Jason was engaged in an important process. He was interpreting and appropriating Catholic tradition within the given Catholic cultures of parish and family life he was raised in, a process that all Catholics should be invited to, but as Baggett maintains, all too often this invitation is completely absent. According to Baggett:

> The Catholic community may do its part in authenticating religious beliefs and practices, but these, in turn, are instrumental in shaping the community and, importantly, determining who ultimately will elect to absent themselves from it. People concerned with the sense of the faithful would do well to pay attention to those no longer present.[22]

Jason's story exposes the confounding fact that in a Church experiencing rapid de-conversion, genuine concern for the young searching "Jasons" of the church is conspicuously absent.

Baggett pinpoints three factors, what he calls "tacit discursive rules," that are operative in the parishes he studied, each one producing a "hushing effect of affective commitment" or a desire to "protect feelings of community" by avoiding disruptive disagreements, conflicts, divisions, and any other kinds of profanations of the cherished sacred space provided by parish life.[23] So strong are these three maxims amongst the faithful—which Baggett de-

---

and employment, and even excommunication.

21. Jerome Baggett, "Becoming Absence-Minded: Sociological Reflections on the Sense of the Faithful," *Proceedings of the Catholic Theological Society of America* 70 (2015) 1–26, http://ejournals.bc.edu/ojs/index.php/ctsa/article/view/8750/7968.

22. Ibid., 22.

23. Ibid., 17–21.

fines as "One Size Doesn't Fit All," "Don't Rock The Boat," and "Neither The Time Nor The Place"—the churches that adhere to them become "sites of synchronized performance whereby people often attempt to jettison those aspects of themselves deemed less religious in order to maintain a collective sense of transcendence among politically hushed actors."[24] Baggett argues that these "tacit discursive rules" are not "imposed upon parishioners from some outside source, but rather come from "parishioners who think of community in distinctively affective terms (i.e., they are privileging feelings of cohesion, sacredness, plurality, etc. in their parishes)."[25]

For example, in the "One Size Doesn't Fit All" rule, parishioners privilege the "multidimensionality" of ways of living the faith according to the "unchallengeable" authority of conscience.[26] If "Peace and Justice" Catholics have conflicting political or religious views with "Holy Rosary Society" Catholics, it's better not to surface them, but rather respect each person's internalized negotiations of conscience, which ultimately is not a matter for public discourse or dispute. The same goes for the "Don't Rock The Boat" rule, which encourages parishioners to stay "on the hush" about divisive political issues, and favors playing one's cards close to the vest to avoid the scandal of infighting.[27] Similarly, parishioners who heed the "Neither The Time Nor The Place" rule highly value sacred space as devotional space, free from the disruption of socio-political chatter.[28]

Each of the three "rules for practicing parish" define public life in the church as performative, a collective walking in step that is construed as a "common good," but in my judgment is more likely a misrecognition of "playing by the rules" of ecclesial authoritarianism, a submission of bodies to symbolic power.[29] By synching their bodies in the performance of parish life, Baggett's parishioners acquiesced to the power "inscribed" in the "training" of their bodies to conform to Church disciplines and upheld the "symbolic order" that defined their sense of thinking and acting like "good Catholics."[30] As Richard Gaillerdetz points out:

---

24. Ibid., 20.
25. Ibid.
26. Ibid., 22–24.
27. Ibid., 24–25.
28. Ibid., 25–27.
29. John Seitz, *No Closure: Catholic Practice and Boston's Parish Shutdowns* (Cambridge: Harvard University Press, 2011) 23.
30. Pierre Bourdieu, *Language and Symbolic Power*, ed. John B. Thompson, trans. Gino Raymond and Matthew Adamson (Cambridge, MA: Harvard University Press, 2003) 169–70.

> Current ecclesiastical documents tend to give more leeway to the possibility of privately withholding assent than they do to the legitimacy of public dissent. Many church officials believe that public dissent is always inappropriate. Others contend that the legitimacy of public dissent depends in large part on underlying motive. If the dissent is motivated by a desire to discredit the teaching office of the Church, then such actions would not be in keeping with authentic church membership.[31]

There is no doubt the parishioners in Baggett's study had clear ideas about what constituted "authentic church membership," but the underlying motives for following these rules needs to be further interrogated. Why is it, then, that Baggett does not dig deeper into the causes of this kind of collusion among the faithful? Surely a collective shutdown of prophetic discourse in favor of censorship and silencing must be interpreted as more than keeping the peace, especially given the fact that Bourdieuian terms, which are geared toward making sense of conflict and political struggle, are at work in the discourse analysis of his informants' reporting in the parish interviews that made up his study. By downplaying the role of conflict, Baggett loses site of the parishes as fields of struggle where power-plays between "those who exercise power and those who submit to it" are continually present and unfolding.[32]

Becoming Absence-Minded and Conflict-Minded

If a researcher in a Catholic religious field wants to understand the "sense of the faithful," he or she cannot avoid assessing and seeking to explain how it brings to the surface a conflict between the directives of authority outside the self and the inner-directedness of authority within the self (or as Richard Gaillardetz refers to it, "substitutionary vs. non-substitutionary authority").[33] Young people on the way to adulthood in the church need guidance from the community so they can learn how to let go of the childhood faith that was founded on the authority and expertise of others who told them how to be "good Catholics," and begin living into an "integral spirituality" that is shaped by an inner-authority in dialogue with a shared community of

---

31. Gaillardetz, *By What Authority?*, 133.
32. Ibid., 170.
33. Richard Gaillardetz, "Power and Authority in the Church: Emerging Issues" in *A Church with Open Doors: Catholic Ecclesiology for the Third Millenium* (eds. Richard R. Gaillardetz and Edward P. Hahnenberg, Collegeville, MN: Liturgical, 2015) 15–17.

equals, companions on the journey toward adult faith.[34] This spiritual path of working out developmental conflicts is part of individuation within community, or what Brad Hinze calls "individuation-in-communion," that is, becoming an adult self in an adult church.[35] Young people like Jason are struggling towards independence, autonomy, and interpretive authority within the Church. They are seeking to establish a new and more mature relationship with the faith handed on to them in childhood and with the faith community that shares in the responsibility of guiding young people on the journey to adult faith. Engaging in this process of becoming an adult self in an adult church—becoming an authentic and discerning "identity in a mutuality of relating"—is something that Jason was not invited, enabled, or allowed to do in a parish culture shaped by the wider landscape of power struggles with the hierarchy in the U.S. Catholic Church.[36] The symbolic power (capital) wielded by the institutional church fosters a parish culture where the silencing, stifling, and stunting of growth and development in faith from childhood to adulthood is all too common, and leaves no room for people like Jason.

In order for American Catholics to heed Baggett's call to become "absence-minded," to pay attention to the dynamics of belief and practice that silence conflict and absent it from thought and discourse in parishes, and to remember the forgotten ones in their midst, so to speak, who absent themselves from communities of belonging where they no longer fit, they must also remember that becoming "absence-minded" entails becoming "conflict-minded" as well. It is critical for American Catholics to become mindful of the suppression of conflict in parish culture that is embedded in the larger culture of U.S. Catholicism marked by an ongoing power struggle for interpretive authority. In order to further explore Baggett's reading of the "sense of the faithful" and how "absence-minded" Catholics cannot give up on the necessity of becoming conflict-minded in their engagement with church tradition, it is important to get a closer look at Baggett's understanding of American Catholic culture as a researcher employing Bourdieu's theory.

---

34. John J. Shea, *Finding God Again: Spirituality For Adults* (Lanham, MD: Rowman and Littlefield, 2005) 97–102.

35. Brad Hinze, *Prophetic Obedience: Ecclesiology for A Dialogical Church* (Maryknoll, NY: Orbis, 2016) 181–98.

36. John Shea, "The Adult Self. Process and Paradox" (*Journal of Adult Development*, Vol. 10, Is. 1, 2003) 24.

Religious Culture: Constructing Meaning and Struggling For Power

In *Sense of the Faithful*, Baggett defines culture in the "signifying or representational sense," meaning that culture "refers to the historically transmitted repertoires of symbols that shape people's perceptions of reality and, at the same time, render that reality meaningful to them."[37] People both make and are made by symbolic worlds (culture), so that being a self in the world is an ongoing "project of identity construction," a self-reflexive "quest" for meaning and authenticity that is relational, "intentional [and] continuously revisable."[38] The Catholic parishioners in Baggett's study are engaged in an "ongoing [negotiation with] and appropriation of Catholic culture," a process he calls "being storied" or situated in a cultural narrative emerging from Catholic tradition. Catholic parishes are "loc[i] of self-expression and meaning-making" or sites of religious culture that serve as "institutional carriers" of a "symbolic repertoire" that is "allocated" to the faithful.[39] Catholics, "sensing themselves as 'cultured' in the representational sense ... frequently take it upon themselves to appropriate whichever symbolic meanings resonate most with who they want to be in the world."[40]

Baggett describes Catholics' sense of "cultural competence to negotiate with their religious tradition" using Pierre Bourdieu's notion of "practical sense," or what Bourdieu calls "having a feel for the game."[41] Every negotiation with culture is the action of embodied agents within "bundles of [social] relations," or the interaction between "habitus and field."[42] For Bourdieu, habitus and field function together, constituting the self as an identity in a mutuality of relating:

> To speak of habitus is to assert that the individual, and even the personal, the subjective, is social, collective. Habitus is a socialized subjectivity.... Social reality exists, so to speak, twice, in things and in minds, in fields and in habitus, outside and inside agents.... Habitus being the social embodied, it is "at home" in the field it inhabits ... [and fosters an intuitive feeling of] coincidence between dispositions and position, between the "sense of the game" and the game, [so] that the agent does what he or

---

37. Baggett, *Sense of the Faithful*, 35.
38. Ibid., 65.
39. Ibid., 38–42
40. Ibid., 65.
41. Ibid., 66.
42. Bourdieu and Wacquant, *An Invitation To Reflexive Sociology*, 16.

she "has to do" without posing it explicitly as a goal, below the level of calculation and even consciousness, beneath discourse and representation.[43]

Just as habitus is "creative [and] inventive, but within the limits of structures," so too is a field an active "space of play . . . that makes room for the organized improvisation of agents," while also being "delimited as a socially structured space in which agents struggle . . . a space of conflict and competition."[44] This notion of the field as a site of power struggles, similar to a "battlefield in which participants vie to establish monopoly over the species of capital effective in it," is central to Bourdieu's sociology. According to Loïc Wacquant, Bourdieu's work is a "sociology of symbolic power . . . [which as a whole] may be interpreted as a materialist anthropology of the specific contribution that various forms of symbolic violence make to the reproduction and transformation of social domination."[45]

It is precisely on this point, the reality of conflict and struggle that situates the relation between habitus and field, that Baggett's use of Bourdieu needs to be more explicit, so as to prevent him from overlooking the power struggles in the Church for interpretive authority regarding issues of structural reform and development of doctrine. In explaining how the parishioners in his study have a "feel for the game"—their intuitive sense of negotiating and appropriating the symbolic repertoire of Catholic tradition and the fields of their particular faith communities—Baggett puts a spotlight on how the faithful claim interpretive authority in regard to Catholic beliefs and practices. Most of the Catholics in his study know that even in the church, "the universe par excellence of rules and regulations, playing with the rule is part and parcel of the rule of the game."[46] Although many of these individuals and communities claim and enact various transgressions of official church teachings and norms, according to their self-reporting in the interviews, they appear to do so "as loyalists . . . [who] are simply not institutional reformers."[47] Believing and acting according to one's conscience is the norm for members of these "deliberative" parishes, in which "the laity's communal discernment on matters pertaining to faith and morals has become as central to religious understanding as are pronouncements from the hierarchy."[48] However, claiming the right to stand apart from the tradi-

43. Ibid., 126–28.
44. Ibid., 17–19.
45. Ibid., 14–15.
46. Ibid., 18.
47. Baggett, *Sense of the Faithful*, 123.
48. Ibid., 18.

tion does not necessarily mean publicly standing against it; in fact many parishioners have "little incentive to engage the difficult work of bringing about institutional change."[49]

"Defecting In Place" vs. Public Dissent

Baggett accounts for the relative ease the faithful display in boldly claiming heterodoxy with three explanations: First, resistance is re-framed within a narrative of "transformation" that honors decisions of conscience as a path to a deeper and more authentic faith and as a way of bearing witness to a world in need of integrity and truth-seeking.[50] Second, many parishes function as "sites of synchronized performance," where the divisive energies of polarizing discourse or open-conflict are sublimated to preserve feelings of cohesion and mutual support within a sacred space.[51] Third, active parishioners thriving as leaders in parishes (who make up the majority of Baggett's informants) view "living out one's faith . . . in terms of a reflexive or self conscious project," which holds open the possibility that being committed to sacramental and communal life does not rule out being critical of the institutional church.[52] As Baggett points out, "many have become accustomed to 'defecting in place' when it comes to whatever doctrines they disagree with."[53]

Although Baggett's work as a researcher is primarily descriptive—situating himself in the field as a "careful sifter of discourse [who] finds conversational shards . . . [that] represent important loci of cultural improvisation"—he does not fully interrogate the laity's relative silence within their parish communities with regard to their beliefs and practices that defy Catholic teaching and the magisterial authority of the hierarchy, to which, through the sacraments of initiation into the Catholic Church, they are held accountable.[54] If an individual believer's "sense of faith" (*sensus fidei*) has led him or her to dissent from Church teaching, and he or she in turn has chosen to internalize and not vocalize their dissent, such persons have made this decision in the larger context of the communal "sense of the faithful" (*sensus fidei fidelium*), which as Ormond Rush points out is one of "the three authorities of the Church's teaching office: the *sensus fidelium* (here

49. Ibid., 123.
50. Ibid., 157.
51. Ibid., 201.
52. Ibid., 75.
53. Ibid., 21.
54. Ibid., 67.

seen as [a] diversity of interpretations), theology, and the magisterium."[55] Any consensus among the faithful (*consensus fidelium*) on the received or authoritative interpretation in matters regarding church teaching and practice, "is best understood as the end product of a process of determining the church's unified diversity of faith regarding a particular matter."[56] Although, according to Rush, "it is the function of the magisterium alone to make such an authoritative statement on behalf of and for the whole church," each of these three sources of authority are in dialogue with each other and inform this process, which means that the dynamics of assent and dissent (*consensus* and *dissensus*) must freely operate in the religious field.

On Bourdieu's terms, the laity in a parish constitutes a habitus in relation to a field, which by its very nature is a site of conflict and struggle. Even where there is "coherence that may be observed in the given state of the field, its apparent orientation toward a common function . . . [is] born of conflict and competition, not some kind of immanent self-development of the structure."[57] Stating this more forcefully, Bourdieu claims: "There is history only as long as people revolt, resist, act."[58] That is not to say that the "sense of the faithful" can be reduced to acts of resistance to church teaching on the part of a rebellious laity, or that the "sense of the faithful" is a univocal assertion of lay interpretive authority, rather than a diversity of voices in dialogue, from laity, to theologians, to bishops.[59] Nonetheless, it is crucial not to back away from conflict that arises within and must be faced by communities of dialogue. While it is pragmatic to say, as Richard Gaillardetz points out, that scholars must be aware of the "tendency to play the hierarchy off of the laity," which could reduce "the sense of the faithful [to] a mere counter-position to official church teaching," this sound word of caution must not be construed as a reason to downplay the importance of prophetic dialogue and the possibility of "prophetic critique" from the laity, especially those on the margins of the church.[60]

---

55. Rush, *Eyes of Faith*, 243.
56. Ibid.
57. Bourdieu and Wacquant, *An Invitation To Reflexive Sociology*, 104.
58. Ibid., 102.
59. Rush, *Eyes of Faith*, 247.
60. Ibid., 260.

Language, Symbolic Power, and the Limits of Discourse Analysis Alone

Not all disputes and dissent in the Church can be characterized as ecclesial face-offs that inevitably lead to schism, but in the case of Baggett's study of Bay Area parishioners, the absence of active church members rallying and siting-in on the steps of the diocesan cathedral does not mean that a researcher shouldn't "lean in" and take a closer look for the signs of power plays and struggles that might not be immediately apparent in discourse analysis alone.[61] In other words, Baggett's claim, based on the narratives of the informants in his study that Catholic parishioners who have made their peace and turned the other cheek in their contentions with the institutional church, causes him to avert his researcher's gaze from the field as a site of competition (or a "battlefield"), which he cannot do if he is fully committed to Bourdieu's sociology. In Bourdieu's thinking, the church (or the "school system, the state . . . political parties, or unions") is not an "apparatus" that can be reduced to a kind of predictable functionalism, but rather, it is a field.[62]

> In a field, agents and institutions constantly struggle, according to the regularities and the rules constitutive of this space of play (and, in given conjunctures, over those rules themselves), with various degrees of strength and therefore diverse probabilities of success, to appropriate the specific products at stake in the game. Those who dominate in a given field are in a position to make it function to their advantage but they must always contend with the resistance, the claims, the contention, "political" or otherwise, of the dominated.[63]

If at the grassroots local level of the church, there is in fact apathy for the project of institutional reform (as Baggett has observed), then this

---

61. Jerome P. Baggett, *Sense of the Faithful*, 56. Baggett points out that while "leaning in" to take a closer look at parishes and comparing them to data collected from parishes around the country, as a researcher he must always keep in mind "there exists no one thing called American Catholicism." In observing a coherent pattern of non-confrontation with Catholic hierarchy and a general disengagement from the work of institutional reform, Baggett's descriptions need to be situated in the variegated landscape of Catholicism in America, which includes reform movements that do engage in open conflict and direct resistance to the institutional church, while often maintaining ties to and drawing on support from local parishes. Similarly, it is important to acknowledge the discourse and practices of the U.S. Catholic Bishops, who have authority and influence over parishes and can impact the cultures of local churches.

62. Ibid.

63. Bourdieu and Wacquant, *An Invitation to Reflexive Sociology*, 102.

lack of open conflict and direct resistance from parishes could be construed as a sign that points to who this inaction serves, specifically the Church hierarchy. As the highest authority in the local church, bishops have the power to produce discourse and take actions that can help foster this passivity in the pews. When it comes to doctrinal positions and interpretations, the bishops as part of the magisterium have the authority to define what constitutes authentic speech and to silence transgressions of authorized discourse. Similarly, bishops can use antagonistic speech (i.e. against the rights of women, LGBT/Q Catholics, divorced and re-married people, to name just a few) and assign to such claims their unassailable and un-debatable nature, premised on the authority of God's revelation within the tradition.

As Bourdieu points out, "*linguistic relations are always relations of symbolic power* through which relations of force between speakers and their respective groups are actualized in a transfigured form."[64] In order to understand the "linguistic habitus," one must pay attention to the "ability to make things happen with words, the power of words to give orders and to bring order [that] is quite magical."[65] Michelle Dillon aptly describes how Bourdieu perceives the functioning of symbolic power, that is, "through self-deception or self-mystification . . . that is socially institutionalized."[66] On Bourdieu's terms, "symbolic power" is established in the religious field through the distribution of "symbolic capital" from the clerical hierarchy, who are sacred "specialists" designated as producers of religious meaning, to the "profane" laity who are "dispossessed of religious capital."[67] Bourdieu's view of the religious field is summarized concisely by Terry Rey, who says it is an "arena of struggle and competition, in which religious agents and institutions vie for the control of the production, accumulation, and distribution of legitimate forms of capital particular to the religious field."[68] In regard to "the sense of the faithful," this struggle is manifested in the ongoing tensions between a plurality of competing claims to legitimate interpretive authority in matters related to Church doctrines, structures, and practices. Catholic parishes are contested sights of meaning made up of variously authorized actors in a religious field of competition. Therefore, as Michele Dillon points out:

---

64. Ibid., 142.
65. Ibid., 147.
66. Dillon, "Pierre Bourdieu, Religion, and Cultural Production," 414.
67. Bourdieu, "Genesis and Structure of the Religious Field," 9–10.
68. Terry Rey, *Bourdieu on Religion: Imposing Faith and Legitimacy* (Oakville, CT: Equinox, 2007) 86.

Although lay Catholics do not have the institutional legitimacy of formal authority that is conferred on Church officials, many nonetheless use doctrine, the specialized language of the church, to counterargue against the reasoning employed by church officials. In short, the pope and the bishops do not have a monopoly on the Church's symbolic resources; the laity, too, have access to doctrinal knowledge and the fund of Catholic capital.[69]

Silence and Apathy in the "Sense of the Faithful"

In *Sense of the Faithful*, Baggett is very much aware of this lay interpretive authority and autonomy as a sociological researcher participating in and observing a Catholic religious field, one in which his parishioner informants are quite outspoken in their formal interviews about their authority as meaning-makers and their freedom as dissenters. While at the same time a close observation of their practices shows that often their lips are sealed when it comes to publicly speaking their truth and they are seated steadfastly in the pews rather than marching in picket lines outside the parish house. It is puzzling, then, why Baggett's discourse analysis does not account more for power struggles in the church and their impact on Catholic parish life, keeping in mind as he listens to his informants that "*authority comes to language from the outside . . . [and] the efficacy of speech [is derived from] . . . the delegated power of the institution.*"[70] While it is true that the "sense of faith" of individual believers (*sensus fidei*) does in fact function "both [as] an imaginative capacity to interpret revelation . . . within the narrative of one's life . . . [and to] construct, consciously or unconsciously, their own concrete catechism" that interprets the meaning of personal religious experience, as well as "Scripture and tradition," the discourse of this "believer's catechism" is always subject to regulation and censure by the institutional church.[71]

Many of the parishioners in Baggett's study know all too well the fact that in the Catholic Church, "[official] access to legitimate language [about the faith] is quite unequal," and that there is a difference between negotiations and innovations with respect to the tradition that are largely internalized, and those that are spoken in protest and acted upon as intentional

---

69. Dillon, "Pierre Bourdieu, Religion, and Cultural Production," 422.
70. Bourdieu and Wacquant, *An Invitation to Reflexive Sociology*, 147.
71. Rush, *Eyes of Faith*, 238.

forms of resistance to the authority of the institutional Church.[72] As a researcher, Baggett doesn't fully account for the stunted impulse for church reform in local parishes, because he does not explicitly situate his observations regarding this absence or silence in the larger web of power relations that define the field. Instead he falls prey to what Bourdieu describes as:

> [The ethnomethodologist's] . . . concern to keep the analysis as close to "concrete reality" as possible which inspires conversational analysis . . . and fuels the "micro-sociological" intention, [which] can prompt [researchers] entirely to miss a "reality" that escapes immediate intuition because it resides in structures that are transcendent to the interaction they inform.[73]

Bourdieu goes on to name an important guiding insight for any researcher engaged in discourse analysis:

> Even the simplest linguistic exchange brings into play a complex and ramifying web of power relations, . . . [and] even the content of the message itself, remains unintelligible as long as one does not take into account the totality of the structure of power relations that is present, yet invisible, in the exchange.[74]

While Baggett does acknowledge the presence and importance of church reform movements and offers accounts of parishioners' active struggles with the clerical hierarchy, his overarching characterization of American Catholics who "have a hard time of making sense of religious authority as being in any way authoritative," does not completely hold up.[75]

The American Catholic landscape is no stranger to a dominant clerical hierarchy that employs a myriad of tactics to assert control over its flock, such as: hostile rhetoric from bishops directed at "liberal Catholics" sometimes backed up by intimidation tactics, like the potential withholding of sacraments; loyalty oaths to Church teachings attached to the contracts of teachers and lay ministers; the silencing of theologians that push the boundaries of orthodoxy; parishes on the margins that have stretched their progressive agenda too far, either in belief or practice, and have been assigned hardnosed pastors to bring them back into line or have even been threatened with *Latae Sententiae* excommunication; thinly veiled bully-tactics such as the Vatican investigation of the Leadership Conference of Women Religious; the de facto liturgical reforms of the New Roman Missal;

---

72. Bourdieu and Wacquant, *An Invitation to Reflexive Sociology*, 146.
73. Ibid., 144.
74. Ibid., 142.
75. Baggett, *Sense of the Faithful*, 122.

unilaterally implemented church and school closings that ignore the input of the people in the pews; and episcopal cover-ups compounded by counter-law suits that deny the suffering of victims of sexual abuse by the clergy. Baggett is accurate in saying that in the face of this, many Catholics leave the church, a small percentage become reformers fighting for change from within, and a good number find a way to remain loyal to their parishes, but he overlooks the reality of competition, conflict, and struggle that unfolds in the drama of the power-plays noted above. As a researcher, Baggett has "leaned in" too closely and has fixed his gaze on a micro-view of parishes at the expense of painting a more realistic macro-view of American Catholicism that is a contested site of ongoing battles for structural transformation and doctrinal reform.

Conclusion

It is onto this Catholic religious field of conflict that the many "Jasons" of the world—searching young people emerging from adolescence and struggling towards adulthood in their twenties and thirties—find themselves looking for a place to ask their questions, engage in "candid conversation," and to find a community of faith willing to walk alongside them as they work through the challenges of identity construction and meaning-making.[76] Yet, in parishes where the communal sense of faith is covered over by a "hushing effect" and the experience of companionship along the rocky path of religious meaning-making is smoothed over by "synchronized performances" of "good" Catholic faith, one finds communities of faith ill-equipped to sustain the journeys of people like Jason, who wind up not fitting into, outgrowing, and letting go of a faith that cannot help them become adults, nor really wants to engage their adult selves. Baggett's challenge to theologians to become "sociologically-minded" in reflecting upon the "sense of the faithful" and to become absence-minded in terms of how the "dynamics of culture" in American Catholicism "engender certain absences," is indeed profoundly important, especially in regard to the large numbers of de-converted Catholics, pushed to various places on the margins and the periphery of the religious field of Catholicism; but becoming absence-minded entails becoming conflict-minded as well.[77] Catholic parishes, as fields of power struggles, are sites of contested meaning-making where prophetic voices, though often silenced, can emerge, where "subversive wisdom" and witness can urge the faithful towards living out their adult faith that names and faces

76. Baggett, "Becoming Absence-Minded," 33.
77. Ibid., 34.

into conflicts, not without a healthy dose of fear and doubt, but also with courage and humility, authenticity and creativity, authority and freedom.[78]

---

78. Ormond Rush, *Eyes of Faith*, 260.

Part 3

Systematic Theology and Social Ethics

9

The *Sensus Fidelium*

Old Questions, New Challenges

— John J. Burkhard, OFM Conv —

There has been renewed interest recently in the teaching of Vatican II regarding the *sensus fidelium* or the "sense of the faithful."[1] The ecclesiological vision of Pope Francis calls for greater collaboration of the bishops among themselves and with the pope, but also for consultation with the lay faithful. Francis has urged the bishops, individually and in their conferences, to ascertain the mind of the faithful regarding the burning issues of the day concerning married and family life, sexual identity, and the pastoral practice of the church regarding divorced and remarried Catholics at the extraordinary synod of 2014–2015. Not since the inquiry by Pius XII in the late 1940s regarding Mary's bodily assumption has there been such broad consultation of the mind of theologians and the faithful at large. Nevertheless, even given the teaching of Vatican II and the most recent papal practice of consulting more broadly in the church, questions still remain about the meaning of

---

1. The literature speaks of the "sense of the faith" [*sensus fidei*] and the "sense of the faithful" [*sensus fidelium*]. The "sense of the faith" is, according to article 12 of the Dogmatic Constitution on the Church, the quality of the gift or grace of faith that bestows on the individual believer "a supernatural sense of the faith." Looked at from the perspective of the totality of those who accept Christian revelation, it is commonly called the "sense of the faithful." In this use it is important to remember that the phrase the "sense of the faithful" refers to everyone in the church, regardless of their status, and not to the lay faithful alone. Again, according to article 12, it refers to "the whole people when 'from the bishops to the last of the faithful laity,' it expresses the consent of all in matters of faith and morals." Translations of the documents of Vatican II are noted in each instance. Here, Norman P. Tanner, ed., *The Decrees of the Ecumenical Councils*, 2 vols. (Washington, DC: Georgetown University Press, 1990) 2:858. Given the ambiguity of the English term "sense" and the fact that the phrase is a technical theological one, I always cite the *sense of the faithful* in quotation marks.

the teaching of Vatican II, its authority, and its relevance for the life of the Church.

Introduction

At least from the time of Melchior Cano (1509–60), theologians have spoken of the infallibility of the whole church when it professes belief in a teaching. Such infallibility, as distinguished from the pope's and the bishops' infallibility in teaching or defining, was never seriously called into question before Vatican II. The infallibility of the whole church in believing Christian revelation might have been hemmed in by distinctions such as "active" and "passive" infallibility, a "teaching church" and "a learning Church," but since the influential nineteenth-century theologians Johann Adam Möhler (1796–1838), Giovanni Perrone (1794–1876), and especially John Henry Newman (1801–90), this infallibility in believing has been understood increasingly as a positive contribution of the faithful in determining the faith. At the very least, the consultation of the faithful by Pius IX in preparation for the definition of Mary's Immaculate Conception (1854) and by Pius XII in preparation for the definition of Mary's Assumption (1950) have sealed the case for a meaningful teaching of the "sense of the faithful" as an active infallibility in believing. When Vatican II opened, some form of the doctrine was undeniably part of the Church's understanding of the tradition. What more can be said, then, about the nature, function, and challenge of the "sense of the faithful" in the life of the Church according to Vatican II?

German Catholic theologian Wolfgang Beinert has defined the "sense of the faithful" as "a free gift granted to all in the Church that imparts to them an interior agreement with the object of faith, and in whose power the Church as a whole expresses its consensus of the faith, knowing and confessing the object of faith in unanimous agreement with the Church's teaching office and with the science of theology."[2] In this essay I attempt to situate the "sense of the faithful" in the context of the ecclesiology of Vatican II and the questions regarding the kind of knowledge or "sense" that past practice in the church and the recent encouragement of the "sense of the faithful" at Vatican II imply.

---

2. "Theologische Erkenntnislehre," in *Glaubenszugänge. Lehrbuch der katholischen Dogmatik*, ed. W. Beinert, 3 vols. (Paderborn: Schöningh, 1995) vol. 1, 167–82, at 169. My translation.

A Listening Church

At this point in the reception of the "sense of the faithful" by the post-conciliar church, the old distinction of a "teaching" and a "learning" Church is thoroughly unhelpful. Frederick E. Crowe, SJ, has left us three seminal essays on the priority of learning in the church—at all levels. In "The Magisterium as Pupil: The Learning Church," he wrote: "Perhaps as a result of Pope John XXIII's initiative, we had in Vatican II a council in which the learning process was more explicit perhaps than it had ever been before, but we do not seem to have kept up the momentum. And so we continue to lay enormous stress on the teaching function, and very little on the learning function."[3] The key, of course, is for all in the church to be listeners, for the church to be a "listening Church." Listening is no easy process. It is active and demanding. It requires openness to the other and courage in the face of the possibly new, frankness in posing questions, the discipline of attending to each other and respecting one another, and finally the humility to acknowledge another's insight.

The priority of listening was emphasized in Vatican II's Dogmatic Constitution on Divine Revelation, when it opened with the words: "Hearing the word of God with reverence and proclaiming it with faith . . ." (article 1).[4] Later, in article 10 it reminded the bishops that although they were entrusted with the task of teaching with authority, the charge could only be fulfilled if they listened to God's word carefully: "The teaching authority is not above the word of God but stands at its service . . . it devotedly listens, reverently preserves and faithfully transmits the word of God."[5] The ideal of the "listening church" is to become a church in dialogue.[6] Believing,

---

3. "The Magisterium as Pupil: The Learning Teacher," *Developing the Lonergan Legacy: Historical, Theoretical, and Existential Themes*, ed., Michael Vertin (Toronto: University of Toronto Press, 2004) 283–93, at 288. The other two studies are "The Responsibility of the Theologian, and the Learning Church" and "The Church as Learner, Two Crises, One *Kairos*," both in *Appropriating the Lonergan Idea*, ed., Michael Vertin (Washington, DC: The Catholic University of America Press, 1989) 172–92 and 370–84 respectively. The challenge was taken up admirably by Margaret O'Gara and Michael Vertin in their co-authored "The Holy Spirit's Assistance to the Magisterium in Teaching: Theological and Philosophical Issues" in *Proceedings of the Catholic Theological Society of America*, vol. 51: *Fifty-first Annual Convention, San Diego, June 6–9, 1996* (CTSA, 1996) 125–42.

4. Austin Flannery, ed., *Vatican Council II: The Conciliar and Post Conciliar Documents* (new rev. ed.; Dublin: Dominican, 1992) 750.

5. Tanner, *The Decrees of the Ecumenical Councils*, vol. 2, 975.

6. See Bradford E. Hinze, "Ecclesial Repentance and the Demands of Dialogue," *Theological Studies* 61 (2000) 207–38, and idem, *Practices of Dialogue in the Roman Catholic Church: Aims and Obstacles, Lessons and Laments* (New York: Continuum,

proclaiming, and teaching all begin with "listening" and come to fruition in dialogue. The observation of the International Theological Commission's document "*Sensus fidei* in the Life of the Church" is to be welcomed: "It is only natural that there should be a constant communication and regular dialogue on practical issues and matters of faith and morals between members of the Church."[7]

The "Sense of the Faithful" and Ecclesiology

People of God

The teaching of Vatican II regarding the "sense of the faithful" should not be isolated from the council's broader ecclesiological accents. If this teaching is to make a difference in the church's life, it must be understood as an indispensable element in its self-understanding. Of particular importance to the meaning of the "sense of the faithful" is the teaching of Vatican II on the People of God, and yet, the reception of Vatican II's teaching remains incomplete. By the early 1980s it was viewed by some as dangerous for its supposed advocacy of democratizing tendencies and its use by liberation theologians. Ideas such as "communion" [*communio*] or sacrament, valid on their own terms, were used to weaken or exclude the influence of the church as the People of God.[8] But the teaching on the People of God stubbornly holds out and from time to time reemerges to claim its centrality in the ecclesiology of Vatican II.[9] Recently, in his apostolic exhortation "The Joy of the Gospel," Pope Francis stressed how the People of God and Christian faith are open to fuller expression in the diverse cultures of the world: "The

2006).

7. "*Sensus fidei* in the Life of the Church," 124, http://www.vatican.va./ roman_curia/congregations/cfaith/cti_documents/rc_cti_201460610_sensus-fidei_en.html. Access date?

8. Dario Vitale has reviewed the post-conciliar discussions of the ecclesiology of Vatican II in his "Il periodo postconciliare," *Popolo di Dio* (Assisi: Citadella, 2013) 153–91. In particular, he points to the Extraordinary Synod of Bishops of 1985 as the catalyst for neglecting the church as the People of God in favor of the church as communion, especially in official Vatican publications. It should be noted that the framers of the 1983 Code of Canon Law showed no such hesitation when they entitled Book II "The People of God" [canons 204–746].

9. The People of God appears in eleven of the sixteen documents of Vatican II. Two recent ecclesiologies that have developed the central idea of the People of God are Gerhard Lohfink, *Does God Need the Church? Toward a Theology of the People of God*, trans., Linda M. Maloney (Collegeville, MN: Liturgical, 1999 and Richard R. Gaillardetz, *Ecclesiology for a Global Church: A People Called and Sent* (Maryknoll, NY: Orbis, 2008).

People of God is incarnate in the peoples of the earth, each of which has its own culture . . . . In the Christian customs of an evangelized people, the Holy Spirit adorns the Church, showing her new aspects of revelation and giving her a new face" (articles 115–116).[10]

Vatican II insisted on the character of the church as the mystery of the Trinity's self-communication to humankind in history. The first chapter of the Dogmatic Constitution on the Church, entitled "The Mystery of the Church," goes on to delineate the reciprocal roles of Father, Son, and Spirit in the divine plan for the church and its realization in history. Central to the council's insights into the nature of the church are the many images and theological concepts it employed. Among these a unique place was given to the image of the People of God. Vatican II envisioned the church as the People of God by taking the idea from its place of origin in the chapter on the laity and giving it a privileged place as chapter 2, before the subsequent chapters on the hierarchy, the laity, and consecrated life in the Church.[11] Of course, the church as People of God does not exclude other images that also elucidate the life and mission of the church. What function, then, does the image of the People of God exercise in the ecclesiology of Vatican II?

First, the People of God has a double perspective. It is an idea taken from religious sociology that communicates specific knowledge about Israel as God's covenant people in history and how the first Christians understood themselves in relation to historic Israel. But it is also a powerful metaphor that acts on the imagination of believers and so stirs them to think creatively and entertain other visions for the church, visions of co-responsibility, collaboration, and participation. Second, the council wanted to emphasize the church as situated in history, not its timeless and unchangeable character, so often emphasized up until then. As a pilgrim people, the church journeys through human history from its beginning to its eschatological conclusion.

Finally, I propose that the People of God as idea and image is inseparable from the function of acting as the horizon for the other images and ecclesiological statements. Apropos, Gilles Routhier has written: "The image of the People of God established as it were the horizon against which the various particular questions in ecclesiology must be situated."[12] The

---

10. "The Joy of the Gospel," (Boston: Pauline Books & Media, 2013), articles 112–114 ["A People for Everyone"] and 115–18 ["A People of Many Faces"].

11. On the Dogmatic Constitution on the Church, see Giuseppe Alberigo, "Major Results, Shadows of Uncertainty," in *History of Vatican II*, vol. 4: *Church as Communion, Third Period and Intersession, September 1964–September 1965*, eds., Giuseppe Alberigo and Joseph A. Komonchak (Maryknoll, NY: Orbis and Louvain, Peeters, 2003) 617–40, especially 617–21.

12. See "La recezione dell'ecclesiologia del Vaticano II: Problemi aperti," in

term People of God is both its content as an idea and image and its added function as horizon.[13] The fundamental content of the idea and image of the People of God is the radical equality of all the baptized and the priesthood or priestly quality of the whole church. The advantage of understanding the People of God in the ways just described—historicity and the prophetic, priestly, and royal dignity of all its members—is that it frees the church to be open to changes that help it realize its mission in new and changing conditions. Greater agreement on the importance of the idea and image of the People of God is imperative for further progress in ecclesiology and for the acceptance of the "sense of the faithful" in particular.

The Threefold Office of Christ

Another important aspect of the church as People of God concerns Vatican II's use of the "threefold office" of Christ as prophet, priest, and king. This division was promoted by the Reformer John Calvin in his *Institutes of the Christian Religion* (1559) and was taken up by the nineteenth-century German Catholic canon lawyers Ferdinand Walter (1794–1879) and George Phillips (1804–72), who incorporated it into their ecclesiologies. The threefold-office schema of Vatican II was the council's preferred way of expressing both the place and role of office and ministry in the church as well as the dignity of the laity in the People of God. All believers participate in Christ's actions of teaching and witnessing, of sanctifying life, and of leading in family, society, and church. Vatican II viewed the threefold-office schema as preferable not only because it avoided a dichotomy between the laity and officeholders in the church, but also because it offered a better explanation of the nature of authority itself in the church than the distinction between two separable "powers"—orders and jurisdiction. The twofold schema, which emerged in the eleventh century among canon lawyers, always had difficulties holding sacramental activity, governance, and the teaching mission together in a fundamental unity. The bishops at Vatican II in the end preferred the more descriptive and flexible threefold-office schema over the standard orders-jurisdiction distinction. It has unimpeachable biblical warrant in the covenant prerogatives listed in Exodus 19:6 and 23:22, explicitly repeated in

---

Associazione teologica Italiana, *La chiesa e il Vaticano II: Problemi di ermeneutica e recezione conciliare* (Milan: Glossa, 2005) 3–45, at 9. My translation.

13. On the epistemological function of a "horizon," see Bernard Lonergan, *Method in Theology* (New York: Herder and Herder, 1972) *passim*. See "Horizon(s)" in the Index, 385–86. I submit that the function of horizon imparts a certain surplus value to the idea and image of the People of God in the context of the ecclesiology of Vatican II.

1 Peter 2:9 ("But you are 'a chosen race, a royal priesthood, a holy nation, a people of his own'"), as well as the advantage of a clearly christological formulation. But the twofold schema has continued to be employed in the post-conciliar period, leaving many unanswered questions about the relationship of the two approaches to one another. Are they compatible? Does one have priority vis-à-vis the other?

These nagging questions cast doubt over the explanatory power of the threefold-office schema where it is used in the documents of Vatican II. They are fundamental questions and until they are answered more satisfactorily the prophetic activity of the "sense of the faithful," for example, will continue to have a fragile hold and will be viewed as a merely secondary exercise by the laity. Furthermore, it is precisely in those passages that refer to the prophetic, sanctifying, and leadership functions of the laity that Vatican II broke new ground in its teaching regarding the inalienable dignity of each believer, of her or his right to collaborate in the mission of the church, and of his or her right to participate in the life of the church at all levels. The real task is to better explain the underlying unity of activity between officeholders and the laity and their mutual relations.[14]

One other question regarding the threefold office in the church involves the relationship of teaching, sanctifying, and leading among themselves. Can these three activities really be so neatly compartmentalized? Doesn't one activity necessarily involve the other two? Is preaching, for example, only an exercise of the prophetic office, or isn't it also sanctificatory and doesn't it at the same time provide direction or leadership to the community receiving it? Aren't the sanctifying sacraments, which take place in the context of a rite that includes announcing the word of God, also proclamatory? What are the implications for spirituality when all three are seen as simultaneously active? In this area, too, much more thought is needed. Without deeper reflection on these points, I fear the "sense of the faithful" as an exercise of the prophetic activity by all believers will be tenuous.

A Restored Understanding of the Church as Communion

An indispensable condition for understanding the "sense of the faithful" is the restoration of a correct understanding of what Vatican II meant by *communio* or communion. As numerous commentators have remarked, the notion has been so theologically reconfigured as to render its original intent

---

14. See Anthony Ekpo, "The *Sensus Fidelium* and the Threefold Office of Christ: A Reinterpretation of *Lumen Gentium* No. 12," *Theological Studies* 76 (2015) 330–46.

all but indecipherable.[15] The task is imperative because in the thought of Vatican II the church as People of God and as communion are intimately connected to one another. If you misunderstand one member of the pair, you distort the other. At the same time, the council's teaching on episcopal collegiality is a concretion of this underlying ecclesiology of communion. Communion without collegiality is ecclesial docetism; collegiality without communion risks becoming ecclesiastical power-grabbing.

Perhaps no one has captured the urgency of fully reinstating Vatican II's ecclesiology of communion more emphatically than Wolfgang Beinert who writes:

> It is imperative that those who hold office in the Church . . . make every effort to assure that what the majority of the bishops at the Second Vatican Council held regarding the ecclesiology of communion will become a reality in the Church today. Some of the particular points of such a program would include more effective connections between the primatial and the collegial exercise of the magisterium, the fostering of forms for their common search for truth, the strengthening of the competencies of the local Churches, respect for the principle of subsidiarity in all the relevant dimensions of the Church, the frank admission and Christian validation of the life-world that the faithful find themselves in today, and the rapid changes that occur daily in their life-world.
>
> It is decisive that a conversion to an ecclesiology of communion be securely anchored in canon law. Individual gestures of good will or the toleration of privileges are not enough. There must be clarity regarding the structural and institutional elements which themselves need to be better explained. It must also not be forgotten that channels of communication must be established that admit the right of action from below toward the top. There must also be reflection as to how lay Christians can become (ecclesial) subjects. Here, impulses from feminist theology can be of help. In all of this, the hierarchical structure of the

---

15. See Gerard Mannion, *Ecclesiology and Postmodernity: Questions for the Church in Our Time* (Collegeville, MN: Liturgical, 2007) 52–54; Joseph A. Komonchak, "Toward an Ecclesiology of Communion," in *History of Vatican II*, vol. 4: *Church as Communion, Third Period and Intersession, September 1964–September 1965*, eds., Giuseppe Alberigo and Joseph A. Komonchak (Maryknoll, NY: Orbis, 1993) 1–93; David McLoughlin, "*Communio* Models of Church: Rhetoric or Reality?" in *Authority in the Roman Catholic Church: Theory and Practice*, ed. Bernard Hoose (Burlington, VT: Ashgate, 2002) 181–90.

Church is in no way being called into question. All that is sought are (institutional) forms that are transparent and fruitful.[16]

Much has been written on the content of the teaching about communion and its importance for understanding the council correctly, but correct understanding alone will not restore communion to the day-to-day life of the Church. We have lost the experience of communion that imbued the church of the first millennium and that experience will not be easy to recover. Concrete practices will be the primary way to retrieve a mentality of communion. Several means have been suggested in recent years, especially by Catholic canon lawyers disappointed by the absence of meaningful references to the "sense of the faithful" in the Code of Canon Law of 1983. These means include improved parochial and diocesan pastoral councils, more frequent use of the diocesan synod, and calls for the holding of national synods. Until the faithful have an experience of being vested partners in the life of the church, a genuine mentality of communion will continue to elude us.

I propose two other actions that can lead to the genuine experience of communion in the twenty-first century. The first is the recovery of the process employed by the United States hierarchy in the drafting of the pastoral letters *The Challenge of Peace: God's Promise and Our Response*[17] and *Economic Justice for All*[18] in the 1980s. Real consultation of all constituents in the church on urgent social, ethical, and pastoral issues has the potential to reconnect the contemporary church with the church of the first millennium and its mentality of communion. The second suggestion is to reopen the issue of the role of all diocesan parties in the process of the appointment of a bishop. In a study devoted to the question of the selection of bishops, German Catholic theologian Gisbert Greshake offered an historical overview of the process in the first millennium, followed by a number of conclusions and suggestions for the present church.[19] Drawing widely on historical studies, Greshake showed how, locally and regionally, the process involved three parties in the case of a diocese in need of a bishop, and reflected a threefold structure of communion as it relates to offices in the church: the

---

16. "Die Rezeptionsgeschehen in der Kirche," *Stimmen der Zeit* 214 (1996) 381–92, at 390–91. My translation.

17. National Conference of Catholic Bishops (Washington, DC: United States Catholic Conference, 1983).

18. National Conference of Catholic Bishops (Washington, DC: United States Catholic Conference, 1986).

19. See "Bischofsernennungen im Lichte einer Theologie des kirchlichen Amtes und einer Communio-Ekklesiologie," in *Zur Frage der Bischofsernennungen in der römisch katholischen Kirche*, ed. Gisbert Greshake (Munich: Schnell & Steiner, 1991) 104–39.

faithful or the laity, the local body of presbyters, and the bishops of the province to which the local Church in question belonged. The "communion of churches" of the first millennium was tripartite, not bipartite—not simply the local church and the universal. It included the local church, the regional church or the ecclesiastical province, and the supra-regional church.[20] This tripartite structure was the way in which the church preserved the christological and the pneumatological dimensions of the church. If we in the West are to recover an understanding of the church as a "communion of churches," we must retrieve this tripartite structure: the local church or diocese, the regional church, including the Bishops' Conference, and the primacy of the see of Rome. For the health of the church, no one element should be isolated from the others. When these two actions are implemented, the faithful will begin to have a real sense of ownership and co-responsibility in the church.

The "Sense of the Faithful" and Revelation, Believing, and Human Cognition

Another series of questions concerns the relationship of the "sense of the faithful" to revelation and to our understanding of revelation. How is the "sense of the faithful" related to human cognition and what kind of knowledge is it?

The Importance of the Dogmatic Constitution on Divine Revelation of Vatican II for Understanding the Faith

In early articles on Vatican II's teaching on the "sense of the faithful," scholars focused attention on article 12 of the Dogmatic Constitution on the Church, where the teaching is presented at the greatest length.[21] Because article 8 of the Dogmatic Constitution on Divine Revelation never explicitly uses the phrases the "sense of the faith" or the "sense of the faithful," its teaching was passed over. More recently, its importance for the ecclesiology

---

20. On the distinction between a bipartite and tripartite structure of communion in the church of the first millennium and its continued importance for today's church, see Will Cohen, "Why Ecclesial Structures at the Regional Level Matter: Communion as Mutual Inclusion," *Theological Studies* 75 (2014), 308–30.

21. Further observations follow in article 35 (the "sense of the faith" on the family and society), the Pastoral Constitution on the Church in the Modern World, article 52 (the "sense of the faithful" on marriage), and the Decree on the Ministry and Life of Priests, article 9 (on the responsibility of presbyters to attend to the gifts and insights of the faithful).

of Vatican II has been noted. Recent commentators, including the authors of the International Theological Commission's "*Sensus fidei* in the Life of the Church," have noted the presence of the reality itself in the text.[22] The appropriate section from the document reads as follows:

> The expression "what has been handed down from the apostles" includes everything that helps the People of God to live a holy life and to grow in faith. In this way the Church, in its teaching, life and worship, perpetuates and hands on to every generation all that it is and all that it believes.
>
> This tradition which comes from the apostles progresses in the Church under the assistance of the Holy Spirit. There is growth in understanding of what is handed on, both the words and the realities they signify. This comes about through contemplation and study by believers, who "ponder these things in their hearts," both through the intimate understanding of spiritual things which they experience, and through the preaching of those who, on succeeding to the office of bishop, receive the sure charism of truth. Thus, as the centuries advance, the Church constantly holds its course towards the fullness of God's truth, until the day when the words of God reach their fulfillment in the Church.[23]

This pioneering passage makes clear that the "sense of the faithful" is more than a static authoritative source of the content of revelation. Instead, it emphasizes the dynamic character of revelation itself by speaking about the church growing into "the fullness of God's truth." The faithful perform an indispensable role in more deeply perceiving this truth and more effectively applying it to life. The "sense of the faithful" is a living, dynamic deepening of the understanding of divine truth that proceeds throughout history as humankind (and the cosmos) moves toward its eschatological goal.

Wolfgang Beinert has pointed out how Vatican II has expanded the very notion of the "sense of the faithful" when compared to the classical notion of an authoritative source of revelation. In an historical presentation of the "sense of the faithful," he characterized the first period as one of being a witness to the tradition, while the second was that of the "sense of the faithful" as an echo of what the popes and bishops have taught, and the third as a witness to the church's dogma when other sources were not

---

22. Articles 46, 67, and 82.

23. Tanner, *Decrees of the Ecumenical Councils*, vol. 2, 974 (adapted slightly). Still to be recommended is the commentary on this passage by then Professor Joseph Ratzinger, *Commentary on the Documents of Vatican II*, 5 vols. (New York: Herder and Herder, 1969) vol. 3, 184–90.

available. Finally, at Vatican II we must say even more: the "sense of the faithful" is a deepening of the understanding of the faith and of the praxis of the faith.[24] Vatican II's understanding is that the "sense of the faithful" not only witnesses to Christian truth but also contributes to the emergence of the understanding of that truth.

Knowing/Sense [*Sentire/sensus*] and Cognition

I asked above how "knowing" is related to "believing." I begin with a prayer attributed to St. Francis of Assisi (1182–1226). It is his prayer before the crucifix of San Damiano, and shows that as early as the thirteenth century the terms "sense" and "knowing" were already closely linked to one another:

> Most High, glorious God,
>
> Enlighten the darkness of my heart
>
> And give me true faith, certain hope, and perfect charity,
>
> Sense and knowledge, Lord,
>
> That I may carry out your holy and true command.[25]

After God's initiative and the gift of the theological virtues, St. Francis adds "sense and knowledge"—words that point to how God's will is to be put into practice. These two terms illuminate one another and move the believer to action—to obeying God's will. They pertain to the order of practical, not primarily speculative, knowledge.

The term "sense" is elusive and evocative. It is not simple "feeling," "intuition," or "blind groping," but is grounded in a true grasp of the faith and its contents. As practical knowledge, and unlike theological discourse, its way of knowing is not especially formal, self-reflective, or self-critical. It is more global and broadly comprehensive knowledge.[26] It doesn't stop to investigate its processes or the complex questions it generates. It homes in

---

24. See "Der Glaubenssinn der Gläubigen in Theologie und Dogmengeschichte: Ein Überblick," in Dietrich Wiederkehr, ed., *Der Glaubenssinn des Gottesvolkes Konkurrent oder Partner des Lehramts?* Quaestiones Disputatae 151 (Freiburg: Herder, 1994) 87–109 [66–131].

25. Regis J. Armstrong et al., eds., *Francis of Assisi: Early Documents*, vol. 1: *The Saint* (New York: New City, 1999) 40.

26. The ITC's "*Sensus fidei* in the Life of the Church" prefers the language of "a sort of perception (*aisthesis*)" (49), "connaturality" (50-51), and speaks of "a natural, immediate and spontaneous reaction" to revealed truth (54), and "a vital instinct or a sort of 'flair' by which the believer clings spontaneously to what conforms to the truth of faith and shuns what is contrary to it" (54).

on how faith is to be lived in truth and incorporated into the whole fabric of one's life and the life of the church. It is impatient with minutiae and shows little difficulty with entertaining a multitude of doubts and problems while embracing lived faith quietly and confidently.

Experience

The "sense of the faithful" pertains to the broad range of knowledge gained from experience. According to Walter Kasper, [The "sense of the faith"] "comes not from abstract theological reflection but from the lived experience of faith."[27] The category of experience is widely invoked by contemporary theologians, even though differences in understanding it can be found. It is a specific form of cognition that is based on expertise, learning by doing, by trial and error, and from insights gained from shared human activity. In particular, experience-based cognition has helped retrieve the ancient idea of praxis as perfective both of the human agent and of her or his society, an insight that is at the heart of a broad range of liberation theologies. Contemporary Catholic theology would be impoverished without the category of experience and its contribution. The "sense of the faithful," too, draws on the richness of experience and experience-based knowledge, refusing to be constrained within the confines of logical, scientific, and discursive reason—however beneficial and indispensable this form of cognition is.

Participatory Knowledge

As practical and experience-based, the "sense of the faithful" is also participatory knowledge. Though some truths can be known by empirical observation and objective reason, it is not the only form. More general in human affairs is what Avery Dulles, SJ, pointed to as participatory knowledge.[28] Some truths can only be known by the knower being immersed in them and by living from them. Dulles spoke of inhabiting and dwelling in them. Knowledge by participation is particularly true when we humans are in search of religious truth. Objective or scientific distance can actually be a hindrance to coming to know in this realm of truth.

The vehicle for discerning and sharing participatory knowledge is the symbol, with its effects of transforming us and influencing our behavior for

---

27. *The Catholic Church: Nature, Reality and Mission*, trans. Thomas Hoebel (New York: Bloomsbury T. & T. Clark, 2015), 407, note 55.

28. "The Symbolic Structure of Revelation," *Theological Studies* 41 (1980) 60–65 [51–73].

the good by uniting us to itself. The vehicle for understanding and expressing participatory knowledge is hermeneutical interpretation, which draws us and the totality of our lives into its self-expressive, holistic, and integrative process. Is there any wonder, then, that the complex and polyvalent knowledge characteristic of the "sense of the faithful" refuses facile and complete analysis? Little wonder, too, that such rich knowledge defies an easy identification of its subjects. Certainly, it includes the great "cloud of witnesses" of the saints (Hebrews 12:1) and all who strive to conform their lives to the Gospel, but not only them, however privileged their witness might be.[29] I continue to resist all attempts to identify only practicing and committed Catholics and Christians as its subjects. Instead, it includes all who are struggling to live their lives in pursuit of and in accord with Christian truth as they inhabit it. This is especially the case when they are struggling with the vast array of issues that promote or restrict human dignity. In the final analysis, there is only one subject of the "sense of the faithful" we can clearly identify—the whole church as guided by the Holy Spirit.

The "Object" of Faith

The "object" of the "sense of the faithful" is the whole content of Christian truth. This observation draws on the teaching of Vatican II regarding the nature of revelation, especially in the Dogmatic Constitution on Divine Revelation. Vatican II did not envision faith as the sum total of divine truths taught in the Scriptures and by the living tradition, but as God's dialogue with humankind in history. In the words of the document: "By this revelation, then, the invisible God, from the fullness of love speaks to men and women as friends and enters into their lives, so as to invite and receive them into relationship with himself" (article 2).[30] Propositional truth gives way to terms that speak about revelation as inter-personal and dialogical communication. After Vatican II the priority resides with faith as God acting on the believer and drawing him or her into God's own life in "trusting faith" (*fides qua*).[31] This insight about faith helps elucidate the "sense of the faithful," too,

---

29. "*Sensus Fidei* in the Life of the Church" stresses the role of holiness and the saints in 99–103.

30. Tanner, *Decrees of the Ecumenical Councils*, vol. 2, 972 (adapted slightly).

31. I have translated the technical term *fides qua* as "trusting faith" for two reasons. First, recent studies by exegetes and theologians have pointed to the elements of "trust" and "committing oneself" to God in faith as the believer's response to God who is preeminently "trustworthy." Second, several twentieth-century theologians have stressed the "personalist" nature of the act of faith, an understanding that builds on mutual trust between persons based on faith as the paradigmatic I-Thou relationship. Moreover,

inasmuch as it points toward the mysterious process of being embraced by God's truth and life prior to all reflection on its concrete content or application in human acts (*fides quae* or "Christian beliefs"). All attempts, then, to formally spell out faith's contents necessarily operate within "trusting faith" as the context of interpretation. Faith cannot be reduced to concepts or terms but seeks to express itself in worshipful trust, service, and acts of justice and love. This does not reduce the "sense of the faithful" to non-rational speech, but to speech that respects the limits of human understanding and how the divine self-communication in grace and truth is expressed. To some extent these "limits" are transcended in our searching and in our faculty of imagination. If we employ words, as we ultimately must, then we do so in a way that goes beyond the boundaries of speech.

Certitude and Epistemological Reserve

We have noted already that the entire "Christian People of God" was considered infallible in what it believed and what the popes and bishops taught in its name. This insight eventually was turned into the expression "sense" or "consensus of all believers" familiar to us today. However, in the wake of the Reformation and the wars of religion, not to mention the effects of the scientific revolution and the claims of Enlightenment thinkers, the idea of infallibility became identified with the human quest for certitude. René Descartes' foundationalist epistemology became the ideal of the certitude of religious knowledge in matters of faith as well. The pursuit of such ecclesial certitude reached its apex in the nineteenth century and at Vatican I in particular. In such a church, nothing less than complete certitude will suffice. In our postmodern condition we do not seek such certitude and the claim to it strikes us as epistemological hubris. We are content with less than absolute certitude, feeling more at home in a world of ideas, values, and truth claims that constitute a coherent world for us. In changed circumstances that valorize epistemological reserve, I often think of the advice of Joseph R. Lerch, SJ, that "infallibility is not the only category that can be opposed to falsity.

---

personalist theologies of faith better explain the dual activities of knowing and willing as mutually conditioning each other in the act of believing. See Jean Mouroux, *I Believe: The Personal Structure of Faith*, trans. Michael Turner (New York: Sheed & Ward, 1959); and Carlos Cirne-Lima, *Personal Faith: A Metaphysical Inquiry*, trans. G. Richard Dimler (New York: Herder & Herder, 1965). A personalist approach would add important nuances to the highly Thomistic presentation of faith in the ITC's "*Sensus fidei* in the Life of the Church," in 49–59 ["The *sensus fidei* as an Instinct of Faith"].

Between it and error there is the whole domain of sufficient certitude."[32] I submit that this advice is quite appropriate to our age and temperament.

The neglect of Fr. Lerch's sage advice has led to an exaggerated zeal in teaching activity, especially by the Congregation for the Doctrine of the Faith in its extension of the category of "definitive doctrine" (*doctrina definitive tenenda*) as practically indistinguishable from infallible teaching. This new teaching has caused unnecessary confusion.[33] Moreover, the multiplication of teachings and directives emanating from Rome, together with strenuous efforts to curtail healthy theological discussion and the normal processing of the meaning of the faith among the faithful, have vainly attempted to perpetuate a church and society that no longer exist—the world of modernity. In Christian hope, we need to come to terms with the ineradicable pluralism, cognitive dissonance, and "ruptures" of postmodernism, even as we struggle to pursue the truth and incorporate our limited insights into a way of living and thinking that proclaims the central claims of Christian revelation and imparts meaning to human lives.[34]

Reception

The "sense of the faithful" leads to the related theme of reception. Wolfgang Beinert has pointed out that reception is concerned with how an action or teaching fits into the whole of faith as lived and not just as something known or epistemologically justified. The primary question is not always, "Is this action or statement objectively true?" but, "Does it function within the faith as a whole?" As "trusting faith," our faith not only makes truth-claims but also constitutes a whole or totality that in the medieval period would have been called *forma vitae* or a "unified pattern of Christian life."[35] Reception answers the question of truth indirectly by primarily addressing the question of appropriation or internalization of the faith. According to Beinert:

---

32. "Teaching Authority in the Church (Magisterium)," in *New Catholic Encyclopedia* (New York: McGraw-Hill, 1967) vol. 13, 959–65, at 964. Fr. Lerch taught Fundamental Theology at St. Mary's College, Kurseong, India.

33. See Richard R. Gaillardetz, "The Ordinary Universal Magisterium: Unresolved Questions." *Theological Studies* 63 (2002) 447–71.

34. See John J. Burkhard, "Apostolicity in a Postmodern World," in *Apostolicity Then and Now: An Ecumenical Church in a Postmodern World* (Collegeville, MN: Liturgical, 2004) 127–63, and the literature cited there.

35. On this notion, see the observations of Giorgio Agamben, *The Highest Poverty: Monastic Rules and Form-of-Life*, trans. Adam Kotsko (Stanford: Stanford University Press, 2013).

Given the necessarily historical condition of magisterial statements, it can happen that its directives are not practicable, are not supportive of life, or in certain socio-cultural situations are not able to be implemented. Precisely because faith is not law it has an inner dynamic that a given directive of the magisterium possibly does not capture. To observe such a directive would be to act contrary to the intention of the magisterium itself to proclaim the faith as something that can be lived . . . It follows that an act of reception or non-reception does not necessarily issue from a judgment. Rather, it consists of the adoption of the contents of the faith in the liturgical life, in one's personal or local spirituality, in the specific praxis of the Church, and so forth . . . Non-reception does not make clear that the content of a magisterial decision is necessarily false, but rather, at least in the here and now (and so possibly not in other places or situations), it does not possess the requisite value to advance ecclesial life. Consequently, the statement is without effect.[36]

Beinert reminds us that there are many situations in the church today, especially when the church is considered as a world church, that defy our ability to spell out the implications of the non-reception of a teaching of the magisterium in terms of its truth or falsity. In some situations the appropriate question is not "Is it objectively true?" but "Is it life-giving?"

Conclusion

We have seen the existence of some form of the "sense of the faithful" in the church from the 1500s onward, and how Vatican II has preserved and extended its importance in the contemporary church. We have also noted some of the questions surrounding the meaning of this rich teaching, questions pertaining to the ecclesiology of Vatican II and to human cognition. The "sense of the faithful" holds out great promise for the life of the church, but there is much that needs to be done to secure it. We need to normalize the practices of dialogue and consensus in the day-to-day life of the post-conciliar Church. Although we have taken significant steps in understanding the "sense of the faithful," we urgently need to institutionalize the forms and structures of dialogue and consultation that will make this teaching

---

36. "Die Rezeption und ihre Bedeutung für Leben und Lehre der Kirche," in Wolfgang Beinert, ed., *Glaube und Zustimmung. Zur Interpretation kirchlicher Rezeptionsvorgänge*, Quaestiones Disputatae 131 (Freiburg: Herder, 1991) 15–49, at 42–44 (my translation).

a reality in a church that better reflects the richness of the church as the People of God and as a "communion of churches."

10

The Church as a Hermeneutical Community and the Eschatalogical Funtion of the *Sensus Fidelium*

Ormond Rush

"Listen to what the Spirit is saying to the churches." The cry rings out seven times in the last book of the New Testament, the Book of Revelation.[1] The essential medium through which the Spirit speaks to the churches is the Spirit's gift of *sensus fidei*. The ecclesial reality of the *sensus fidei*—given by the Holy Spirit in baptism to baptized individuals and to the church as a whole—is a significant affirmation in *Lumen Gentium*'s second chapter on the People of God.[2] This "sense of/for the faith," the council teaches, enables the church to continue responding faithfully to God's loving self-revelation, i.e., to be infallible in believing. In the fifty years' reception of the council, the implications of this teaching have hardly begun to affect the official learning and teaching processes of the Catholic Church. However, it appears the Catholic Church is entering into a new phase in the recep-

---

1. Rev 2:7, 11, 17, 29; 3:6, 13, 22 (NRSV translation).

2. *Lumen Gentium* 12 states: "The holy people of God has a share, too, in the prophetic office of Christ, when it renders him a living witness, especially through a life of faith and charity, and when it offers to God a sacrifice of praise, the tribute of lips that honour his name. The universal body of the faithful who have received the anointing of the holy one, cannot be mistaken in belief. It displays this particular quality through a supernatural sense of the faith in the whole people when 'from the bishops to the last of the faithful laity,' it expresses the consent of all in matters of faith and morals. Through this sense of the faith which is aroused and sustained by the Spirit of truth, the people of God, under the guidance of the sacred magisterium to which it is faithfully obedient, receives no longer the words of human beings but truly the word of God; it adheres indefectibly to 'the faith which was once for all delivered to the saints'; it penetrates more deeply into that same faith through right judgment and applies it more fully to life." Tanner translation.

tion of this significant teaching of the Second Vatican Council. The faithful have an increasing awareness of the importance of their own sense of the faith for revitalizing the church in an age of unbelief; theologians are giving more attention both to the *sensus fidei* as a topic for systematic reflection and, accordingly, to the *sensus fidei* of their local communities; and, among the hierarchy, Vatican II's doctrine of the *sensus fidei* seems to be receiving greater acknowledgement. Of significance here is the prominent role the *sensus fidei* of the whole People of God plays in the ecclesial vision of Pope Francis.

Early in his pontificate, in an interview with the editor of the Jesuit periodical *La Civiltà Cattolica* during August 2013, Pope Francis revealed something of his personal ecclesiology:

> The image of the Church I like is that of the holy, faithful people of God. This is the definition I often use, which is the image of *Lumen Gentium*, no. 12. Belonging to a people has a strong theological value ... The people themselves are the subject. And the Church is the people of God on the journey through history, with joys and sorrows. *Sentire cum Ecclesia* [to think and to feel with the Church], therefore, is my way of being a part of this people. And all the faithful, considered as a whole, are infallible in matters of beliefs, and the people display this *infallibilitas in credendo*, this infallibility in believing, through a supernatural sense of the faith of all the people walking together. This is what I understand today as the "thinking with the Church" of which St. Ignatius speaks. When the dialogue among the people and the bishops and the Pope goes down this road and is genuine, then it is assisted by the Holy Spirit. So this thinking with the Church does not concern theologians only ... And, of course, we must be very careful not to think that this *infallibilitas* of all the faithful I am talking about in the light of Vatican II is a form of populism. No, it is the experience of the "holy mother the hierarchical Church," as St. Ignatius called it, the Church as the people of God, pastors and people together. The Church is the totality of the people of God.[3]

A few months later, Pope Francis echoed these same thoughts in his Apostolic Exhortation *Evangelii Gaudium*.[4]

---

3. Pope Francis, *My Door Is Always Open: A Conversation on Faith, Hope and the Church in a Time of Change. Pope Francis with Antonio Spadaro* (London: Bloomsbury, in association with *La Civiltà Cattolica*, 2014) 49–50. This interview took place over three meetings in August 2013.

4. "In all the baptized, from first to last, the sanctifying power of the Spirit is at

In this chapter, I propose that the ecclesial reality and authority of the *sensus fidelium* can be fruitfully explored by employing the "background theory" of hermeneutics.[5] Of course, as Jürgen Habermas noted in his critique of Hans-Georg Gadamer's hermeneutical notion of tradition: "Hermeneutic consciousness remains incomplete as long as it does not include a reflection upon the limits of hermeneutic understanding."[6] Other background theories, such as critical theories, can well aid the church in developing its theology of the *sensus fidei* by opening up further perspectives on the complexity of the world in which the faithful live the Gospel.

The background theory of hermeneutics I believe is especially relevant for interpreting four major teachings of the Second Vatican Council. First, divine revelation is not only, nor primarily, a series of doctrines and morals formulated throughout church history, although it includes these in a secondary and qualified sense. Rather revelation is primarily a personal encounter with the Living God in all ages throughout history; and it is the Holy Spirit who enables the reception of revelation by bestowing the gift of faith (DV 2; 5). Secondly, along with the gift of faith (*fides*), the Holy Spirit bestows on baptized individuals and the whole community of faith a hermeneutical skill, a *sensus fidei*, i.e., "a sense for" understanding, interpreting and applying the faith through time (LG 12). With the gift comes the ability both to receive the gift and to contextualize the gift. Third, this divine revelation, and its accompanying gift of *sensus fidei*, are communicated to, not just the pope and bishops (as if we were some gnostic sect of select *illuminati*), but to the whole People of God, the *universitas fidelium*

---

work, impelling us to evangelization. The people of God is holy thanks to this anointing, which makes it infallible *in credendo*. This means that it does not err in faith, even though it may not find words to explain that faith. The Spirit guides it in truth and leads it to salvation (*Lumen Gentium*, 12). As part of his mysterious love for humanity, God furnishes the totality of the faithful with an instinct of faith—*sensus fidei*—which helps them to discern what is truly of God. The presence of the Spirit gives Christians a certain connaturality with divine realities, and a wisdom which enables them to grasp those realities intuitively, even when they lack the wherewithal to give them precise expression." Pope Francis, *Evangelii Gaudium. Apostolic Exhortation of the Holy Father Francis: On the Proclamation of the Gospel in Today's World* (London: Catholic Truth Society, 2013), art. 119, at 62–63.

5. On the function of "background theories" in theological method, see Francis Schüssler Fiorenza, "Systematic Theology: Task and Methods," in *Systematic Theology: Roman Catholic Perspectives*, ed. Francis Schüssler Fiorenza and John P. Galvin, 2nd and revised ed. (Minneapolis: Fortress, 2011), 1–78, at 56–58.

6. Jürgen Habermas, "The Hermeneutic Claim to Universality," in *The Hermeneutic Tradition: From Ast to Ricoeur*, eds., Gayle L. Ormiston and Alan D. Schrift (Albany: State University of New York Press, 1990), 245–72, at 253. For Gadamer's approach, see Hans-Georg Gadamer, *Truth and Method*, 2nd rev. ed. (New York: Crossroad, 1989).

(LG 12). Fourth, in this way (as *Dei verbum* 8 teaches), "God, who spoke in the past, continues to converse with the spouse of his beloved Son. And the Holy Spirit, through whom the living voice of the Gospel rings out in the church—and through it in the world—leads believers to the full truth and makes the word of Christ dwell in them in all its richness." In other words, revelation is happening here and now, and the Spirit's gift of *sensus fidei* enables its faithful interpretation.

Reading these four teachings in a hermeneutical key opens up avenues for exploring the ecclesial implications of the dialogue that God continues to have with the church in our own time. And, it thus opens up ways of understanding the eschatological character of Christian truth; the story is never finished, until the eschaton. God continues to surprise us and to provoke us. And the *sensus fidei* is the antenna for sensing those surprises and provocations. Furthermore, the background theory of hermeneutics is particularly helpful for articulating the dynamics at work in interpreting those divine surprises and provocations.

Around the time of his appointment, Blase Cupich, the new Archbishop of Chicago, spoke of the uncomfortable provocation Pope Francis is currently presenting for the Catholic Church. He said: "One of the lines that [Pope Francis] uses [is] '*realities* are greater than ideas.' . . . I think the pope is giving us *a new epistemology, a new way of learning, of knowing—another way in which we're informed.* We can really get caught up in living in our own little bubble of an idea or an illusion of things the way they have been in the past. It's important not to have just a 30,000 feet perspective on life but to really be there in the reality of the situation and pay attention to the observables right now around you."[7]

The hermeneuts among you may have heard evoked in Archbishop Cupich's words something of the so-called "hermeneutical circle" or "spiral": i.e., we get a sense of the whole (in theological terms, the doctrinal perspective) by getting down into the detail (the pastoral perspective); and from the perspective of the detail, we have to form a revised and more "real" sense of the whole; and so it continues in an ongoing hermeneutical circle. Observing the valley below from 30,000 feet gives *one* sense of context; landing the plane, getting out, and walking through the villages in the valley gives a very different sense of things.

The church well knows this dynamic, with its ongoing challenge, however much it might sometimes try to avoid the challenge. But, *from its*

---

7. Joshua J. McElwee, "Exclusive: Chicago's New Archbishop Talks about 'Stepping into the Unknown,'" *National Catholic Reporter*, May 24, 2015, http://ncronline.org/news/people/exclusive-chicagos-new-archbishop-talks-about-stepping-unknown (emphasis added).

very origins, the church has always been a hermeneutical community—it is embedded in our DNA. In the process that gave rise to the New Testament, those early disciples, even pre-Easter, were interpreting Jesus, trying to "make sense" of his words and deeds, and of his identity in relationship with the God whose kingdom he was so focused on. But, as someone like a Paul or the evangelist Luke asked, What does all that mean for my community? The canon of 27 writings, chosen by the early church to stand thereafter as a canon regarding the faith for all time, is a testament to plurality and diversity in the church's earliest proclamations of the one faith in Jesus Christ. Here, in these writings from the 80 or so years of the so-called Apostolic Period, we see local hermeneutical communities interpreting the faith *from within* their own context and *for* their own context. There is at work here what I have called elsewhere an "apostolic hermeneutic": an interpretive dynamic, within the first few generations of the church, regarding Jesus Christ and the implications of his teaching and way of acting within the changing circumstances of economic, social, cultural, and political life.[8] This "apostolic hermeneutic" (as a dynamic way of interpreting the Gospel) is normative for all times, and indeed our own. We too must operate out of an apostolic hermeneutic, and be equally creative for the sake of fidelity to the same God, still revealing and saving in Christ through the Spirit in our own time.

The forthcoming Synod on marriage and the family is not only about moral and sacramental theology, and the church's doctrinal teaching. It is, more basically, about hermeneutics—and about keys issues in fundamental theology (revelation and faith) and ecclesiology (the salvific mission of the church). The previous 2014 synod has already exposed deep conflicts in interpretation, deep rifts regarding what the church should be all about, and in particular the interrelationship between doctrine and pastoral realities. It has ignited *a hermeneutical battle* that rages on now, as we approach this year's synod.

The German philosopher Odo Marquard, in his essay "The Question, To What Question Is Hermeneutics the Answer?" situates a significant point in the origins of the modern hermeneutical tradition in the religious wars of the seventeenth century following the Reformation.[9] He depicts the devastating Thirty Years War (1618–48) as "a civil war of the absolute text"

---

8. See Ormond Rush, *The Eyes of Faith: The Sense of the Faithful and the Church's Reception of Revelation* (Washington, DC: Catholic University of America Press, 2009) 116–29.

9. Otto Marquard, "The Question, To What Question Is Hermeneutics the Answer?," in *Farewell to Matters of Principle* (New York: Oxford University Press, 1989) 111–37.

between Catholics and Protestants.[10] The word "hermeneutics," he notes, is first found in 1654, six years after the end of the Thirty Years War with the so-called Peace of Westphalia. Marquard's thesis is that "hermeneutics gives an answer to this experience of the deadlines of the hermeneutic civil war over the absolute text by inventing—thus turning itself into pluralizing, which is to say literary, hermeneutics—the nonabsolute text and the nonabsolute reader."[11] He makes a distinction between "singularizing hermeneutics" and "pluralizing hermeneutics." For singularizing hermeneutics there is only "the one correct reading . . . the one absolute reading (for salvation) of the Bible."[12] Pluralizing hermeneutics "traces out many possible meanings and the most various kinds of spirit in one and the same literal form."[13] In the religious wars both sides were working out of their own singularizing hermeneutics, with tragic consequences, as Marquard observes:

> The dogmatic quality of the claim to truth that is made by the unambiguous interpretation of the absolute text can be deadly: that is the experience of the religious civil wars. When, in relation to the sacred text, two interpreters assert, in controversy, "I am right; my understanding of the text is the truth, and in fact—and this is necessary for salvation—in this way and not otherwise": then there can be hacking and stabbing. Hermeneutics, when it turns into pluralizing hermeneutics, gives an answer to precisely this situation when it asks: "Could this text not be understood, after all, in still another way, and—if that is not sufficient—still another way, and again and again in other ways?"[14]

The text thus invites a dialogue down through history. This ongoing process of pluralizing hermeneutics is evident within the Bible itself.[15] Applying such a pluralizing hermeneutics to the human interpretation of divine revelation is not a denial of the status for Christians of the Bible as the written Word of God and its function as the canon of the Christian faith.[16]

---

10. Ibid., 122.
11. Ibid.
12. Ibid., 121.
13. Ibid., 122.
14. Ibid., 123. Marquard's approach has affinities with that of Paul Ricoeur's notion of a text's "surplus of meaning," which the reader makes of the text. See, for example, Paul Ricoeur, *Interpretation Theory: Discourse and the Surplus of Meaning* (Fort Worth: Texas Christian University Press, 1976).
15. See, for example, Mogens Müller and Henrik Tronier, eds., *The New Testament as Reception* (London: Sheffield Academic, 2002).
16. On the Bible as not being "revelation" as such for Christians, but rather a

Nor is it some capitulation to a dictatorship of relativism in interpretation, but rather a recognition that "realities are greater than ideas" in the transmission of revelation in new contexts.

Certainly the distinction between singularizing and pluralizing hermeneutics captures something of the tension within the Catholic Church in our own time. There have been some who have publicly voiced their concern over the present pope, his privileging of "mercy" in the interpretation of Scripture and tradition, and, what they perceive as his promotion of "a weaker, pastoral permissiveness and a Christianity-lite, a way of being Christian at a reduced cost. So they see in mercy a kind of 'fabric softener' that undermines the dogmas and commandments and abrogates the central and fundamental meaning of truth."[17] Walter Kasper speaks of the pope's lens for interpreting and applying the Gospel in a new context as a "hermeneutical principle," in a way that appears to want to avoid any singularizing hermeneutics:

> One can . . . characterize this highlighting of mercy—as a foundational hermeneutical principle—as a paradigm shift: from a deductive method to a method in the sense of see-judge-act, which begins inductively at first and, only in a second step, introduces theological criteria. Such a paradigm shift can elicit irritations and misunderstandings . . . as if what had been previously said was no longer valid. However, rightly understood, the paradigm shift does not change the previously valid content of what has been taught, but certainly changes the perspective and the horizon in which it is seen and understood."[18]

The appeal of Pope Francis' opponents to the absolute character of Scripture and the absolute character of the church's doctrinal tradition on those texts does sound a bit like a "singularizing hermeneutics," and indeed, like a declaration of war—without perhaps the bloody devastation of 1614–48. But it does seem to be an ecclesial conflict as significant as that hermeneutical battle between Paul and Peter in the early church over the

---

"revelatory text," requiring interpretation from different worlds "in front of the text," see Sandra M. Schneiders, *The Revelatory Text: Interpreting the New Testament as Sacred Scripture*, 2nd ed. (Collegeville, MN.: Liturgical, 1999).

17. Walter Kasper, *Pope Francis' Revolution of Tenderness and Love: Theological and Pastoral Perspectives* (New York: Paulist, 2015) 34. On the opposition to Pope Francis from certain cardinals and bishops, see, for example, Massimo Faggioli, "The Italian Job: Can Pope Francis Manage His Local Opposition?," *Commonweal* (August 15, 2014) 17–20.

18. Kasper, *Pope Francis' Revolution of Tenderness and Love*, 35.

implications of the Gospel in a new non-Jewish context.[19] As we approach the forthcoming synod, can we dare to hope: could the October synod achieve the *consensus fidelium* achieved at the Council of Jerusalem, where, through the diverse *sensus fidei* of the community gathered in "council," they were able at the end of it to say: "It has seemed good to the Holy Spirit and to us . . ." (Acts 15:28).[20] A pluralizing hermeneutics can lead to dialogue, and through dialogue, to a *consensus fidelium*.

Of course, often in the church today the underlying debate is not only about the appropriate hermeneutic for the interpretation of Scripture and tradition, but also another fundamental hermeneutical issue: the most appropriate hermeneutic for interpreting the Second Vatican Council. And generally related to that is the council's teaching on revelation as not simply some e-mail attachment with propositional statements of divine truths sent by God to humanity in every age, but rather revelation as primarily a personal (and ongoing) encounter with the Living God in Jesus Christ through the Holy Spirit, in the messiness of human history.

Cardinal Luis Tagle has recently made a distinction between "problems" and "dilemmas." "Problems," he said, can be solved; but "dilemmas" don't have clear and universal solution. Learning how the faithful have faced dilemmas, he went on, can only be accessed by listening to their stories. "Tell stories of people who have navigated through those murky waters of dilemmas . . . You don't need a solution. You need meaning. You need hope."[21] Listening to the stories of the People of God, and the dilemmas they have faced in their journey through the murky waters of their lives, is simply listening to their *sensus fidei,* their "senses of the faith".[22] Those *sensus fidei* may very well have been formed in conversation with the Holy Spirit who graced them with that gift in their baptism. Those *sensus fidei* reveal how they have sensed the Gospel and have decided to act in their circumstances. Hearing those stories is hearing stories of *the Holy Spirit at work,* the one

---

19. Gal 2:11–14: "But when Cephas came to Antioch, I opposed him to his face, because he stood self-condemned; for until certain people came from James, he used to eat with the Gentiles. But after they came, he drew back and kept himself separate for fear of the circumcision faction. And the other Jews joined him in this hypocrisy, so that even Barnabas was led astray by their hypocrisy. But when I saw that they were not acting consistently with the truth of the gospel, I said to Cephas before them all, "If you, though a Jew, live like a Gentile and not like a Jew, how can you compel the Gentiles to live like Jews?" (NRSV translation).

20. NRSV translation.

21. Joshua J. McElwee, "Cardinal Tagle: Church Should Not Look to 'Idealized Past' with Nostalgia," *National Catholic Reporter*, http://ncronline.org/news/global/cardinal-tagle-church-should-not-look-idealized-past-nostalgia.

22. The plural form is also *"sensus."*

who is the Enlightener, the Interpreter, the Hermeneut. Through the exercise of their sense of the faith, in the reality of their constrained lives in the changing contexts of human history, God is in dialogue with humanity throughout that history (*Dei Verbum*, 8). This is not to be cheaply dismissed as some "situation ethics" or just one more example of the "dictatorship of relativism," but rather *a deeply theological affirmation*, grounded in the New Testament and the tradition of the church, concerning the activity of the Holy Spirit whose enlightenment brings about understanding, interpretation, and application of the Christian Gospel in the realities of life, in sinful, yet grace-filled and often selflessly loving, human lives—down in the valley.

And here we get to the rub—*history*. The hermeneutical tradition is above all concerned with having a historical consciousness at all turns, and even—in more recent times, with the "urging" of critical theories—turning historical consciousness critically upon ourselves as interpreters of the past in the present. On this score, I think the present pope is once again prophetically messing with the minds of Catholics, bringing us back to basics. Like the historian pope he seems to be modeling himself on, St. John XXIII, Pope Francis is bringing into play the Holy Spirit, who urges us to descend the plane from 30,000 feet and land down in the valley—and, from the valley, where Jesus walked, to go back up to a renewed perspective on reality from 30,000 feet. From Pope Francis's perspective, there are lots of smelly sheep wandering across this valley; and the hermeneutical church must take on "the smell of the sheep."[23] That hermeneut Martin Heidegger continues to challenge us as an ecclesial hermeneutical community: "What is decisive is not to get out of the [hermeneutical] circle but to come into it in the right way."[24] And the privileged way for us as a church to get into the hermeneutical circle of interpreting God's revelation is the *sensus fidelium*.

Yes, the *sensus fidelium* is a diffuse sense. That's why we need local theologians to bring it to expression and judge it against Scripture and tradition. But we must not forget that already, within faith and the functioning of the *sensus fidei*, there is "theologizing" being done, before the scholarly theologians get to work.[25] The *sensus fidei* is already itself a capacity for intuitive

---

23. *Evangelii Gaudium*, 24.

24. Martin Heidegger, *Being and Time* (New York: Harper & Row, 1962) 195.

25. Karl Rahner writes: "Since the analysis by the hearer of what he is told is an inevitable moment in the process of hearing itself, and since utter non-understanding destroys even the hearing itself, *a certain degree of theology belongs as an inner moment to hearing itself*, and the mere hearing in faith is already a human activity in which man's own subjectivity, together with its logic, its experience, native concepts and perspectives, already enters into play. What we call theology and hence dogmatic statement in the strict sense is therefore merely a further development, an unfolding, of that basic subjective reflection which already takes place in the obedient listening to the Word of

judgment of what rings true to the Gospel, and what doesn't. Theologians must tap into the trajectory of this intuitive theologizing. At the local level they have a particular role to play in bringing to systematic expression the oftentimes-diffuse expressions of insight into the Gospel by the faithful. In this way, theologians help to coalesce these insights into "local theologies" that are genuine expressions of the lived faith inspired by the Holy Spirit through the exercise of the *sensus fidei*. Theologians, then, are mediators of the Holy Spirit in helping to bring international awareness across the universal church of the particularities of the one faith in different contexts. And bishops, assisted by the same Holy Spirit, are called to listen to the lived faith of the church local and universal, and are aided by theologians to be open to the possible challenges coming from the Spirit-inspired *sensus fidelium*.

Thus, the church's interpretation of divine revelation can be imagined as a circle, a hermeneutical circle, of understanding. And around the circle are the five constitutive points of reference: Scripture, tradition, the *sensus fidelium*, theology, and the magisterium. Getting into the hermeneutical circle marked by these five points can only be via those who live in the valley; it must be through the lived faith of the church in history enabled by the Holy Spirit, i.e., via the *sensus fidelium*. This, of course, does not make the *sensus fidelium* the final arbiter in the formulation of matters of faith and morals. But even though the magisterium is that final arbiter, its role is to safeguard the church's *faith*. And faith has its sensing organ that the Spirit has guaranteed. The guarantee to the magisterium of a "charism of truth"[26] is not a gift over and above the guarantee of infallibility in believing assured of the church as a whole, through the *sensus fidei* given to all the baptised; there is a condition to the charism of truth that must be realized: "in maintaining, practicing and professing the faith that has been handed on there is a unique interplay (*conspiratio*) between bishops and the faithful."[27] Truth, as the "council" of Jerusalem found, is arrived at through dialogue. And theologians too, in their "faith seeking understanding," are beholden not only to their own perceptions, but more so to the faith of the communities

---

God, i.e. in faith as such. From this it follows, however, that dogmatic reflection and its statement can and must never separate themselves completely from the source from which they spring, i.e. from faith itself. This refers always, as has been said, not merely to the object of faith but also to its exercise. The latter remains the basis and support of the dogmatic statement as such itself." Karl Rahner, "What Is a Dogmatic Statement?," in *Theological Investigations* (New York: Seabury, 1975) 5:49 [42–66] (emphasis added).

26. DV 8.

27. DV 10.

of faith they serve. Through their attention to the *sensus fidelium*, their local theologies can contribute to a so-called "development" of doctrine.[28]

Development of doctrine can come through new encounters with God's otherness within human history, and new perceptions of the meaning of Scripture and tradition. It is incumbent on all the baptized to be attentive to these "signs of the times" (Gaudium et Spes 4), especially the signs of God's presence in shifting human perspectives (GS 11). And here the Spirit's activity through the *sensus fidei* of the faithful is vital. Yves Congar writes of the promise of new knowledge, which the Holy Spirit bestows to the church: "In his discourse on the coming of the Spirit, Jesus combines the affirmation of a non-autonomy of the Spirit with the promise of new knowledge: 'He will guide you into all the truth; for he will not speak on his own authority, but whatever he hears he will speak, and he will declare to you the things that are to come . . . He will take what is mine and declare it to you.' Such a pendulum-swing between *the already acquired* and *the new*, between what has preceded and what has yet to come, should not perplex anyone with a sense of Tradition, *for it is the very law of Tradition*. To be the genuine transmission of something, Tradition must be at once criticism, creativity, and reference. It is the active presence of a principle at every moment of its history, the permanence of identity in what renews itself and changes."[29]

This element of criticism is fundamental for the vitality of the living tradition. The *sensus fidelium*, actively at work receiving the Gospel and passing it on to others in a meaningful and truthful way, constitutes the living tradition of the church. This *sensus fidelium* therefore should function in a critical way in the processes of the church learning and teaching, in its hermeneutical circle of understanding. In his commentary on *Dei Verbum*, Joseph Ratzinger noted that *Dei Verbum* unfortunately did not allow for a critique of tradition by Scripture.[30] A similar statement can be

---

28. For a hermeneutical approach to the organic notion of "development", see Ormond Rush, "Reception Hermeneutics and the 'Development' of Doctrine," *Pacifica* 6 (1993) 125–40.

29. Yves Congar, "Renewed Actuality of the Holy Spirit," *Lumen Vitae: International Review of Religious Education* 28.1 (1973) 24 [13–30]; emphasis added. Congar is quoting from John 16:13-14 and cites John 14:26.

30. Ratzinger writes: "Not every tradition [in the narrow sense] that arises in the Church is a true celebration and keeping present of the mystery of Christ. There is a distorting, as well as a legitimate, tradition. . . . Consequently, tradition must not be considered only affirmatively, but also critically; we have Scripture as a criterion for this indispensable criticism of tradition, and tradition must therefore always be related back to it and measured by it. . . . On this point Vatican II has unfortunately not made any progress, but has more or less ignored the whole question of the criticism of tradition." Joseph Ratzinger, "Chapter II: The Transmission of Divine Revelation," in Herbert Vorgrimler, ed., *Commentary on the Documents of Vatican II*, Vol. 3 (New York: Herder,

made regarding the role of the *sensus fidelium* as a necessary critique of tradition. *Dei Verbum* 12c intimates the role of the Holy Spirit for a proper ecclesial reading of Scripture: that Scripture must be interpreted with the same Spirit with which it was written. The same Holy Spirit, who inspired the Scriptures—which, as Ratzinger highlights, must act as a critical norm of the tradition—evokes in believers, through the gift of *sensus fidei*, interpretations and applications of Scripture that must be allowed to function as a critique of the tradition.

The cry still challenges the Catholic Church: "Listen to what the Spirit is saying to the churches." Finding better ways to listen to, discern, and determine the sense of the faithful throughout the world church is fundamental for responding to that scriptural injunction—and for implementing the vision of the Second Vatican Council fifty years on.

1969) 185–86 [181–98].

11

Whose *Sensus*? Which *Fidelium*?

Justice and Gender in a Global Church

───── Cristina L. H. Traina ─────

As the other essays in this volume demonstrate, the theology of *sensus fidelium*—the church's corporate sense of revelation—has been inflected in myriad ways. Gender provides a particular challenge to discussion of the *sensus fidelium* because gender is irrelevant to central doctrines of salvation; formally at least, sin, grace, mercy, and salvation apply equally and identically to all. But gender is not at all irrelevant to sacramental theology, ecclesiology, or ethics, which explains why gender is such a contentious issue in both theology and ecclesial life. In addition, gender provides richly resonant material for the symbols and metaphors on which all theology depends. Maybe most importantly, gender also figures prominently and differently in the shape that lived lay Christianity takes in particular times and places. And as Anne Arabome, SSS and Gemma Tulud Cruz point out in this volume, the *sensus fidelium* resides partly in this lived, communal practice of faith, which is also deeply inflected by culture.[1] Given the diversity of global cultures, gender's centrality to daily religious life on the ground seems to doom the search for a universal theological sense or taste for gender to failure. In particular, cultural diversity sets empirical investigation of the *sensus fidelium* around gender on a collision course with the universalist, essentialist theology of gender generated by John Paul II in recent decades.

───

1. See also Jerome P. Baggett, "Becoming Absence-minded: Sociological Reflections on the Sense of the Faithful," *CTSA Proceedings* 70 (2015) 2 [1–26]. Even the International Theological Commission finds a place for lived religion in the *consensus fidelium*; see International Theological Commission, "*Sensus Fidei* in the Life of the Church" (2014) 3. http://www.vatican.va/roman_curia/congregations/cfaith/cti_documents/rc_cti_20140610_sensus-fidei_en.html.

The conflict between diversity and uniformity is supremely evident in Pope Francis' recent discussions of gender. This is a matter not just of the content of Francis' theology of gender but also of its methodological framing. Despite great continuity with John Paul II—for instance, his tendency to treat gender as an issue only when women are under discussion—Francis and his administration have introduced both new concerns and new modes of questioning that have the potential to move gender away from the "universal, eternal, and essential" category and toward the cultural "signs of the times" column.

To be sure, these developments are not univocal or consistent. Unfriendly to fungible readings of gender, Francis recently asserted that "the gender theory" "disfigure[s] the face of man and woman."[2] But this essentialism is balanced by a keen concern about abuse of power. Like feminist and gender-inclusive theologians, Francis asks how a global church can talk about gender meaningfully and justly in a culturally diverse world still suffering from colonialism and coercive ideological movements. I argue that Francis's anti-elitist concern for cultural autonomy, along with a modernist idea of progress (both inherited from Pope Paul IV), and their implications shape much of Francis' and the Vatican's current speech about gender.[3] Further, Francis and the Pontifical Council for Culture outline on gender released under his watch make important connections with gender theory, even as they often claim to condemn it. All of these reflections hold important implications for the use of gender in theology and in doctrine, opening the door for a broadly conceived *sensus fidelium* around issues of gender. In brief, Francis's culturally critical stance undercuts his dogmatic, essentialist tendencies, opening—although not guaranteeing—new possibilities for theologizing gender.

To trace this progression, I begin by describing gender theory. Next, I describe Francis' experience of gender theory in the context of his worries about coercive ideological colonization. Further, I explain how these concerns, combined with a progressive vision of theological development, yield a version of "equality with difference." After detailing the inevitable conflict between Francis's adoption of "paradigm" language and his insistence on a universal binary, I argue that theology of gender must be both flexible and

---

2. Quoted in Joshua McElwee, "Francis Strongly Criticizes Gender Theory, Comparing It to Nuclear Arms," *National Catholic Reporter* online (February 13, 2013) http://ncronline.org/news/vatican/francis-strongly-criticizes-gender-theory-comparing-nuclear-arms.

3. On Francis's anti-elitism, see Massimo Faggioli, "Populism and the Anti-elitism of Pope Francis," *Global Pulse Magazine* (August 3, 2015). http://www.globalpulsemagazine.com/news/populism-and-the-anti-elitism-of-pope-francis/1640.

open-ended at the symbolic and metaphoric levels but insistent on the matter of universal, basic rights.

Gender Theory in Theory

The first task is to distinguish between the "gender theory" Francis explicitly decries and the gender theory he implicitly embraces. Theories make sense of data, or experience. They are heuristic grids created to relate existing data meaningfully and logically. On this basis, they predict future eventualities; then, they are evaluated by their accuracy; finally, they are edited to improve it. They are often multiple, coexisting, overlapping, and somewhat contradictory (think of light as a wave and as a particle). They are open to and vulnerable to new data. And every so often, when even revision will not account for the new data, they are replaced (think of Ptolemy's epicycles, superseded by Copernicus's circular orbits, superseded again by Kepler's elliptical ones). Theories are "truths" inasmuch as they really do organize, describe, and explain the data we have before us. But they are "only" theories inasmuch as they are always open to revision by new experience. The most comprehensive theories create paradigms, or frames though which people view reality.[4] Theory is the opposite of ideology, which is a singular, totalizing, hegemonic, apparently static doctrine that is in practice closed to being challenged, questioned, or revised by the experiences of the people on whom it is imposed. As Francis himself remarks, "ideology obstructs a clear vision of reality."[5]

Broadly speaking, gender theory begins from the observation that different behaviors are attached to "masculinity" and "femininity" in different places and times and that we inevitably adopt one set or the other or a combination of the two, with or without "making ourselves" into a person who does not match our biological sex. For instance, is it feminine to cry out in labor or to be silent? It depends on where one lives. Is it feminine to cover one's legs? It depends upon culture and religion: it may be forbidden, required, or optional. Is it masculine to wear narrowly tailored pants? It depends on where and when. Gender theory also has a place for data

---

4. See Mimi Marinucci, *Feminism Is Queer: The Intimate Connection between Queer and Feminist Theory* (New York: Zed Books, 2010), 7-10. The author of paradigm theory is Thomas S. Kuhn; see especially his *The Structure of Scientific Revolutions* (Chicago: University of Chicago Press, 1962).

5. Pope Francis, "Address of His Holiness Pope Francis to the Participants in the Plenary Assembly of the Pontifical Council for Culture" (February 7, 2015). https://w2.vatican.va/content/francesco/en/speeches/2015/february/documents/papa-francesco_20150207_pontificio-consiglio-cultura.html.

beyond biological male and female: ambiguously sexed or intersexed persons, or persons who identify strongly with a gender not expressed in their bodily features, are invisible from the masculine/feminine binary but are visible to gender theory. And, gender theory is not one thing; it is a body of (in theory) equally privileged, overlapping, and occasionally contradictory theories that are struggling to comprehend the complex existing data of sex, sexuality, and gender and are always open to new experience.

Gender Theory in Francis

Pope Francis's experience of gender theory is a bit different. He often tells a story about a loan for the construction of schools for the poor. Its approval was contingent on the minister of education accepting and mandating a textbook that the funders prescribed in which, Francis says, "gender theory was taught." It's clear from the context that the situation was coercive: if you want our money, you will use the book that we approve. In Francis's eyes,

> This is ideological colonization. They introduce an idea to the people that has nothing to do with the people. With *groups* of people yes, but not with the people. And they colonize the people with an idea which changes, or means to change, a mentality or a structure . . . certain loans in exchange for certain conditions . . . Why do I say "ideological colonization"? Because they take, they actually take the need of a people to seize an opportunity to enter and grow strong—through the children.[6]

Francis's first objection to the gender theory textbook is colonization. It is almost impossible to overstate Francis's distaste for colonization, which he sees as an ongoing imperial project.[7] Colonization was on his lips constantly during his 2015 visit to the Philippines. He has spoken regularly—even immediately after canonizing Jesuit missionary Junipero Serra—of the endless series of sins committed during the colonization of the Americas.[8] He not only points out that the Virgen de Guadalupe was a mestiza, but he

---

6. "In-Flight Press Conference of His Holiness Pope Francis from the Philippines to Rome" (January 19, 2015). http://w2.vatican.va/content/francesco/en/speeches/2015/january/documents/papa-francesco_20150119_srilanka-filippine-conferenza-stampa.html.

7. "In-Flight Press Conference of His Holiness Pope Francis from the Philippines to Rome."

8. Pope Francis, "Visit to the Joint Session of the United States Congress: Address of the Holy Father" (September 24, 2015), https://w2.vatican.va/content/francesco/en/speeches/2015/september/documents/papa-francesco_20150924_usa-us-congress.html.

specifically says that she chose to reveal herself to a non-colonial, the simple, humble, married native man, Juan Diego. For Francis, Mary becomes mother to the Americas—specifically, saving mother to the colonized Americas, and not to their colonizers.[9] Thus for Francis, the education loan was a moment of colonial coercion: an economically strong country or international agency imposed its will as a condition for giving the aid needed by—and one might even argue owed to—a weaker one. And, it targeted the most impressionable, whose education depended on the funds: children.

Second, for Francis the story of the loan is a story about the integrity of cultures. In the version he told in his press conference on the way home from the Philippines, Francis explained,

> Every people has its own culture. But when conditions are imposed by colonizing empires, they seek to make these peoples lose their own identity and create uniformity. This is spherical globalization—all points are equidistant from the centre. And true globalization ... is not a sphere. It is important to globalize, but not like the sphere but rather, like the polyhedron. Namely that each people, every part, preserves its identity.[10]

Here Francis upholds cultural integrity in much the same way Paul VI did.[11] Human similarity yields variety across time and place. Cultures are systems of meaning; they have their own interdependent systems of traditions, which are valuable to the people who practice them. Thus, no one should arbitrarily force change from outside. Uniformity—whether of cultures, or of women and men—is distasteful, unnatural, and coercive.

The third dimension of his critique explains why Francis is so insistent on this point. He argues that the act of attaching the book to the loan was also ideological. In other words, to recall our earlier definition, it enforced a singular, totalizing, hegemonic, apparently static doctrine that was in practice intended to be closed to challenge, questioning, or revision by the

---

9. "Los primeros dos años de la 'Era Francisco' en entrevista a Televisa" (March 13, 2015). http://www.news.va/es/news/los-primeros-dos-anos-de-la-era-francisco-en-entre. On ideological colonization in Africa, Madagascar, and Lithuania, see also http://w2.vatican.va/content/francesco/en/speeches/2015/february/documents/papa-francesco_20150207_conferenze-episcopali-africa-madagascar.html and http://w2.vatican.va/content/francesco/en/speeches/2015/february/documents/papa-francesco_20150202_ad-limina-lituania.html.

10. "In-Flight Press Conference of His Holiness Pope Francis from the Philippines to Rome."

11. For instance, see Pope Paul VI, *Populorum progressio* (March 26, 1967), 10. http://w2.vatican.va/content/paul vi/en/encyclicals/documents/hf_p-vi_enc_26031967_populorum.html.

experience of the people on whom it was to be imposed. It was supposed to "bulldoze" children's inherited cultural traditions and replace them with foreign ones. In the interview, Francis recalls Nazi and Fascist indoctrination of youth before and during the Second World War.

To be clear, although it was certainly anti-elitist, Francis's objection was not romantic, reductionistic, or paternalistic. Was he extolling the purity of a "simple" culture in contrast to a decrepit one, and did he think the book was bad in itself? No, he says it was "a well-thought-out book, didactically speaking" and did apply to "some people";[12] thus he clearly believes that gender ideas that are "foreign" to one culture are "at home" in another. Did the ideological colonization succeed? No, again. He applauds the minister's solution: she had another book printed that she thought fit the cultural situation better, and she distributed both books to the new schools. Does he think cultures should be "siloed," protected from one another? No, he implies that children can be exposed to gender ideas originating from more than one culture; they just should not be force-fed a single point of view. There is a kind of cultural autonomy, but there is also the implicit possibility of mutual critique and cross-fertilization. So, we have Francis opposing gender *ideology* and implicitly embracing something akin to a gender *theory* perspective: in this case, the idea that there are multiple ways to live out gender and assign meanings to maleness and femaleness, and that these ways can be put in conversation. And, we have him assuming that people can recognize and manage these differences on their own. What is more, even though colonization is immoral and bullying, the adults among the colonized are not vulnerable innocents; they can evaluate, and they can parry.

So, for Francis, cultures are many and diverse. And, they have integrity. The obvious conclusion for the *sensus fidelium* around gender is that there is not one *sensus fidelium*, but many, and that they are legitimate: we can expect differences in the ways human communities live out gender and express themselves theologically about it.

Gender Theory, Revisited

Francis's response to the story about the book and the loan raises one troubling question for the preceding analysis: If all cultures are really equal and distinctive, and if Francis approves of diversity in culture, and if diversity in culture implies diversity in views of gender, and if diversity in views

---

12. "In-Flight Press Conference of His Holiness Pope Francis from the Philippines to Rome."

of gender implies gender theory, then why does he equate gender theory with ideology? His language is strong: gender theory is one of the "Herods" that "destroy, that plot designs of death, that disfigure the face of man and woman, destroying creation":

> Let's think of the nuclear arms, of the possibility to annihilate in a few instants a very high number of human beings . . . Let's think also of genetic manipulation, of the manipulation of life, or of the gender theory, that does not recognize the order of creation . . . The design of the creator is written in nature.[13]

In my reading, Francis does not in fact put all cultures on equal footing. His constant references to "throwaway culture" make it clear that he characterizes Euro-American cultures primarily by their consumerism.[14] He worries about the "planned obsolescence" not just of manufactured goods but also of people, the systematic marginalization of the elderly, children, the ill, the poor, and the natural world.[15] Pointedly, Francis argues that this attitude is one and the same as colonial imperialism:

> Rejection . . . makes us see our neighbour not as a brother or sister to be accepted, but as unworthy of our attention, a rival, or someone to be bent to our will. This is the mindset which fosters that "throwaway culture" which spares nothing and no one: nature, human beings, even God himself.[16]

Francis decries the growth of this consumerist attitude. The obvious assumption—and one that must be taken seriously as a critique, even if it can be answered—is that views of gender that issue from consumerist cultures are suspect, not because they directly contradict traditional Catholic teaching, but because they are infected with imperialism, selfishness, and consumerism, and because they have the interests of the issuers, not the recipients, at heart. In addition, they are applied ideologically, to the extent that the economies and politics of the two-thirds world are coercively

---

13. Quoted in McElwee, "Francis Strongly Criticizes Gender Theory."

14. "Address of Pope Francis to the European Parliaments" (November 25, 2014). http://w2.vatican.va/content/francesco/en/speeches/2014/november/documents/papa-francesco_20141125_strasburgo-parlamento-europeo.html.

15. See especially Pope Francis, *Laudato Si* (May 24, 2015). http://w2.vatican.va/content/francesco/en/encyclicals/documents/papa-francesco_20150524_enciclica-laudato-si.html.

16. "Address of His Holiness Pope Francis to the Members of the Diplomatic Corps Accredited to the Holy See" (January 12, 2015). http://w2.vatican.va/content/francesco/en/speeches/2015/january/documents/papa-francesco_20150112_corpo-diplomatico.html.

shaped by Euro-American values and institutions. From this perspective, Euro-American gender theories are inevitably ideologies, whether they contradict Catholic teaching on gender or not. And we could say that they therefore forcibly disrupt the local *sensus fidelium*. So, from a perspective that seems highly inflected by liberation theology, Francis seems to be saying that all cultures have their own gender ideas, but the gender ideas of colonizing cultures are particularly suspect. This is a conclusion that we ought to take seriously and self-critically. To what degree does our hegemonic position shape Euro-American theologies of gender, even feminist and queer theologies?

Despite this caution, Francis does not imply that the gender ideas of colonized cultures are inherently superior. The strongest hints in this doubly qualified direction are the outline document for the Plenary Assembly of the Pontifical Council for Culture and his later address to the Assembly.

Equality and Difference

Early in 2015, an anonymous group of women created a discussion document on gender guided by anonymous "Members and Consultors" in preparation for the February 2015 meeting of the Pontifical Council for Culture. The document and its presentation were problematic in countless ways, starting with contradiction between the document's express condemnation of "sexual allusion and debasement" in the presentation of women's bodies and the pouty, come-hither demeanor of the blonde model chosen for the advertisement inviting women to contribute additional commentary. Overall, however, the outline had two features that probably surprised readers accustomed to John Paul II's and Benedict's writings. First, it was titled "Women's Cultures," not "Women's Culture"; it did not assume uniformity. Also, it seemed to contain at least three ideas of gender. Parts spoke in very familiar papal language of needing to discover and understand "the feminine specificity," as if there were a single one and as if "the masculine specificity" were already clear. Second, there seemed to be a whiff of psychoanalytic difference feminism,[17] which puts generativity, the womb, at the center of women's identity. Third, liberal feminism was unmistakable in the outline's critique of the church's "obsolete feminine iconography" and

---

17. Based in critical appropriation of Sigmund Freud and Jacques Lacan, psychoanalytic feminism roots masculine and feminine difference not just in the body but also in the psychological dynamics of early mother-child relations. French feminists Luce Irigaray, Helene Cixous, and Julia Kristeva are among its proponents. For further information, see "Psychoanalytic Feminism" in the Stanford encyclopedia of Philosophy, http://plato.stanford.edu/entries/feminism-psychoanalysis/

"preconceived models" of participation as well as in the often spunky questions, in themselves a novel feature of a document on gender. The outline can, then, be read as *de facto* evidence that faithful women with different theories of gender can coexist in one church, that the *sensus fidelium* on gender can be plural.

The document can also be read another way, in light of Francis' address to the Plenary on February 7. In that address, Francis applauds the fact that the patriarchal model—as he defines it, men's social subordination of women—has nearly been wiped out in the West but still lingers in other areas. This is praise for colonizing cultures but criticism for the two-thirds world. It is also consistent with his other writings. Elsewhere, Francis decries social patriarchalism, correcting St. Paul's patriarchal analogy, husband is to wife as Christ is to the church, arguing that husband and wife are equal, and *mutual* submission between equals is the point[18]; he calls gendered pay disparities "an absolute disgrace"[19]; and he insists that the opinion that women's emancipation stresses marriage is "a form of male chauvinism."[20]

Yet, the address does not end with his condemnation of patriarchy and patriarchalism. Francis also condemns a model of absolute gender equality "applied mechanically."[21] This is criticism of liberal feminism, which for Francis implies the belief that there is no sexual difference, which for Francis implies a colonizing gender theory. It is also implied praise for parts of the world that have not yet adopted this point of view. Later in 2015, he explained further, asking whether "the so-called gender theory is not, at the same time, an expression of frustration and resignation, which seeks to cancel out sexual difference because it no longer knows how to confront it."[22]

Finally, Francis describes his own paradigm—his word, implying a theoretical frame—as being neither patriarchal nor liberal, but drawing the best from both worlds, and therefore the best from human culture. His paradigm is "*reciprocity*, in equivalence and difference": men and women "possess an identical nature, but each with its own modality"; together "they

---

18. Pope Francis, general audience: "The Family 13: Marriage (II)" (May 6, 2015). https://w2.vatican.va/content/francesco/en/audiences/2015/documents/papa-francesco_20150506_udienza-generale.html.

19. Pope Francis, general audience: "The Family 12: Marriage" (April 29, 2015). https://w2.vatican.va/content/francesco/en/audiences/2015/documents/papa-francesco_20150429_udienza-generale.html.

20. Ibid.

21. Pope Francis, "Address to the Participants in the Plenary Assembly of the Pontifical Council for Culture."

22. Pope Francis, general audience: "The Family 10: Male and Female (I)" (April 15, 2015). https://w2.vatican.va/content/francesco/en/audiences/2015/documents/papa-francesco_20150415_udienza-generale.html.

truly complete the fullness of the person."[23] For instance, engagement and marriage are essential in part because one can learn about the other gender, and therefore one's own, primarily through one's intimate relationship with one's partner;[24] without marriage men and women would be foreigners, despite their common humanity. Read from this perspective, even the outline's sexual difference, equal dignity, and "feminine specificity" may not be multiple voices; they may all fit within Francis's paradigm, with femininity "in full collaboration and integration with the male component," as the outline says.[25]

Francis embraces the language of paradigm, but he characterizes his own position on gender as combining something from patriarchal approaches—difference, but without the hierarchy—and something from liberal approaches—equality, but without the sameness. The thesis-antithesis-synthesis structure of the argument implies that he has discerned the true terminus of a millennia-long Western process of theorizing gender, that he has arrived at a final truth.

Sowing the Seeds of Change?

But here we run into a problem. Francis labels his vision a paradigm, implying that it is a model responsive to experience. And yet, the content conjures a 20-year-old essentialist vision. John Paul II's 1995 letter to women also invokes an ontological "duality of the 'masculine' and the 'feminine,'" alludes to "'the mystery of woman'" with her "'feminine genius,'" "feminine 'tradition,'" and "feminine dignity," but (with its confusing proliferation of scare quotes and italics) begs the question of exactly what sort of reality is being evoked in each usage of "feminine."[26] Francis likewise sees men and women as essentially different, in specific ways that most readers of this essay would probably see as products of culture rather than of created nature. For instance, he argues that women possess "delicacy, particular sensitivity and

23. Pope Francis, "Address to the Participants in the Plenary Assembly of the Pontifical Council for Culture."

24. Pope Francis, general audience: "The Family 16: Engagement" (May 27, 2015). https://w2.vatican.va/content/francesco/en/audiences/2015/documents/papa-francesco_20150527_udienza-generale.html. See also his general audience of April 15, 2015.

25. "Women's Cultures: Equality and Difference" (2015). http://www.cultura.va/content/dam/cultura/docs/pdf/Traccia_en.pdf.

26. Pope John Paul II, "Letter of Pope John Paul II to Women" (June 29, 1995). https://w2.vatican.va/content/john-paul-ii/en/letters/1995/documents/hf_jp-ii_let_29061995_women.html.

tenderness,"[27] and "know how to ... give time rather than occupy space, to welcome rather than exclude."[28] Men take care of and protect their families as St. Joseph did,[29] correcting "with firmness" and "without humiliating."[30] Women, although stressed by the need to juggle work and family, appear to be immune to consumerist, self-centered cultural trends; men, seemingly weaker, often become "so concentrated on themselves and on their work and at times on their career that they even forget about the family."[31] Francis infamously referred to female theologians as the all-too-rare "strawberries on the cake" and winked that female housekeepers ensure that male priests account for women's perspectives, as if women were identical and one woman could represent "womanhood" to male hierarchs.[32]

Thus, again, here is the conflict: on one hand Francis presents himself—and culture—as moving through paradigms of gender and gender relations. In fact, in his address to the Pontifical Council for Culture, he presents the model of reciprocity as having "arrived" and needing only to be "announced." This suggests a kind of open-endedness and replaceability even for the model of "reciprocity in equality and difference" and implies that the transformations have a certain "bottom-up," populist character rooted in lived culture.

On the other hand Francis presents the earlier patriarchal and liberal paradigms as products of sin, implying that reciprocity is the final, correct mode, bringing to fruition what had been implied in creation. In addition, Francis is certain that permanent psychic and emotional differences divide men and women, and he sees gender exclusively in terms of masculinity and

27. Pope Francis, "Address to the Participants in the Plenary Assembly of the Pontifical Council for Culture."

28. Ibid.

29. Pope Francis, "Meeting with Families: Address of his Holiness Pope Francis" (January 16, 2015). http://w2.vatican.va/content/francesco/en/speeches/2015/january/documents/papa-francesco_20150116_srilanka-filippine-incontro-famiglie.html. See also Pope Francis, general audience: "The Family 1: Nazareth" (December 17, 2014), https://w2.vatican.va/content/francesco/en/audiences/2014/documents/papa-francesco_20141217_udienza-generale.html.

30. Pope Francis, general audience: "The Family 3: The Father (second part)" (February 4, 2015). https://w2.vatican.va/content/francesco/en/audiences/2015/documents/papa-francesco_20150204_udienza-generale.html.

31. Pope Francis, general audience: "The Family 3: The Father (first part)" (January 28, 2015). https://w2.vatican.va/content/francesco/en/audiences/2015/documents/papa-francesco_20150128_udienza-generale.html.

32. For these and some of Pope Francis's other off-handed references to women, see David Gibson, "Seven Pope Francis Quotes That Make Women Wince," *The Huffington Post* online (December 11, 2014). http://www.huffingtonpost.com/2014/12/11/pope-francis-women_n_6307822.html.

femininity. In other words, a "correct" vision of sexual difference implies that there is a uniform, permanent ideal of both masculinity and femininity; although it may never be fully realized in actual human relations, it is a universal standard.

But a demand for uniformity among cultures—according to Francis himself, with his analogy to the sphere and the polyhedron—should always make us suspicious that something else is afoot: ideology. In this case, Francis seems to be calling for enforcement of a view of the world that, in his own words, obscures reality: a view of gender that ignores the data of other experiences of masculinity and femininity and that ignores the data of intersex, to name just two examples.

Enforced uniformity is also, again according to Francis, usually a symptom of colonization, an effort to impose a view of reality that benefits the colonizers. Historically, Catholic bishops and popes have been tempted in the direction of ideological coercion when they have tried to tie a universal doctrinal claim too tightly to a theory without which it seemed incredible. Not all of these cases were matters of literal colonization. The cases of Copernicus and Galileo are examples. As Galileo realized, the Catholic clergy's conviction that it could not worship a God who had not placed the earth at the center of the universe forced the clergy to ignore the growing, then overwhelming evidence of a heliocentric system. As the *sensus fidelium* shifted, and the tie between a particular astronomical theory and faith in God's power weakened, the holders of the magisterium still resisted the change. Similarly today, although Francis understands ideology, culture, coercion, colonization, and even paradigm shift, the need he perceives to uphold other longstanding doctrines by keeping a gender binary clear forces him to ignore the data of human experience. His caution would be justified if all of that data were coming from the colonizers, as caution would have been justified if all the astronomers of Galileo's time had been scholars whose primary intent was to unseat Christianity. But the data is not arising only from the colonizers; it is global.

Justice, *Sensus Fidelium,* and Gender: Where To?

These concerns do not imply that we should not theologize with gender; theologizing with gender is inevitable because the experience of gender is inevitable (on this, Francis is correct). To be gendered, to be in culture, is a fundamental human experience out of which rich theological meaning can and must be made. What this trip through Francis's recent thought shows us is that because gender is cultured we will never have a *sensus fidelium*, singular, of gender; when it comes to gender, we will always have, to some degree, a *sensus fidelium*, plural. That means we ought never to base a universal doctrine on a particular cultural vision of gender, but we should accept multiple, shifting theologies of gender.

This realization should lead us to theological humility, on all sides. Because gender means different things in different places, and gender is the necessary context rather than the content of faith, no one should attempt to ensconce a single set of gendered metaphors, ideals, and images as universal, propositional theological truths about human beings.

It should also lead to patience. As the International Theological Commission insists, the charism of fidelity belongs to the church as a whole, and it often works slowly. In the early centuries of Christian history, the lay faithful preserved essential christological doctrine when the bishops were at odds.[33] More recently, lay articulation of and advocacy for human rights helped redirect the magisterium from the sweeping condemnations of Pius IX's 1864 Syllabus of Errors to the appreciation of diversity rooted in human dignity that was expressed in the 1965 document *Dignitatis humanae*.[34] Obviously, decades or even centuries of disagreement over central theological questions are par for the course. Just as obviously, awards for fidelity and good judgment can be granted only in hindsight; the lay beliefs that the bishops and popes ultimately accepted came in for strong episcopal criticism during both periods of controversy. Today, Francis's respect for local culture and his worries about coercion, combined with the complexity of lived practices and symbolism drawing on gender, caution against making definitive, final theological proclamations about gender, its implications, and its meaning. They counsel waiting.

Humility and patience might imply relativism and inaction. They should not. First, that theology is meaning-making, and that meaning-making is both local and often gendered, does not necessitate that theologies inspired by gender are either limiting or lacking in critical power. For instance, Mercy Amba Oduyoye's analysis of African women's theologies presents an approach that theologizes richly from particular understandings of womanhood: hospitality, for example, which might not be gendered female everywhere.[35] Hospitality is one starting point for imagining the Christian life. But in Oduyoye's sources, such an approach does not limit women to hospitality, exclude women from other activities like teaching,

---

33. International Theological Commission, "*Sensus Fidei* in the Life of the Church" (2014) 26.

34. Ibid., 3.

35. Mercy Amba Oduyoye, *Introducing African Women's Theology* (Cleveland: Pilgrim, 2001).

or forbid men to practice hospitality. Rather, it makes hospitality a ground, a first step, for helping women imagine how to teach effectively and inspiringly. Neither does it frown on men's hospitality, although it might imagine their hospitality as grounded in another culturally gendered quality. Rather, common humanity and the requisites of flourishing are the criteria for judging whether you are acting well and whether I am being treated well or ill.

Second, culture embroiders gender onto a canvas of genuine givens for which just provision must be made. Francis's and John Paul II's insistence on difference must be heard, even if the conclusions they draw from it are often uncritical and hasty. It simply is, and has always been, true that some people can accomplish emotional, physical, and spiritual intimacy—total self-gift—only with a person of their own biological sex. It simply is, and always has been, true that some people find their biological sex incompatible with their self-understanding. It simply is, and always has been, inescapably true that fertile women's capacity to bear children subjects them (not to mention their offspring) to personal, domestic, and social vulnerability. It is also, and always has been, true that men's reproductive biology make them susceptible to life-threatening diseases.

Any adequate theology of gender must take these data into account. It might even use some of them as starting points for theological reflection: maternity, for instance, is a profound, flexible, and expansive image for the church and for God. But, like the doctrine of Jesus Christ's simultaneous humanity and divinity, or the profound implications of human dignity, authentic theologies of gender would acknowledge and reflect expansively from, rather than use as limits, the genuine differences that give rise to gender in culture. Only in this way can it honor, rather than limit, human dignity.

These universal experiences also signal that justice requires some universal claims for the protection of human flourishing and the honoring of human dignity. We should not wait patiently for these. As in Galileo's time, as well as in the interim between the Syllabus of Errors and *Dignitatis Humanae*, real lives are lost, real Christians are excommunicated, and real callings are lost to the Catholic Church when Catholics embrace positions that the magisterium currently condemns but eventually embraces. In these cases the church itself, and not its enemies, unnecessarily creates martyrs for the faith. In addition, the experience of scandal, persecution, or abandonment that results from this contradiction unnecessarily drives people away from the Catholic Church. From this perspective, a church concerned to evangelize and seek justice cannot simply rest sanguinely in confidence that its central teaching on gender will eventually right itself through the automatic development of the *sensus fidelium*. It must invest honest critical effort in advancing the cause. If history is any indication, much of the impetus for this effort must come from willing, creative lay people. It behooves the pope and the bishops to lessen the risks undertaken in doing us this service.

Here theologians have not had much encouragement from recent popes. Francis' approach, imperfect as it may be, is a welcome sign of possible change.

12

Beyond "Who Am I to Judge?"

The Sensus Fidelium, LGBT Experience, and Truth-Telling in the Church

Brian N. Massingale

"If someone is gay, and searches for the Lord and has good will, who am I to judge? We shouldn't marginalize people for this. They must be integrated into society."[1] With this single, seemingly spontaneous press conference comment, Pope Francis decisively moved official Catholic discourse on LGBT persons away from what one high ranking prelate had called "a theology of contempt" for gay persons.[2] Yet, this papal intervention was immediately characterized as signaling no change in official church doctrine, but only a more compassionate and pastoral tone in its presentation. This same line of argumentation—compassionate tone without doctrinal shift—was also marshaled in light of the public attention given to the 2014 Synod on the Family's treatment of gay and lesbian persons,[3] especially in light of the mid-term summary of its discussions. I argue to the contrary. There is a change of tone, to be sure. But the tone masks a definite doctrinal development now underway—a change of beliefs that is cautious, incremental,

---

1. Pope Francis, "On Gay Priests, Pope Francis Asks, 'Who Am I to Judge?'" *The New York Times* (July 29, 2013). www.nytimes.com/2013/07/30/world/europe/pope-francis-gay-priests.html.

2. Archbishop Emeritus Rembert G. Weakland, personal communication to the author, August 31, 2002: "On the gay issue, the level of fears is so high that the official teaching of the church skates so very close to the edge of a new "theology of contempt." Why is it presupposed—and I can tell you from correspondence and some writings of late that it is—that gays have less sexual "self-control" than heterosexuals and are thus dangerous?"

3. I will use the term, "gay and lesbians," as opposed to the more preferred acronym LGBT, because magisterial teaching is largely silent on the issues of bisexuality and transexuality.

tentative, tense yet nonetheless real. This paper examines the shifts in magisterial discourse on gay and lesbian persons in light of Pope Francis's interventions and the 2014 Synod on the Family. I will also argue that these shifts would be impossible without the *sensus fidelium* of lesbian and gay persons in the church, and its empathic reception by the larger faith community. This situation thus becomes a case study that raises a larger question: Is the *sensus fidelium* only of pastoral value, or does it have doctrinal authority?

The Shifts in Magisterial Discourse and Teaching

To accurately understand the major shifts and tensions that mark Pope Francis's remarks and the interim report of the 2014 synod, we have to recall the previous state of Catholic teaching on homosexual persons as it has developed since the 1980s.[4] Same-sex behaviors (usually left unspecified) are judged an objective intrinsic evil that cannot be made morally right under any circumstance; that is, they are always morally wrong, although the individual's subjective culpability is to be judged with prudence. Moreover, homosexuality is not considered a true "sexual orientation." Rather, it is spoken of as an "inclination," or a "condition," or a "tendency" which, because it orders a person to intrinsically moral evil acts, is judged to be an "objective disorder."[5] This does not mean that homosexual persons are

---

4. I use the term, "homosexual persons," as it is the term used in most magisterial documents. The terminology, as we will see, especially the avoidance and/or acceptance of the term "gay," is part of the shift that is happening. The official teaching summarized here is found in the following documents: Congregation for the Doctrine of the Faith (hereafter, CDF), *Letter to the Bishops of the Catholic Church on the Pastoral Care of Homosexual Persons* (1986).

www.vatican.va/roman_curia/congregations/cfaith/documents/rc_con_cfaith_doc_19861001_homosexual-persons_en.html; CDF, *Some Considerations Concerning the Response to Legislative Proposals on Non-Discrimination of Homosexual Persons* (1992); CDF, *Considerations Regarding Proposals to Give Legal Recognition to Unions between Homosexual Persons* (2003). www.vatican.va/roman_curia/congregations/cfaith/documents/rc_con_cfaith_doc_20030731_homosexual-unions_en.html; and Congregation for Catholic Education, *Instruction concerning the Criteria for the Discernment of Vocations with Regard to Persons with Homosexual Tendencies in View of Their Admission to the Seminary and to Holy Orders* (2005).

www.vatican.va/roman_curia/congregations/ccatheduc/documents/rc_con_ccatheduc_doc_20051104_istruzione_en.html.

5. CDF, *Letter to the Bishops of the Catholic Church on the Pastoral Care of Homosexual Persons* (1986) 3. On the usage of "inclination" or "same-sex attraction," see among others, United States Conference of Catholic Bishops, *Ministry to Persons with a Homosexual Inclination: Guidelines for Pastoral Care* (2006).

http://www.usccb.org/about/doctrine/publications/upload/ministry-to-persons-of-homosexual-inclination.pdf.

incapable of moral rectitude outside of their sexual activities; their sexual condition "does not mean that homosexual persons are not often generous and giving of themselves." Yet, "when they engage in homosexual activity they confirm within themselves a disordered sexual inclination which is essentially self-indulgent."[6]

The documents speak of the human dignity of homosexual persons. They are to be welcomed sensitively and compassionately. Yet, this dignity is highly qualified and conditional. All "unjust discrimination" against homosexual persons is proscribed and condemned. Yet, this phrasing allows for "just" or legitimate forms of discrimination. Indeed, it is explicitly taught that discrimination and inequalities in the areas of housing, teaching, coaching, adoption/foster care and military service are not only justifiable but indeed at times mandatory.[7] This ostensibly is required to protect the unique status of heterosexual marital and familial love.[8] Moreover, legal protections of homosexual persons are judged unnecessary since the "chaste homosexual" is usually unwilling to call attention to his/her status. Since few would, or should, know of his/her condition, there would not be a cause for discrimination or social harm.[9] The not so subtle implication is that if one is discriminated against, it's one's own fault. Even violence against homosexuals is not considered surprising when they advocate "for protecting behavior to which no one has any conceivable right."[10]

This negative judgement of same-sex love and intimacy is underscored in official documents issued in the twenty-first century. For example, when speaking against efforts to grant legal recognition to same-sex unions/relationships, the Congregation for the Doctrine of the Faith emphasizes that "marriage is holy."[11] The clear implication is that same-sex unions are not—

---

6. CDF, *Letter on Pastoral Care*, 7.

7. CDF, *Some Considerations Concerning the Response to Legislative Proposals on the Non-Discrimination of Homosexual Persons*, 11 and 12: "Among other rights, all persons have the right to work, to housing, etc. Nevertheless, these rights are not absolute. They can be legitimately limited for objectively disordered external conduct. This is sometimes not only licit but obligatory."

8. CDF, *Considerations*, "Forward" and 15

9. CDF, *Considerations*, 14: "An individual's sexual orientation is generally not known to others unless he publicly identifies himself as having this orientation or unless some overt behavior manifests it. As a rule, the majority of homosexually oriented persons who seek to lead chaste lives do not publicize their sexual orientation. Hence the problem of discrimination in terms of employment, housing, etc., does not usually arise."

10. CDF, *Letter on Pastoral Care*, 10.

11. CDF, *Considerations Regarding Proposals to Give Legal Recognition to Unions between Homosexual Persons* (2003), 4.

and therefore unworthy and undeserving of civil recognition or protection. Indeed, Catholic civil authorities and political leaders are required to make clear their absolute opposition to efforts to legally recognize or protect same-sex relationships.[12] Moreover, in speaking of the inadmissability of gay men—that is, those "struggling with deep-rooted same-sex attraction" to the priesthood—the Congregation for Catholic Education gives as a reason that those with this unfortunate condition cannot mediate or fulfill the "spiritual paternity of Christ" to the faithful because they lack the "affective maturity" required to relate "correctly to men and women."[13] In short, they cannot truly love. This congregation also notes that anyone who has any connection with the "gay" community as being unqualified for admission. Why? Because of what "gay" signifies in official Catholic discourse: namely, belonging to a sub-culture or social minority that defines itself through sexual activity and public advocacy opposed to Catholic moral teaching.[14] Homosexual persons—those with "deep-seated homosexual tendencies"—thus are not only morally suspect but also spiritually impaired and emotionally stunted. This renders them unfit for positions of leadership within the Catholic community.[15]

Thus current magisterial teaching, up until 2013, not only viewed homosexual *sex* as unconditionally morally illegitimate but it also judged homosexual *persons* as civilly unequal, spiritually hobbled, and psychologically damaged. One is left with the impression that these are an unfortunate group of people with a tragic affliction. Never is it stated or suggested that they have a positive contribution to make to church and society. At best, they merit our compassion and sympathy. Yet in the name of "truth," they cannot be extended a welcome on the basis of their sexuality.[16]

---

12. CDF, *Considerations Regarding Proposals to Give Legal Recognition to Unions between Homosexual Persons* (2003), 10.

13. Congregation for Catholic Education, *Instruction Concerning the Criteria for the Discernment of Vocations with regard to Persons with Homosexual Tendencies in view of their Admission to the Seminary and to Holy Orders* (2005) 2 and 3.

14. Congregation for Catholic Education, *Instruction Concerning the Criteria for the Discernment of Vocations*, 2.

15. Cf. Congregation for Divine Worship and the Discipline of the Sacraments, *Letter* (16 May, 2002) in *Notitiae* 38 (2002) 586: "Ordination to the diaconate and the priesthood of homosexual men or men with homosexual tendencies is absolutely inadvisable and imprudent and, from the pastoral point of view, very risky. A homosexual person, or one with a homosexual tendency is not, therefore, fit to receive the sacrament of Holy Orders," http://www.zenit.org/en/articles/vatican-response-on-possibility-of-ordaining-homosexuals-to-priesthood.

16. Congregation for Catholic Education, *Instruction Concerning the Criteria for the Discernment of Vocations*, 2.

Given the fact that human sexuality is a constitutive dimension of the human person and affects the way one relates to and is present to the world,[17] one cannot avoid the conclusion that the Catholic Church judges not only gay *sex*, but also gay *persons*, in a negative and even destructive light. Their very humanity is somehow deficient. The implicit yet operative Christian anthropology and soteriology at work here is problematic, to say the least. Gay and lesbian persons are saved—after all, they are enjoined to link their sufferings to the cross of Christ[18]—but not in or through their sexuality. Not as gay and lesbian persons. This is at best. But insofar as they are advocates for social equality and ecclesial acceptance, their presence is viewed with suspicion and their existence with hostility. In their efforts at civil justice and recognition they must be considered a dangerous "contagion" that needs to be contained and combated, if not eradicated.[19]

It is necessary to recall the official stances of the magisterium in order to truly appreciate the seismic implications of Francis's statement, "Who am I to judge?" The difference is not only tonal but substantive, in the following ways:

1) He uses the word "gay" in English. Francis does not employ the circumlocutions of same sex "attractions," "tendencies," "inclinations," or "condition." If part of respect is calling a group by the terms it chooses, and avoiding terms that give offense, this is a necessary prelude to effective Catholic engagement and a significant shift. Moreover, it marks a major departure from the previous teaching given in the priesthood document and other prior statements. Implicitly, Francis recognizes that people can be "constitutionally gay" as opposed to experiencing "deep-seated" or "more or less strong" sexual "tendencies" that can and should be overcome with discipline and grace.

2) There is a clear recognition that gay people have spiritual lives, spiritual strivings and loving relationships with God. Moreover, this spiritual life is *not* solely or principally centered upon a struggle against sexual sin or a repudiation of their sexual nature. "If a gay man seeks the Lord and has good will . . . ." This phrasing acknowledges that as sexual beings, gay people can and do have vital relationships with God. This is a major shift in official Catholic discussion.

---

17. Congregation for Catholic Education, *Educational Guidance in Human Love*, 1983.

18. CDF, *Letter on Pastoral Care*, 12.

19. CDF, *Considerations Regarding Proposals to Give Legal Recognition to Unions between Homosexual Persons* (2003), 5.

3) Finally, Francis's statement is an official recognition that gay men serve as spiritual leaders and guides.[20] It also conveys that this is a legitimate reality in the Christian community. It acknowledges that God can and does call such people to the priesthood. This is more than a disciplinary change. There is the clear implication that gay men (and by extension, lesbian women) can and do make positive contributions to the faith community. They can and do serve as models for holiness, edification and leadership. Indeed, Francis's statement proclaims that gay persons can image Christ by acting *in persona Christi capitis* in the traditional understanding of priesthood. "Gay" men can be an *alter Christus,* another Christ, to and for the faith community.

Thus Pope Francis's intervention is not only a shift in tone or a mere pastoral overture to gay Catholics. This is a significant change in official teaching. I argue that it constitutes a doctrinal development.

The Current Tensions in Magisterial Teaching

But I have to somewhat qualify that assertion in light of discussions that occurred at the 2014 Synod of the Family. The deliberations of the synod's participants then (and now) revealed significant tensions and fault lines in magisterial reflection, which I will make evident by contrasting the "midterm" report of the 2014 synod with its final document.

Midway through the synod, a public report was issued that summarized the discussions up to that time. What generated copious news coverage was the positive appreciation expressed for gay and lesbian Catholics and their committed relationships:

> Homosexuals have gifts and qualities to offer to the Christian community: are we capable of welcoming these people, guaranteeing to them a fraternal space in our communities? Often they wish to encounter a Church that offers them a welcoming home. Are our communities capable of providing that, accepting and valuing their sexual orientation, without compromising Catholic doctrine on the family and matrimony?
>
> Without denying the moral problems connected to homosexual unions it has to be noted that there are cases in which mutual aid to the point of sacrifice constitutes a precious support in the life of the partners. Furthermore, the Church pays special attention to the children who live with couples of the

---

20. Recall that Francis made his observation in response to a question concerning the status of a gay priest working in the Vatican.

same sex, emphasizing that the needs and rights of the little ones must always be given priority.[21]

Note how this summary continues and further develops the more positive directions indicated by Pope Francis's 2013 remarks. Gay and lesbian persons have "gifts and qualities to offer" the faith community. The church is challenged to provide a welcome "to these people." Granted that this is not the most felicitous of phrasings, yet the attitude of welcome, and the onus placed upon the faith community to provide such welcome, is striking given previous official teaching. Even more, the church is exhorted to "accept and value their sexual orientation." This is remarkable, given that the prior teaching was that homosexuality was not an "orientation" but a "condition" or "tendency" that constitutes an "affliction." Finally, there is a positive value attributed to same-sex committed relationships. Even though they have unspecified "moral problems," there is an implicit yet clear break with the previous teaching that same-sex acts are an "intrinsic evil," that is, behavior that has no conceivable justification regardless of the circumstances. For if the behaviors in such relationships provide "precious support" to the "partners," how can it follow that such sexual behaviors have no possible ethical justification (i.e., are intrinsically evil)? Rather, this mid-term report maintains that such relationships—and the children in such relationships—can be and ought to be received as occasions of grace.

This intervention received considerable pushback and impassioned opposition from more traditionally inclined participants, including Cardinals Burke of the U.S. and Pell of Australia. They challenged both the English translation of the midterm report and the accuracy of its summation of the synodal discussions. Thus, another translation was posted on the Vatican's website, one that replaced the summons to "welcome" with "providing for these people." There was also a small but important shift where same-sex relationships were characterized as "mutual assistance to the point of sacrifice is a valuable support in the life of these *persons*"—the word "partners" is avoided or changed. Presumably, this is to guard against recognizing that form of partnership as kind of committed relationship analogous to heterosexual marriage. (This reflects the clear concern of the conservative faction that the mid-term report did not adequately highlight the value and distinctiveness of traditional marriage.)[22]

21. Synod 14—Eleventh General Assembly: "Relatio post disceptationem" of the General Rapporteur, Card. Péter Erdő, 13.10.2014. 50 and 52, http://en.radiovaticana.va/news/2014/10/13/synod_on_family_midterm_report_presented,_2015_synod_announ/1108442.

22. Accessed June 9, 2015, http://press.vatican.va/content/salastampa/en/bollettino/pubblico/2014/10/13/0751/03037.html.

The final document of the 2014 synod also contained none of the more positive language found in the mid-term report. Homosexual persons are treated in the following two paragraphs, in a section revealingly entitled, "Pastoral Care for Persons with Homosexual Tendencies"

> 55. Some families have members who have a homosexual tendency. In this regard, the synod fathers asked themselves what pastoral attention might be appropriate for them in accordance with Church teaching: "There are absolutely no grounds for considering homosexual unions to be in any way similar or even remotely analogous to God's plan for marriage and family." Nevertheless, men and women with a homosexual tendency ought to be received with respect and sensitivity. "Every sign of unjust discrimination in their regard should be avoided" (Congregation for the Doctrine of the Faith, *Considerations Regarding Proposals to Give Legal Recognition to Unions Between Homosexual Persons*, 4).
>
> 56. Exerting pressure in this regard on the Pastors of the Church is totally unacceptable: it is equally unacceptable for international organizations to link their financial assistance to poorer countries with the introduction of laws that establish "marriage" between persons of the same sex.

Here we see a vigorous reassertion of the traditional moral doctrine, as well as a strong assertion that any outreach to those with "homosexual tendencies" is a pastoral move only that must not even appear to compromise traditional teachings on homosexual activity, the homosexual inclination, or heterosexual marriage. Gone is any suggestion that "homosexual unions" have even a "remote" positive significance or value.

Yet, it is significant that these paragraphs (as well as those dealing with the reception of communion for the divorced and remarried) did not receive the two-thirds majority usually required for inclusion into a final synodal document. Many synod participants explicitly did not endorse these for they did not go far enough in developing new directions or perspectives. These paragraphs were included only at the insistence of Pope Francis, respecting his desire for total transparency in the synod's deliberations.[23]

23. "The secretary general of the synod said the real news of the final report 'is that the Holy Father chose to publish it immediately in its entirety, including the paragraphs that did not reach the supermajority of two-thirds of the votes.' *According to the synod's regulations, paragraphs that do not receive a supermajority of two-thirds have not gained a consensus, and thus customarily are not published in the final report.* At the 2014 synod, two contentious paragraphs on the divorced and remarried, and one about homosexuals, failed to garner two-thirds of votes—though they did receive a simple majority." See "For Cardinal Baldisseri, consensus at the Synod of Bishops

Thus the conservatives carried the day. Or did they? The fact that the issues of gay and lesbian persons, and the intimate committed loving bonds they form, generated such vigorous discussion and open disagreement with what was previously a closed and settled issue indicates that the matter is far from settled. Indeed, the synodal discussions then and since the synod reveal stark divisions and deep tensions within the hierarchy over these matters. At the very least, the traditional teaching on same-sex morality does not reflect the "consensus" of the synod's participants.

The synod's deliberations thus are a microcosm of the larger ferment that has been going on within the Christian churches for several decades over the moral status of same-sex intimacy and persons. To put this matter theologically, the strong and forthright debates at the synod demonstrate that traditional magisterial teaching on these matters is no longer unqualifiedly "received" not only by many of the laity, but by significant members of the hierarchy as well, including the Pope himself. Of course, it is hardly "breaking news" that there is a rift or chasm between the official teachings on sexual morality and the convictions of the majority of Catholics, not only in the West, but globally. But the lasting significance of the synod may well lie in the fact that it gave bishops permission to engage in an already existing conversation and debate—a debate from which they had insulated and isolated themselves, and indeed actively proscribed and condemned.[24]

---

remains important," *Catholic News Agency/EWTN News* (October 10, 2014), http://www.catholicnewsagency.com/news/for-cardinal-baldisseri-consensus-at-the-synod-of-bishops-remains-important-51492/.

24. This is a very important point that merits further discussion. I believe that what Pope Francis is doing through the synods on the family is bringing the magisterium—the bishops—up to speed on conversations about sexuality that the rest of the church (the 99%) has been having for the past 45+ years. But these discussions are ones from which the magisterium, for the most part, has absented and insulated themselves—if not attempted to suppress, censor, and derail. For example, it is safe to say that the majority of current seminarians and younger clergy ordained since the 1990s have had little exposure to so-called "dissenting" theologies of sexuality in their seminary studies. Or, if they were studied, it was to the end of showing their error and how to lead the laity to embrace the fullness of "authentic" sexual teaching. Those theologians or scholars who advanced differing approaches to human sexuality found themselves removed from the lists of approved speakers in many dioceses. Thus the faithful were also curtailed or inhibited from such discussions. It is safe to say that the magisterium, on the whole, did its best to censor and silence such opinions and views. Indeed, they were mandated to do so (cf. John Paul II, *Veritatis Splendor* [1993], 110, 116). This makes Francis' encouragement of open discussions and debates at the 2014 and 2015 synods all the more remarkable—and difficult, since the majority of those participating were appointed to the episcopacy ostensibly because they possessed aptitudes for curbing such discussions, not facilitating or engaging in them.

The *Sensus Fidelium* of Gay and Lesbian Believers

But what gave rise to such debate and ferment? What accounts for the doctrinal developments in same-sex morality that have already taken place and, arguably, are still continuing? One can point to the deliberations of theologians and the influence of biblical scholarship regarding scriptural verses long considered as supporting a negative moral judgment on same-sex behavior. But most decisive, in the minds of many, is the testimony of committed gay and lesbian members of the faithful.

For example, Catholic ethicist Margaret Farley declares that such testimonies are pivotal for the renewed evaluations and vigorous discussions that are fermenting in the Christian churches.[25] In line with this observation, one can ask: how could Pope Francis know that a gay priest "is searching for the Lord" and "has good will" without listening to the testimonies from and his own experience of spiritually mature and wise gay men? Indeed, how could the 2014 synod's participants know of "the precious support" that same-sex partners offer one another apart from the testimonies of such partners and the bishops' own experience of loving gay and lesbian persons in committed relationships? The shifts in both tone and doctrine that have and are occurring—as cautious and tentative as they may be—would be impossible without a new ecclesial experience, that is, without gay and lesbian persons speaking of their faith-filled and loving experiences within and to the church.

How does this *sensus* manifest itself? I argue that the *sensus fidelium* of LGBT persons expresses itself in the same manner as that of other faithful believers. The *sensus fidei* is a pre-conceptual, non-discursive form of knowledge, a graced sensitivity on the part of the faithful that enables them to grasp what is congruent or in harmony with the faith—not understood as conformity to doctrine but as adherence to the person of Christ. It stands to reason, then, that expressions of the faith-consciousness of believers will not always be in the language of dogmatic formulation or theological discourse. In order to be sensitive to the activity of the Spirit in ordinary believers, one must pay attention to forms of expression that have not traditionally been utilized by the hierarchy and the theological community. For example, the various theologies of liberation have shown that the ordinary believer's awareness of faith is often expressed by way of narratives and personal testimony.[26] Similarly, Catholic ethicist John Milhaven has pleaded with his

---

25. Margaret Farley, *Just Love: A Framework for Christian Sexual Ethics* (New York: Continuum, 2006) 286–88.

26. Herbert Vorgrimler, "From *Sensus Fidei* to *Consensus Fidelium*," *Concilium* 180 (April 1985) 8; and Hans Waldenfels, "Authority and Knowledge," *Concilium* 180 (April

fellow ethicists to pay greater attention to those genres that are most likely to communicate the direct experience of the faithful: convinced eloquence, creative writing, dramatic acting, films, accounts of real cases, and detailed, evocative phenomenology.[27]

Such testimonies from LGBT Christians abound. These take the form of formal articulations and declarations from groups as organized as Dignity USA, which declares in its "Statement of Position and Purpose," "We believe that gay, lesbian, bisexual and transgender persons can express their sexuality in a manner that is consonant with Christ's teaching. We believe that we can express our sexuality physically, in a unitive manner that is loving, life-giving, and life-affirming."[28] They also include anguished testimonies from young gay Catholics, whose struggles to live as the official teaching demands led to emotional isolation and suicidal thoughts and attempts.[29] They even come from otherwise self-described social conservatives such as Republican presidential contenders Scott Walker and Marco Rubio, who both spoke of being present at and supportive of the same-sex marriages of family members.

Such testimonies alone are not doctrinally determinative. But they are indispensable. They become doctrinally significant when these testimonies arouse a deep empathy within the Christian community, such that the *sensus fidei* of the LGBT Christian becomes the *sensus fidelium* of the broader faith community. John Noonan has persuasively demonstrated how developments in official moral doctrine, such as slavery, usury, and marriage, are preceded by an empathic hearing of new experiences:

> ... experience and empathy are necessary before a practice can be definitively known as good or bad. . . . The great formulas of moral theology have needed to be fed by the most extensive empathy. . . . Neither "intrinsic" nor "unnatural" are always decisive. . . . A new understanding of old human nature nourished by empathy is at the heart of profound change. . . . Empathy with those seen as brothers and sisters leads to the rejection of practices formerly considered to be compatible with Christianity

---

1985) 40.

27. John G. Milhaven, "The Voice of Lay Experience in Christian Ethics," *Proceedings of the Catholic Theological Society of America* 33 (1978) 51.

28. Dignity USA, "Statement of Position and Purpose," http://www.dignityusa.org/purpose.

29. Among the many places one can find LGBT Catholics speaking of their struggles to reconcile their faith and sexuality, see the website http://owningourfaith.org.

such as the enslavement of human beings and persecution for the sake of religion.[30]

This is perhaps the deepest theological issue that lurks just underneath the synodal developments I have outlined. The intervention of Pope Francis and the LGBT debates at the 2014 Synod on the Family (and those yet to come) are so contentious because they "call the question" over the role of the *sensus fidelium* in doctrinal development, especially shifts in ethical beliefs. Moral doctrine changes in the light of a deeper examination of human experience, preceded or accompanied by the empathic listening to new voices and new experiences; by empathic identification with the other; in a word, by love. This is not to undermine the political conflict and social struggle that very often also accompany doctrinal shifts. But such struggles and conflicts will not lead to doctrinal change without an empathic reception of new experiences and truths in the church. In this way, the *sensus fidelium* becomes a catalyst for doctrinal development and change of magisterial teaching, even teaching long-held to be immutable for it proscribes "intrinsically evil" behavior.

Thus the underlying neuralgic question confronting the synod, and the whole church, at this moment is this: Does the *sensus fidelium* of LGBT Christians and others have *pastoral* significance and import only—that is, it must be attended to in order that the officials may more convincingly or sensitively present the current teaching—or does it have genuine *doctrinal* weight such that human experience and reflection upon that experience can affect and shift official faith commitments and moral beliefs?

Even traditionalists concede the pastoral significance of new experiences. For example, the International Theological Commission notes that a divergence between official moral teaching and the lived experience of the faithful challenges the magisterium to "reflect on the teaching that has been given and consider whether it needs clarification or reformulation in order to communicate more effectively the essential message."[31] Also, Archbishop Diarmuid Martin of Dublin famously remarked that the Irish Church needed a "reality check" in light of the overwhelming approval given to same-sex marriage during a referendum in that traditionally Catholic country in the spring of 2015. Noting that the majority of young people voting in favor of same-sex marriage were products of at least twelve years of Catholic

---

30. John T. Noonan, *A Church That Can and Cannot Change: The Development of Catholic Moral Teaching* (Notre Dame: University of Notre Dame Press, 2005), 211, 213, 215.

31. International Theological Commission, *Sensus Fidei in the Life of the Church* (2014) no. 80.

education, he said "there's a big challenge there to see how we get across the message of the Church."[32] Both of these sources concede the pastoral significance of the *sensus fidelium*.

But the analysis I provided of Pope Francis' remarks and the discussions of the 2014 synod indicates that much more is at work here. His "who am I to judge" comment was not simply the voice of a pastor; it manifested a genuine doctrinal shift. To be sure, it is a shift that many in the LGBT community judge to be inadequate. (For example, Francis has signaled his opposition to same-sex marriage, though he has expressed some openness to other forms of legal recognition).[33] But there has been a shift nonetheless, one that would be impossible without the LGBT *sensus fidelium* in the church. This, I suggest, is the reason for the impassioned concern that some are directing at Francis and his overtures, namely, the inchoately articulated awareness that the *sensus fidelium* has *doctrinal* significance and authoritative weight.

Speaking Truths to and for the Church

Mark Jordan concludes his insightful and wise book, *Telling Truths in Church*, with this moving reflection on speaking and listening for truth:

> Truth proclaimed builds up the community of believers who are enjoined to love one another. One sign that they do love is that they can tell truths to one another—which means that they can hear truths from one another. We might then understand that here *agape* includes committed respect and trust, the mutual gifts of attention and encouragement, that are required for full telling of the truth ... Since we can only talk about *agape* through *eros*, we might say, more succinctly: the church must be a community with *eros* for truth. It must be an erotic community.[34]

My hope is that, regardless of apostolic exhortation that Pope Francis will issue in light of the family synods of 2014 and 2015, his overtures and remarks thus far will create an atmosphere in the Church—a genuine "culture of encounter"—where the truth of LGBT lives can be more openly shared

---

32. http://www.theguardian.com/world/2015/may/24/ireland-same-sex-marriage-dublin-archbishop-catholic-church-needs-reality-check.

33. John L. Allen, Jr., "Pope Sends Mixed Signals on Civil Unions for Gay Couples," *The Crux* (January 27, 2016), www.cruxnow.com/church/2016/01/27/pope-francis-sends-mixed-signals-on-civil-unions-for-gay-couples/.

34. Mark D. Jordan, *Telling Truths in Church: Scandal, Flesh, and Christian Speech* (Boston: Beacon, 2003) 105.

and empathically received. For this is the necessary, even if not sufficient, condition for doctrinal development in human sexuality.

13

Who Are the *Fideles* and What Is Their *Sensus*?

Insights from Bernard Lonergan

William P. George

Early on in the International Theological Commission's 2014 study of the *sensus fidei*, the ITC recalls Pope Francis' encounter with "a humble, elderly woman he once met," who said to him, "If the Lord did not forgive everything, the world would not exist," about which the pope commented with admiration, "that this is the wisdom that the Holy Spirit gives." In the judgment of the ITC, "The woman's insight is a striking manifestation of the *sensus fidei*, which, as well as enabling a certain discernment with regard to the things of faith, fosters true wisdom and gives rise, as here, to proclamation of the truth."[1] There is no reason to question the ITC's judgment in this case. But juxtapose to this woman's words those of another, a distraught Muslim in the suburbs of Chicago, whose nineteen-year-old son had been arrested for attempting to provide material support to the Islamic State. "Leave our children alone," she pleaded on camera to the leaders of this group. "The venom spewed by these groups and the violence committed by them," she went on to say, "find no support in the Quran and are completely at odds with our Islamic faith."[2]

Drawing on insights from Bernard Lonergan, in this essay I want to suggest, among other things, that this woman—not a baptized Catholic or

---

1. International Theological Commission, *Sensus Fidei in the Life of the Church*, 2014, 2.

2. "Mom of teen terror suspect tells ISIS to 'Stop recruiting our kids,'" Channel 7 (Chicago) CBS News: http://abc7chicago.com/news/mom-of-teen-terror-suspect-tells-isis-to-stop-recruiting-our-kids/473421/.

even the baptized Christian envisioned by the ICT,[3] and presumably not a highly educated Islamic scholar—might also be counted among the *fideles* to whom the church ought to listen, and that her protest in this case might also be construed as a "proclamation of the truth" prompted by the Holy Spirit. In other words, I wish to argue that prevailing understandings of the *sensus fidelium*, as articulated in the ITC report, appear overly restrictive, failing to move beyond the bounds of Christianity to other religious traditions. But beyond that, I want to suggest that the *fideles* also reside outside of explicitly religious traditions altogether, for instance—in the example I will give—in the highly secularized world of international lawyers and the law they practice.

This paper is more suggestive than conclusive, and many questions must be set aside. It might also be viewed as speculative: How different, one might ask, would the ITC report on the *sensus fidei* have read had Lonergan, or one of his students, been an influential member of the commission? For there are, I propose, a number of insights from Lonergan that might help us to rethink and to broaden the notion of the *sensus fidelium*. Here, I will focus all too briefly on four: (1) Lonergan's observation about Catholic tardiness in staying abreast of the times; (2) his distinctive understanding of natural law; (3) his emphasis on God's universal salvific will and a concomitant emphasis on the activity of the Holy Spirit; and (4) his related notion of "the emerging religious consciousness of our time."

Catholic Tardiness

At the end of *Insight*, in commenting on the church's less than successful response to modern science and the challenges it posed to the Christian faith, Lonergan remarked that Catholicism arrived on the scene a "little breathlessly and a little late."[4] While one must be careful not to generalize, leading to conclude that Catholicism is always "behind the times," Lonergan's observation about this one case leads one to ask whether, in matters not only of faith, but also of morals—my primary emphasis here—some outside the Catholic and wider Christian communion have been in possession of a *sensus fidei* at least as vital as that of baptized Catholics and the magisterium.

Let me give an example: In its report, the ITC acknowledges that Christians not in communion with Rome can also be in possession of the *sensus*

---

3. ITC, *Sensus Fidei* ¶ 186.

4. Bernard Lonergan, Jr SJ, *Insight. A Study of Human Understanding*, 3rd ed. (New York: Philosophical Library, 1970), 733.

fidei. It also acknowledges that the church grows in its understanding of the implications of the Christian faith. So, for instance, it recalls the church's changed thinking on usury, social issues, and religious liberty.[5] Significantly, it seems to overlook what John T. Noonan considers a prime case to consider when asking about "a church that can and cannot change," namely, slavery.[6] One might argue that Catholicism formally condemned slavery only in 1965 during the Second Vatican Council.[7] Could it not be said that, compared to some other Christians, the magisterium arrived on this scene a little breathlessly and a little late? That some, such as the Quakers, were more in tune with and acted upon the *sensus fidei* than was the case with many if not most Catholics?[8] And to press the point further: Is it possible that those abolitionists quite outside the Christian tradition—perhaps even at odds with it—were acting out of their own *faith*, that cornerstone of the *sensus* discussed by the ITC?

Obviously, there is more to discuss here, but let me make one observation or, better, pose a question: Is there such a thing as a *selective sensus fidei*? That is, might a person or a community be faithful to the movements of the Spirit in one respect and yet quite resistant in another? The ITC report details some rather stringent criteria, a set of recognizable "dispositions," for identifying "the faithful." These include participation in the life of the church; listening to the Word of God; openness to reason; adherence to the magisterium; holiness—humility, freedom and joy; and seeking edification

---

5. ITC, *Sensus Fidei*, 4

6. John T. Noonan Jr., *A Church That Can and Cannot Change* (Notre Dame: University of Notre Dame Press, 2005).

7. For a brief review of Catholicism's mixed attitude towards slavery, see Daniel K. Finn, *Christian Economic Ethics: History and Implications* (Minneapolis: Fortress, 2013) 183–90. Finn relies heavily on John Francis Maxwell, *The History of Catholic Teaching on the Moral Legitimacy of Slavery* (Chichester, UK: Rose, 1975).

8. "A further reason for the long delay [in condemning slavery] appears to be that the use of charismatic gifts by the Catholic laity has normally not been accepted as a means of putting right social injustices and providing a remedy for unjust pharisaism and legalism . . . The few members of the Society of Friends (Quakers) in the early eighteenth *century who appear to have been open to the direction of the Holy Spirit concerning slav*ery, exercised an enormous influence, first on their fellow Quakers, and then on all North American Protestants . . . On the other hand, the graces received by most of the eighteenth and nineteenth century Catholic laity from the traditional Latin prayer and liturgy were apparently insufficient to awaken their consciences to the unjust slavery-legislation in Latin America, North America, West Africa, etc., and insufficient to overcome the baneful influence of Roman civil law concerning slavery on Catholic moral theology and canon law" (Maxwell, *Catholic Teaching on Slavery* 20–21, emphasis added).

of the church.⁹ And yet, we know that some otherwise very faithful Catholics have been—or are—racist in their attitudes or practices.¹⁰ Could it be that those with a solid *sensus* about the wrongness of slavery could be right about this and yet be in error in other matters of faith and morals—or, the other way around: wrong about slavery, right on other matters? After all, for a time, even one of the greatest Catholic opponents of slavery, Bartolomé de Las Casas, had his blind spots regarding that very issue.¹¹ In any event, for the sake of argument and keeping in mind all that Lonergan has to say about biases of various kinds,¹² I propose that there might be a "selective" or quite imperfect *sensus fidelium*—clear-sighted on some issues, blind on others—and if this is so, then this alone may broaden the field of *fideles* and expand the notion of the *sensus* upon which they, and the church, may call as they live out their lives.

Natural Law

The topic of natural law raises so many thorny issues that I hesitate to bring it into the discussion at all. Yet it is indeed germane, and thus deserving of at least brief comment. On the one hand, Catholicism has maintained a rather optimistic view towards natural law, trusting in the human capacity, wounded but not totally eviscerated by sin, to know the true and the truly good. At the same time, there has been within the tradition an abiding reticence to conflate reason and faith, nature and grace, the natural with that which is revealed. Lonergan himself is careful to distinguish the "natural

---

9. ITC, *Sensus Fidei*, 88–105.

10. Consider, as but a single example, what Francis Cardinal George had to say about presumably faith-filled Chicago Catholics in his 2001 pastoral letter on racism: "Forced to live on the near south and west side of the city in often substandard housing owned by landlords living elsewhere, many African American families that could afford better housing could not move into nearby neighborhoods because of the color of their skin. Catholics, loyal to their parishes, often made up the bulk of the white population in neighborhoods near the expanding African American sections of the city. Sometimes these same Catholics mixed parish loyalty with racial prejudice in a desperate, always unsuccessful, effort to 'save' particular neighborhoods by preventing the entrance of black people." Francis Cardinal George, *Dwell in My Love: A Pastoral Letter on Racism*, 10th Anniversary Edition. Archdiocese of Chicagohttps://www.archchicago.org/Cardinal/pdf/DwellInMyLove_10thAnniversary.pdf, 8.

11. Gustavo Gutiérrez, *Las Casas: In Search of the Poor in Jesus Christ* (Maryknoll, NY: Orbis, 1993) 324–30.

12. Lonergan, *Insight*, Chapter 7; see also Bernard J. F. Lonergan, *Method in Theology*, 2d ed. (New York: Herder & Herder, 1972) 230–31.

order" from the "supernatural order."[13] Yet, if, as Aquinas points out in his discussion of the natural law, all human beings have "a *natural* inclination to *know* the *truth* about *God*,"[14] then maybe that "natural inclination" can be related to if not identified with the *sensus fidei*. On the face of it, this is doubtful, since the tradition wants to maintain that the desire to know God is indeed "natural," while at least according to the ITC, when it comes to the *sensus fidei*, the emphasis is subjectively on the gift of faith and, objectively, on revealed truth.[15] To this, Lonergan has responded in part with reference to the natural knowledge of God affirmed by Vatican I: "*I do not think that in this life people arrive at natural knowledge of God without God's grace, but what I do not doubt is that the knowledge they arrive at is natural.*"[16] In other words, on theological grounds there is reason to assume that human beings everywhere, if they are truly attuned to the "natural law," are in fact aided by saving grace to know God and other matters related to the natural law, for example, "to live in society."[17] If this is so—if God's grace, and not just "nature," is always in the picture—could one not understand the dynamics of the natural law as another way of discussing the *sensus fidei* and the *sensus fidelium*?

This suggestion is strengthened when one considers Lonergan's own apparent reluctance to discuss "the natural law," a reluctance that might be motivated by worries about a classicist understanding of natural law that would obscure the natural law's more fundamental "inclinations"—that is, the inclinations of the self-transcendent subject in history.[18] As some have argued, Lonergan does in fact hold for a dynamic, heuristic notion of natural law, a notion that may be thematized in terms of the transcendental precepts: Be attentive, Be intelligent, Be reasonable, Be responsible.[19] And

---

13. Lonergan, *Grace and Freedom: Operative Grace in the Thought of St. Thomas Aquinas*, ed. J. Patout Burns (New York: Herder & Herder, 1971) 13–19.

14. Thomas Aquinas. *Summa Theologica*, trans., Fathers of the English Dominican Province, 5 vols (Westminster, MD: Christian Classics, 1981) I-II 94, 2.

15. ITC, *Sensus Fidei*, 48, 56.

16. Lonergan, "Natural Knowledge of God," in *A Second Collection*, ed. William J. F Ryan, SJ and Bernard J Tyrell, SJ (Toronto: University of Toronto Press, 1974), 133 [117–35] (emphasis added).

17. *ST* I-II 94, 2.

18. Lonergan, "Natural Right and Historical Mindedness" in Frederick E. Crowe, SJ, ed., *A Third Collection: Papers by Bernard Lonergan* (Mahwah, NJ: Paulist, 1985) 169–83.

19. For a discussion of Lonergan's view of natural law in terms of the transcendental precepts, see Patrick McKinley Brennan, "Asking the Right Questions: Harnessing the Insights of Bernard Lonergan for the Rule of Law," *Journal of Law and Religion* 21 (2006) 1–38.

if one adds to the list, Be loving, it hardly seems a stretch to argue that the loving—but also attentive, intelligent, critical, and responsible—attitude and action of, say, the Muslim woman introduced at the outset of this essay might, *de facto*, be expressing the *sensus fidei*, at once natural *and* graced. If this is so, then those outside the Catholic fold might be expressing the *sensus fidei* in ways that the church, including the magisterium, needs to engage, attentively, intelligently, reasonably, responsibly, and lovingly, even when, perhaps especially when, the magisterium's own possibly restrictive reading of natural law is at issue.

God's Universal Salvific Will and the Activity of the Holy Spirit

Years ago when I was a "missionary" in Zambia, a man I met on one of my visits to a rural village asked me why I was trying to learn the local language. I explained to him that, long before the Europeans came to Africa, God was already working there, and that by learning Citonga I might get a better idea of what God had been doing all that time. In saying this, I was hardly espousing some radically new and original way of thinking. I was pretty much expressing what I had been taught by the Jesuits and others, beginning, perhaps, with what I had read about the Jesuit missionaries in late sixteenth and early seventeenth-century China.[20] At the end of our conversation, as we parted my new Tonga friend said, "*Twaiiya kabotu sunu*"—"We have learned well today." He was right about that, in more ways than one. Not only had we *both* learned from the exchange, but our lesson was about evangelization itself: not one person imparting to another knowledge of God brought from afar but, through conversation, attending to and educing through words the God already present, active, and in some way known to us.

I recall this pastoral encounter because it seems in tune with what Lonergan stressed so often, namely, the "universal salvific will of God" and the universality of grace—God's love flooding our hearts through the Holy Spirit.[21] As Robert Doran argues, this fundamental conviction is given further theological depth and nuance by focusing on the Holy Spirit.[22] In

---

20. George H. Dunne, SJ, *Generation of Giants: The Story of the Jesuits in China in the Last Decades of the Ming Dynasty* (Notre Dame: University of Notre Dame Press, 1962).

21. Frederick E. Crowe, SJ, "Lonergan's Universalist View of Religion," in Michael Vertin, ed., *Developing the Lonergan Legacy: Historical, Theoretical, and Existential Themes* (Toronto: University of Toronto Press, 2004) 111–41.

22. Robert M. Doran, "Functional Specialties for a World Theology," *Lonergan Workshop* 24 (2013) 99–111.

what Doran considers a foundational article, Frederick Crowe sought to move beyond our "binarian" tendencies (God is Father and Son) by positing that God's first sending into the world was/is not the Son but rather the Spirit. This reversal of order, in Crowe's view, has immense implications for Christian attitudes towards and relations with other world religions.[23] To put it in terms of our topic, it might be argued that if the Spirit is present in the other religions—including indigenous religious thought and practice such as one finds in Africa—and if fidelity, or "faith," within those traditions means attunement and responsiveness to the promptings of that Spirit, then the *sensus fidelium* may be found in other religions. And if that is the case, then consulting the faithful on matters of faith and morals will, on the part of the church, require and entail engagement of those other traditions.

But, as stated at the outset, I wish to take the argument a step further, beyond the bounds of explicit religious belonging and commitment, in this case venturing into the highly secularized world of international lawyers and law. This may appear to be overreaching, but I do not think this to be the case. If I may again appeal to personal experience, this time of a more scholarly kind: A few years after the 1993 Chicago meeting of the Parliament of the World's Religions and its attempt to articulate a global ethic,[24] I wrote an article for the *Journal of Religion* titled "Looking for a Global Ethic? Try international Law."[25] There I argued that, "in seeking an ethic worthy of the name global, religious ethicists ought to pay very close attention to, and actively engage, that complex, contested, and multidimensional carrier of meaning and value called international law."[26] The article was reissued, with slight revisions, as the last of 22 chapters in a 1999 volume entitled *Religion and International Law*, edited by two scholars of international law.[27] This book was then reviewed for the *American Journal of International Law* by Harold Berman, a leading expert on law and religion.[28] Towards the end

---

23. Frederick E. Crowe, SJ, "Son of God, Holy Spirit, and World Religions," in *Appropriating the Lonergan Idea*, ed. Michael Vertin (Toronto: University of Toronto Press, 1989) 324–43.

24. Parliament of the World's Religions, "Declaration toward a Global Ethic," Chicago, U.S.A., 4 September 1993.

25. William P. George, "Looking for a Global Ethic? Try International Law," *Journal of Religion* 76 (1996) 359–82.

26. Ibid., 360.

27. Mark W. Janis and Carolyn Evans, eds., "Looking for a Global Ethic? Try International Law," in *Religion and International Law* (Lancaster: Kluwer Academic, 1999) 191–208.

28. Harold J. Berman, "Review of Janis and Evans, eds., *Religion and International Law.*" *Religion and International Law*, in the *American Journal of International Law* 94 (October 2000) 800–803.

of his review, Berman posed a question: "In a multicultural, multireligious world, what, if any, common faith can provide a basis for legal institutions that will support world peace against potential aggressors, and universal human rights against oppressive governments?" He then turned to my own contribution for "one answer," which was, in Berman's words, "surprisingly," the proposal of "a common faith in the underlying 'global ethic' of international law itself."[29]

After discussing my contribution at some length, Berman concluded his review in this way: "This, indeed, may be the final word in the analysis of the interaction of religion and international law in a multicultural and multireligious world: that not only Roman Catholicism and Protestantism, as in the Grotian paradigm, but all great faiths, including some forms of humanism, may unite in affirming the presence of a transcendental spiritual element—a holy spirit—in the process of making, interpreting, and applying international law itself."[30] And there can be little doubt what—or who—in Berman's mind, this "spiritual element" might be. Yes, "holy spirit" is in small case letters here. But other of Berman's writings are quite explicit: It is the "Holy Spirit" of his Trinitarian Christian faith to which Berman refers. In fact, what one finds in Berman's writings, with titles such as "The Holy Spirit: The God of History"[31] and "World Law: An Ecumenical Jurisprudence of the Holy Spirit,"[32] is not altogether different from what Frederick Crowe is drawing out from Lonergan's work: a clear conviction about the Holy Spirit's unbounded animating presence in the world, and thus, for our purposes, the possibility of a *sensus fidei* to be found even in the dynamic, largely secular world of international or global law.

The Emerging Religious Consciousness of Our Time

I will return to international law, but it will advance that return and our topic in general if we focus for a moment on Lonergan's remarkable essay, "Prolegomena to the Study of the Emerging Religious Consciousness of Our Time."[33] First of all, in discussing religious consciousness, Lonergan distin-

29. Ibid., 802.

30. Ibid., 803.

31. Harold J. Berman, "The Holy Spirit: The God of History," *The Living Pulpit* (April–June 2003).

32. Harold J. Berman, "World Law: An Ecumenical Jurisprudence of the Holy Spirit," *Emory Public Law Research Paper No. 05-4*, February 2005; see also "Law and Logos." *DePaul Law Review* 44 (1994) 143–65.

33. Bernard Lonergan, JF, SJ, "Prolegomena to the Study of the Emerging Religious Consciousness of our Time." In *A Third Collection*, ed., Frederick E. Crowe, SJ, 55–73

guishes between "infrastructure" and "suprastructure."[34] The infrastructure is unthematized experience captured in feelings, intimations, insights prior to reflection upon those insights, and so on—in short, the data of consciousness. The suprastructure, on the other hand, thematizes this experience, making it conceptually and linguistically explicit and communicable to others. Second, the religious consciousness to which Lonergan is referring is an *emerging* consciousness. Thus it is a new consciousness in search of some way, of some convention, to articulate it. Now, Lonergan says, "when the choice [of a convention] falls to Christianity," Paul's statement about God's love flooding our hearts through the Holy Spirit, and the account of Christian origins in "God sending his only Son through death and resurrection and the sending of the Spirit" provide a suprastructure, and it is that suprastructure, not the emerging consciousness as infrastructure, that distinguishes Christianity from other traditions.[35] Third, for Lonergan, this emerging religious consciousness is closely tied to an emerging *global* consciousness that seeks unity of the human family but does not escape alienation and bias.[36] In terms of the *sensus fidei*, this *sensus* might be manifest not only in the "simple faith" of the woman who met Pope Francis, but also in the anguish of the Muslim woman who, not unlike the biblical Rachael, was weeping for her children—or, more generally, in the cry of the poor, of immigrants from war-torn countries seeking refuge in Europe and other lands, or of those of any faith—or of no explicitly religious faith—who are tortured in body or spirit.

Putting these considerations together, one might argue not only that diverse religious traditions, each with its own suprastructure, seek to articulate and advance this emerging consciousness, but also that international law, with, in Berman's words, its "spiritual element," its "holy spirit," also provides a suprastructure for articulating the "emerging religious consciousness of our time." Or, put otherwise, international law might provide a suprastructure for expressing the underlying *sensus fidei* in and of an emerging global law.

If this still seems like a theological stretch, let me possibly close the gap in three ways. First, is the worry expressed by the ITC that the *sensus*

(Mahwah, NJ: Paulist, 1985).

34. Ibid. 71.

35. Ibid. One way to read the ITC report on *sensus fidei* is in terms of infrastructure and superstructure, as the document seeks to describe what this pre-thematic "sensus" might be. The pre-thematic *sensus* soon—and necessarily—gives way to the superstructure of theologically informed articulation and explanation of what this *sensus* is and how it is to be understood in relation to the Catholic tradition.

36. Ibid. 30–40.

fidelium not be confused with public opinion.³⁷ This is a legitimate concern, but one that may be lessened in the case of international law since international law is itself a very long, dynamic, developing, and self-correcting tradition, with complex institutions, multiple "sources," guiding norms, and room for negotiation. International law may indeed be attuned to "world opinion" but it cannot be reduced to it. One should not underestimate the winnowing process that international law represents.

Second, international law is certainly not without its flaws. But it need not be perfect in order to embody, at some unarticulated level, "the emerging religious consciousness of our time," or potentially to express the *sensus fidelium*. After all, the laity in the time of St. Jerome found the bishops to be mostly in error; in other words, the very notion of a *sensus fidelium* assumes the possibility of imperfections on the part of some that the *sensus* of others may counter or correct. As I have argued elsewhere, sometimes international law lags behind particular religious traditions. But occasionally, it runs ahead.³⁸

Third, when it comes to the question of whether international law, again, highly secularized, just might be a locus of the *sensus fidei*, one could argue that the fact proves the possibility. That is, just as the ITC could point to the example of the "simple woman" who met Pope Francis as a sure example of the *sensus fidei,* so there appear to be similarly good examples among the practitioners—or, in Lonergan's terms, the "subjects"³⁹—of international law. Let me call to mind two such subjects, one briefly and one at more length. Consider the first example: In reflecting on his experience as a lawyer and judge appointed to important international tribunals, the late Antonio Cassese, an avowed secularist, tells of how his encounter with people who had been raped, tortured, or otherwise brutally treated both had an impact on his legal practice and led him to the works of Primo Levi and Martin Buber in hopes of gaining perspective on the very real problem of evil.⁴⁰ Is it too far afield to suggest that Cassese's encounter with victims was itself a profound experience of "I-thou" relationality that may echo, in stark and painful ways, John Henry Newman's motto, *"Cor ad cor loquitur"*? A heart-speaking-to-heart conversation that might be expressive of a shared *sensus fidei* of lawyer and victim?

37. ITC, *Sensus Fidei*, 113–19.

38. George, "Looking for a Global Ethic? Try International Law," 368.

39. Lonergan, "The Subject," in *A Second Collection*, ed., William J.F. Ryan, SJ and Bernard J. Tyrell, SJ (Toronto: University of Toronto Press, 1974) 69–87.

40. Antonio Cassese, "Soliloquy," in *The Human Dimensions of International Law. Selected Papers,* lxv–lxviii (Oxford: Oxford University Press, 2008) lxix.

The second example is that of a former World Court judge, indeed its vice-president for a time: Judge Christopher Weeramantry of Sri Lanka. Weeramantry (b. 1926), is a prolific writer whose works include titles such as *Islamic Jurisprudence: An International Perspective*, *The Lord's Prayer: Bridge to a Better World*, and *Tread Lightly on the Earth: Religion and the Environment*. And these titles, with their pointers to religious consciousness, only hint at the range of his moral and legal concerns, such as the threat of nuclear weapons about which he wrote at length in his remarkable dissent from the 1996 ICJ advisory opinion on the legality of threat or use of those weapons.[41] Perhaps no international lawyer of his stature has taken so seriously the role of religion in the world, including the world of international law itself.

Weeramantry is a committed Catholic layperson, but this is not always apparent in his writings, including his lengthy memoirs,[42] so at home he appears to be with other traditions—some of which he grew up with in Ceylon before it was Sri Lanka. Indeed, elsewhere I have tried to show how Weermantry and his life's work might be paradigmatic of the "emerging religious consciousness of our time."[43] Here, I want to suggest that his life and work may also exemplify the *sensus fidei* not only of a baptized Catholic, but precisely of one whose *cor ad cor loquitur* extends at once to other religions, to his legal and academic colleagues, *and* to the diverse human subjects engaged in or affected by an ever-emerging international law. But I want to emphasize something else: Weeramantry is a very sophisticated thinker and doer who, in his own way, has managed to negotiate and integrate what Lonergan calls the realms and functions of meaning[44] as well as the scale of values[45]—a scale that Doran suggests may stand as "an extraordinary litmus test regarding the major authenticity of the various religious traditions of our world."[46] Weermantry's faith may be a simple faith

---

41. ICJ Advisory Opinion on the Legality of the Threat or Use of Nuclear Weapons, July 8, 1996, Dissenting Opinion of Judge Weeramantry.

42. Judge C. G. Weeramantry, *Towards One World, Memoirs of Judge C.G. Weeramantry*. Vol. 1: The Sri Lanka Years; Vol 2: The Australian Years; Vol. 3: The International Court and Thereafter (Moratuwa, Sri Lanka: OPRO Printing and Publishing Solutions, 2010, 2012, 2014).

43. William George, "Emerging Religious Consciousness.: The Examples of Eboo Patel and C.G. Weeramantry," paper delivered at the 41st Lonergan Workshop, Boston College, June 2014.

44. With regard not only to "functions" and "realms" but also to other relevant aspects of meaning, see *Method*, 57–100.

45. Ibid., 31–32.

46. Doran, "Functional Specialties," 101. Doran explains that, "Like functional specialization, the scale of values is a complication of the structure of intentional

(he makes no strong claim to be a theologian) but it is by no means a simplistic faith, which is perhaps one more reminder that Lonergan's remark in *Insight* about a church that arrives a little breathless and a little late in the modern world remains relevant today. Yes, the *sensus fidei* may be alive in the "humble, elderly woman" who encountered the pope. But it may be equally alive in theologically and otherwise sophisticated women and others whom the church ought to consult more effectively and more often on matters of faith and morals.[47]

Conclusion

I know I have overlooked a lot and have skirted a number of questions. I have said nothing, for instance, about the *sensus fidelium* in relation to the kinds of conversion so central to Lonergan's thought and method, even though some thoughts about conversion may be implied from what I have said. Nor have I made any attempt to work out suitable "rules for discernment," to borrow from St. Ignatius of Loyola's *Spiritual Exercises*, for determining just what is and is not evidence of the *sensus fidei* as it exists outside the Christian tradition, or outside of any explicit religious tradition—for example the largely secularized world of international law. My intent has been more modest: simply to suggest with the help of Lonergan that our understanding of the *sensus fidei* and the *sensus fidelium* may be too narrow and restricted. If I have offered some openings to broader understandings, openings that demand further discussion, then I will be satisfied for now.

---

consciousness elevated by divine grace, one that opens on the collective responsibility that is made operative as grace takes on social and cultural effectiveness" (100, 2).

47. One might argue that this is precisely what is happening as the Vatican enters into dialogue with experts on climate change and related environmental issues.

14

A Rahnerian Reading of "*Sensus Fidei* in the Life of the Church"

— Michael M. Canaris —

Because of the lasting impression the great German theologian Karl Rahner has wrought on contemporary theology, and since his ecclesiological contributions dovetail with so many of the themes addressed in it, the aim of this piece is to analyze the International Theological Commission's 2014 document "*Sensus Fidei* in the Life of the Church" through a Rahnerian lens. I posit that this is a worthwhile endeavor in that Karl Rahner's optimism towards the Church's integral appreciation of the People of God, broadly understood, recognizes the contributions of the faithful in handing on, receiving, and actively living out the faith. It seems fitting then to read the recent document through the lens of this legacy, and to explore what questions it raises and what insights Rahnerian theology can provide, perhaps all the more so with a Jesuit pope, who shares Rahner's Ignatian heritage and appreciation for spiritual discernment, now pressing for greater synodal and collegial conversations in curial circles and church governance. Let me begin then with just *very brief* introduction to the specifics of the ITC document itself, before moving into the agenda proper.

The 2014 text obviously sought to address theological issues involved in the understanding of the *sensus fidelium* that have arisen since its explicit phrasing in the council's writings.[1] There has been little change to the Commission that produced this text, and that which wrote the 2012 document titled *Theology Today: Perspectives, Principles, and Criteria*. The

---

1. For the purposes of this essay, I will follow Ormond Rush's distinction between the *sensus fidei fidelis* (or *sensus fidei*) as the sense of the faith of an individual believer, and the *sensus fidei fidelium* (or *sensus fidelium*) as the communal sense of all the faithful. Cf. "*Sensus Fidei*: Faith 'Making Sense' of Revelation," *Theological Studies* 62 (2001) 232 [231–62].

subcommittee listed as drafting both is in fact exactly the same, made up mostly of clerics, but also including a woman, Sara Butler, and a lay man, Thomas Söding. The texts were, however, authorized by two different Prefects of the CDF—Cardinal William Levada for the former, and Cardinal Gerhard Müller for the latter. Obviously, other more substantial changes in tone and ecclesial governance were underfoot between the publication of the documents, as Pope Benedict XVI's resignation and the election of Pope Francis also took place in the intervening years.

The general structure of the relevant text at hand includes an introduction, four thematic chapters with a number of subsections in each, and a conclusion. The chapters contain reflections on the *sensus fidelium*, and derivatively of the *sensus fidei*, in terms of (1) Scripture and Tradition, (2) the personal life of the believer, (3) the life of the Church, and (4) the need to develop strategies for discerning authentic manifestations of such a *sensus*.

Most of the conversation regarding the document, which at a macrocosmic level really hasn't been all that much, surrounds its interpretation of the relationship between the magisterium, theologians, and the wider faithful; the theology of the laity present in or undergirding the text; and particular applications of the *sensus fidelium* in terms of both what the text calls 'popular religiosity' and of public opinion. The historical background to the concept's development in the life of the church and its endorsement in the conciliar texts is fairly straightforward, and accordingly has warranted little further attention. However, the relevance of the *sensus* to ecclesiological reception and its heightened role in the ecumenical movement would seem to be one area where the document could have practical significance moving forward.[2]

Interesting to note is the text's explicit and repeated references to the theology of Yves Congar, who it is claimed "contributed significantly to the development of the doctrine [of the *sensus fidelium*]" and whose thought was reflected in the work of the council.[3] He is posited as being instrumental in arguing for the organic unity between the *ecclesia docens* (the teaching church) and the *ecclesia discens* (the learning church), which is a crucial theme consonant with the *sensus fidelium* and with wider developing notions of theological reception. Karl Rahner is nowhere mentioned,

---

2. Cf. for example Paul D. Murray, ed. *Receptive Ecumenism and the Call to Catholic Learning: Exploring a Way for Contemporary Ecumenism* (Oxford: Oxford University Press, 2008); William Rusch, *Ecumenical Reception: Its Challenge and Opportunity* (Grand Rapids: Eerdmans, 2007); and Joint Working Group between the Roman Catholic Church and the World Council of Churches, *Reception: A Key to Ecumenical Progress* (Geneva: World Council of Churches, 2013).

3. ITC, *Sensus Fidei* in the Life of the Church (hereafter SFLC) 43–44.

either in the body of the text or footnotes; perhaps as is fair, for as Pamela McCann recently pointed out in a 2013 article in *Philosophy and Theology*, Rahner "provided no systematic treatment of the topic of the *sensus fidelium*," though he does allude to it and related concepts both implicitly, and even explicitly in some of his later writings. She argues that ecclesiologists do often reference his contributions to these discussions.[4] Again, the ITC chose not to do so directly in the final text.

McCann's article on Rahner and the *sensus fidelium*, which is a distillation of her larger dissertation, argues that his influence on theological thinking about the topic can be felt mainly in two general areas: what she calls attending to the "right relation" between the faithful and the magisterium and in attention to communal consensus building in terms of dialogue and experiment in the church.[5] Her analysis has proved invaluable in this project, and in assessing Ranhner's contribution to these questions both in Catholic circles, and beyond.

I will begin by introducing what Rahner and the ITC text each envision in terms of the interaction among the magisterium, theologians, and the wider church, here understood in a Catholic context—though, as noted, much of this can have ecumenical implications as well. I will then explore what I see as the two most important applications of the *sensus fidelium* in terms of issues important to Rahner (and, not unrelatedly, at the fore of this pontificate): "popular religiosity"; and determining authentic expressions of the *sensus* vis-à-vis statistical majorities, or public opinion. I will conclude with some comments on Rahner's dream of "the church to come" and its relevance to the conversation.

The Interplay between the Magisterium, Theologians, and the Faithful at Large

The ITC text claims, "As the faith of the individual believer participates in the faith of the Church as a believing subject, so the *sensus fidei (fidelis)* of individual believers cannot be separated from the *sensus fidei (fidelium)* or *sensus Ecclesiae* of the Church herself."[6] Its terminology then equates the

---

4. Pamela McCann, "Karl Rahner and the Sensus Fidelium," *Philosophy and Theology* 25 (2013) 313 [311–35].

5. Ibid., 316. See also her dissertation "Karl Rahner as a Resource for the Theology of the *Sensus Fidelium*: The Canonical Impications of His Vision," PhD diss., University of Toronto, 2011.

6. SFLC, 66.

sensus fidelium with the *sensus Ecclesiae,* and follows this shortly later with two concise and powerful statements:

1. "The magisterium listens to the *sensus fidelium*,"[7] which it goes on to call unequivocally "the living voice of the people of God."[8]

2. "The magisterium nurtures, discerns, and judges the *sensus fidelium*."[9] Again, adding "Judgment regarding the authenticity of the *sensus fidelium* belongs ultimately not to the faithful themselves nor to theology but to the magisterium."[10]

While the document does discuss "reception" of this judgment by the wider community, and goes on to describe the role of the theologian in this exchange, its emphasis seems to remain on how "resistance, *as a matter of principle*, to the teaching of the magisterium is incompatible with the authentic *sensus fidei*."[11] No discussion follows concerning that phrase—"as a matter of principle"—on which the whole meaning of the statement would appear to turn.

Theologians are described as helping "the faithful to know with greater clarity and precision the authentic meaning of Scripture, the true significance of conciliar definitions, the proper contents of the Tradition, and also which questions remain open."[12] While there is an allusion in this section to those "areas [where] a revision of previous positions is needed," as a whole the vocation of the theologian appears here, to my mind at least, to have a less robust and dynamic role than most theologians would describe themselves as having, and as Rahner almost certainly would. What does it mean to "resist" the teaching of the magisterium within a faith context when the theologian has not only the right but the duty to do so? Is this the same thing as "resisting as a matter of principle"? Certainly resisting, "as a matter of principle," related corruptions or pathologies present even in the church's official teaching office, which can obfuscate instead of illumine the gospel, is not only allowable, but obligatory for a Catholic theologian.

See as evidence of a different perspective Rahner's much more nuanced position in his essay reacting to 1973's *Mysterium Ecclesiae,* where he makes clear that there are mutually conditioning elements within the

---

7. SFLC, subheading 2a, immediately preceding 74.
8. SFLC, 74.
9. SFLC, subheading 2b, immediately preceding 76.
10. SFLC, 77.
11. SFLC, 80, emphasis mine.
12. SFLC, 84.

church. He rhetorically asks whether the "hierarchy *alone* has the exclusive task of teaching the Gospel authentically," and goes on to answer:

> The Church is governed by a mutually conditioning relationship, as must be the case in a unity consisting of pluralistic elements: the community of faith would not exist at all if it did not have institutional form; in that way the faith of the whole Church is essentially co-conditioned by the specific function of its authentic teachers. *On the other hand*, their function is conceivable only as *one aspect* of the eschatologically indestructible community of faith. It does not supervene from outside, by means of an authorisation which is simply conceived of in juridical terms. A true understanding of the Church's infallibility is possible only if we heed this relationship between the authority of the magisterium and the whole Church's invincible grace of faith, from [and in] which even the office-bearers, with their specific function, live.[13]

He goes on:

> To put it honestly and soberly: the Roman authorities apparently proceed from the assumption that they have to state correct doctrine and issue the correct edicts, appealing to their formal authority; and that when they have done this they have performed their task adequately. They still presuppose as a matter of course that what they have in front of them is an obedient flock.[14]

Rahner is unambiguous regarding his stance that theology is to be of service to the church in both preaching and teaching, and thus possibly in "resisting." The authority of the bishops—for him a real, authentic, and permanent dimension of the Catholic faith—can never, however, replace theological discourse.[15] The magisterium then, as he puts it, "learns and should continue to learn" from the actual faith of the People of God, of whom theologians are of course a part. He emphasizes that in many past times, "in the Church's awareness of the faith, the accent has shifted."[16] Perhaps we are ready for—or already beginning to undergo—such a shift in accent or emphasis during this pontificate, when (at least some) voices within the

---

13. Karl Rahner, *Mysterium Ecclesiae*: on the Declaration of the CDF on the Doctrine of the Church," *TI* 17, 145 (emphasis mine).

14. Ibid.

15. See McCann, "Karl Rahner and the Sensus Fidelium," 329; and Rahner, "Dialogue in the Church," *TI* 10.

16. Karl Rahner, "What the Church Officially Teaches and What the People Actually Believe," *TI* 22:173 [165–75].

hierarchy appear to be less willing to silence or reproach theologians who appear critical of static understandings of some doctrinal articulations or of propositional, proof-text ecclesiologies more suited to the manual theology of the past, than to the incredibly literate and inter-connected world of today. The ITC text does not deny any of this, but could further emphasize such insights.[17]

Popular Religion and the *Sensus Fidelium*

The ITC text is quite positive in its appraisal of what it calls "popular religiosity," citing such sources as CELAM, the catechism, and Scripture itself (Matt 11:25; Luke 10:21; Rom 5:5). It continues to emphasize the need to evangelize popular religion if it tends toward distortions or superstitions, but on the whole when "well-oriented" and appropriately "ecclesial," both popular religious expression and the *sensus fidei*—which the texts describes as "underl[ying] it"—are "great resources for the Church's mission" and "work of the Holy Spirit."[18]

Rahner, too, spoke positively about the role of popular religion in the lives of the faithful. In an article in *Theological Investigations* 22, Rahner argues that popular religion has a more substantial role to play in the life of the church than merely one of subordination to the teachings of the magisterium and the explanations of theology.[19] Rather, an active reception process, as has been recently developed more fully in the work of Ormond Rush, Richard Gaillardetz, and Paul D. Murray, and which can be understood to be present and operative in popular religion, "exerts on theology itself an influence what is to some extent normative and creative."[20] There is a more dialogical reality at play here than a sheer passive acceptance of official church teaching of bishops and theologians by the "simply pious." In point of fact, Rahner argues that in many cases popular religion can be seen to be "superior" to theology—because it is closer to "the first source of genuine religiosity and real faith that consists in God's universal standing invitation to accept divinization."[21]

---

17. The reflections on digital media and their ecclesiological significance by Anthony Godzieba and Vincent Miller could prove helpful here. Cf. Richard Gaillardetz, ed., *When the Magisterium Intervenes: The Magisterium and Theologians in Today's Church* (Collegeville, MN: Liturgical, 2012), especially 140–74.

18. All of these quotations are from SFLC, 112.

19. Karl Rahner, "The Relation between Theology and Popular Religion," *TI* 22:142 [140–47].

20. Ibid., 143.

21. Ibid, 145.

Of course it is important to define what we mean by popular religiosity in a Christian context.[22] To my mind, it describes the interface between the faith-lives and praxis of believers, both in their local church settings and private devotions, always rooted within the wider cultural context in which they live. It can of course include such things as individual and communal prayer, pilgrimages, veneration of relics, saints, Marian apparitions, or inspiring figures (e.g. Dorothy Day, Martin Luther King Jr., Matteo Ricci, the Jesuit martyrs of El Salvador), Eucharistic adoration, and major events like World Youth Day, the World Day of Peace, or the Week of Prayer for Christian Unity. But it also includes wider realities such as artistic and literary expression, charitable work undertaken in a religious context, musical expression, participation in charismatic movements and Christian Life Communities (CLC's), and a wide variety of holistic articulations of a life of faith expressed in a particular place and time. As *Lumen Gentium* §8 and §12 make clear, it is not to be exclusively identified with the Roman Catholic Church, but is rather to be seen as rooted in the vocation of the baptized.

Pope Francis has repeatedly endorsed the Spirit's role in fostering such articulations, saying to a gathering of 50,000 European members of confraternities of faith, many of whom share an emphasis on lay spirituality: "Popular piety is a road which leads to what is essential, if it is lived in the church in profound communion with your pastors.... You have a specific and important mission," he said, "that of keeping alive the relationship between the faith and the cultures of the peoples to whom you belong. You do this through popular piety. You express this faith, born of hearing the word of God, in ways that engage the senses, the emotions and the symbols of the different cultures," he said. "In doing so, you help to transmit it to others, and especially the simple persons whom, in the Gospels, Jesus calls the little ones."[23]

Evangelii Gaudium echoes such themes (cf. §§122–126) and strikes a different tone entirely than the Congregation for Divine Worship's earlier *Directory on Popular Piety and the Liturgy* (2001), which is decidedly more muted and hesitant in its analysis. That earlier document argued that "forms of popular religiosity can sometimes appear to be corrupted by factors that

---

22. Obviously, the sociological reality of collective religious expression exists outside of Christian contexts as well, arising at least as questions in fact "in every human life." However, the document is speaking about the "more specific usage" of the term in reference to "the great variety of manifestations of Christian belief found among the people of God in the Church, or, rather, to refer to 'the Catholic wisdom of the people' that finds expression in such a multitude of ways." SFLC, 108

23. "Pope Celebrates Diversity of Popular Piety, Unity of Church" CNS, 6 May 2013, http://www.catholicnews.com/data/stories/cns/1302012.htm. This and all websites hereafter were accessed October 1, 2015.

are inconsistent with Catholic doctrine. In such cases, they must be patiently and prudently purified through contacts with those responsible and through careful and respectful catechesis—unless radical inconsistencies call for immediate and decisive measures" (§5). This fear of popular piety still finds its way into the ITC text, which is in many ways closer to such a vision than to the pope's.

Walter Kasper has argued that much of Francis's ideas about popular piety are influenced by the Argentinian *teologiá del pueblo*.[24] Although more associated with Juan Carlos Scannone than Rahner, there are obvious points of intersection ecclesiologically. The pope has repeatedly employed an "expression he really likes": the *santo pueblo fiel de Dios*, "the holy faithful people of God."[25] His consistent use of such a phrase, obviously resonant of the *sensus fidelium*, embraces such a theological vision, realizing that in popular piety we find both "missionary power" and "an active evangelising power which we must not underestimate[, for] to do so would be to fail to recognise the work of the Holy Spirit."[26] He cites the Aparecida Document in praising the "people's mysticism," one "incarnated in the culture of the lowly."[27]

Rahner's famous analysis that we were moving into the third great epoch of church history (after a brief Judeo-Christian one and a lengthy Hellenistic/Eurocentric one) calls for a greater attention to the polycentric nature of contemporary Christianity and to the plurality of voices and popular expressions of the faith around the globe, and thus manifests a greater openness to popular piety and *all* the faithful as the title of this volume puts it. The "lowly" and voiceless, long praised with platitudes but in reality excluded from making authentic contributions in terms of leadership and church governance, are coming to be appreciated in more dialogical ecclesial exchanges. Rahner's, Scannone's, and Francis's visions converge at points, as is evident in what the former calls the rise of the *Weltkirche*. Rahner proffers an optimistic image of just such a process of mutual enrichment in a commencement speech he once gave:

> I am envisioning a Catholic theology that is courageous and does not shun relative and restricted conflicts with Church authorities. I am thinking of a theology which can no longer be

24. Walter Kasper, *Pope Francis' Revolution of Tenderness and Love* (Mahwah, NJ: Paulist, 2015) 37–46.

25. Cited from a 2012 radio interview with Juan Isasmendi by Austen Ivereigh, *The Great Reformer: Francis and the Making of a Radical Pope* (London: Allen & Unwin, 2014) 111.

26. SFLC, 112. The relevant section of *EG* is §126.

27. *EG*, 124. Cf. Fifth General Conference of the Latin American and Caribbean Bishops, *Aparecida Document*, 29 June 2007.

uniform in a Neo-scholastic approach . . . I envisage a theology which in the Church at large must be a theology of a worldwide Church. This means a theology which does not recite its own medieval history but, one that can listen to the wisdom of the East, to the longing for freedom in Latin America, and to the sound of African drums. I envisage a systematic theology that is an inner unity and what trinitarian theologians call (literally a dancing around together) perichoresis of fundamental and dogmatic theology. I envisage a theology that enables human beings of our time to have a real grasp on the message of freedom and redemption, a theology that courageously abandons external stanchions of seemingly self-evident truths and things, something which does not stem necessarily from what is Christian, but rather from the changing historical situation structured by its intellectual and social elements. I envisage a theology that does not only move along the numbers in our familiar friend 'Denzinger,' interpreting old ecclesiastical pronouncements, but a theology which breaks new ground for new pronouncements of the Church. . . . [This theology] would not pride itself upon its clear concepts but would force them to open over and over again into the incomprehensibility of God himself. . . . [O]ur time calls also us theologians sleeping under the broom tree of orthodoxy like Elijah in the old days: *Surge, grandis tibi restat via*—Arise, a long journey lies ahead of you."[28]

While the ITC document does recognize the right to exist and positive role of the popular expressions of the faith that are implied by Rahner's 'grand vision,' it perhaps does not emphasize them to the degree he, or for that matter Pope Francis, might, especially in terms of the disenfranchised.

The *Sensus Fidelium* and Statistical Majorities

In my view, §113–126, "The *sensus fidei* and public opinion"—the second of two particular applications given under the heading "How to discern authentic manifestations of the *sensus fidei*"—is the most important passage in the ITC document.

The text makes clear that the church respects democracy, but is not itself structured strictly along such lines. As such, "public opinion cannot, therefore, play in the Church the determinative role that it legitimately plays

---

28. Karl Rahner, "Foreword," in *Theology and Discovery: Essays in Honor of Karl Rahner, SJ*, ed. William Kelly, SJ (Milwaukee: Marquette University Press, 1980) vii.

in the political societies that rely on the principle of popular sovereignty, though it does have a proper role in the Church."[29] As a consequence, "there can be no simple identification between the *sensus fidei* and public or majority opinion. These are by no means the same thing."[30]

Yet there is room for an analysis of differing perspectives within the church, which by their very nature can result in majority and minority positions, at least in terms of raw statistics.[31] The important thing to make clear is that being in the numerical majority does not ensure orthodoxy or a greater grasp of the sense of the faithful. John Henry Newman's study of the Arian crisis repeatedly emphasizes that there very likely were times the orthodox position of Christ's divinity had fewer vocal proponents among the bishops than those at least tacitly endorsing the positions eventually condemned.[32]

As Ormond Rush employs Rahnerian theology to explain: "The object of the *sensus fidei*, therefore, is ultimately the revelatory and salvific event of God's self-communication in history, i.e., revelation itself."[33] Thus, while, as Rahner pointed out, there can be discrepancies between what the church officially teaches and what the average person actually believes (especially one

---

29. SFLC, 114.

30. SFLC, 118. It is interesting to note that both Pope Francis and Pope Benedict XVI encouraged the ITC to reflect upon this distinction in addresses to that body. See Pope Francis' December 6, 2013 address and that of Pope Benedict on December 7, 2012. Both are available at the Pontifical Speeches page under the ITC section of the Vatican website: http://www.vatican.va/roman_curia/congregations/cfaith/cti_documents/rc_cti_index-discorsi-pontif_en.html.

31. Of course, the multifaceted and complex issues at hand necessitate that majority and minority are here understood in a more nuanced way than "for" or "against" a particular point, doctrine, teaching, or prudential application. Yet, pluralities of opinion are always present and need to be studied and reflected upon as such, for the faith can never be understood in a monolithic sense, nor one in which propositions need merely be intellectually affirmed.

32. "[I]n that time of immense confusion the divine dogma of our Lord's divinity was proclaimed, enforced, maintained, and (humanly speaking) preserved, far more by the '*Ecclesia docta*' than by the '*Ecclesia docens*;' that the body of the episcopate was unfaithful to its commission, while the body of the laity was faithful to its baptism; that at one time the Pope, at other times the patriarchal, metropolitan, and other great sees, at other times general councils, said what they should not have said, or did what obscured and compromised revealed truth; while, on the other hand, it was the Christian people who, under Providence, were the ecclesiastical strength of Athanasius, Hilary, Eusebius of Vercellæ, and other great solitary confessors, who would have failed without them." *On Consulting the Faithful in Matters of Doctrine*, 213. http://www.newmanreader.org/works/rambler/consulting.html

33. Ormond Rush, "*Sensus Fidei*. Faith 'Making Sense' of Revelation," *Theological Studies* 62 (2001) 241 [231–62].

not fluent in Denzinger), to those who respond in the depths of their being to God's offer of self-communication, they participate in the Holy Spirit's charism of the "sense of the faith."[34] This happens regardless of whether or not they outnumber others holding contradictory positions, and certainly whether or not they are ordained.

To counterbalance the polarization that takes place when the numerical majority (whether in line with the CDF's position on a particular issue or not) is set over and against a contrary position, we can turn to Rahner's argument for an "open Church."[35] Because of the nature of society today—and even Rahner's pre-internet world was quite different than ours when it comes to social connection and immediacy of information—he calls for an increased role of lay participation in official decision-making and charisms in the church, even in terms of governance.

This finds strong resonance in the ITC text, where the authors trace concrete and practical ways of consulting the laity to gauge the *sensus fidelium*, including particular councils, diocesan synods, and pastoral councils at the diocesan and parish level. While clear that an "insufficiently critical embrace of contemporary culture" can lead to aberrations in the *traditio* and *receptio* processes, the authors readily admit that "in some cases [these problems] indicate that certain decisions have been taken by those in authority without due consideration of the experience and the *sensus fidei* of the faithful, or without sufficient consultation of the faithful by the magisterium"[36] This, while not unprecedented, is a refreshingly honest and potentially fruitful position to articulate in terms of the more dialogical church envisioned by Rahner, and I would argue, by Pope Francis.[37]

As Rush's interpretation of Rahner makes clear, a diversity in expression of the faith is neither purely negative, nor a reality that can ever be denied. "Even given optimum education," he says, "diversity in interpretation will still remain, and indeed cannot be avoided. It is the concreteness and distinctiveness of both a person's *fides qua* and *fides quae* which enables a sense of the faith that is grounded in their Christian experience."[38] This

---

34. Cf *TI* 22:165–75.

35. Karl Rahner, *The Shape of the Church to Come*, trans. Edward Quinn (London: SPCK, 1974) 93ff.

36. SFLC, 123.

37. On similar statements where the magisterium's need to be open to further, ever-clearer articulations of teachings in light of developments in knowledge or as the result of consultation, see *Mysterium Ecclesiae* 5 and Pope John XXIII, "Opening Address to the Second Vatican Council" October 11, 1963. *Acta Apostolicae Sedis* 54 (1962) 792.

38. Rush, "Making Sense," 245.

is applied not only to individuals, but also to the communal wrestling with doctrine and prudential applications thereof. Thus, "minority" expressions and voices have always and will continue to exist in the church, both as a result of the beneficial presence of legitimate pluralism and of the brokenness of the human condition. An asymptotic *metanoia* and life-long process of conversion toward Christ and towards his community enlivened by the Spirit must continue to form and shape one's sense of the faith, whether in the majority or minority on a particular issue. As the ITC text puts it nicely: "Structures of consultation such as those mentioned above can be greatly beneficial to the Church, but only if pastors and lay people are mutually respectful of one another's charisms and if they carefully and continually listen to one another's experiences and concerns. Humble listening at all levels and proper consultation of those concerned are integral aspects of a living and lively Church."[39]

Conclusion: A Dream on Its Way to Fulfillment?

In conclusion, let us return to Rahner's writing directly, and especially a "hopeful dream" he describes having had.[40] Its prescience is noteworthy:

> With a former student of mine I was going up one of the fine staircases in the Vatican. Oddly enough this student had been employed as a theologian in the Vatican itself. This was not something that might have been taken for granted. For my students are more likely to be regarded there with suspicion. But sometimes things turn out well . . .
> 'I am taking you with me' said the student, 'to one of the sessions which are taking place here at the present time, at which about a dozen of the leading representatives of the Christian Churches from all over the world come to meet the Pope for a friendly conversation about the possibility at last of the ecumenical movement going beyond non-committal expressions of friendship by church leaders . . . The churchmen sit at a round table, so that it is not obvious who is above and who is below . . .
> Soon the session started. The people really had come from all parts of the world. You could see it in their faces. The whites were very numerous, but no longer a majority. The actual participants at first stood around talking in a relaxed way, then the Pope also came. Mutual greetings took place without ceremony, as between old friends. An African Protestant clergyman said a

39. SFLC, 125.
40. Karl Rahner, "Dream of the Church," *TI* 20:133–42.

prayer. I did not get the impression that this was a mere ritual, of the kind usual before official church business is transacted. The Pope gave an impression of frankness and cheerfulness, reminding me by his lack of solemn dignity agreeably of John XXIII. He spoke English. What else could he have done?

Notwithstanding Francis's obvious recent efforts to strengthen what is very clearly a tertiary language for him, Rahner's description cannot but bring to mind some of the events unfolding in our day. (Though even *he* didn't have the audacity to predict a candidate from his own religious order.) However, we see more stunning similarities in the content of this chimerical pontiff's address about a re-envisioned Petrine ministry, years before *Ut Unum Sint*'s invitation to think more along these lines.

> Gentlemen, dear brothers! . . . In an *ex cathedra* decision, the Pope acts as head of the Church and of the whole episcopate as an authority that is restricted by the Church as a whole and its infallible faith. Consequently, in preparing *ex cathedra* decisions, the Pope must necessarily have recourse to the sense of the faith of the whole Church, not in the form of a public opinion poll, but by looking at what is truly the Church's sense of the faith. But the Pope does not possess or receive any such revelation. He is the authentic spokesman of the Church's sense of the faith and for this he has the assistance of the Spirit, an assistance which must not be understood as psychological inspiration, but which must mean the success, actually coming in the last resort from God, of his appeal to the infallible sense of faith of the Church as a whole.

How does he determine this *sensus*?

> It is obvious such consultation today would have to take place in certain forms now possible of explicitness, transparency, facilitating dialogue, discussion with theologians, investigation of the believers' sense of the faith, and so on—in a word, in straightforward sincerity and making use of the publicity now taken for granted—even though I must admit that even up to recent times these procedures have not been considered clearly enough or practised in Rome, as is evident from a glance at very recent dogmatic declarations by the Congregation for the Doctrine of the Faith.

Rahner's imagined pope, like our current one (who, to be fair, often cites his predecessors on this point), iterate that the *sensus fidelium* cannot be ascertained merely in opinion polls, for, as Rahner said elsewhere "the Church is more than a theological debating society."[41] Yet, the fictional pontiff's calls for transparency, dialogue, and collaborative input seem to have direct correlations with reality more in recent months than in any time since the council. Unfortunately, these themes are not expressed with concomitant dynamism and commitment to practical co-responsibility to the same degree in the ITC text. *Sensus Fidei in the Life of the Church* is unarguably a theologically sound, carefully written, and worthwhile statement on the history and importance of the *sensus fidelium*. But it remains tentative and guarded when read vis-à-vis Rahner's hope-filled reveries on a future where leadership-in-*diakonia* and previously silenced voices are appreciated across all cultural, geographical, and intra-ecclesial boundaries. For all of its many beneficial contributions, the ITC's trust for the sense of the faith present elsewhere than the hierarchy (and perhaps in some limited ways in the academy) remains tentative and muted. The text's approach to its related expressions in popular piety still in many ways echoes the tone of the CDW's 2001 *Directory*, which expressed worry that all of this discussion of the people's role in decision making and as fully active participants in the community of the church, while authentically admirable and salutary, is a reality also precipitously close to devolving into superstition, theological imprecision, doctrinal error, or potential dissent.[42] Notwithstanding its caution, the work is certainly a praiseworthy step in the right direction, and one that inspires us to continue to dream and hope for the "shape of the church to come."

---

41. Karl Rahner, "Theology and Authority After Council," *TI* 9:95 [83 100].
42. Such a tone is also struck in *Donum Veritatis*, 35–38.

Part 4

Insights on the *Sensus Fidei* for World Christianity

15

Sensus Fidelium, Dissensus Infidelium, Consensus Omnium

An Interreligious Approach to Consensus
in Doctrinal Theology

—————— PETER C. PHAN ——————

EVER SINCE VINCENT OF Lérins (died ca. 445) formulated in his *Commonitorium*, written in 434 under the pseudonym "Peregrinus," his three criteria for orthodoxy, namely, geographical ubiquity, temporal antiquity, and numerical unanimity (*quod ubique, quod semper, quod ab omnibus creditum est*), have played a determinative role in the Catholic understanding of Tradition, and within it, of the *sensus fidei/fidelium*.[1] This role is briefly mentioned by the International Theological Commission (ITC) in its 2014 document titled *Sensus Fidei in the Life of the Church*, which refers to Vincent of Lérins' triple criterion for discerning the *sensus fidei*: "Vincent of Lérins (died c. 445) proposed as a norm the faith that was held everywhere, always, and by everyone (*quod ubique, quod semper, quod ab omnibus creditum est*)."[2]

---

1. The best critical edition of Vincent of Lérins's *Commoniutorium* is by Roland Demeulenaere in *Corpus Christianorum Series Latina* 64 (1985) 127–95. An older edition, with a very informative introduction, is Reginald Stewart Moxon, *The Commonitorium of Vincent of Lérins* (Cambridge: Cambridge University Press, 1915). The English translation of the *Commonitorium* is by C. A. Heurtley in *Nicene and Post-Nicene Fathers. Second Series*, vol. 11, ed. Philip Schaff and Henry Wace (Buffalo, NY: Christian Literature Publishing, 1894). It is revised and edited by Kevin Knight and is available at http://www.newadvent.org/fatherd/3506.htm.

2. International Theological Commission, "*Sensus Fidei* in the Life of the Church," 24, http://www.vatican.va/roman_curia/congregations/cfaith/cti_documents/rc_cti_20140610_sensus-fidei_en.html.

The purpose of this essay is neither to expound the Lérinian's teaching on the three criteria for discerning Christian truth in his *Commonitorium*[3] and the various theses of the ITC's document *Sensus Fidei*, nor to evaluate and compare them as a whole and in detail. Obviously, such a task is impossible within the allotted space, as the issue of the *sensus fidei/fidelium*, as the ITC rightly notes, is intimately connected with a host of complex Christian doctrines such as biblical revelation; the prophetic function of Christ, the church and in particular the laity; doctrinal development; the distinctive roles of the magisteria of bishops and theologians; hermeneutics; ecumenical unity; theological and spiritual qualifications of the subjects of the *sensus fidei*; popular religiosity; public opinion; and so on. Rather I focus on the narrow question of whether Vincent's three criteria of orthodoxy are to be modified and extended to be serviceable at all in the contemporary contexts of Christianity.

While Vincent's three criteria for orthodoxy appear unassailable in the abstract, there have been vigorous debates about their concrete applicability and usefulness. Doubts have been expressed as to whether any Christian doctrine can meet these three criteria fully, and whether it is possible to verify with historical accuracy the extent to which it satisfies them. More to the point of my inquiry, questions may be raised about the geographical extent of the *ubique*, the temporal length of the *semper*, and the people to be counted (and more disturbingly, *not* counted) among the *omnibus*. Obviously Vincent's "everywhere" (*ubique*) did not extend beyond the Mediterranean world and Africa; his "always" (*semper*) did not extend back to the beginning of Christianity by more than five hundred years; and his "all" (*omnibus*) were exclusively Christians, and indeed mainly bishops, and these within a severely circumscribed area. It is highly unlikely that Vincent could envision, from his cell in a secluded monastery on an island in southern Gaul, the world of exuberant, often conflicting, socio-political, cultural, and religious diversity and multiplicity that is ours today.

Given the globalized, and most importantly, multicultural and multireligious character of our contemporary world, and given the emergence of what is referred to as "world Christianity," my essay will explore the necessity of going beyond the theological ambit of the Vincentian canon. Even though Vincent never uses the expression *sensus fidei/fidelium* in his *Commonitorium*, it is beyond doubt that this concept, as will be shown below, is operative throughout the work. In light of world Christianity and in our current multireligious context, my question may be rephrased as follows:

---

3. A helpful recent commentary on the *Commonitorium* is Thomas G. Guarino, *Vincent of Lérins and the Development of Christian Doctrine* (Grand Rapids: Baker Academic, 2013).

What is the context in which the *sensus fidei* is formed today and should the *sensus fidelium* be corrected, complemented, and enriched by the *dissensus infidelium* in order to build up the *consensus omnium*, that is, an interreligious understanding and reformulation of Christian doctrines among believers of diverse religious traditions?

I begin with a brief commentary on the import of the Vincentian canon in the *Commonitorium*. Next I argue that today Vincent's three criteria for orthodoxy—ubiquity, antiquity, and universality—must be expanded to reflect the contemporary context of world Christianity and religious pluralism. Furthermore, I propose that Christian theologians take into account the *dissensus infidelium*, taking *dissensus* to mean not only doctrinal diversity but also difference, and *infidelium* to refer to the adherents of other faiths (the so-called non-Christians). In my view it is no longer possible to do Christian theology by drawing only on the *sensus fidelium*, with *fidelium* restricted to Christians. Rather, Christian theology must be an interreligious discipline; learning from the *dissensus infidelium* must be a constitutive part of the theological method. By radically expanding and redefining the three elements of the Vincentian canon, I hope to show that the *consensus omnium*, inclusive of *sensus fidelium* and *dissensus infidelium*, is a historically conditioned and dynamic reality that finds its root and fulfillment in God's plan of salvation.

The Vincentian Double "Rule" in the Commonitorium

The objective of Vincent of Lérins's work is well stated in its title: "For the Antiquity and Universality of the Catholic Faith Against the Profane Novelties of All Heretics"[4] The Lérinian's aide-memoire (*commonitorium*) is intended as a defense of what he takes to be the two essential characteristics of the true Catholic faith, namely, *antiquitas* and *universalitas*, in contrast to which all heresies are "*profanae novitates*." Little is known about the life of the author of *Commonitorium* except that he was a monk of Lérins, a mon-

---

4. *Pro catholicae fidei antiquitate et universalitate adversus profanas omnium haereticorum novitates*. Vincent's own title might simply be: *Commonitorium Peregrini adversus haereticos* (*haereses*). The work is currently made up of 33 chapters. At the end of chapter 28, however, the editor of the manuscript notes: "The Second Book of the Commonitory is lost. Nothing of it remains but the conclusion: in other words, the recapitulation which follows." Clearly then chapters 29–33, which deal with the council of Ephesus—which took place three years prior to the composition of *Commonitorium*—are part of the Second Book. Vincent argues that the council of Ephesus defends the doctrine of the *Theotokos* against Nestorius precisely on the ground of its ubiquity, antiquity, and universality. Quotations of the text are followed by the number of the chapter and the paragraph given in the English translation, e.g., 2, 4.

astery in southern Gaul, who styled himself *peregrinus* (pilgrim). However, nothing is more certain and obvious about him than his all-consuming love for the truth of the Catholic faith, the obverse of which is his deep-seated obsession—not too strong a word—with heresies and heretics. Hence, his dogged determination to discover "how and by what sure and so to speak universal rule" with which we can "distinguish the truth of Catholic faith from the falsehood of heretical depravity" (2, 4). Vincent finds this rule first and foremost (*primum*) in the Scripture or "Divine Law," which is "complete, and sufficient of itself for everything, and more than sufficient" (2, 5) and next (*deinde*) in the "Tradition of the Catholic Church" (2, 4).

However, as Vincent notes, because Scripture is "capable of as many interpretations as there are interpreters" (2, 5) and because heretics themselves are fond of quoting Scripture in defense of their novel teachings, he deems it necessary to formulate a "rule for the right understanding of the prophets and apostles . . . in accordance with the standard of ecclesiastical and Catholic interpretation" (2, 5). His formulation of this rule (which we will call "First Rule") deserves full quotation:

> In the Catholic Church itself, all possible care must be taken that we hold that faith which has been believed everywhere (*quod ubique*), always (*quod semper*), and by all (*quod ab omnibus*). For that is truly and in the strictest sense "Catholic," which, as the name itself and the reason of the thing declare, comprehends all universally. This rule we shall observe if we follow universality (*universitatem*), antiquity (*antiquitatem*), consent (*consensionem*). We shall follow universality if we confess that one faith to be true which the whole Church throughout the world (*tota per orbem terrarium ecclesia*) confesses; antiquity, if we in no wise depart from those interpretations which it is manifest were notoriously held by our holy ancestors and fathers (*sanctos maiores ac patres*); consent, in like manner, if in antiquity we adhere to the consentient definitions (*definitiones*) and determinations (*sententias*) of all, or at the least of almost (*paene*) all priests (*sacertodum*) and doctors (*magistrorum*) (2, 6).

Later, in chapter 27, Vincent spells out in greater detail the process of distinguishing truth from falsehood in interpreting the Scripture. The basic method is to interpret the Scripture "according to the traditions of the Universal Church and in keeping with the Catholic doctrine" and adhere to universality, antiquity, consent: "And if at any time a part opposes itself to the whole, novelty to antiquity, and the dissent of one or a few who are in error to the consent of all or at all events of the great majority of Catholics," then they must prefer "the soundness of the whole to the part," "the religion of antiquity to the profanes of novelty," and with regard to consent, "to the temerity of one or of a very few they must prefer, first of all, the general decrees, if such there be, of a Universal Council, or if there be no such, then, what is next best, they must follow the consentient belief of many and great masters" (27,70). Among the other *loci theologici* of the Catholic faith, the Lérinian mentions the bishop of Rome, the *apostolica sedes* (6, 15), who acts within the whole college of overseers/bishops (*totum corpus praepositorum*, 22, 27), and all the faithful (*universa ecclesia*, 22, 27).

In insisting on ubiquity, antiquity, and universality as criteria of orthodoxy, Vincent is by no means insensitive to doctrinal development. On the contrary, to the question of whether there has been progress (*profectus*) in the church, he enthusiastically replies: "Certainly; all possible progress" (23, 54). He hastens however to draw a sharp distinction between "profectus" (progress) and "permutation" (alteration): "Yet on condition that it be real progress (*profectus*), not alteration (*permutatio*) of the faith. For progress requires that the subject be enlarged in itself (*res amplificetur*), alteration, that it be transformed into something else (*in aliud transvertatur*). The Lérinian goes on to formulate what might be called his "Second Rule," which deserves to be quoted in full:

> The intelligence, then, the knowledge, the wisdom as well of individuals as of all, as well of one person as of the whole Church, ought, in the course of ages and centuries, to increase and make much and vigorous progress, but yet in its own kind (*in suo genere*), that is to say, in the same doctrine, in the same sense, and in the same meaning (*in eodem dogmate, eodem sensu, eadem sententia*) (23, 54).[5]

To explain this kind of organic development, Vincent uses two analogies: that of a child growing into an adult, and of a seed becoming a fully formed plant. Just as in the child that has become an adult, in spite of all the changes, "his nature is one and the same, his person is one and the same," and just as in the seed that has grown into a plant, in spite of all the changes in shape, form, clarity (*species, forma, distinction*), "the nature of each kind must remain the same," so Christian doctrines can "follow the same laws of progress, so as to be consolidated by years, enlarged by time, refined by age, and yet, withal, to continue uncorrupt and unadulterated, complete and

---

5. This text is quoted by Vatican I in its *Dogmatic Constitution on Catholic Faith*, chapter 4. See Joseph Neuner and Jacques Dupuis, eds., *The Christian Faith in the Doctrinal Documents of the Catholic Church* (New York: Alba House, 1982) 136. John Henry Newman adopts Vincent's rule in developing his own theory of development of doctrine. See T. Guarino, *Vincent of Lérins*, 43–80.

perfect in all the measurement of its parts, and, so to speak, in all its proper members and senses, admitting no change, no waste of its distinctive property, no variation in its limits" (23, 56).

For the Lérinian, in a genuine development of doctrine, there must remain *idem sensus* (the same meaning). To describe this *profectus* he uses words such as: *crescere* (to grow), *proficere* (to advance), *evolvere* (to develop), *florere* (to flower), and *maturescere* (to mature). He never tires of repeating 1 Tim 6:20: "O Timothy, guard the deposit that has been entrusted to you." In this development, what is only permitted is the effort to express the universal and ancient doctrinal consensus (the *ubique, semper, et ab omnibus*) in a new way (*noviter*) and not new things (*nova*). Hence, the slogan: *noviter, non nova*. Therefore there can never be substantive novelty, let alone reversal. That would be *permutatio fidei*, a clear and unmistakable sign of heresy. Vincent's array of terms to characterize this *permutatio* includes: "pervert," "adulterate," "corrupt," "maim," "mutilate," and "innovate." He abhors the "madness of novelty" (8, 13), the "profane novelties," which he calls the "garbage of heretical novelty" (8, 21). Contrary to heretics who itch for and peddle novelties, "the true Church of Christ, the careful and watchful guardian of the doctrine deposited in her charge, never changes anything in them, never diminishes, never adds, does not cut off what is necessary, does not add what is superfluous, does not lose her own, does not appropriate what is another's, but while dealing faithfully and judiciously with ancient doctrine, keeps this one object carefully in view—if there be anything which antiquity has left shapeless and rudimentary, to fashion (*accuret*) and polish (*poliat*) it, if anything already reduced to shape and developed, to consolidate (*consolidet*) and strengthen (*firmet*), if anything already ratified and defined, to guard (*custodiat*) it" (23, 59).

Sensus Fidelium and World Christianities

From the Vincentian double rule of *"ubique, semper et ab omnibus"* and *"in eodem dogmate, eodem sensu, eadem sentential"* it is abundantly clear that for the Lérinian the principal and primary task of the church is to preserve what he calls the *"depositum"*—the faith "once delivered to the saints" (Jude 3) and to guard the *"regula fidei"* (and the plural *"regulae fidei"*) and the *"regula credenda."* As he puts it pithily, the deposit is "a matter brought to you, not put forth by you, wherein you are bound to be not an author but a keeper, not a teacher but a disciple, not a leader but a follower" (22, 53). What Vincent means by *depositum* and *regula fidei* is referred to today as *sensus fidei* or *sensus fidelium*, the former referring to the instinct of faith possessed by "all" and "the whole church," and the latter, that possessed by "individuals" and "one person" (23, 54).[6]

From Vincent's historical context, though we know next to nothing about his personal life, we may safely assume that by *ubique*, even though he does use the expression *orbis terrarum* (the whole world, 2, 6),[7] he has in mind (southern) Gaul, the countries where the councils of Nicea, Ephesus, and Ariminum were held (Asia Minor, Greece, and Italy respectively), and the cities where the various people he mentions lived, chiefly: Rome (Popes Celestine, Felix, Julius, Sixtus, and Stephen), Milan (Ambrose), Alexandria (Origen, Arius, and Cyril), Carthage (Cyprian and Donatus), and Constantinople (Nestorius). For a fifth-century monk who confesses to be dwelling "in the seclusion of a monastery, situated in a remote grange" (1, 2), this geographical list is admittedly impressive. Nevertheless, it is quite negligible when compared to the world in which Christianity existed in his day, especially beyond the Roman Empire, and of course, as it exists today. The *semper*, that is, the ancient world in which the New Testament (leaving aside the Hebrew Bible) was composed, and the centuries in which the two chief doctrines that Vincent expounds, namely, Trinity and Christology, amounts to no more than five hundred years. Finally, the *omnes/omnibus* comprises chiefly ecumenical councils (Nicea and Ephesus), the bishops of Rome, other bishops, theological doctors, and, to a much lesser degree, "all the faithful of all ages, all the saints, the chaste, the continent, the virgins, all the clergy, deacons and priests" (24, 61).

However generous an interpretation is given to the Lérinian's double rule, taking his *ubique* to mean the inhabited world (the *oikoumene*), his *semper* to extend into the foreseeable future after his death, his *omnibus* to include all the Christians of the first five Christian centuries, and his *idem sensus* to connote the essential continuity between the original meaning of a Christian doctrine and all its virtual and enfolding meanings (John Henry Newman's "preservation of type"),[8] it is highly doubtful that Vincent's triple criteria for orthodoxy and his theory of doctrinal development are adequate

---

6. On the distinction between *sensus fidei* and *sensus fidelium*, see the ITC, *Sensus Fidelium*, 4. The "subject" of the former is the church as a whole, whereas that of the latter is the individual believer. Needless to say, the two realities are intrinsically linked with each other to form the *consensus fidelium*.

7. Vincent speaks of "so many islands, provinces, kings, tribes, kingdoms, nations, in a word, almost the whole earth, have been incorporated in Christ the Head, through the Catholic faith" (24, 61). Still this enumeration of places is more for rhetorical effect and does not evince Vincent's real knowledge of them.

8. This is the tack taken by T. Guarino, whose magnanimous and spirited defense of Vincent's double rule as relevant for ecumenical unity is unpersuasive.

for the peculiar contexts of Christianity of today. Of these I will mention only two, namely, the emergence of world Christianity and religious pluralism.

In the last two decades a sizable body of literature, especially in church history and missiology, has highlighted the emergence of what is called "world Christianity," or better still, "world Christianities." To cite just an example: The last two volumes of the massive nine-volume *Cambridge History of Christianity* bear the subtitle *World Christianities*. Briefly, by "world Christianity" is meant Christianity as it currently exists globally, with a polycentric structure, that is, as a "world religion," and not a religious institution with centers of ecclesiastical power located in the West for the past several centuries, including Europe and North America, which was exported to other parts of the world through the missionary enterprise and colonial conquest. Since the twentieth century there has been a massive shift of the Christian population from the global North to the global South. As the church historian Justo L. González summarizes it crisply:

> At the beginning of the twentieth century, half of all Christians in the world lived in Europe. Now that figure is less than a quarter. At the beginning of that century, approximately four out of five Christians were white. At the end of the century, less than two out of five. At the beginning of the century, the great missionary centers of Christianity were New York and London. Today more missionaries are sent from Korea than from London, and Puerto Rico is sending missionaries to New York by the dozen. A hundred years ago, there were less than 10 million Christians in Africa, less than 22 million in Asia, and some 5 million in Oceania; now those numbers have risen to 360 million, 312 million, and 22 million respectively. Meanwhile, growth in the North Atlantic has been much less spectacular (from 460 to 821 million), and in most cases has not kept up with population growth.[9]

This demographic shift requires a radical redrawing of the map of Christianity. A new cartography is needed to reflect this shift of the center of gravity of Christianity, a shift that Vincent of Lérins of the fifth century and, truth to tell, even many of us of the twenty-first century could not even remotely imagine when we hold on to the *ubique* and the *ab omnibus* as criteria of orthodoxy. There have been of course shifts of the centers of Christianity in the past—from Jerusalem to Antioch, to Constantinople, to Western Europe, and to the North Atlantic, and each time the map of

---

9. Justo L. González, *The Changing Shape of Church History* (Saint Louis: Chalice, 2002) 9.

Christianity got bigger. The Lérinian was familiar with the first three shifts, and his triple criteria of orthodoxy might well be serviceable then. But this time the shift is different. While in the previous shifts, one center was largely replaced, politically, economically, and ecclesiastically by the next; by contrast, today, world Christianity is *polycentric*, that is, it has many concurrent centers, so that there are Christianit*ies*, each being a local/regional/national Christianity and none capable of claiming superiority over and normative for the others. In other words, it is not simply a geographically larger Christianity but a qualitatively *different* Christianity.

Another extremely significant factor in world Christianity is the improbable and massive explosion of Evangelicalism/Pentecostalism across the globe in the last 50 years, currently with over 500 million members worldwide. Again, it is not so much a matter of number—though of course it is—as a theologically *different* type of Christianity, which emphasizes elements that are suspect to, if not despised, by mainline Christians, such as belief in biblical inerrancy and apocalypticism, free-ranging styles of worship, unregulated ministries, and practices such as literalist interpretation of the Bible, prophecy, glossolalia, exorcism, miraculous healing, and conservative ethics, especially in sexual matters. The ITC's *Sensus Fidei* is to be applauded for its affirmation that separated Christians do participate in and contribute to the *sensus fidelium* (86). The document states that "the Catholic Church therefore needs to be attentive to what the Spirit may be saying to her by means of believers in the churches and ecclesial communities not fully in communion with her" (56). This is highly commendable, but it may be wondered whether the ITC is fully aware of the extreme complexity if not sheer impossibility in discerning the *sensus fidei* underlying these types of Christianities.

In addition to a new cartography, as Justo González suggests, world Christianity requires a new topography. Maps are flat and do not represent the terrain accurately. Hence, the saying: "The map is not the territory." However, what is badly needed is not the familiar church topography, but a new topography, one that represents the systemic changes brought about by world Christianity. The old topography of church history is basically orography; it focuses on mountains and mountain chains. To shift the metaphor, the old topography of church history gives prominence almost exclusively to ecclesiastical leaders such as popes, bishops, and ecumenical councils. It is the ecclesiastical counterpart of the ancient secular historical genre *De viris illustribus* [note *viris*—males], as practiced by the Father of church history Eusebius of Caesarea in his *Church History*. In this genre, church history is the narrative of the achievements of ecclesiastical elites and intellectual virtuosi; it is the equivalent of the contemporary idol and celebrity television shows. It is from these church elites and virtuosi—popes, bishops, councils, the Roman Curia, academic theologians—that the *sensus fidei* is derived and proclaimed in dogmatic formulas accompanied by anathemas, or encyclicals, or notifications. While such a narrative can be informative and useful, it tends to lead to distortions and misrepresentations, as if these people were the only ones that constitute the church and the magisterium. No doubt Vincent of Lérins operates with an orographic topography that focuses on the mountains and mountain ranges of the church. His *Commonitorium* contains a long list of heroes and villains—the former including popes, bishops, ecumenical councils, and theological doctors among the *omnes* guarding the ancient *depositum fidei*, and the latter being heretics with their "profane novelties," all of them equally elites and virtuosi. As noted above, Vincent does mention "all the faithful of all ages" (24, 61) and highlights the powerful witness to the truth by martyrs "adhering to religious antiquity" (5, 13), but their role in *producing* and discerning the *sensus fidei* remains woefully undervalued.

By contrast, what is needed today in world Christianities is a new topography that highlights the valleys out of which mountains arise, a *koiladology*—to coin a new word—which shows the beliefs and practices of the ordinary Christians. Without them, church leaders could not have achieved the feats celebrated in past church history textbooks. Without their contributions, the *sensus fidei* could not have been produced and transmitted. Without them, in Newman's memorable phrase, the church would look foolish. Consequently, the new *koiladology* will privilege the voices of the poor and the marginalized, including women, the colonized, the dalits, the people of color, the migrants and refugees, the young, and the people of the so-called Third World, where nearly four out of five Christians will live in 2050. The ITC's document deserves high praise for noting that "in the history of the people of God, it has often been not the majority but rather a minority which has truly witnessed to the faith" (118, ii) and that "sometimes the truth of the faith has been conserved not by the efforts of theologians or the teaching of the majority of bishops but in the heart of believers" (119). The million-dollar question is of course where these believers are to be found in world Christianity and how to listen to their hearts.

Among the practices of the common faithful that merit highlighting is popular religion/religiosity. The ITC pays great tribute to popular religiosity since "both as a principle or instinct and as a rich abundance of Christian practice . . . popular religiosity springs from and makes manifest the *sensus fidei*, and is to be respected and fostered" (110). Again, the question is how to discern the *sensus fidei* in popular religion when theologically we continue to speak of the liturgy as *fons and culmen* of Christian life and relegate popular religion to the rank of "devotions"?

Dissensus Infidelium: *Sensus Fidelium* and Other Religions

Another striking feature of world Christianity, which is of course totally foreign to the monk of Lérins, and which is not even mentioned in the ITC's document, is its constant encounter with other religions. Thanks to globalization and migration, our world is becoming increasingly not only multicultural but also multireligious. Religious pluralism is now the air we breathe, so that being religious today is being interreligious. Given this fact of enormous theological significance, how is the *sensus fidelium* formed and preserved in the context of religious pluralism? For the Lérinian, who deals with trinitarian and christological doctrines and heresies in an exclusively Christian context, to ignore other religions is understandable. However, for us, members of world Christianities, who live our Christian faith amidst the followers of other religions, as a tiny minority in many parts of the world, framing the issue of the *sensus fidei* apart from the different, and at times conflicting, perspectives of the other faiths—the *dissensus infidelium*—would be a serious lacuna.

By *dissensus* is meant here simply beliefs and practices that are different from those of Christianity. It is to be remembered that these have not been formulated *over against*, in contradiction to and in dissent from the Christian ones. This is obviously the case with world religions such as Hinduism, Jainism, Buddhism, Confucianism, and Daoism that predate Christianity by several centuries. Some of the beliefs and practices of these religions are different, others similar to (though not identical with) those of Christianity. By *infidelium* is meant not infidels or unbelievers, as these terms are used pejoratively in older apologetical and missiological literature, but simply non-Christian believers or faithful. The *infideles* are simply the counterparts of Christian *fideles*. Contrary to *Dominus Iesus*, I hold that the adherents of other religions than Christianity do not have simply "belief" but faith. I call them *infideles* not because they have no faith but because they have a faith different from that of Christians.

The question then is: Can the *dissensus infidelium*, that is, the *sensus fidei* of non-Christians contribute to the shaping of the *sensus fidelium* of Christians? Were he asked this question, Vincent would definitely answer with a resounding Barthian *Nein*! So would also be, I suspect, the answer of many Christians, especially if they accept the position of *Dominus Iesus*.

The ITC's document, as mentioned earlier, acknowledges the possibility of a positive contribution to the *sensus fidei* from the "separated Christians" of other churches and ecclesial communities, and its argument for its affirmative position is well-taken. It does not however raise the question that is being asked here.

In the light of teaching of the hierarchical magisterium, especially that of Saint John Paul II as well as that of the Asian Bishops' Conferences, and adopting the insights of many theologians of interreligious dialogue and comparative theology, and drawing on the experiences of countless Christians of world Christianity who live among the faithful of other religions, I propose an affirmative answer to this question.

Perhaps one helpful way to support this thesis is to take a cue from the ITC's document *Sensus Fidei*. To the question whether non-Catholic Christians can contribute to the *sensus fidei*, the ITC gives an affirmative answer and explains the reason for it: "The Catholic Church acknowledges that 'many elements of sanctification and truth' are to be found outside her own visible boundaries, that 'certain features of the Christian mystery have at times been more effectively emphasized' in other communities and that the ecumenical dialogue helps her to deepen and clarify her own understanding of the Gospel" (86, ii).

Since the faithful of other religions have faith, we may say that the *dissensus infidelium* can "deepen and clarify" the *sensus fidelium,* since "the Catholic Church rejects nothing of what is true and holy in these religions. It has a high regard for the manner of life and conduct, the precepts and doctrines which, although differing in many ways from its own teaching, nevertheless reflect a ray of that truth which enlightens all men and women . . . . Let Christians, while witnessing to their own faith and way of life, acknowledge, preserve and encourage the spiritual and moral truths found among non-Christians, together with their social life and culture."[10] There is an obvious parallel between what Vatican II affirms about non-Catholic Christianities and what it affirms about non-Christian religions. In both cases there are "elements of truth and grace"; in both cases, there are non-Catholic Christians and non-Christians who live lives of holiness that, to quote John Paul II, put Catholics to shame; in both cases, ecumenical and interreligious dialogues, respectively, help the Catholic Church "deepen and clarify her own understanding of the Gospel." In a word, the *dissensus infidelium* is necessary for the *sensus fidelium,* and vice versa.

The question then is not whether the *dissensus infidelium* can "deepen and clarify" the *sensus fidelium* (and vice versa) but how to bring about this

---

10. *Nostra Aetate,* 2.

process of mutual enrichment. This is a highly complex question, and a host of literature has been produced in recent years on interreligious dialogue and comparative theology to find ways in which Christian Scripture and Tradition can be corrected, complemented, and enriched by non-Christian religions and vice versa. There have been helpful works on what I call "interreligious" trinitarian theology, Christology, pneumatology, ecclesiology, ethics, and spirituality, just to name a few *loci theologici*. Many of these works have been written by members of CTSA, and I can only refer readers to them here.

Vincent of Lérins's triple canon formulated in his celebrated dictum: "That which has been believed everywhere (*ubique*), always (*semper*), and by all (*ab omnibus*)," which is commonly appealed to in conservative circles in defense of orthodox tradition, is given a new and surprising twist in light of world Christianities. Geographical ubiquity, temporal antiquity, and numerical unanimity, which are often attributed to Western tradition as proof of its universality and normativity, are now turned on their heads. For the first time, it may be argued, these three Vincentian criteria of Christian orthodoxy have been met—albeit never perfectly and unambiguously: Only in world Christianities is "everywhere" found, "always" instantiated, and "by all" realized. In world Christianities, Western tradition of the past as well as the present is not given a privileged, much less normative, status. Western Christianity is not related to world Christianities as center to periphery with all the privileges attendant to the center; rather it is only one Christianity among other Christianities, no more and no less, and its traditions, often maintained through power and imposed by force, legal and otherwise, must be seen for what they really are: local, context-dependent, and culture-bound historical particularities. In world Christianity, the *sensus fidelium* and the *dissensus infidelium* work hand-in-hand, in mutual learning and teaching, with the hope that there may emerge one day the *consensus omnium*.

16

A Mosaic of Identities of the *Sensus Fidelium*

The Realities of African Ecclesial Communities in Diaspora

— SimonMary A. Aihiokhai —

Introduction

THIS PAPER INVITES US to journey with African Catholic immigrants here in the United States who quietly contribute to the rich tapestry of gifts that make up the community of believers. Their presence invites as well as challenges us to take seriously our vocation as providers of hospitality to strangers. They help us to expand our understanding of what it means to be a community of believers. Using the words of Michele Hershberger, "Community is an essential part of our faith . . . the church is called to live as a gathered community of persons who celebrate together, support each other, seek accountability together, listen to and challenge each other, forgive and heal each other. . . . When people look at the church, the thing that usually matters to them first is not our doctrines or our worship, but rather how we live together."[1] These words best summarize what Jesus commands in what history has recorded as the *mandatum novum* and celebrated at the most solemn period of the Christian calendar, the *Holy Triduum*.

Christian hospitality goes beyond *ad extra*; it has an innate component to it—*ad intra*—for to love those outside of our fold, we must first draw from the gifts and talents of those who constitute our members. When we

---

1. Michele Hershberger, *A Christian View of Hospitality. Expecting Surprises* (Scottdale, PA: Herald, 1999) 186.

are attuned to the promptings of the Spirit we become fully aware of not just our strengths but also our weaknesses. We become alert to how we constitute ourselves; those we favor, those we disfavor, those we are glad to see and those whose presence cause us discomfort.

Methodologically, I will proceed by first telling my story to demonstrate a sense of membership within the *sensus fidelium* of the local church here in the United States. I will then attempt to tell the story of the many brothers and sisters of our churches who embody not just the narratives of immigrants but in a beautiful way, the catholicity and *koinonia* that bonds the sister churches not only in the heads of the churches but in the members. I know that to tell a story is to do harm to the rich experiences of the ones whose stories are told. I will therefore tell the stories with a sense of great humility and gratitude. Finally, I will reflect on the narratives and argue for a fuller sense of being church today in the context of broad pluralism.

My Hermeneutic and Theological Locus

The curia document *Sensus Fidei in the Life of the Church* speaks of the twofold relationship that exists between the theologian and the sensus *fidelium*. The theologian's vocation as one who voices the received truths of the faith is given legitimacy by the lived expressions of the faith in the lives of the faithful as well as being a source of guidance for the faithful to understand the truths of faith taught primarily by the magisterium.[2] It is important also to include a third element in that relationship that focuses on the theologian as part of the *sensus fidelium* and not outside of it. Recognizing the location of the theologian calls for the following: one ought not forget how, where, and what mediates the content of one's work and how one brings their particularities to that mediation. In other words, the theologian is called to be aware always of the factors shaping one's perspectival location. Borrowing the perspective of Ann E. McManus Holroyd, the theologian's "own foreprojections are born from [one's] history, culture, language and sociopolitical experiences, and constitute the familiar horizons of [one's] lifeworld."[3] This said; it is important I state the following so you may fully discern my own theological perspective along with its strengths and weaknesses.

---

2. International Theological Commission, *Sensus Fidei in The Life Of The Church* (2014), 80–81, http://www.vatican.va/roman_curia/congregations/cfaith/cti_documents/rc_cti_20140610_sensus-fidei_en.html#3._The_sensus_fidei_and_theology.

3. "Interpretive Hermeneutic Phenomenology: Clarifying Understanding," *Indo-Pacific Journal of Phenomenology* 7:2 (2007) 4, http://www.tandfonline.com/doi/pdf/10.1080/20797222.2007.11433946. Words in parentheses are mine.

I am an African theologian living and working in a North American church that is currently grappling with the realities of cultural pluralism as the faces, names, and languages of its members are fast becoming diverse. I am a Roman Catholic whose religiosity is shaped by African Religions, Islam, and of course Christianity. I reside in the margins not out of leisure but as an existential marker culturally and religiously. I am a member of a tribe in Nigeria that has a total population of less than three thousand in a country with more than 170 million.[4] I am a black man living in the United States who has to juggle the burdens and prides of what blackness means historically in this country and in a church that has not always reflected the perfection of the Christian message in its body and leadership. It is in these loci of being that I have come to encounter God, the world, my fellow humans, and myself. I am an immigrant myself. The stories you are about to hear are not those only of others. In them, my voice is always heard. They are our stories. They are the stories of our church, of our collective humanity. In the beautiful theological piece written by Christine D. Pohl, the story of the church is one of marginality and hospitality. It is a church with an "alien status."[5] It is a church called to be at the margins and from its marginality share with the world divine hospitality experienced in and through Jesus Christ.

The Archdiocese of Los Angeles

"A church that does not acknowledge the different gifts of its members will not be relevant in the third millennium. Neither will such a church be a viable vessel for the Spirit of the Lord to renew the face of the earth." Words of wisdom from Roger Cardinal Mahoney during a dinner meeting I had with him in 2002 as a first-year seminarian of the Archdiocese of Los Angeles. When one looks at the statistics of the global Roman Catholic Church today, one is struck not only by the shift of centers of population but also by the rainbow of cultural expressions present in the local churches. In the Archdiocese of Los Angeles, masses are celebrated on Sundays in forty-two languages.[6] In a country where the popular expectation is for citizens to speak the English language, the realities of migration and pluralism have

---

4. This is the 2014 information on Nigeria from The World Bank, "Nigeria," http://data.worldbank.org/country/nigeria.

5. Christine D. Pohl, *Making Room: Recovering Hospitality as a Christian Tradition* (Grand Rapids: Eerdmans, 1999) 105.

6. See Roger Cardinal Mahoney, "Welcome to Your Cathedral," *Cathedral of Our Lady of the Angels*, http://www.olacathedral.org/.

necessitated the demand that all seminarians studying for the priesthood in the archdiocese learn a pastoral language to better minister to the different members of the body Christ present in the local church.

As the church in the United States began to experience its own purgation due to scandalous sex abuses of minors and cover-ups, the Archdiocese of Los Angeles began its ninth synod. The synod was convoked in 2000. I was fortunate to be part of the synodal process and can attest to the gifts of the Spirit fully manifested in the members of the local church. The representatives of the local church that participated in the synod came from all works of life. Fifty-seven percent of the participants were members of the laity. The other percentage comprised the ordained and religious. The synod was carried out in many languages representing the major languages of the members of the local church. Even with all these differences and particularities, everyone felt a sense of unity and it came from the collective desire to nurture to maturity a church that all its members can be proud of, not because it suits what they egoistically want but what they understand to be the vision of the Spirit of the Lord for the people of the archdiocese and to the world whom they minister to collectively and individually.

The synod representatives engaged in three years of collaborative dialogue which began at the parish level. In each parish community, leaders were formed to help facilitate the conversations among the parishioners on what type of church they want to see and be part of. In some parishes, the pastors facilitated this conversation. Some parishes were creative enough in their theological understanding of *koinonia* of the community of believers and chose to reflect together as neithborhood sister parishes. The conversations and deliberations continued at the regional levels, where the issues raised in the parishes within the respective regions were discussed with the aim of reaching a consensus as well as prioritization of the issues. The final stages of discussions were on the archdiocesan level. Representatives were chosen, appointed, and voted to be members of the respective levels of dialogue to ensure that the breadth of concerns and gifts of the church were acknowledged. The people of God came up with six initiatives that continue to guide the pastoral initiatives of the hierarchy in the local church. What is fundamental and peculiar about this synod is that it was truly a synod of the entire church, not as sometimes understood by the Roman Church, where the people of God is often understood as represented by the ordained and major superiors of the older institutes of consecrated life. If the church is truly a community of the baptized who embrace fully their baptismal commitments, it is important that the church fully represents in its governance the breadth of our baptismal membership. Without denying the role of those with ministerial ordination, the role of the royal priesthood ought always to be emphasized not reflecting a spiritual idealism but grounded in the concrete life of the church. What is wrong with having members of the laity as participating members in a general council and synods with deliberative powers as do the hierarchy?

Let me return to the context of the church of Los Angeles. The synod revealed some paradoxes. Fifty-six percent of the synod participants were of European descent; an ethnic group that does not fully represent the majority of the people of God in the local church but that still has the financial power. In a church that is fast becoming Hispanic, the delegates that were of Hispanic heritage were 29 percent. What does this say? Should church governance be conditioned by the length of the pockets of the members or by the gifts of its members? Should church governance be conditioned by a nostalgic affection for the past when it was dominated by one culture and ethnic group or by a tapestry of the peoples and cultures?

A missed opportunity was not to create an avenue for the synod participants to participate in cultural settings with which they were comfortable. While some parishes took the initiative of organizing the discussions in the respective languages of their members, there was no consideration for cultural location to the best of my knowledge. As those conversant with the dynamics of mediating meaning know, language derives its status of conveying meaning not solely in itself but through the complex nuances that culture mediates as well. In my own experience as an immigrant to the United States from a country whose official language is English, it was only after spending many years in this country that I began to understand the unspoken meaning that language embodies even in the very spoken words. Simply stated, cultural context is relevant to proper communication even when using a common language. No attempt was made by the organizers of the synod to address the cultural location of the participants. For example, all blacks whether African Americans, African Europeans, African Caribbean, or Africans were all categorized together and expected to speak to the realities and experiences of being Catholic in the archdiocese. Those of us who have not shared the experiences of one another found ourselves lost and unable to articulate any relevant response to the synodal discussions. It began to dawn on me that the synod lacked knowledge of the rich and diverse experiences that define blackness. As the meetings progressed, issues brought up by others where simply not issues some of us could address. Let me use a clear example to demonstrate my point. In an archdiocese that has existed for more than 200 years, only a handful of priests are blacks. Of these, only one, to the best of my knowledge is African American. This lack of ministry to this group of Catholics in the archdiocese was not articulated in the synodal discussions. Perhaps one will argue, as was argued when I raised it during my years as a seminarian for the archdiocese, that African Americans tend to be Baptists or members of freestanding churches. Something is definitely wrong with that picture. The reception of blacks in the Catholic Church in America is not something we Catholics can be proud of. It does more injustice to both them and other cultural groups of African descent and those of non-African descent when we fail to take time to understand the particularities of our neighbors. Hospitality is not simply about providing shelter for the homeless, it is also about embracing the homelessness of the homeless and journeying together to find a new home and undoing the shackles of oppression that makes one homeless. Let me quickly touch on some markers that have defined and continue to shape the continent and people living in Africa as well as show what narratives the African ecclesial communities in the United States embody.

Markers of African Communities—Sacred and Profane

"What is Africa?" This is the title of an essay written by Dr. Daniel Tetteh Osabu-Kle of Carleton University, Canada.[7] In it he calls attention to the complexities that shape what the West has called Africa. The coloration of the skin has come to be understood by many to speak to the identity markers of who is African, of African descent, and so forth. I invite us to reflect briefly on a very beautiful work written by one of Africa's beautiful minds, which many may have read and which I find very compelling due to its poetic innocence. It also offers a powerful insight in capturing the existential dislocation of meaning in the agenda of the British colonial power during its imperial and colonial occupation of Africa. It is the work written by Ngugi wa Thiong'o titled *Weep Not Child*.[8] What a simple title and yet saturated with a surplus of meaning. The novel addresses the tensions existing between colonial British officers and the Kenyan people. It focuses on the crisis resulting from the displacement of the Kenyans from their lands by the British colonial agents. Underneath the beautiful prose form that draws its readership into a literary marriage with the characters are rivers of hermeneutic significance. Let me briefly explore one of them that is especially relevant to the theme for this paper. It has to do with identity. The child that weeps in Ngugi wa Thiong'o's novel is Africa and her children. They weep not because of the presence of the guests, the European powers, colonialists, missionaries, or adventurers. No! They weep because

---

7. Daniel Tetteh Osabu-Kle and Daniel Tetteh, "What Is Africa?" http://carleton.ca/africanstudies/wp-content/uploads/What-is-Afrrica.pdf.

8. Ngugi Wa Thiong'o, *Weep Not Child* (Harlow, UK: Heinemann, 1964).

they have lost the sense of who they are as a people. This theme resonates very well also with the work of another of Africa's child, Chinua Achebe of Nigeria in the novel *Things Fall Apart*.[9] Achebe pointedly voices what plagues Africa in light of the colonial agenda of Victorian Britain: What we have always held on to as the symbol of our identities has been taken away from us. We are no longer a people. We have become pilgrims scattered all over the land in a land that no longer calls us children. The mother earth has rejected us because we have failed to reciprocate the maternal affection that exists between a mother and a child.

To understand African identity, one must understand what land means to Africans. I say Africans not in relation to a twenty-year-old kid born in metropolitan Lagos, Nigeria or Cape Town, South Africa. I speak of an African in relation to their ancestors who live in and through their collective memories, silently guiding them to maintain a balance between the sacred and the profane. Postcolonial Africa seems to have lost this virtue. It has become a continent plagued by unfathomable greed and corruption. It has become a land that constantly flows with rivers of innocent blood of its people sacrificed to the senseless wars perpetuated by forces internal and external.

Africa today is faced by many social ills; some directly linked to its colonial past, others caused by absence of healthy narratives as a result of a systematic destruction of the mindset of the people. This is what colonialism does to a people; it affects a violent break with the past and forces them to embrace a new identity that is alien and manipulative. For many in postcolonial Africa, what is authentic must essentially be from the "whiteman."[10] This is what Ayi Kwei Amah, a Ghanaian novelist, wrote about in the nicely written novel, *The Beautiful Ones Are Not Yet Born*.[11] The story speaks of postcolonial Ghana. Yes! Ghana is free. Yes! Kwame Nkrumah is now the Prime Minister of the Great and Free Ghana. Yes! Ghana is calling for Pan-Africanism. But wait! Lest you forget, what image, vision, narrative is shaping the new and free Ghana? Amah reminds us that it is the colonizing vision. Now, what is worse is that it is the vision perpetuated not by the "whiteman" but by fellow Africans, who simply drove the "whiteman" out and occupied the colonial bungalows.

Tribalism, a conscious tool used by colonial agents to divide and conquer Africa in order to colonize it, has become the scourge of Africa today.

9. Chinua Achebe, *Things Fall Apart* (New York: Anchor, 1994).

10. This is a term in Pidgin English that refers to anything coming from those of the European context.

11. Ayi Kwei Armah, *The Beautiful Ones Are Not Yet Born* (Harlow, UK: Heinemann, 1989).

The church is not free from this cancer. In fact, the church has perpetuating this even in its ranks of the ordained. Candidates for the priesthood or bishopric are now being chosen on the grounds of tribal affiliations in some of Africa's local churches.

The African Church reflects the strengths and weaknesses that categorize the colonial realities of Africa. It is a church that has come to see itself essentially in light of the polarities tied to language. Each national church operates within the boundaries of the linguistic connections with the colonial powers it has with Europe. The African Church has been accused and sometimes rightly so to be a very docile church that always acquiesces to the directives from the Roman Curia at the expense of doing grave injustice to its indigenous insights. It has most often become a church that has resisted any call to engage the mother religions of Africa. It continues to sing the language of and use the appellations of the colonial churches and agents to describe the faith of ancestral Africa, paganism, fetishism, animism, and so forth.

On the flip side, many of the local churches are becoming churches that embrace a sense of African religiosity. They look at the churches in the colonizing West and are shocked at the disarray that seems to have held them captive; a persistent and somewhat frightening reality of lack of vocations in the missionary churches of the West. They are reluctant to embrace wholeheartedly the reforms being advocated by the West for fear of suffering the same fate.

On a positive note, present-day Africans want to be free not only from the vestiges of colonialism but also from the failed leadership of its own leaders. Africans want functioning democracies where the rule of law is the mark of their societies. The recent elections in Nigeria clearly represent this aspiration. For the first time in the country's history as an independent nation since 1960, a democratically elected government was voted out of office and accepted the will of the people without annulling or manipulating the election.

North American Vision of African Catholic Migrant Communities

For many of the sister churches in the United States, African Catholic immigrant communities represent a vibrant church with its members wearing beautifully colored dresses and headgears. They joyfully sing and dance to songs and rhythms foreign to western musical heritage. They dance with their entire bodies, beating drums and instruments that produce sacred melodies that point to the diversity of sacred music previously unknown to an American audience. The Eucharistic liturgies go on in *kairos* time that defies western appreciation of brevity.

On a very positive note, African immigrants are slowly but consistently becoming active voices in the hosting sister churches. They are studying for the priesthood, entering religious life, becoming lay theologians like my humble self. Others are active leaders in their parish communities and helping to build the church in this part of the world.

Many, if not all, the dioceses in the United States have African priests and religious as part of their communities. These priests bring the gifts and challenges from their mother churches in Africa to their hosting communities. Something also has to be said about African priestly and religious vocations within the seminaries and formation houses here in the United States. I can attest to this fact. During my years in the seminary studying for the Archdiocese of Los Angeles, we had nine seminarians from African churches studying for different dioceses here in the United States. Something is striking, though, which ought to be addressed. While the numbers of African vocations are on the rise here in the United States, there seem to be no increase among African American communities. Why is this the case? Is it that our churches are more interested in seeking foreign vocations from Africa and less interested in homegrown vocations from our minority communities, or are there other factors shaping this?

It is also important to note that in the Archdiocese of Los Angeles, vocations coming from the African communities are vocations nurtured and sustained within the communities themselves and not by the wider archdiocesan community. This calls for a reengagement with the African communities by the larger local churches here in America. By doing so, they can consider ways of broadening the nurturing of these vocations because these men and women will minister in a church larger than their respective cultural communities.

Some parishes here in North America have also begun the practice of adopting sister parishes in Africa. For instance, the Archdiocese of Los Angeles has entered into a sororal partnership with some dioceses in Africa to help train their candidates for the priesthood. These are fruits worth celebrating and giving thanks to the Spirit that calls all believers to a union of friendship in Christ.

On the flip side, while the presence of African immigrants in our local parishes is cherished, their presence has not always been seen as a positive one. Tensions continue to arise as a result of cultural differences. As one of the participants at the recently concluded conference of the Catholic Theological Society of America opined, "These Africans are viewed as taking over our churches. They want their celebrations to go on forever, and it affects the other activities of the community."[12] Perhaps there needs to be a visible effort to work towards mutual cultural understanding between the hosting western cultures and the African immigrants. The United States Conference of Catholic Bishops has begun this effort through its ethnic diversity department, but it needs to go beyond just the ordained and the religious. The laity also needs to be helped to integrate fully into the hosting cultures. While the guest brings to the host the joyful message of the resurrection, the host embodies Christ's hospitality. Both the host and guest must see each other as partners in the Lord and together build a community where love and friendship in the Lord is at its best.

Conclusion

The unity of the church as *koinonia* is and ought to always be validated not only by faithful adherence to ethical promulgations coming from the Roman Curia but by the continuous engagement with the members within each local church and among the sister churches. In other words, each Christian embodies in his or her being through the sacraments of initiation the ability and mandate to make concrete this unity of the church as people of God. *Koinonia* thus entails the fruition of charity in friendship in the members. The church of God, must, in my reading of *Lumen Gentium*, be a church that is incarnated in its members. The church cannot simply be an abstract reality that we all talk about without any point of reference. To speak of the church is to speak of the lives of the baptized Christians. If this is the case, then, we ought to ask ourselves as members of sister churches who today are characterized by the realities of migration; what form of hospitality are we showing to the migrant members of our churches? How much are we aware of their gifts, burdens, joys, and pains? These are questions that today demand urgent responses as we experience globally a shift in societal makeup. Migration has become the marker of defining our age. It means that both our ecclesial focus and identity must explore and reflect the beauty of diversity as well as be able to engage the challenges that come along.

Finally, the call of Pope Francis to Christians globally to embrace the evangelizing mission of the church ought not to be understood solely in the context of making Christ known to non-Christians. It involves also the call to the local churches to embody in the totality of their being a trinitarian hospitality to which all Christians are drawn by virtue of their baptism.

12. This comment was made during the questions-and-answers section after I presented the initial draft of this paper.

This is the discernment that the local church is called to undertake today.[13] Each local church is called to constantly read the signs of the times and see within the chaos of history the path the Spirit is leading the church to follow in the twenty-first century. It is definitely one that involves openness to alterity in all its manifestations. Our churches cannot be preoccupied with issues related to sexuality alone. Yes, these issues are important. However, the local churches cannot forget about the poor, the hungry, the refugees, the marginalized, the oppressed, and the voiceless. These are issues our diaconal vocation must address as well with all forcefulness and urgency. This said; the church of today ought to always be a community of believers where all are welcome, irrespective of their race, ethnicity, culture, language, or gender orientation. To be Christ to the world, the church must be Christ to itself in word and action.

---

13. Pope Francis, *Apostolic Exhortation, Evangelii Gaudium* (November 24, 2013), 30, http://w2.vatican.va/content/francesco/en/apost_exhortations/documents/papa-francesco_esortazione-ap_20131124_evangelii-gaudium.html#II.%E2%80%82Pastoral_activity_and_conversion.

17

The Institute for Black Catholic Studies

Culture, the Sensus Fidelium, and Practical Theological Agency

M. Shawn Copeland

> *I've got a home in a-that Rock.*
> *Don't you see? Don't you See?*
> *Between the earth and sky,*
> *thought I heard my Savior cry,*
> *I've got a home in a-that Rock.*
> *Don't you See?*
>
> —AFRICAN AMERICAN SPIRITUAL

THIS ESSAY SEEKS TO bring to wider attention the work of the Institute for Black Catholic Studies (IBCS) of Xavier University of Louisiana, New Orleans. In particular, it highlights the institute's support of the exercise of the *sensus fidelium* among the black Catholic faithful with regard to their experience of the relation of culture and faith. The work of the institute has resulted in critical appropriation of African American cultural aesthetics and in careful formation of practical theological agency. Through its various degree and continuing education programs, the institute has increased the capacity of black Catholics and those who minister with and among them to respond holistically to pastoral needs in the black community and make a gift of their ministry to the church universal. To this end, the institute takes as its own the challenge Paul VI laid at the feet of African intellectuals:

African Americans, black Catholics, the church universal need "your study, your research, your art, your teaching. [Y]our specific task is to ensure the vitality of the values of the human mind and spirit."[1]

The Institute's Educational Mission and Geographic Setting

The Institute for Black Catholic Studies is the first and primary laboratory for research, study, and practical theological analysis and reflection on African American Catholic experience. The curricula of its constituent programs (graduate studies in pastoral theology and continuing education in youth ministry, catechist formation, leadership in the faith community) are developed from "an interdisciplinary and participative vantage point, shaped around solid theological core courses, and focused on critical reflection regarding pastoral work."[2] Since its inception in 1980, the institute has dedicated itself to the formation and nurturance of a black Catholic religious *praxis*, i.e., conscious affective, moral, aesthetic, and cognitive responsiveness to Divine Mystery expressed through sensibilities, styles, and *practices* rooted in an African-derived heritage recognized and understood as diverse and plural. Moreover, this praxis aims for critical and practical theological engagement with the black lifeworld. To accomplish this, the Institute appropriates and transmits Roman Catholic doctrinal and theological traditions and engages its faculty and students in serious historical, theological, cultural, sociological research, teaching, study, and action for critical cultural interventions in local parishes. The comprehensive theological orientation of the institute provides "a black articulation of Catholic faith and a Christian interpretation of black experience."[3]

New Orleans provides more than an incidental geographic setting for the institute. New Orleans has been, at once, a site of and witness to profound spiritual, cultural, historical, and aesthetic agony and power. The city is home to the only black and Catholic university in the Western Hemisphere, Xavier University of Louisiana, which traces its foundation in 1915 to the work of St. Katharine Drexel and the Sisters of the Blessed Sacrament.

---

1. Paul VI, *Africae Terrarum* (10. 29. 1967).

2. Institute for Black Catholic Studies, Xavier University of Louisiana, New Orleans, Louisiana, "Educational Philosophy," 8, http://www.xula.edu/ibcs/index.php.

3. Joseph Nearon, "Introduction," in Thaddeus J. Posey, ed., *Theology: A Portrait in Black, Proceedings of the 1978 Black Catholic Theological Symposium* (Pittsburgh: Capuchin, 1980) 5.

In the nineteenth century, as the leading city of the lower South, New Orleans rivaled New York, Philadelphia, Baltimore, and Charleston in commercial activity and prosperity; but, in large measure, its success rested on trade in black bodies. The first ship carrying captured Africans for sale arrived in Louisiana in 1719, and "over the next dozen years roughly 6,000 bound men, women, and children entered the colony through the slave trade."[4] Nearly a century later, New Orleans hosted the largest slave market in the United States.

Historian Gwendolyn Midlo Hall contends that like other colonial cities in the Americas, New Orleans was the site of vivid, "intense and often violent contacts among people of varied nations, races, classes, languages, and traditions." But in New Orleans, she concludes, "the African imprint was formidable."[5] Indeed, traces of Bakongo, Mandé, and Yoruba cultures reverberate throughout the city: in Congo Square, where enslaved Africans drummed and danced well into the nineteenth century; in the Tremé district, where St. Augustine's Catholic Church holds the tomb of the Unknown Slave; in the French Quarter's Royal Orleans Hotel and Café Maspero where slave traders and slave holders conducted the sale and purchase of black human flesh; in the "cities of the dead," the eighteenth- and nineteenth-century cemeteries St. Louis I and II, where Mandé blacksmiths and their descendants left coded symbols wrought in iron on grave vaults; in the dance movements of second-line parades; in the spices and peppers, greens and roux that flavor the cuisine; in the polyphony and polyrhythm, dissonances and synchronicities, grotesque and beauty of daily life.

These distinctive and identifiable cultural signifiers along with practices of masking and music, drumming and dance, storytelling and speech, vivid vesture and vivacious gesture coalesce as a fertile, variegated, and dense religious-aesthetic-cultural ground. In African American cultural consciousness, New Orleans radiates power and liminality: Here the dead and the living vie for space; here spirit and flesh bare themselves, couple and uncouple, heal and astonish; here love supreme subverts culture and race to sculpt new identities and possibilities; here blues fugues a transcendental aesthetic that welds mourning and joy. In the tensive contact of history, culture, and memory, New Orleans forms a *lieu de mémoire*, that is, a

---

4. Emily Clark and Virginia Meacham Gould, "The Feminine Face of Afro-Catholicism in New Orleans, 1727–1852," par 9, *The William and Mary Quarterly* (April 2002) http://www.historycooperative.org/cgi-bin/justtop.cgi?act=justtop&url=http://www.historycooperative.org/journals/wm/59.2/clark.html.

5. Gwendolyn Midlo Hall, "The Formation of Afro-Creole Culture," in Arnold R. Hirsch and Joseph Logsdon, eds., *Creole New Orleans: Race and Americanization* (Baton Rouge: Louisiana State University Press, 1992) 58.

"material, symbolic, and functional"[6] site of historical consciousness, iconic religiosity, and sensuous imagination. New Orleans offers a unique space for in-depth engagement with and development of critical cultural consciousness and competency for ministry and for creative theological research and reflection.

Critical Cultural Consciousness and Competency in Ministry

In addition to the unique site and witness New Orleans affords, from its outset two events stimulated the institute's commitment to the histories, cultures, and memories of the black lifeworld. The first is the scholarly and popular interest accorded to black cultures during the intellectually creative, artistically productive, and politically volatile decades of the 1960s and 1970s. Although the Institute's engagement ought not to be understood as a mere "by-product" of the climate of that period,[7] its keen and serious interest may be located properly within the horizon of the black radical tradition. The institute's commitment to appropriate black culture aligns comprehensively with the drive for freedom animating black life since that fateful encounter with European man and his dynamics of domination.[8]

Certainly, chattel slavery problematizes black collective cultural memory. The violent tearing away and suppression of embodied gestures, behaviors, languages, styles, dispositions, rhythms, taboos, and norms from natal matrices unmoors their expressions from their original meanings and values, and leaves them fragmented and scattered throughout the Americas. Centuries of bondage, physical and sexual abuse, lynching, segregation, and discrimination have not eradicated completely cultural memories within black communities. Anthony Pinn contends such events have left those

---

6. Pierre Nora, "Between Memory and History: Les Lieux de Mémoire," 295, in *History and Memory in African-American Culture*, eds., Geneviève Fabre and Robert O'Meally (New York and Oxford: Oxford University Press, 1994).

7. Richard J. Powell, "Art History and Black Memory: Toward a 'Blues Aesthetic,'" 182, in *The Jazz Cadence of American Culture*, ed., Robert G. O'Meally (New York: Columbia University Press, 1998).

8. See Fred Moten, *In the Break: The Aesthetics of the Black Radical Tradition* (Minneapolis and London: University of Minnesota Press, 2003), Edouard Glissant, *Caribbean Discourse: Selected Essays*, trans., J. Michael Dash (Charlottesville: Caraf/University Press of Virginia, 1989), Sylvia Wynter, "Unsettling the Coloniality of Being/Power/Truth/Freedom: Towards the Human, After Man, Its overrepresentation—An Argument," *The New Centennial Review* 3.5 (2003) 257–337.

memories "fragile and cultural artifacts decontextualized."[9] Detached from their contexts, these memories and cultural artifacts have been disfigured and distorted by the dominant culture.[10] Artifacts of African American culture have been made to vanish, rendered invisible, considered as belonging to no one. Even African Americans sometimes wonder if African Americans have a culture. Still, "fragile memory," Pinn remarks, is [not] worthless; rather simply fragile."[11]

The *second event* animating the institute's commitment to culture is the Second Vatican Council. Prior to the council, black Catholics experienced themselves as living in two distinctive and separate worlds. The prevailing culture mediated by Roman Catholic worship and practice was considered normative and universal, aloof from and resistant to change. Culture meant "acquiring and assimilating the tastes and skills, the ideals, virtues and ideas" of what, in fact, were the values, prudence, and wisdom of Western European culture. To this culture black Catholics—all Catholics—were taught to aspire and imitate since that culture conveyed "stability, immutability, [and] fixity."[12] Conceived along these lines, Western European culture rightly could be named classicist. The sights and sounds, tastes and smells, textures and shapes of this culture mediated the Catholic imaginary and, reflexively, presented that particular culture as identical with the Gospel. Certainly, Western European culture stands as a powerful instance of cumulative human development, but in a classicist manifestation it failed to grasp the basic and radical openness of the human spirit in its capacity for attentive, intelligent, reasonable, and responsible adaptations to various, different, differing, and differentiated human experiences and situations.[13]

For black Catholics, the significance of the conjunction of black cultural and social movements in the 1960s and 1970s and the convening of the Second Council cannot be overstated. Black Catholics yearned to belong in their church, to come to worship, as Sister Thea Bowman once proclaimed, "fully functioning," that is bringing to the church their black selves, bringing

> all that [they] are, have, hope to become . . . [their] whole history, traditions, experiences, culture, song and dance and gesture

---

9. Anthony Pinn, *Varieties of African American Religious Experience* (Minneapolis: Fortress, 1998), 190, 192. Here I follow his argument closely.

10. Franz Fanon, "On National Culture," 149, in *The Wretched of the Earth*, Kindle Edition, trans. Richard Philcox (1963; New York: Grove, 2004).

11. Pinn, *Varieties of African American Religious Experience*, 190, 192.

12. Bernard Lonergan, *Doctrinal Pluralism* (Milwaukee: Marquette University Press, 1971) 4, 5.

13. Ibid., 8.

and movement and teaching and preaching and healing and responsibility as gifts to the church."[14]

The council carved out a graced opening through which black Catholics might enter bringing *their whole selves*, might *be* themselves for their church, might *be* church as black *and* Catholic.

As theologian Michael Gallagher observes, the council "initiated a whole new wavelength for Roman Catholic understanding of culture."[15] In *Gaudium et Spes*, the council outlined this new understanding in detail and sketched a theological anthropology that linked culture intimately and decisively with the dignity of the human person and with the call of freedom to become more fully and authentically human.[16]

> It is one of the marks of the human person to reach true and authentic humanity only through culture, that is, by cultivating natural gifts and values. Wherever human life is involved nature and culture are intimately connected.
>
> In its general sense, the word 'culture' stands for everything by which human beings refine and develop their various capacities of mind and body. It includes efforts to control the cosmos by knowledge or by work, as well as ways of humanizing social life within the family or civic community through the progress of customs and institutions (#53).[17]

While the document at some points elides classicist and pluralist assumptions about culture, nonetheless, it accepts and approves the plurality of cultures. Quite importantly, for the work of the institute, *Gaudium et Spes* recognized "an increase in the number of men and women who are conscious that they themselves are the authors and the artisans of the culture of their community" (55). The document encouraged a notion of culture as communal, as concrete expression of a people's self-understanding, beliefs and meanings or visions of life; commitments, ethics, and values or norms

---

14. Thea Bowman, "To Be Black and Catholic: An Address to the U. S. Catholic Bishops, 1989," 40, *In Her Own Words*, ed. and compil. Maurice J. Nutt (Liguori, MO: Liguori, 2009).

15. Michael Paul Gallaher, *Clashing Symbols: An Introduction to Faith and Culture* (Mahwah, NJ: Paulist, 1998) 36.

16. Ibid., 37.

17. *Gaudium et Spes* (The Pastoral Constitution on the Church in the Modern World), December 7, 1965. http://www.vatican.va/archive/hist_councils/ii_vatican_council/documents/vat-ii_cons_19651207_gaudium-et-spes_en.html   Paragraphs 53-62 comprise the encyclical's second chapter, "The Proper Development of Culture." Unless stated the translation is taken from that provided by the Vatican. The translation of 53 is taken from Gallagher, *Clashing Symbols*, 37.

for behavior and action; customs, practices, and traditions—all manifest and rooted in various institutions that preserve and transmit them (56).

Proper, adequate, and nourishing pastoral ministry for *all* the faithful requires critical cultural consciousness and competency; this is the goal of inculturation. But the church's historic timidity in evangelization of African Americans as well as its acquiescence to prevailing social propriety regarding their inclusion has been well documented.[18] To limit the church to the theatre of one culture is a dangerous attempt to restrict the Holy Spirit whose presence and power make the church. For the Holy Spirit can and shall never be confined by our socially constructed boundaries of age or social condition or ecclesiastical appointment or race or culture or custom or country or sex or gender. As the source and principle of the life of the church, the Spirit dwells among *all* the faithful and is at work in them and in the most decisive acts of our life as church. The Spirit animates the church and gives to its members those gifts or charisms necessary for growth and ongoing life, and helps to structure its gifts.[19]

Black Catholic Faithful and Exercise of the *Sensus Fidelium*

That black Catholics have participated in the explication and elaboration of the truths and experience of Christian faith and assumed responsibility for the care of souls compose a well-documented dimension of black Catholic ecclesial life since the late nineteenth century. With only a handful of indigenous clergy and several dozen vowed women religious, between 1889 and 1894, educated, dedicated, and proactive black lay Catholics organized and sustained a national movement among black Catholics.[20] Their motive

---

18. See Cyprian Davis, *The History of Black Catholics in the United States* (New York: Crossroad, 1990); Cyprian Davis and Jamie T. Phelps, eds., *"Stamped with the Image of God:" African Americas as God's Image in Black* (Maryknoll, NY: Orbis, 2003); Katie Grimes, "'Christ Divided': White Supremacy as Corporate Vice in the Body of Christ," Ph.d. diss., Boston College.

19. Cf. Yves Congar, *Tradition and Traditions: An Historical and Theological Essay* (1960; 1963; London: Burns & Oates, 1966).

20. These congresses attracted delegates from across the nation who met in assemblies to read and hear papers, evaluate the results of surveys of the treatment of black Catholics in parishes and dioceses, proposed recommendations for the education of youth as well as for sound catechesis, urged the recruitment of blacks to the priesthood and vowed religious life, and pledged to engage in evangelization among the larger black community, see Davis, *The History of Black Catholics in the United States*, 163–94; and *Three Catholic Afro-American Congresses* (Cincinnati. The American Catholic Tribune, 1893, reprint ed., New York: Arno, 1978).

and goal was the pastoral care of the black community, promulgation of the Gospel, and advancement of the church. These black lay people took courage and inspiration from their baptismal charism to carry out pastoral ministry. They exercised the *sensus fidelium*: reading the signs of the times, evangelizing, supporting and sustaining their co-religionists in faith. The institute is heir to and builds on this legacy of black Catholic *traditio*, of handing on the faith.

Evangelization, that is, clarifying and teasing out meanings of the Gospel within its own culture, then announcing and re-contextualizing its message in other cultures calls for both "assertive fidelity" and "assertive discernment."[21] Carrying out these two tasks characterize the *praxial* work of the Institute for Black Catholic Studies. For without assertive fidelity and assertive discernment Catholic theology can neither take firm root within African American culture, nor fully express black ecclesial experience. While this *praxial* work demands attentiveness to the teaching authority of the church, it also insists upon thoroughgoing attentiveness to black Catholic faithful, who, by virtue of baptism, are "incorporated in Christ [and] constituted as the people of God."[22] Sharing with other believers a "true equality regarding dignity and action by which they all cooperate in the building up of the Body of Christ according to each one's own condition and function."[23]

With the phrase "assertive fidelity," I refer to a self-confident and insistent commitment—commitment without arrogance or self-abnegation, coercion or manipulation. The institute exercises assertive fidelity in word and worship to the God of Jesus Christ, to the "good news" he promulgated, to the church's teaching *magisterium*, and to holistic pastoral care of black souls. Such fidelity is nurtured through study of the Scriptures and sound exegesis, attention to and engaged dialogue with magisterial teaching, interpreting the signs of the times and analyzing and evaluating the social situation and condition of the black lifeworld and proposing appropriate solutions as warranted. Moreover, in its exercise of assertive fidelity, the institute insists upon listening to the experience and questions of the black

---

21. I derive, interpret, and modify the phrases—"aggressive fidelity" from Johann Baptist Metz, "Do We Miss Karl Rahner?" 93, in *A Passion for God: The Mystical-Political Dimension of Christianity*, ed. and trans. J. Matthew Ashley (Mahwah, NJ: Paulist, 1997) and "aggressive discernment" from Michael Paul Gallaher, *Clashing Symbols: An Introduction to Faith and Culture* (Mahwah, NJ: Paulist, 1998) 131. The interpretation of these phrases is my own.

22. http://www.vatican.va/archive/ENG1104/_INDEX.HTML

23. http://www.vatican.va/archive/ENG1104/_INDEX.HTML

faithful even as it seeks discussion with the wider church on a range of practical, cultural, and social issues in living Christian faith effectively.[24]

With the phrase "assertive discernment," I refer to self-confident and insistent reflection and evaluation—without arrogance or self-abnegation, coercion or manipulation. The institute exercises assertive discernment in the structure of theological educational programs and their curricula and in cultural appropriation. The institute carefully selects and supports faculty who value student participants of all racial-ethnic and cultural groups as "whole" persons and, thus, educate head and heart, spirit and hand. Further, exercise of assertive discernment calls for educational programs and curricula that take seriously critical retrieval, sifting, study, and evaluation. Exercise of assertive discernment distinguishes and critiques: rejects whatever may be romanticized and unexamined as well as what may be stereotypical and debilitating in theological and pastoral, historical and cultural representation.[25]

Through sound and rigorous teaching in biblical exegesis, catechesis, ethics, evangelization, history, and theology, and in culture, dance, liturgy, and performance the institute plays a significant role in the holistic formation of black Catholics and those who minister with and to them and supports black Catholics in their ongoing exercise of the *sensus fidelium*.

Formation of Practical Theological Agency

While black Catholics may and do matriculate in other pastoral programs of study, *as far as I know, only* the Institute for Black Catholic Studies carries out a comprehensive pedagogical and practical pastoral program of study through which African American Catholic and Protestant cultural specialists, historians, liturgists, musicians, experts in ministry and spirituality, and theologians collaborate to hand on the faith and to discern and

---

24. "*Sensus fidei* in the Life of the Church," 124, http://www.vativan.va/roman_curia/congregations/cfaith/cti_documents/rc_cti_20140610_senssu-diei_en.html.

25. See Jamie T. Phelps, "African American Culture: Source and Context of Black Catholic Theology and Mission," *Journal of Hispanic/Latino Theology* 3 (February 1996) 43–58; Phelps, ed., *Black and Catholic: The Challenge and Gift of Black Folk: Contributions of African American Experience and Thought to Catholic Theology*, 2nd ed. (Milwaukee: Marquette University Press, 2002); Diana L. Hayes and Cyprian Davis, eds., *Taking Down Our Harps: Black Catholics in the United States* (Maryknoll, NY: Orbis, 1998); M. Shawn Copeland, "Theological Education of African American Catholics," in *Theological Education in the Catholic Tradition: Contemporary Challenges*, eds., Patrick W. Carey and Earl C. Muller (New York: Crossroad, 1997) 318–39; M. Shawn Copeland, ed., with LaReine-Marie Mosely and Albert Raboteau, *Uncommon Faithfulness: The Black Catholic Experience* (Maryknoll, NY: Orbis, 2009).

instantiate gifts of African American culture within the Roman Catholic Church. On the one hand, this collaboration meets a longstanding and continuing deficiency in the national ministerial priorities of the American Catholic Church. For too long a time now, African American Catholics have been perceived as numerically insignificant and presumed to be a religious "other" (read: Protestant). As Dominican theologian Jamie T. Phelps states: "African American Catholics experience a double invisibility, and devaluation. In the Black world we are marginalized because of our religious identity as Catholics, and in the Catholic world we are marginalized because of our racial identity as African Americans."[26] Under these circumstances this collaborative mode unveils the moral fortitude and uncommon faithfulness of African American Catholics.

The Institute provides an intellectual, worshipful, and aesthetic experimental laboratory in which black Catholic laity are "educated in ways of knowing, perceiving, relating, and acting that enable" effective leadership in service to the mission of Jesus.[27] The institute accords primacy to daily Eucharist and daily communal prayer, and is imbued with an active commitment to the liberation of the Christian message in order to bring about a way of living that nurtures reconciliation between human persons and God, among human persons of *all* races and cultures, and between humankind and all creation. To this end, the institute takes up the formation of black Catholic practical theological agents. This entails (1) instruction in critical and theological, historical and cultural studies necessary for ministry in local parishes; (2) sound training in doctrine; (3) competence in theological reflection; and (4) development of a practicum project, a critical cultural intervention that concretely and practically demonstrates the integration of interdisciplinary pastoral study and theology and that contributes to local parish life or to diocesan program.[28] A sample of more than three decades of such critical cultural interventions include a program for training catechists in pedagogies drawing on African American culture, a plan for reviving spirituality among inactive black Catholics, cultural strategies to enhance self-esteem among black Catholic female adolescents, approaches to the use of African American literature to enhance faith witnessing and shar-

---

26. Phelps, "Introduction: Theology from an African American Catholic Perspective," 21, in *Black and Catholic*.

27. Dorothy C. Bass and Craig Dykstra, "Introduction," Loc. 20/4865, *For Life Abundant: Practical Theology, Theological Education, and Christian Ministry*, Kindle Edition (Grand Rapids, MI / Cambridge, UK: William B. Eerdmans, 2008).

28. The Institute for Black Catholic Studies, Xavier University of Louisiana, *The Master of Theology, Handbook* (2013) 24, http://www.xula.edu/ibcs/documents/degree-Handbook.pdf.

ing within families, a program to introduce African American culture to a religious order of men, correlations between African American practices of discernment and the Spiritual Exercises of St. Ignatius of Loyola, constructing an oral history of a black Catholic parish, and formulation of models of communal parish theological reflection.[29] These and many, many other critical cultural interventions in parishes in Baltimore, Brooklyn, Chicago, Houston, Lake Charles, Louisiana, St. Louis, and Washington, DC, have enabled African American Catholics (and their collaborators) to live out practical theological agency in handing on the faith. As agents of practical theology, African American Catholics enrich parish intellectual life with the goods of passionate and rigorous research and saturate parish liturgical life with the Spirit's gifts of embodied prayer, spontaneous responsorality, dance, chant, and song.

The Ritual Practice: Commemoration of Ancestors

The annual Commemoration of Ancestors forms the primary public popular religious practice of the institute. This event is held on or close to the United States day of independence, the fourth of July. The choice of date directly contests any simplistic celebration and interpretation of freedom in the United States and raises the memory of chattel slavery, which the nation so slyly obscures. For several years, the institute has partnered with the Ashé Cultural Center of New Orleans in commemorating *Maafa*. The word *maafa* is of Kiswahili origin, means "great" or "horrific" tragedy, and refers to the trauma of the Middle Passage. Commemoration of *Maafa* takes place on the Saturday closest to the fourth of July.[30] This event begins at Congo Square with drumming, libation, intercession and prayer, and, perhaps, one or two brief speeches are made. Accompanied by drumming, participants process in relative silence through the French Quarter and pause at sites historically associated with the slave trade. The procession concludes at the banks of the Mississippi River, although on some occasions the group has ferried across the river to pay homage at Algiers Point, the site of an African village during the period of enslavement. Finally, participants are welcome to feasting at the cultural center.

---

29. These topics of *critical cultural interventions* were proposed and carried out by Juanita Blackshear, LaReine-Marie Mosley, Willa Ellis Golden, Richard M. Potts, J. Timothy Hipskind, Thomas Clark, and Donald Chambers.

30. Developed by Dr. Marimba Ani, the concept of *maafa* denotes the experience of the Middle Passage.

An established, if flexible, rubric orders the Commemoration of Ancestors, even as improvisation and adaptation to circumstance contribute energy and acknowledge particularity. Nonetheless, several more or less common features and a general structure of the ceremony may be outlined as follows: summons of the drum to gather the community and guests, libation and prayer, processional, readings, singing, storytelling, "walking" the circle, and feasting with the ancestors, guests, and members of the institute community.

The drum calls participants to the appointed place of gathering and holds their waiting. Ordinarily, the director of the institute presides over the ritual, but a female or male member of the institute faculty (ordained or non-ordained) also may assume this role. Male and female dancers and drummers—some professionals, others students—all take part. Institute community elders, female and male, pour libation (most often water) onto the ground as an offering of respect to the One Holy Triune God and to the ancestors. Libation enables the symbolic and ritual participation of the ancestors and is accompanied by a litany addressing them and those canonized as saints of the church. Among those who are petitioned for guidance and protection and invited to be present are Mary, Our Mother of Africa, Daniel Rudd, Harriet Thompson, Booker Ashe, Dolores Harrall, Joseph Davis, Lucy Williams, Beatrice Jeffries, Leon Roberts, St. Katharine Drexel, St. Josephine Bakhita, Venerable Pierre Toussaint, Servant of God Elizabeth Lange, and Venerable Henriette Delille.

When the recitation of the litany has been completed, the gathered assembly moves in silent procession to the site of commemoration, swaying and dancing, led by an incense bearer and dancers, the drums setting the pace and rhythm. Once participants reach the site of the ceremony, singing follows, the music chosen from the Spirituals. Next, a person or persons (male and female) serving as the *griot*, the keeper and teller of the story, recites the origin of the institute, placing it in the context of black and black Catholic history. Since the ancestors "are not mental concepts, but historical people,"[31] the *griot* identifies, names, and calls upon the local or familial ancestors of the institute. The gifts and achievements of these beloved dead are publicly recited, received, affirmed, and reincorporated into the black Catholic story.[32] When the prayers to and for the dead and the living are

---

31. Nwaka Chris Egbulem, *The Power of Afrocentric Celebrations: Inspirations from the Zairean Liturgy* (New York: Crossroad, 1996) 91.

32. The reader should note that among most African cultures *not every deceased person becomes a true ancestor*. According to Egbulem, "Moral excellence, bravery, successful social and family life, and other qualities are important criteria in establishing who is truly an ancestor. In some tribes it is still true that people who do not have

completed, when meditation, drumming, and singing cease, the ceremony flows into dancing and tears, joy and sorrow, and feasting with the ancestors, guests, and the institute community.

The Commemoration of Ancestors poses a correspondence with the communion of saints, for the unity of the dead and living forms an ancient and treasured part of the faith. On Catholic teaching, the very term "communion of saints" intimates communion in holy things (*sancta*) and communion among holy persons (*sancti*) who brought together by the Lord to his own table, fed from his own hand on his own flesh and blood that they might grow in the communion (*koinonia*) of the Holy Spirit and communicate the gospel's message to a broken and hurting world. The notion of organic solidarity provides the interpretative key that unlocks theological resonances between these two memorials. The ancestors are a "source of solidarity, communication, and reciprocity among the living."[33] Not only do they command reverence and remembrance, the ancestors bind *a people* one to another in acts of mutual love and compassion, respect and shared responsibility for the present. Thus, the dead *mission* the living to *all* those whom the dominant society excludes, consigns to the prison-industrial complex, criminalizes by homelessness, substance abuse, and poverty; and the living resolve to respond and participate with greater determination in Christ's redemption of the future.

Commemoration of Ancestors as an African Diasporic Practice

The term *African diasporic practice* denotes the religio-cultural and aesthetic sayings and doings of people of African descent in the Americas. Diasporic practices reflect the influence of certain African aesthetic principles including "dominance of a percussive performance; call and response; battles of aesthetic virtuosity between two singers, or two dance groups, and so forth."[34] These principles are best recognized, understood, and appreciated

---

offspring may never be regarded as ancestors, since they have no descendants to perpetuate their names" (*The Power of Africentric Celebrations*, 60). The institute addresses the ancestors without name, yet infers that certain beloved black Catholic dead may be counted among their company.

33. F. Eboussi Boulaga, *Christianity without Fetishes: An African Critique and Recapture of Christianity*, trans., Robert Barr (Maryknoll, NY: Orbis, 1984) 82.

34. Robert Farris Thompson, "Recapturing Heaven's Glamour: Afro-Caribbean Festivalizing Arts," in *Caribbean Festival Arts: Every Little Piece of Difference*, ed. John W. Nunley and Barbara A. Bettelheim (Seattle: University of Washington Press, 1988) 19.

when we know, what Robert Farris Thompson calls, their "atomic weight," which I take to mean the quality of resonance of a particular practice or performance relative to an indigenous standard. In the case of the complex practice of Commemoration of Ancestors, those standards "lie embedded in the aesthetic vocabularies of the Yoruba of Nigeria and Benin, and the Bakongo of Congo, Bas-Zaire, and Angola."[35]

African diasporic practices figure as "utopian eruptions of space into the linear temporal order" of modernity.[36] Whereas casual onlookers or the uninitiated or inattentive might see in diasporic practices only the exotic or outlandish, prepared participants or those informed by African cultures recognize processioneering or solemnized walking as the rerouting of habitual geographic circuits, forming a circle for ritual action as claiming and commanding and marking sacred a space and place—all in the mediation of dense religio-cultural significations. Most importantly, these practices make present those living memories that cannot be erased: the very bodies of the descendants of the Africans who survived the Middle Passage and enslavement provoke the dangerous memory of a past that is only obscured and must be confronted.

In structuring the ritual practice of the Commemoration of Ancestors, the institute draws upon properties of Bakongo culture.[37] This ritual practice brings together Roman Catholic and Bakongo regard for the dead: the African American Catholic community embraces and addresses the Many Thousand Gone of the Middle Passage, intercedes for African and African American ancestors as well as the Church Suffering, and remembers those African American Catholic dead who are the very seed of our faith. Moreover, this ritual practice represents more than an annual and solemn necrology, although it *is* this; Bakongo and Roman Catholic regard for the dead compenetrate one another. The honored dead, both those who died long ago and the deceased of more recent memory, remain, even in death, most intimately connected to the living—involved in daily affairs, bestowing blessing or meting out punishment.

Great care is taken with the environment of the ritual space. No liturgical or ritual activity is "simply an activity of the spirit," writes Nwaka Egbulem, "the eyes, the nose, the ears, the hands, the feet, the mouth all have

---

35. Ibid.

36. Paul Gilroy, *The Black Atlantic: Modernity and Double Consciousness* (Cambridge: Harvard University Press, 1993) 198.

37. Philip Curtin, *The Atlantic Slave Trade, A Census* (Madison: University of Wisconsin Press, 1969); see also Robert Farris Thompson and Joseph Cornet, *The Four Moments of the Sun: Kongo Art in Two Worlds* (Washington, DC: National Gallery of Art, 1981) 32, 27.

to be involved in one way or another [to realize] a unifying experience."[38] Pattern and color caress the eye: a crucifix draped in kente cloth commands prominence, baskets and gourds filled with flowers and fruits are artfully arranged, material imprinted with Adinkra symbols from Ghana's Akan culture cover tables and pedestals. Finally always, photographs of those deceased recognized as founders of the institute, Thaddeus J. Posey, OFM, Cap., Ph.D, the Reverend Joseph Nearon, SSS, STD, Sister Thea Bowman, FSPA, PhD, and Brother Bede Abrams, OFM, Conv., STL, are displayed along with deceased elders of the community.

A circular "social geometry"[39] features in this ritual. The visual and physical arrangements of chairs and/or stools and, often, pebbles on the floor of the room literally replicate the Bakongo cosmogram. This figural rendition offers a way of stating in ideograph or picture writing the vitality and significance of the connection of the community of the living to the visions and hopes of the dead. Participants, ordinarily dressed in white traditional West African attire, enter the site moving in a counterclockwise direction and take their seats. This counterclockwise movement accords with Bakongo belief that the rhythm of human life (ontology) follows the rhythm of nature (cosmology). Bakongo hold that human life has no end, that it constitutes a cycle.[40] That cycle signifies the four moments of the sun: (1) rising—meaning birth or beginning, (2) ascendency—indicating maturity and responsibility (e.g., initiation, taking of titles, marriage, and so on), (3) setting—meaning death as a transition or transformation, (4) midnight—inferring existence in the other and ancestral world and reincarnating birth. Moreover, counterclockwise movement echoes the four winds and four corners of the earth. For the men and women and children who underwent the trauma of the Middle Passage, this ocean journey physically charted the *kalunga line*, the boundary line that reckoned the unity of the living and the dead; but the Middle Passage would have disoriented the captive Africans' sense and experience of time, of life, of death, and life in death.

Members of the institute community may be invited to "walk" the circle for or on behalf of the dead. Each person moves counterclockwise around the space. This ritual walk honors the Many Thousand Gone, the Ancestors of the Middle Passage, and the honored and beloved black and black Catholic dead. Moreover, as Estella Conwill Majozo points out, this ritual walk makes present "the pilgrimage path upon grounds made holy

38. Egbulem, *The Power of Afrocentric Celebrations*, 129.

39. Thompson, "Recapturing Heaven's Glamour: Afro-Caribbean Festivalizing Arts," 20.

40. Thompson, *Flash of the Spirit: African and Afro-American Art and Philosophy* (New York: Random House, 1984) 108.

by the tears, sweat, and blood of our people."[41] With regard to the local or familial ancestors of the institute, it allows for their personification, and, in this way, the memory of a particular man or woman is vivified in the body of another. Often, institute elders, administrators or faculty, visiting national or diocesan or local parish leaders are invited to walk the circle as their contributions to church, community, and society are publicly recited, received, affirmed, and incorporated into the African American Catholic story. The walk marks, performs, and resonates: the walk marks a point of contact between the worlds of the living and the dead. It performs the duty of attending the pilgrimage of the dead to their place of rest. Finally, the walk resonates with parading in Yoruba and Bakongo cultures: As Thompson observes: "[T]o parade, with or without masks, was a serious matter in Kongo. Bakongo believe the ritual processioners ideally carry fortune and spiritual rebirth to a village that they circle [and] that processioneering around a village can mystically heal its hidden problems, can 'cool' the entire settlement with circling gestures of felicity and good faith."[42]

The Commemoration of Ancestors as an African diasporic practice, insinuates a continual return of the past in order to revivify and reconstitute both the institute as a community and each member who forms and is formed within that community. Thus, the ritual strengthens communal and personal faith, reinvigorates purpose, enfolds participants in black and black Catholic history, and energizes weary spirits. At the same time, the ritual evokes and performs mourning and loss. Mourning for the dead of the Middle Passage, mourning for the unnamed and unknown enslaved women and men who survived on whispers, hopes, and prayers of freedom for their children's children's children can never be completed. Always, weight must be and is given to ambiguity, opacity, and incalculability of loss. Finally, as an African diasporic practice, Commemoration of Ancestors *choreographs* movements of nature, of being, and of history. Respectfully and delicately appropriating Bakongo belief regarding the unity of nature and human being, tensively holding a history at once terrifying and terrifyingly beautiful, the ritual practice of commemorating the ancestors reiterates the ethical responsibility of memory and the "ethical impossibility of forgetting."[43]

---

41. Estella Conwill Majozo, *Libation: A Literary Pilgrimage through the African-American Soul* (New York: Harlem River, 1995), 11.

42. Thompson, "Recapturing Heaven's Glamour: Afro-Caribbean Festivalizing Arts," 20.

43. I take the term choreograph from Sara Kaplan, "Souls at the Crossroads, Africans on the Water: The Politics of Diasporic Melancholia," *Callaloo* 30.2 (2007) 518, 522 [511–26].

Evoking *Mythos*, Making Meaning

"But, where is home? In a fragmented state, home is a mythic place to which there is no return."[44] G.M. Gonzalez asks and answers a poignant longing, one that fragile cultural memories yearn to answer, yet shall never do so fully. Popular religious practices and, in particular, ritual practices gesture toward home, evoke myth, make meaning—make home. For a people whose black bodies are despised, whose faith praxis comes under suspicion, whose culture is dismissed as nonexistent or pathological or deprived, popular religious ritual practices provide a crucial mediation for human subjectivity. These practices evoke *mythos* through which meaning is made and sustained, even if only for a few minutes, as flashes of consciousness of home erupt and "heaven's glamour"[45] embraces those in longing. The Spiritual asserts:

> *I've got a home in a-that Rock.*
> *Don't you see? Don't you See?*
> *Between the earth and sky,*
> *thought I heard my Savior cry,*
> *I've got a home in a-that Rock.*
> *Don't you See?*

The ceremony of Commemoration of the Ancestors functions in at least five ways: first, as a critical cultural intervention in devotional practices in the American Catholic Church, the ceremony advances recognition of this regional church as a diverse and plural community of differing races, cultures, ethnicities, and nationalities, with differing gifts and needs, differing challenges and difficulties, yet drawn together for the mission of Jesus. Second, the ritual illustrates the practical theological competence of trained African American Catholics—women and men, lay and ordained—and their desire and willingness for collaboration. Third, for African American Catholics, the ritual practice promotes the remembrance of the dead who have lived and worked for, among, alongside, and on behalf of this community. The ritual practice lifts up their lives for example and allows those lives to influence and shape the lives and ministries of members of the black Catholic community. Fourth, the ritual allows the living co-creators of black Catholic thought and praxis to be seen by the institute community. Through

---

44. G. M. James Gonzalez, "Of Property: On 'Captive' 'Bodies,' Hidden 'Flesh,' and Colonization, 133, in *Existence in Black: An Anthology of Black Existential Philosophy*, ed., Lewis R. Gordon (New York: Routledge, 1997).

45. Thompson, "Recapturing Heaven's Glamour," 17.

their public presentation to the ancestors and to the whole African American Catholic community as represented by the institute, this cadre of leaders and teachers, vowed religious and priests and laity, are challenged and strengthened to live a life worthy of their calling. Moreover, the leadership these women and men exercise is recognized publicly as African American Catholic and acknowledged as rooted in baptismal charism and in educational and cultural competence, as self-initiating and attentive to the signs of the times, as committed to social justice in the concrete, as collaborative, and as prayerful. And, the entire community is invited to personal and communal self-examination. Fifth, the ceremony teaches the African American Catholic story as one of uncommon faithfulness and love, perseverance and service, courage and integrity. Telling and performing the story nurtures an intimate bond with the ancestors and between and among the institute and its new members, both students and faculty, and reaffirms that bond between returning members. Finally, as members of a church in which all too often they have been denied the joys, challenges, and possibilities of intersubjective community, the very elemental meaning of belonging, African American Catholics seek and find communion, belonging, and home with the ancestors and the beloved black Catholic dead. To pour out libation to them signifies conscious and willing acceptance of the wisdom, comfort, and courage of that great cloud of witnesses, whose visitation descends in accord with the Spirit.

18

Learning to Discern the *Sensus Fidelium Latinamente*

A Dialogue with Orlando Espín

Edward P. Hahnenberg

The SENSUS FIDELIUM is notoriously difficult to nail down. Vatican II's claim that the "whole body of the faithful" cannot be mistaken in belief thanks to a "supernatural sense of the faith" is great *in theory*, but what practical role does the category play in the life of the church?[1] Just the attempt to identify this "supernatural sense" proves frustrating—never mind trying to appeal to the "sense of the faithful" for guidance in situations of disagreement or controversy. Most theologians agree that the concept cannot be reduced to polling data, nor is it simply a secondary affirmation of what is first taught by the magisterium.[2] Rather, the *sensus fidelium* seems to fall somewhere between these two extremes, where it exists as a kind of shared spiritual instinct, a sacred common sense. But how do you analyze an intuition? How do you study a sense?

Behind these practical questions are at least three theological challenges: First, we are dealing here with a peculiar type of knowledge that belongs to each individual Christian, a *sense* of the faith—*sensus fidei fidelis* ("sense of the faith of the faithful one," usually abbreviated *sensus fidei*). As a sort of non-discursive spiritual instinct, the *sensus fidei* eludes easy analysis by theology, a discipline traditionally oriented around texts, concepts, and rational argumentation. Second, this individual sense of the faith (*sensus*

---

1. *Lumen Gentium*, 12, in *Vatican Council II: The Basic Sixteen Documents*, ed., Austin Flannery (Northport, NY: Costello, 1996).

2. International Theological Commission (ITC), "Theology Today: Perspectives, Principles and Criteria," 35, http://www.vatican.va/roman_curia/congregations/cfaith/cti_documents/rc_cti_ doc_20111129_teologia-oggi_en.html.

255

fidei) also exists at the communal or ecclesial level—*sensus fidei fidelium* ("sense of the faith of the faithful," usually abbreviated *sensus fidelium*).[3] But how do we move from the individual to the communal? What do we mean by the "instinct" or "intuition" of a corporate body like the church? And where, within this community, does the intuition reside? Finally, given the inevitable diversity of individual and communal expressions of this sense, how is the theologian to discern authentic articulations of the *sensus fidei* or the *sensus fidelium*? And what normative force does any particular expression hold?

To its credit, the 2014 document by the International Theological Commission (ITC), "*Sensus Fidei* in the Life of the Church," acknowledges these challenges, taking up each, in turn, in its second, third, and fourth chapters. The document offers a positive treatment of the *sensus fidei/sensus fidelium*, tracing the biblical and historical roots of these ideas, and presenting a systematic theological account using the categories of what the ITC authors call "classical theology."[4] As we will see, the ITC authors use the phrase "classical theology" as shorthand for a particular set of scholastic and neo-scholastic distinctions, read through the lens of the organic, developmental notions of church that emerged in the nineteenth-century. This "classical" interpretation of the *sensus fidelium* reached a high point in the work of John Henry Newman and entered into official Roman Catholic teaching at the Second Vatican Council.

Without denying the genuine contribution of "classical theology" to our understanding of the *sensus fidelium*, the present essay is built on the premise that a lot has changed since the nineteenth century. The simple narrative of development, which imagines doctrine progressing over time from insight to greater insight, is today complicated by stories told from the margins, stories told from the underside of "development" in all its modern forms. The confident claim to universal truths held "everywhere, always, and by everyone," is challenged today by the irrepressible diversity of cultures and worldviews.[5] The reality of our present, postmodern, pluralistic context calls for alternative approaches to the *sensus fidelium* than that provided by "classical theology."

---

3. A third term also appears in the literature, *consensus fidelium*, which describes a convergence or consensus of belief among all of the faithful. See International Theological Commission (ITC), "*Sensus Fidei* in the Life of the Church (2014)" 3. http://www.vatican.va/roman_curia/congregations/cfaith/cti_documents/rc_cti_20140610_sensus-fidei_en.html.

4. ITC, "*Sensus Fidei*," 48.

5. The phrase is that of Vincent of Lérins, cited in ITC, "*Sensus Fidei*," 23.

In what follows, I explore one particularly promising alternative in the work of Cuban-American theologian Orlando Espín. Espín has written incisively on the *sensus fidelium* as part of a larger project that seeks to reimagine the theological enterprise from a Latino/a perspective (*latinamente*). His attention to culture and to popular Catholicism—an emphasis shared by many of the Latino/a theologians with whom he is in conversation—suggests a form of intercultural dialogue that is necessary for any theology that wants to attend to the actual, lived faith of the people. But dialogue implies shared life (*convivir*) and shared work (*en conjunto*)—it implies community. Thus, it is the communal, contextual nature of Espín's work that challenges the individualistic presuppositions of "classical theology," inviting the whole church to learn what it might mean to discern the *sensus fidelium latinamente*.

Entering into this dialogue with Espín, I am keenly aware of my own inescapable cultural context. I raise these issues from the perspective of a white North American heterosexual male, socialized quite comfortably within the dominant discourse of "classical theology." In reflecting sympathetically on Espín's work, I do not pretend to be a voice for him or for other Latino/a theologians. Nor do my critical questions for "classical theology" lead to the conclusion that it ought to be left behind. Rather, I imagine this essay as an initial and halting attempt at the intercultural dialogue enjoined by Espín, which unfolds as an ever-deepening and continuing conversation, one in which truth is discovered, over and over, "through mutual witnessing, contrasting dialogue, and non-colonizing reflection."[6]

To Know the *Sensus Fidei*

In his first Angelus address, Pope Francis spoke of the special insight granted to the humble believer, quoting the words of an elderly woman he once met: "If the Lord did not forgive everything, the world would not exist." "That," the pope exclaimed, "is the wisdom which the Holy Spirit gives."[7]

The ITC document "*Sensus Fidei* in the Life of the Church" uses this vignette to introduce the *sensus fidei* as a supernatural instinct intrinsically linked to the gift of faith. It goes on to flesh out this "instinct" in language that reflects the many ways theologians have described it. A quick survey of the literature reveals the following descriptions: The *sensus fidei* is a sort of

---

6. Orlando O. Espín, *Idol and Grace: On Traditioning and Subversive Hope* (Maryknoll, NY: Orbis, 2014) 63.

7. Pope Francis, Angelus address, March 17, 2013, cited in ITC, "*Sensus Fidei*," 2. http://www.news.va/en/news/angelus-if-god-didnt-forgive-everyone-the-world-wo.

spiritual instinct, a form of spontaneous and natural knowledge, a perception, an intuition, a faculty, a capacity, a capability, a sensibility, a spiritual "sixth sense," a particular and profound form of knowledge that is not the result of rational deliberation, a different order than objective knowledge,[8] an imaginative grasp, analogous to aesthetic reception, an "organon" of faith, an interpretive instrument for understanding, interpreting, and applying salvific revelation,[9] a mode of understanding that is "less discursive or rigorously logical, more global, more instinctive, and deeply responsive to an underlying sense of evangelical authenticity,"[10] a sympathy, being attuned, congeniality, a pre-conceptual, transcendental experience of reality, a natural, immediate, and spontaneous reaction, comparable to a vital instinct, a sort of "flair" for the gospel, "an experiential knowledge based on what has been lived."[11]

Often to appear in discussions of the *sensus fidei* is the classic Catholic category of "connaturality," drawn from the epistemology of Thomas Aquinas. In his discussion of wisdom in the *Summa Theologiae*, Aquinas illustrates what he means by the term. One comes to a decision, Aquinas writes, in one of two ways: either through the "perfect use of reason" or by way of "a certain connaturality with the matter" at hand.[12] His example is chastity. The chaste man (*sic*) makes good ethical decisions either because he knows everything the catechism says about the sixth commandment (through the perfect use of reason), or because he feels a deep resonance—a connaturality—between his being and his doing.

The ITC document appeals to this "classical theology" in order to explain the *sensus fidei* as a kind of connatural knowledge, established by the infused virtue of faith:

---

8. ITC, "Sensus Fidei," 49–50.

9. Ormond Rush, *The Eyes of Faith: The Sense of the Faithful and the Church's Reception of Revelation* (Washington, DC: Catholic University of America Press, 2009) 63–70.

10. John J. Burkhard, "Sensus Fidei: Recent Theological Reflection (1990–2001) Part I," *Heythrop Journal* 46 (2005) 454.

11. Zoltán Alszeghy, "The Sensus Fidei and the Development of Dogma," in *Vatican II: Assessment and Perspectives Twenty-Five Years After (1962–1987)*, vol. 1, ed. René LaTourelle (New York: Paulist, 1988) 139. John Burkhard has produced an excellent series of reviews of the literature on the *sensus fidei* since Vatican II. See John J. Burkhard, "Sensus Fidei: Theological Reflection Since Vatican II: 1965–1984," *Heythrop Journal* 34 (1993) 41–59; John J. Burkhard, "Sensus Fidei: Recent Theological Reflection (1990–2001) Part I,"; id., "Sensus Fidei: Recent Theological Reflection (1990–2001) Part II," *Heythrop Journal* 47 (2006) 38–54.

12. *Summa Theologiae* II-II, 45, 2.

The *sensus fidei fidelis* arises, first and foremost, from the connaturality that the virtue of faith establishes between the believing subject and the authentic object of faith, namely the truth of God revealed in Christ Jesus. Generally speaking, connaturality refers to a situation in which an entity A has a relationship with another entity B so intimate that A shares in the natural dispositions of B as if they were its own. Connaturality permits a particular and profound form of knowledge. For example, to the extent that one friend is united to another, he or she becomes capable of judging spontaneously what suits the other because he or she shares the very inclination of the other and so understands by connaturality what is good or bad for the other. This is a knowledge, in other words, of a different order than objective knowledge, which proceeds by way of conceptualization and reasoning. It is a knowledge by empathy, or a knowledge of the heart.[13]

In this passage, the ITC employs the metaphor of friendship to describe the peculiar type of knowledge that is the *sensus fidei*. In the realm of faith, connatural knowledge arises from a closeness, a kind of co-existence or intimacy, between the believing subject and the ultimate object of faith, "the truth of God revealed in Christ Jesus." In other words, God's gift of self in Christ and our response in faith makes each of us a friend of God. And because we are friends, we *just know* what is faith-full and what is not.

Its appeal to the broader epistemology conveyed by the concept of connaturality is not original to the ITC document; nevertheless, it offers a helpful starting point for dialogue with U.S. Latino/a theologians. For decades, Latino/a theologians—including María Pilar Aquino, Alex García-Rivera, Roberto Goizueta, Orlando Espín, and others—have questioned the unquestioned premises of dominant modes of thinking. Their critique has focused primarily on the modern reduction of reason to the narrow rationalism that emerged out of the European Enlightenment, with its drive for mastery and its desire to discover some presupposition-free foundation for all thought. Goizueta sees this critique broadly: "From quantum physics to poststructuralist literary theory, across diverse disciplines, the contemporary academy is today unmasking the pretentious, underlying claims of modern epistemologies—especially as these presuppose an autonomous subject and the possibility of a universal knowledge."[14]

---

13. ITC, "*Sensus Fidei*," 50. See also Francis A. Sullivan, "The Sense of Faith: The Sense/Consensus of the Faithful," in *Authority in the Roman Catholic Church: Theory and Practice*, ed. Bernard Hoose (Aldershot, UK: Ashgate, 2002) 85–93.

14. Roberto S. Goizueta, "Foreword," in *The Faith of the People: Theological Reflections*

In the realm of theology, Espín argues that what makes Latino scholarship Latino is not the ethnic background of its practitioners, nor its citation of Latino sources or its appeal to Latino experience. Rather, for Espín, "The very core of the distinctiveness must be, above all else, our work's epistemological claims and premises."[15] "Epistemology is cultural too," he reminds his readers.[16] And what "counts" as reasonable is usually determined by the particular rationality of the dominant cultural group. This has the effect of marginalizing all other forms of understanding, excluding those whose very way of knowing is dismissed as "irrational." For Espín, the dominant epistemology in the United States is a type of modern, Enlightenment rationality that manages to keep Latinos "in their place."[17] He argues that the American theological establishment has uncritically embraced this epistemology, serving to marginalize Latino/a ways of knowing, and disqualifying one of their most important sources for theological insight: popular religion. Under the hegemonic epistemology of the modern academy, popular religion can only appear as an embarrassment to Catholic theologians—"the superstitious result of religious ignorance, a product of syncretism, a vestige of the rural past."[18]

Goizueta shares Espín's critique of the modern reduction of truth to theoretical reason, where the only thing admitted to rational discourse is what can be objectified, universalized, or generalized.[19] But his reservations about the sterile rationalism of modernity are equally matched by his suspicion of the postmodern swing toward irrationality. Affect and the aesthetic cannot be extolled at the expense of intellect. For lurking beneath the postmodern celebration of ambiguity and indeterminacy is a hearty dose of sexism, racism, and classism. "Only those persons whom the dominant culture already considers 'rational' have the luxury of 'opting' for irrationality," Goizueta writes.[20] More deeply, he asks whether the embrace of irrationality renders impossible any communication at all among particularities. As María Pilar Aquino puts it, this postmodern extreme "represents a radical break in the conditions that would permit any possible basic consensus on

---

on *Popular Catholicism*, by Orlando O. Espín (Maryknoll, NY: Orbis, 1997), xii.

15. Orlando Espín, *The Faith of the People: Theological Reflections on Popular Catholicism* (Maryknoll, NY: Orbis, 1997), 157.

16. Ibid., 5.

17. Ibid., 94.

18. Ibid., 63.

19. Roberto S. Goizueta, *Caminemos Con Jesús: Toward a Hispanic/Latino Theology of Accompaniment* (Maryknoll, NY: Orbis, 1995), 134.

20. Ibid., 147.

the fundamental truths that ground human dignity, justice, or the integrity of the world."[21]

Over against both modern foundationalism and postmodern deconstructionism, Goizueta proposes an epistemology understood as aesthetic praxis. He is clear that the aesthetic is not to be seen—as in many postmodern accounts—as a *replacement* of reason. Instead, it is "an *expansion* of our criteria of rationality beyond the logical, theoretical criteria of modern Western thought."[22] Thus reason is defined not as "logical certainty" but as "understanding." The metaphor shifts from subject-object to subject-subject. If all understanding operates analogously to our efforts to understand one another, then we begin to see that all understanding demands relationship. It is embodied. It calls for encounter and arrives through participation. It engages affect and intellect. It is a knowledge by empathy or connaturality, a knowledge of the heart.

To Know *Latinamente*

The ITC's appeal to connaturality offers an opening for dialogue with Latino/a epistemological concerns. Coming out of quite different contexts, both articulate (with their own words and within their own cultural frameworks) a common insight: There are many ways "to know." And some of the most important things "to know" are truths that cannot be counted or commodified, measured or mastered by the universalizing, instrumentalizing rationality of modernity. Within Latino/a theology, this insight flows naturally out of the embodied and communal knowing that is popular religion, or popular Catholicism. For, as Goizueta puts it, "In popular Catholicism, theological truth is encountered not in clear and distinct ideas but in relationships; not in universal, abstract concepts but in particular, concrete sacraments, or symbols; not through observation but through participation, by kissing the statue, or walking with Jesus, or kneeling alongside Mary, or singing to Mary."[23]

Popular religion—the daily religious practices, beliefs, understandings, devotions, and ways of relating that belong to "the people"—has been the living heart of Orlando Espín's theological project from the beginning.

---

21. María Pilar Aquino, "Theological Method in U.S. Latino/a Theology: Toward an Intercultural Theology for the Third Millennium," in *From the Heart of Our People: Latino/a Explorations in Catholic Systematic Theology*, ed., Orlando O. Espín and Miguel H. Díaz (Maryknoll, NY: Orbis, 1999), 12.

22. Goizueta, *Caminemos Con Jesús*, 139.

23. Ibid., 140.

He challenges the tendency of theologians to concentrate on written texts from the past, pointing out that this decision effectively privileges the perspectives of the social and religious elite.[24] It overlooks the simple fact that, over the course of Christian history, the vast majority of Christians have been illiterate. These Christians were not producing texts, but they were, and they are, handing on the faith ("traditioning") in ways that are just as important as (if not more important than) the written word. Thus, for Espín, it is not only the theoretical limitations of modern rationality, or its oppressive marginalization of other modes of discourse that demand critique; it is, more importantly, the lived experiences of Latino/a people that witness to alternative ways of knowing. To put it another way, it is not so much that a more capacious epistemology lets popular religion in; it is that popular religion opens out into a more capacious—even subversive—epistemology.

In an essay on the problem of suffering, Espín claims that popular religion is itself a way of knowing; it is itself an epistemology.[25] In an experimental and provisional way, he describes Latino/a popular religion as an "epistemological network"—a model that helps to illuminate the knowledge-constituting nature of culture.[26] By "network" Espín means a communication relationship among interconnected nodes, each of which has the capacity to transfer and receive data from other nodes. Within the network of Latino/a popular religion, the various nodes include beliefs, ethical expectations, rites, and experiences. In their interrelationship, these nodes are assumed as plausible premises for explaining reality, "real and true for those who hold them, but probably not self-evident for those who do not."[27] What gives shape to this network is the *experiencia* of Latino/a communities—a word that is richer that the English "experience," evoking an active "living and reflecting upon reality."[28] Any particular node—whether it be a deeply-held conviction, an ethical commitment, a concrete practice, or a personal experience of God—takes on meaning and truth only through lived life, that is, within the context of Latino/a historical, communal, and familial *experiencia*.

---

24. Espín, *The Faith of the People*, 65. See also, id., *Idol and Grace*, 8–13.

25. Espín, *The Faith of the People*, 158.

26. Ibid., 163.

27. Ibid.

28. "In Latino usage, people gain *experiencia* as they live and reflect upon their lives and contextual reality," which is one reason older members of the community (especially women) are seen as wiser—"precisely because they have lived and reflected upon reality better and longer than most others." Espín, *The Faith of the People*, 177 n26. See Jeanette Rodríguez, "Experience as a Resource for Feminist Thought," *Journal of Hispanic/Latino Theology* 1 (1993) 68–76.

In speaking about the mystery of God that is at the heart of the faith experience, Espín argues that any truth we claim about this mystery is only and at best *verosimilitud*.[29] As Espín points out, the Spanish noun *verosimilitud* cannot be reduced to the English "verisimilitude," the "appearance of truth." In its everyday use, *verosimilitud* evokes that which is "very close to truth," that which "can be or is *regarded* as true." In making a claim to *verosimilitud*, the speaker is not pointing to an abstract concept or an independent fact. Rather, the speaker is *claiming a connection*, implying that the *context* of both the claim and the claimant are what make the statement reasonable and trustworthy. The interlinking of persons, practices, and prior commitments are what make something *verosimilitud*. "The relationship established by the claimant regarding the claim is the point here, not the truthfulness or facticity of the claim."[30]

The concept of *verosimilitud* thus serves to elaborate Espín's distinctive contextual epistemology. A network of relationships (among persons, places, ideas, practices, commitments, and convictions) establishes a context within which any particular claim appears reasonable or not. Different contexts and different cultures construct different rationalities, which imply different standards for what "counts" as reasonable. Thus, in a very real way, the reasonableness of a particular claim cannot be assessed by outsiders— "unless colonization or the imperial is the aim."[31] If this starts to sound relativistic, Espín reminds his readers that worrying about relativism is itself a cultural construct. An honest look into history may very well reveal that this worry has more to do with "power structures and hegemonic pretensions" than we care to admit. "In other words, the cultural fear of relativism might be discovered to have less to do with truth itself and more to do with some groups' need to make universal validity claims, which have historically accompanied the exercise of dominant power."[32]

While this warning may serve as an important check against those who would confuse the dominant with the universal, Espín does not simply dismiss the effort to move toward convergence, consensus, and mutual understanding. Indeed, his commitment to genuine communication across cultural divides—explored in the paragraphs that follow—is one of the strengths of his project. At this point, I simply want to make explicit the implicit epistemological commitments that lie behind Espín's treatment of the *sensus fidelium*. His model of "epistemological networks" offers a relational

---

29. Espín, *Idol and Grace*, 57.
30. Ibid.
31. Ibid., 164 n59.
32. Ibid., 66.

approach to knowing that parallels the ITC's metaphor of friendship, just as the ITC's appeal to connaturality echoes Espín's own call for a broader epistemology—one that is less discursive, more subjective, and relational in nature.

However, there are differences between the two approaches, and it may be helpful to say more about the assumptions behind the ITC document in order to draw the contrast. Earlier in this essay, I made the claim that the ITC uses the term "classical theology" to refer to a set of scholastic categories read through the lens of nineteenth-century developments in ecclesiology. The ITC's approach is entirely defensible, given the fact that some version of this "classical theology" is found in the documents of the Second Vatican Council, particularly in *Lumen Gentium* and *Dei Verbum*. These texts, in turn, reflect the legacy of no less a figure than John Henry Newman, whose writings on doctrinal development and the *sensus fidelium* hold near-canonical status in modern Catholic theology.

Newman's contribution is too significant to summarize here. I would simply draw attention to an observation made a number of years ago by Paul Crowley; namely, that while Newman was not insensitive to issues of interpretation, his account of the *sensus fidelium* was thoroughly epistemological in nature.[33] That is to say, Newman approached the question of the sense of the faith from the point of view of the individual mind—the idea—that then served as a guiding metaphor for the church as such. Not only in his famous *Rambler* article of 1859 ("On Consulting the Faithful in Matters of Doctrine"), but also in his earlier *Essay on the Development of Christian Doctrine* (1845), Newman drew a parallel between the mind of the individual and the mind of the church. His argument moved from the former to the latter. A single idea, seen from the unique perspective of each person, takes possession of many people, becoming the common possession of a community. Like a diamond, this idea reflects—in its unity—a variety of facets and perspectives.[34] The process of development unfolds gradually, shaping the "mind" of the church:

> The multitude of opinions formed concerning [an idea] . . . will be collected, compared, sorted, sifted, selected, rejected, gradually attached to it, separated from it, in the minds of individuals and of the community. It will, in proportion to its native vigour and subtlety, introduce itself into the framework and details of

---

33. Paul G. Crowley, "Catholicity, Inculturation and Newman's *Sensus Fidelium*," *The Heythrop Journal* 33 (1992) 168.

34. Ibid., 164.

social life, changing public opinion, and strengthening or undermining the foundations of established order.[35]

The beauty of the prose here may disguise the logical difficulties of extrapolating "from the descriptive psychology of the individual to a theory of doctrinal development."[36] The smooth movement from the mind of the individual to the "mind" of the church can easily gloss over the conflicts and power structures endemic to social existence, and minimize the complexity of crossing cultural horizons. What is understandably underdeveloped here is the role that interpretation plays at every step in the process. According to Crowley, "The major philosophic development of our time, the shift from epistemology to hermeneutics, from the idea to language, must be taken into account if the *sensus fidelium* is to serve as an effective principle for relating the catholicity of faith to its inculturated forms."[37]

Unfortunately, "*Sensus Fidei* in the Life of the Church" misses this philosophic shift, and thus it reflects more the concerns of the nineteenth century than those of the twenty-first. Despite repeated reminders that the *sensus fidei* is always an ecclesial reality, the document's treatment of the *sensus* in relation to the virtue of faith is surprisingly individualized and interiorized. Beginning its systematic analysis with the believer's *sensus fidei* (chapter 2), the document struggles to move on to the *sensus fidelium* (chapter 3). The text does not build from one to the other; it simply turns the page, noting that the *sensus fidei* "cannot be separated" from the *sensus fidelium*.[38] And the rich, relational notion of connaturality developed at length in chapter 2 is never heard from again. When the document turns to the question of discernment in chapter 4, it lists several subjective dispositions that indicate a believer's authentic participation in the sense of the faith. While these dispositions are thoroughly ecclesial, embedding the believer in the life of the church and the teaching of the magisterium, they nevertheless presuppose that discernment is the act of an individual. The individual may not be alone, but is largely working it out alone, in the interiority of his or her conscience. When popular religion finally appears at the end of the document, it is listed as one of several "applications"—and thus

---

35. John Henry Newman, *An Essay on the Development of Christian Doctrine*, 1878 rev. ed., ed., C. F. Harrold (London: Longmans, Green, 1949) 31; cited in Crowley, "Catholicity, Inculturation and Newman's *Sensus Fidelium*," 164.

36. Nicholas Lash, "The Notions of 'Implicit' and 'Explicit' Reason in Newman's University Sermons: A Difficulty," *The Heythrop Journal* 11 (1970) 49.

37. Crowley, "Catholicity, Inculturation and Newman's *Sensus Fidelium*," 168.

38. ITC, "*Sensus Fidei*," 66.

has no substantive impact on the theological framework established earlier in the text.

In contrast, Espín leads with popular religion, and his concern for epistemology is embedded in hermeneutical questions about interpreting the lived faith of the people. In adopting the scholastic category of connaturality, with its links to the virtue of faith, the ITC emphasizes the individual and the internal. Espín's attention to popular religious culture emphasizes instead the communal and the external. If simple binaries fall short (psychology vs. sociology, spirituality vs. ecclesiology, belief vs. belonging, personal intuition vs. common sense), then a more accurate description of the difference here is to say that the ITC document reads the "sense of the faith" through the lens of the *sensus fidei fidelis* (the sense of the faith *of the faithful one*); Espín reads the "sense of the faith" through the lens of the *sensus fidei fidelium* (the sense of the faith *of the faithful*). For the former, it is the individual believer who frames the discussion; for the latter, it is the believing community.

To Know the *Sensus Fidelium Latinamente*

In identifying popular religion as an authentic bearer of the *sensus fidelium*, Espín is neither naïve nor romantic. To study the real faith of the real Christian people is fraught with difficulty. First of all, the object of study, the *sensus fidelium* as traditionally understood, exists at the level of an intuition. It is a "sense" made possible by faith, which is nothing less than *"a lived life wager"* in which Christians "bet their lives on the subversive hope that effective compassion towards the disposable of the world is worth all the risks."[39] This "sense" is never found in some kind of pure state. It is always mediated through the symbols, language, and cultures of the people of God.[40] But the great variety of cultures, the diversity of languages, the distance of both history and geography, and all kinds of other variations make studying these expressions of faith extremely complex.[41] Moreover, these expressions are marked by our fallen nature, and thus the "faith-full" mediations of the *sensus fidelium* are inevitably mixed together with, and often obscured by, human sinfulness and error.[42] Amidst the diversity of cultures—permeable, overlapping, mutually-influencing—that constitute the church, where is unity to be found? And how is the theologian, or the

39. Espín, *Idol and Grace*, 23, 22 (emphasis in original).
40. Ibid., 24.
41. Espín, *The Faith of the People*, 65.
42. Ibid., 78–81.

ordinary Christian, to know which expressions of the *sensus fidelium* are faithful and which are not?

Espín responds to this challenge by developing a theology of intercultural dialogue, drawing on the Cuban philosopher Raúl Fornet-Betancourt.[43] As Espín explains, Fornet-Betancourt's notion of interculturality is not "inculturation," which works on the assumption that there is a "canonical something" that exists independent of culture and that can be "poured" from one culture into another, taking a new shape in a new vessel. Such an approach rests on the faulty assumption that this "canonical something" (e.g., a particular belief, practice, or the gospel itself) interprets itself, when in fact it only has meaning within a particular cultural horizon. Thus what gets passed on (almost always from dominant cultures to marginal ones) is always culturally infused.[44]

Interculturality is something else entirely. It emerges from an open dialogue in which someone from another cultural context witnesses to me what she or he understands and lives as truth. I engage that truth—*from within my own cultural context*—contrast it, and perhaps even adopt it, "because *I have discovered it as truth* within and from within my cultural horizon."[45] In turn, I witness to the other what I have come to understand and live as truth (always within my own cultural perspective), "inviting the other to question and grow *in what that other person understands and lives as truth*." Espín concludes, "Thus we move the process into an ever-deepening and continuing dialogue where truth is discovered and affirmed, over and over, through mutual witnessing, contrasting dialogue, and non-colonizing reflection."[46]

It is only in and through this process of contrasting, intercultural dialogue that universally relevant truth claims appear. Espín avoids the language of "universal validity," which for him inevitably involves one culture positing its particular, culturally conditioned truth claim as applicable for all people everywhere, thus imposing its worldview on other cultures. Instead,

---

43. María Pilar Aquino highlights the work of Fornet-Betancourt in "Theological Method in U.S. Latino/a Theology," 10–11.

44. Espín, *Idol and Grace*, 62–63. This treatment appears earlier in Orlando O. Espín, "Intercultural Thought," in *An Introductory Dictionary of Theology and Religious Studies*, Orlando O. Espín and James B. Nickoloff, eds. (Collegeville, MN: Liturgical, 2007) 639–45.

45. Espín, *Idol and Grace*, 63.

46. Ibid. Espín reflects on the implications of the *sensus fidelium* for interreligious and ecumenical dialogue in "Migrations and Unexpected Interreligious Dialogue," *Journal of Hispanic/Latino Theology* 12 (2007), http://www.latinotheology.org/2007/migrations. See also *Building Bridges, Doing Justice. Constructing a Latino/a Ecumenical Theology*, ed., Orlando O. Espín (Maryknoll, NY: Orbis, 2009).

he speaks of "universal relevance." Universally relevant truth emerges through an unfolding process in which a truth claim is *offered*, from within a specific culture, to others who find this claim "useful, suggestive, or even true" from within *their own* cultural perspective, opening up the possibility for new perspectives.[47] Such truth claims are what Espín calls "particular universalities"—those culturally specific and concrete insights that launch us out into dialogue with other insights from other cultures. These "particular universalities" flow from the contingency of our own truth claims and flow toward universally relevant truth.[48] As María Pilar Aquino writes, "the 'whole' of truth occurs in the very process of exchange among culturally plural 'truths.'"[49]

Intercultural dialogue is thus intercultural *discernment*, a process of moving toward truth. The emphasis on discernment as a *process* of "ever-deepening and continuing dialogue" illuminates the question of discerning the *sensus fidelium*. Vatican II taught that tradition makes progress in the church through the study and contemplation of theologians, through the teaching and preaching of bishops, and through "the intimate understanding of spiritual realities" that believers experience (*ex intima spiritualium rerum quam experiuntur intelligentia*).[50] Thus the sense of the faithful contributes directly to the church's "growth in insight . . . always advancing towards the plenitude of divine truth, until eventually the words of God are fulfilled in it."[51] Espín frames this eschatologically infused vision of tradition in terms of intercultural discernment: "In this model, Catholic tradition occurs in every Catholic generation and in every Catholic community, as the Catholic communities throughout the world acknowledge one another again and again, in every historical present, as bearers and witnesses of universally relevant truth."[52]

The historical norms for this process of discernment have primarily been written texts—Scripture, writings of early Christians, decrees of councils and popes. Espín proposes another criterion: "*whether a doctrine or practice is in coherence or coincidence with the people's present religion.*"[53] Written texts are appealed to occasionally and as needed, but the daily life

---

47. Ibid., 65.
48. Espín, "Intercultural Thought," 642.
49. Pilar Aquino, "Theological Method in U.S. Latino/a Theology," 21.
50. *Dei Verbum*, 8. See ITC, "Sensus Fidei," 46.
51. *Dei Verbum*, 8.
52. Orlando O. Espín, *Grace and Humanness: Theological Reflections Because of Culture* (Maryknoll, NY: Orbis, 2007), 27.
53. Ibid., 28 (emphasis in original).

practice of the faith (popular religion) is the constant, ordinary way in which tradition is handed on, interpreted, and constructed anew from one historical-cultural context to another. The diverse expressions of popular religion are the principal manifestations of the *sensus fidelium*, by which the baptized hold to what is true. The sense of the faith of the *whole* Christian people is not found in some kind of conceptual uniformity or abstract consensus. It exists *in* the mutual dialogue among these diverse expressions. Espín writes:

> Perhaps our theological reflection on the *sensus fidelium* might admit that the latter exists mainly, if not only, as a Spirit-led process of intercultural contrasting dialogue (on all sorts of faith-related issues) that occurs among and within Catholic communities world-wide, leading (again as a Spirit-led process) toward universally relevant claims that could in time be consensually acknowledged by Catholic communities.[54]

This evocative passage stands in some tension with language elsewhere in Espín's work, where he describes the *sensus fidelium* as an intuition that is distinct—though inseparable—from its expression. Here the *sensus fidelium* is not a preconceptual awareness; it is not a set content nor a static capacity; it is a process. The sense of the faith of the faithful is the dialogue itself. The truth claims made by the Christian tradition over time—those doctrines and dogmas that the church community believes to be universally relevant—are important. But they are not the *sensus fidelium* or even its most important expression. The most important expression—the most important truth—is lived.

In another context, Espín says that we must "pluck our understanding of truth from the prison of concepts." We should seek truth not primarily in ideas, but in our "inter-comprehension" with others.[55] Genuine intercultural dialogue—with all that it demands in terms of vulnerability, risk, and solidarity—is really an act of compassion, an act of "enduring with" others. For Jesus, "[n]othing was more important than compassion," because God is compassionate.[56] God was compassionate toward Israel, and God remains compassionate toward all those who are marginalized and oppressed. Thus a *consensus fidelium* is found not when we arrive at some common denominator or de-contextualized truth, but when we open ourselves to others with the compassion of God, seeking and living the truth of that compassion in and with one another.

54. Ibid., 29.
55. Espín, *Idol and Grace*, 66.
56. Espín, *Idol and Grace*, 4.

Conclusion

In the work of Espín, we discover resources for addressing the three challenges noted at the beginning of this essay. First, the type of intuitive knowledge involved in the believer's sense of the faith (*sensus fidei fidelis*) is not the detached rationality of modernity. Rather, it is a thoroughly relational knowledge that comes by way of actual engaged living (*experiencia*) within the network of relationships that find their primary expression in popular religion.

Second, by beginning with the community rather than the individual, Latino/a theology eliminates the problem of moving from an individual, interior "sense" to a communal, ecclesial "sense." Instead, it is the network of relationships constituting the community that shapes the intuitions, attitudes, and ideas of the believer. The network is the context within which any particular claim appears reasonable and true. And the most important truths are only known *verosímilmente*. They are "very close" to the truth—and thus reasonable—because of the connections, relationships, and trust among human persons living in community.

This brings us to the final challenge. The problem of discerning authentic expressions of the *sensus fidelium* implies—in the word "authentic"—a relationship between particular cultural expressions and the shared beliefs of the universal church. This convergence or consensus of faith among the faithful (*consensus fidelium*) is made up of those universally relevant truths of the faith that are discovered in and through a process of intercultural dialogue. Believers—each shaped by particular cultures carrying their own particular "sacred common sense"—witness to and learn from one another. The truth claims that emerge are valuable, but not as valuable as the process of "inter-comprehension" and the compassion demanded by any genuine dialogue.

In bringing the Latino/a experience of popular religion front and center, Orlando Espín expands the sources for studying the *sensus fidelium*. However, this expansion should not be seen as the opening up of new markets, providing more raw material for colonial exploitation. To know the *sensus fidelium latinamente* is not simply to subject the "real faith of the real Church" to modern modes of rational analysis. Nor does Latino/a theology merely "enrich" dominant accounts, "making a contribution" to Eurocentric methods that, in the end, remain unexamined and unchallenged. On the contrary, the intercultural dialogue proposed by Espín is much more unsettling. Genuine dialogue means "risking our assumptions and methods by contrasting them with the assumptions and methods of others."[57] We must be willing not only to witness, but also to learn, to see our own commitments as contextual and contingent, to be prepared to let some of them go, and to let others enter in.

Such a process requires an environment conducive to real mutuality. Thus intercultural dialogue calls participants to become genuinely present to one another, to "live with" (*convivir*) others, to spend time together, to share in the daily lives of people "in ways that each considers sufficiently meaningful and sufficiently mutually respectful."[58] But such mutual presence alone is not enough. In order to establish the conditions necessary for serious intercultural dialogue, participants must be willing to face the cultural asymmetries and the political, social, economic, gendered, and racial structures that continue to marginalize some cultures and privilege others. Facing context *is* the context for dialogue. Otherwise dialogue becomes an ideological exercise that fails to recognize that those speaking from the margins, including those speaking *latinamente*, are full "theologizing subjects"—equal voices at the theological table and authentic interpreters of the *sensus fidelium*.[59]

---

57. Ibid., 70.
58. Ibid., 64.
59. Espín, "Intercultural Thought," 643.

19

Latina Lives, Latina Literature

A Narrative Camino in Search of the Sensus Fidelium

NATALIA IMPERATORI-LEE

MY OLDEST SON IS ten years old. Like most children his age, he can be a bit of a know-it-all at times. When we have bacon at breakfast, for example, he will claim that it is merely "digested and processed grass and grain," implying that bacon can be somehow reduced to its humble, vegetarian origins. "Sure it is," his parents reply, "but it is so much more glorious by what the pig brings to it!" Might I suggest that the *sensus fidelium* is like this? It is not the grass; it is not the pig; it is the bacon. Because the *sensus fidelium* brings together doctrine, culture, and narrative in the context of everyday life, it (like the bacon) is more than the sum of its parts. The analogy can be deepened: like the bacon, the *sensus fidelium* can be seen as the scaffolding holding together the body of Christ—shared meanings, shared devotion, shared intuitions about salvation ultimately underlie unity, not some imagined doctrinal uniformity. Moreover, just as a bacon-rich diet can lead to a multitude of health issues, the *sensus fidelium* has presented some vexing problems for theologians and ecclesiologists in particular.

The first and most pressing problem the *sensus fidelium* presents is its elusiveness. What, after all, is a sense and how do you know you have found it? Scholars such as Edward Hahnenberg have pointed out that the *sensus fidelium* has served more often as a retrospective category, which is to say we know it only after it has manifested itself. How, then, can ecclesiologists utilize this as a category without the ability to elaborate what exactly the *sensus fidelium* is, if it is anything at all? Moreover, if it is an empty category, and if no one can point to it, then why deploy it? More importantly, why say it participates (when manifested as the *consensus fidelium*) in the infallibility of the church? Can we say that there has ever been a clear *consensus fidelium* in a church where the nature of Christ was debated for centuries?

If the primary problem of the *sensus fidelium* is the elusive content of this *sensus fidelium*, a related issue can be said to be the terminology used to describe it. Many scholars distinguish between the *sensus fidelium* and the *sensus fidei*, between the subjective aspect (the intuition of the believer) and the objective (that which is believed), but the ways in which they do so do not always overlap. Thus there tends to be muddying of *sensus fidei*, *sensus fidelium*, and *consensus fidelium*, when only *sensus fidei* appears in the documents of Vatican II. Ormond Rush parses this category most efficiently, sorting out the terminology, distinguishing between the *sensus fidei* of the individual, the *sensus fidei fidelium* of the community, and the *consensus fidelium* which applies to the agreement of the whole church on a matter of faith.[1]

Grammatically, we can see that the difference between *sensus fidei* and *fidelium* is one of number, but within these categories, Rush seeks to maintain both the subjective and objective meanings of *sensus fidelium*. He defines them as follows: firstly the *sensus fidei fidelium* is "a spirit given capacity that enables Christians within the struggle of their daily lives to make sense of revelation and understand it,"[2] thus it is a process of understanding (subjective). In addition it "is the particular sense that an individual makes, understanding, interpretation, and application of the faith."[3] Here he means sense not as an intuition but as the sense, or meaning, one makes from the application of the faith. In this way, Rush preserves subjective and objective meanings for the *sensus fidei/fidelium*, and allowing us to move forward to examine not only how an individual or a community makes sense of the faith but what meaning is being gleaned, what Rush calls the "interpretive experience of revelatory salvation."[4]

This differs from John Henry Newman's insight about the *sensus fidelium*, outlined in the International Theological Commission's "Sensus Fidei in the Life of the Church."[5] For Newman, the *sensus fidelium* forms part of a three-part process that begins with articulation (where most people would locate the expressions of the *sensus fidelium* like those suggested by Orlando

---

1. Ormond Rush, "*Sensus Fidei*: Faith Making Sense of Revelation" *Theological Studies* 62 (2001) 231–61, at 231.

2. Ibid., 239.

3. Ibid., 240.

4. Ibid., 244.

5. International Theological Commission, "The *Sensus Fidei* in the Life of the Church," 34, 39, http://www.vatican.va/roman_curia/congregations/cfaith/cti_documents/rc_cti_20140610_sensus-fidei_en.html.

Espín and others, popular religion, liturgy, prayer, actions, etc.) followed by pedagogy, which allows the magisterium to shape the articulations into doctrines (preexistent ones or new ones, as needed) and then is followed by reception, where once again through the *sensus fidelium* the whole people of God decide whether the doctrines as presented are congruent with their initial articulations. In this way, the process of traditioning is a dialectical movement between the magisterium and the laity, between the hierarchy and the non-hierarchy. But it is also, as Hahnenberg points out in his essay in this volume, an imposition of dominant rationality, a forcing-into-boxes of the *sensus fidelium* as expressed in what are perhaps deemed nonrational or more likely, alternatively rational ways, like art and storytelling.

It is my belief that Vatican II intended to move away from this clergy/lay dialectic with its emphasis on the baptismal dignity of all believers. Or, to put it differently, I think Newman's method should be revised. To do this, I will present a story from a contemporary Puerto Rican author, Rosario Ferré, who details in her story "The Battle of the Virgins" an alternative vision of devotion to Our Lady of Guadalupe. Ferré's vision exemplifies one of the varied ways in which the faithful make salvific meaning out of doctrines, even those that have already been "received" and accepted, and continue making the church new in different cultural and historical contexts.

"She Gets Things Done"

The brief personal essay "The Battle of the Virgins," by Rosario Ferré, is a prime example of narrative as theological resource. Ferré's essay foregrounds the tension Orlando Espín describes between religious elites and the faith of the common people, and it reveals a complex faith that is rooted in traditional devotional prayer practices and subversive of a repressive patriarchal system this faith-tradition seems to endorse. The story is narrated by a girl of the upper class who is about eight years old. She describes life in Ponce, a city on the southern coast of Puerto Rico, with her caregiver, Gilda, with whom she understandably spends a great deal of time. Gilda is clearly poor but a profound influence on the young narrator. Gilda's approach to religiosity exemplifies, to my mind, a lot of the theoretical material Hispanic theologians are getting at when they talk about popular religious practices, devotions, and most especially, the role of women in preserving and transmitting these practices. So here's a scene from that essay, which takes place at the cathedral in Ponce, where the elites worship, which is dedicated to La Inmaculada (the Immaculate Conception who is also, incidentally, the patroness of the United States). In this scene, Gilda takes the narrator with her to pray at a side altar where there is a statue of Guadalupe.

> No sooner has she [Gilda] begun to pray when I asked, "Why is *la Guadalupe* black? All the other Virgins I know are white and blond, and they have blue eyes."
> "She's not black, she's brown. She was buried in the ground for eight hundred years. The dirt stuck to her and now she's the same color as the earth."
> "Why was she buried in the ground for eight hundred years?" I whispered.
> "Because some bad men wanted to harm her. I saw the story in Tizoc, a Mexican movie I went to. Pedro Infante tells how la Guadalupe was hidden away in a cave in the mountains because they wanted to destroy her image. It was such a beautiful movie! Every time María Félix appeared on the screen, Pedro Infante and his mariachis played the guitar for her just like Eusebio does for me in El Tibidabo once in a while."[6]

This scene represents the first catechetical moment between the narrator of Ferré's short story (likely Ferré herself) and Gilda Ventura, the nanny in the story.[7] It also exemplifies the difficult nature of getting at the *sensus fidelium* by looking at popular religious practices and beliefs; namely, that these beliefs tend to be extra-doctrinal or non-doctrinal, informed as much by popular belief and customs (and in this case, movies and popular culture) as they are by magisterial Catholic teaching. What we think is going on when we see two young women kneeling before a statue of Guadalupe is not too close to what Gilda is whispering to Rosario about a movie starring Maria Felix and Pedro Infante (two famous Mexican movie stars) and conflating the Guadalupe de Extremadura with the Mexican virgin who appeared to Juan Diego at Tepeyac. We cannot equate popular Catholicism with the *sensus fidelium*. The *sensus* is primarily a Spirit-infused intuition, and you can't point to an intuition. It requires interpretation, or, as Hahnenberg would note, it requires a willingness to enter into a connatural relationship.[8] This does not render the practices and beliefs irrelevant however. In fact, the opposite holds true: I believe this scene represents the way in which diver-

---

6. Rosario Ferré, "The Battle of the Virgins" in *Goddess of the Americas: Writings on the Virgin of Guadalupe*, ed. Ana Castillo (New York: Riverhead, 1996), 81.

7. The story is told in the first person, so while it is safe to assume, given the similarities with Ferré's life, that the author is the narrator, I will nevertheless refer to the protagonist as "the narrator" because a name is not given.

8. See Edward Hahnenberg's essay in this volume, "Learning to Discern the *Sensus Fidelium Latinamente*: A Dialogue with Orlando Espín."

gent strands of knowledge and complex systems of sense-making coalesce into a fundamental understanding of divine activity in the world that fits both with the central teachings of Christianity and the faith of Christians themselves. For thinkers like Rick Gaillardetz and Ormond Rush, the *sensus fidelium* doesn't just mirror or rubber-stamp or reject Tradition, it contributes to Tradition, it adds to doctrines through inculturation, interpretation, application.

When the narrator joins Gilda at the cathedral of the Immaculate Conception (La Inmaculada) in Ponce, praying at a side altar before la Guadalupe, the child is engaged in a traditional religious practice. Outwardly, it would appear that two women kneeling in prayer in front of a Guadalupan statue is nothing out of the ordinary. It is Gilda's gloss on the Virgin's story that makes it extraordinary. Gilda's interpretation is influenced by a conflation of the stories of the Virgin of Montserrat, the Virgin of Guadalupe de Extremadura and the story of the Mexican virgin told in the *Nican Mopohua*, coupled with a movie that includes the Guadalupan apparition.[9] From this intercultural stew, Gilda gleans a lesson that subverts the traditionally pious message of marian devotion and replaces it, or at least nuances it with an understanding different than traditional mariologies.

Later in the story, the narrator asks Gilda about the rays, which she thinks are swords, pointing out from behind Guadalupe. Gilda tells the little girl: "La Guadalupe is a very powerful virgin! You don't want her as your enemy. Those swords are her thunderbolts. She's not a namby-pamby virgin like the ones in the other churches. She gets things done and she protects people who fight for what they want."[10] Here, Gilda has picked up on the narrator's "misreading" of the rays of light surrounding Guadalupe as samurai swords and uses this misreading to emphasize the power of the Virgin. Guadalupe stands in contrast to the "other" virgins, like the Immaculate Conception imported by the English-speaking settlers and revered by the religious elites. These elites are personified in the narrator's mother and the rest of the high society in Ponce, as well as the Irish bishop, James MacManus, who is referred to most irreverently as "Marshmallow" for his lily-white skin and propensity to drive the few blocks from his home to the church to avoid sunburn. He sweats profusely. The narrator observes that Bishop MacManus tends to focus his homilies on the Immaculate Conception and female purity. Unlike the image of the Immaculate Conception, Guadalupe

9. That movie, *Tizoc*, featured Mexican actors retelling the narrative Guadalupe as a love story between a native man and a white European woman (played by Maria Felix) who symbolizes the virgin. *Tizoc: Amor Indio*, directed by Ismael Rodriguez (1957; Mexico; Azteca Films).

10. Ferré, "The Battle of the Virgins," 82.

is not passive, long-suffering, placidly standing on a bed of lilies. Guadalupe represents, for Gilda and for her charge, a powerful woman who protects those who follow their passions.

This endorsement of passion and self-determination was indeed a subversive message for the young female narrator to hear, and for Gilda to proclaim. Both the narrator and Gilda were expected to conform to the socio-cultural expectations of their respective classes, expectations that very much fit the mold of marianismo outlined by sociologist Evelyn Stevens.[11] For Stevens, women in Latin America were expected to perform public acts of mourning and sadness, including the wearing of all-black clothing, essentially from the time they were middle aged. Joy, passion, and sexual interest were associated with unserious women, and somberness or sadness were the marks of a "good" woman. The first hints of this phenomenon come early in Ferré's story, when the narrator is contrasting Gilda's joy and exuberance with her mother's somber sadness, indicated by the mother's performance of expected mourning rituals. "Gilda was beautiful . . . with nut-brown skin and finely chiseled features. She always wore brightly colored clothes, and her enameled nails looked like cherry-red daggers. Her mouth was a perfect bow and shot arrows at you when she laughed. Mother on the contrary was always sad. She dressed only in black because she was in mourning."[12] The child sees her caregiver as a joyous, passionate person, in contrast to her mother's performance of public mourning and outward drab dress and melancholy demeanor.

For the narrator, a child from a wealthy family, class expectations nevertheless meant aspiring not to an education but to a placid family life where, by denying herself pleasure (particularly sexual pleasure, as demanded by the marianismo paradigm) she would guarantee her soul's entrance into

---

11. Evelyn Stevens, "Marianismo: The Other Face of Machismo in Latin America," *Female and Male in Latin America*, ed., A. Decastello (Pittsburgh: University of Pittsburgh Press, 1973). It is important to note that since the publication of Stevens' work, scholars such as Tracy Ehlers have critiqued the universalizing impulse in Stevens' use of marianismo, arguing that the paradigm does not apply with the same force to cultures outside of Mexico, and perhaps only applies to middle- or upper-class women. Others have claimed that marianismo does not speak out strongly enough against the reality of domestic violence that characterizes the specific forms of patriarchy at work in Latin America. While these critiques are valid, I nevertheless contend that what Ferré depicts in this short story reflects a real, and though not physically violent, spiritually and hermeneutically violent strain of marianismo that operates in many parts of Latin America, including Puerto Rico and the Spanish-speaking Caribbean. See Tracy Ehlers, "Debunking Marianismo: Economic Vulnerability and Survival Strategies among Guatemalan Wives," *Ethnology* 30:1 (Jan 1991), as well as Miguel de la Torre, "Marianismo," in *Hispanic American Religious Cultures* (Santa Barbara: ABC-CLIO, 2009) 346–48.

12. Ferré, "The Battle of the Virgins," 82.

heaven. This lesson is emphasized in the preaching of Bishop MacManus, who explains the notion of sinlessness as something that "could be achieved only if the wife managed to keep herself detached from earthly passion. Even during the holy act of procreation . . . ."[13] The narrator confronts the constricting expectations of marianismo in the church's official voice, but experiences a different, though no less religious, reality when praying with Gilda. Still, Ferré makes clear that the expectations for a woman of the upper class included spiritual purity, attained through avoidance of pleasure and sin, particularly sexual sin.

For a woman of Gilda's class, the expectations were far more extreme: her family's poverty made it nearly impossible to fathom an education or any sort of liberation from the life of poverty to which she was surely doomed. And yet, at the end of the story neither woman has conformed to the marianista norms expected of them. Gilda improbably was able to leave the island and complete an education, become a nurse, and marry her true love Eusebio. The narrator gains the courage to leave the island for boarding school and college in the U.S.

Ferré's story ends with a shocking observation on the part of the now-adult narrator: "Gilda's life had been heroic; she was a fit example of a devotee of [Guadalupe] the Virgin of the conquistadors."[14] While the majority of Latin America (and other colonized cultures) would likely disagree with the characterization of conquistadors as heroic, I'd like to focus here on the juxtaposition of Gilda, a victim of the double-rejection of being a woman and a Latina of the lower class in Puerto Rico and the mainland U.S., with the heroic virtue of Guadalupe as understood by Gilda and the narrator: a smart, powerful Virgin who protects those who fight for what they want. What Gilda wanted for herself and for her young charge was to break away from the predetermined feminine roles and into a life of one's own, a life marked by love, passion, freedom, and education. Both Gilda and the narrator find this, by leaving their homeland and seeking out something new. In rooting their liberative praxis in devotion to the Guadalupe in Ponce's church, Ferré ties popular Catholic practice to goals that would be characterized as feminist: the self-actualization of women, their education, and their capacity for self-determination.

There are, however, unsettling questions that remain after reading a story like this. Why must the women leave the island to find fulfillment? Why does the author hold up migration to the United States as the symbol of liberation? Is there no salvation to be found within one's culture, but only

13. Ibid., 84.
14. Ibid., 87.

outside it? Moreover, what sense can be made of equating Guadalupe with the conquistadors or characterizing them as heroic? Without interviewing the author, it's not possible to know for sure. Hermeneutically, however, readers create meaning as much as an author does. It is possible to glean important insights about the ways in which the sense of the faithful functions through popular religion and narrative in this story, even if the story presents us with a superabundance of signification, not all of which can be characterized as relevant to this line of ecclesiological inquiry.

Conclusion: Narrativity or Normativity or Both?

Ultimately Ferré presents us with an uncomfortable narrative that highlights the ways in which endemic issues of race and class are reinscribed by devotionalism and popular religion, and also points to the ways in which people make sense, in this case liberative sense, of the faith. What we have in Ferré's presentation is more than intuition; it is content, albeit surprising and at points disturbing. It is certainly NOT your mother's marian devotion, or the one presented as "Hispanic" in the media. This telling reorients Newman's method and puts pedagogy in the hands of all the faithful not merely the magisterium. Further, it highlights the importance of Latina lives in traditioning, in cooperating with the Spirit in a connatural way to make all things, even marian devotion, new.

The *sensus fidelium* is one of several *loci receptionis* for Rush.[15] Within this locus, narratives have a special place, both because narratives are a primary way in which we understand ourselves, and because narratives have the capacity to elicit a certain connaturality in the reader. By entering into the world of the text the reader participates in the hermeneutical task of meaning-making. This is precisely what the *sensus fidelium* does—invites the whole people of God to participate in the task of meaning-making when it comes to salvation. Ferré's narrative of the *sensus fidelium* in a particular life, a particular life story, historical moment, and familial relationship—like all instances of the *sensus fidelium*—contributes to the tradition. It does not merely confirm what came before and it certainly does not conform. In this way, the *sensus fidelium* also serves as a primary vehicle of inculturation. As Rush notes: it (the *sensus*) always exceeds the proposition (of faith); it bridges the gap between past and present, and enables the faith to be constantly rejuvenated.[16] To my mind what Ferré provides in her story is a radi-

---

15. Ormond Rush, *Still Interpreting Vatican II: Some Hermeneutical Principles* (New York: Paulist, 2004) 53.

16. Rush, "*Sensus Fidei*: Faith Making Sense of Revelation," 239.

cal rejuvenation of Guadalupan devotion, or at least a vision of Guadalupan devotion that is the in-breaking of something new.

Ultimately the *sensus fidelium* must conform to norms, but following Ormond Rush, I am tempted to go with the norm of salvation. He writes, "The sense one has made of the faith is an individual's interpretive experience of revelatory salvation."[17] This interpretive experience necessarily includes social, geographic, and other aspects of an individual's location. Not all the senses or understandings of the faith need to conform or be uniform . . . indeed, this is impossible in each case. But the understandings must be salvific; they must point to the liberative message of Christ, and lead the believer on a pilgrimage, a *camino* to that salvation. To my eyes, the story of Rosario and Gilda in "The Battle of the Virgins" represents salvation for both women, liberation from oppressive structures put in place by colonialism, sexism, and even very specific marianista expectations that plague women in Latin America and to some extent, the U.S. Karl Rahner felt that Christians may interpret doctrines in a variety of ways and indeed that this was a necessary feature of the global church.[18] Our duty as theologians then, is to witness to the loci where these interpretations take place. Narratives like Ferré's give us insight into how devotions work through storytelling, a cornerstone of the life of faith and of Christianity, a religion based in gospel stories of the teacher-storyteller Jesus.

---

17. Ibid., 244.

18. Karl Rahner, "The Abiding Significance of the Second Vatican Council," *Theological Investigations* 20, trans. Edward Quinn (New York: Crossroad, 1981), 90–102.

20

"Who Do You Say that I Am?"

Uncovering the Chinese Sensus Fidelium in Images of Jesus in Pre-Communist Chinese Catholic Devotional Art from the 1930s to 1940s

JONATHAN Y. TAN

IN THE ANNALS OF evangelization in the history of the Chinese Catholic Church, art often played a major role as a catechesis tool that enabled many new Chinese Catholic converts, especially the unlettered, to grasp and express the *sensus* of their newly-embraced Catholic faith. In the 1930s, Chinese Catholic art underwent a shift from European artistic styles (*xihua* 西畫) to Chinese artistic styles (*guohua* 國畫) that enabled a new generation of Chinese Catholic artists, many of whom were converts, to express their *sensus* of their new faith through layers of Chinese cultural, philosophical, and spiritual influences.

This essay explores the contours and articulates some tentative understandings of the early twentieth century Chinese Catholic reception and *sensus* of foundational christological principles in Chinese Catholic devotional art that were produced by the leading Chinese Catholic artists from 1930s–1940s. It discusses how these Chinese Catholic artists expressed their understanding of the Catholic faith and their sense of the soteriological significance of Jesus Christ in their artistic oeuvre. In doing so, it seeks to unpack how these Chinese Catholic artworks reveal the *sensus fidelium* of the Chinese Catholic community on the christological question. As space does not permit an exhaustive discussion of the entire range of Chinese Catholic art, the focus of this discussion is primarily on paintings from the collection of the Ricci Institute for Chinese Western Cultural History at the University of San Francisco, supplemented by appropriate or comparable images from other collections.

Celso Costantini

The emergence of a distinctive Chinese artistic style (*guohua* 國畫) for Chinese Catholic art owes its beginning to Celso Costantini (1876–1958), who was appointed by Pope Pius XI as the first apostolic delegate to the then newly established Republican China on August 12, 1922. As apostolic delegate, Costantini arrived in China with a clear agenda to indigenize the Chinese Catholic Church according to the vision outlined by Pope Benedict XV in his apostolic letter, *Maximum Illud* (1919). By the time he returned to Rome in 1933 to take up his new appointment as secretary of Propaganda Fide, he left behind a list of remarkable achievements, including the convocation of the First Plenary Council of the Chinese Catholic Church in Shanghai in 1924, the establishment of the Catholic University of Peking (*Beiping Furen Daxue* 北平輔仁大學) in 1925, and making episcopal history with the episcopal ordination of six indigenous Chinese bishops by Pope Pius XI in 1926, marking the beginning of the transition of the Chinese Catholic Church from a mission church to an indigenous local church.[1] Jeremy Clarke sums it up succinctly when he states that Costantini "successfully shepherded the Chinese church towards maturity, helping transform it into a church that was no longer merely missionary, but one that became fully localized."[2]

Costantini was an ardent proponent of using the genius of Chinese indigenous artistic and architectural forms rather than importing Western forms for use in China. He was highly critical of the pervasive presence of western architectural and artistic forms in the Chinese Catholic Church. In his own words:

> Within the Gothic style, the roofs come to a rapid point in order to hasten the fall of snow from them, and the rising gothic spires are in magnificent harmony with the countryside of Northern Europe, but I am not in any way able to say the same about the gothic towers that I have seen nestled among bamboo groves during my journey throughout China.[3]

---

1. For an overview of Celso Costantini's contributions and accomplishments in China, see Sergio Ticozzi, "Celso Constantini's Contribution to the Localization and Inculturation of the Church in China," *Tripod* 28 (Spring 2008) 11–28. This is a special issue commemorating the fiftieth anniversary of Costantini's death with essays by Sergio Ticozzi on Costantini's contributions to the inculturation of the Chinese Catholic Church, Anthony Lam on Costantini's role in the First Plenary Council of Shanghai (1924), and Francis Chong summarizing Costantini's principal contributions to the Chinese Catholic Church.

2. Jeremy Clarke, The *Virgin Mary and Catholic Identities in Chinese History* (Hong Kong: Hong Kong University Press, 2013), 121.

3. English translation taken from Clarke, *Virgin Mary*, 125. For the original text,

Writing to the two Apostlic Prefects, Columban missioner Edward J. Galvin of Hanyang, Hubei and Maryknoll missioner James Edward Walsh of Jiangmen, Guangdong on April 23, 1923 soon after his arrival in China,[4] Costantini minced no words when he insisted on the following points:

1. Western art is a style unsuited to China.
2. Western art in mission areas gives the impression that the Church is a foreign religion.
3. It has been a policy of the Church to adopt local art forms and incorporate them into the Christian tradition.
4. Chinese art (and culture) offers favorable possibilities for adaptation.[5]

A year later, at the First Plenary Council of the Chinese Catholic Church in Shanghai (1924), Costantini pushed hard for the Council to adopt the following proposal: "In constructing and decorating the sacred buildings and residences of the missionaries, styles of foreign art should not be employed, but, as far as possible and according to the opportunity, forms of the native art of the Chinese people should be used."[6]

In this regard, Costantini was not introducing something novel but implementing the original vision of the Sacred Congregation for the Propagation of the Faith in its instruction to its newly appointed apostolic vicars, François Pallu and Pierre Lambert de la Motte, in 1659 on the eve of their inaugural mission to Tonkin and Cochinchina respectively:

> Do not in any way attempt and do not on any pretext persuade these peoples to change their rites, customs and mores unless these are clearly contrary to religion and good morals. For what could be more absurd than to bring France, Spain, Italy, or any other European country over to China? It is not these countries but faith that you must bring, the faith that does not reject or jeopardize the rites and customs of any people as long as these are not depraved, but rather desires to preserve and promote

---

see Celso Costantini, "L'universalité de l'art chrétien," in *Dossiers de la Commission synodale. Numéro special sur l'art chrétien chinois* 5 (1932) 413.

4. See Costantini, "Universalité de l'art chrétien," cited in Nicolas Standaert, ed., *Handbook of Christianity in China*, Vol. 2 (Leiden: Brill, 2010) 734 n.2.

5. These four points are taken from Lawton, "A Unique Style in China," 472. For an alternative translation of these four points that Costantini made, see Ticozzi, "Celso Costantini," 18–19. For primary source of these four points, see Celso Costantini and Maoxue Sun, 中國天主教美術 *Zhongguo Tianzhujiao Meishu* [Catholic Art in China] (Taizhong: Guangqi, 1968,) 12.

6. English translation in Ticozzi, "Celso Costantini," 19.

them . . . Admire and praise whatever deserves praise. As to things that are not praiseworthy, they should not be extolled, as is done by flatterers. On the contrary, exercise prudence in either not passing judgment on them or in not condemning them rashly and exaggeratedly. As for what is evil, it should be dismissed with a nod of the head or by silence rather than by words, though without missing the opportunity, when people have become disposed to receive the truth, to uproot it without ostentation.[7]

With support and encouragement from Costantini, the foundation for the Catholic University of Peking (*Beiping Furen Daxue* 北平輔仁大學) was laid in 1925 and its art department was created in 1930. Costantini held high hopes for Furen, which was administered by Benedictines of St. Vincent Archabbey (Latrobe, Pennsylvania) from 1925–1933 and the Society of the Divine Word from 1933–1952. Indeed, he envisaged that this university "would be a centre of high culture, religious and humanistic."[8] Under the aegis of Furen in the pre-Communist Chinese Catholic Church, a number of Furen's Chinese Catholic art professors and their students produced a diverse array of Chinese artistic images of Jesus drawn from infancy narratives, Madonna and Child, the Holy Family, as well as the life and ministry of Jesus for both public ecclesial and private devotional use. Mary S. Lawton notes that the period between 1939 and 1959 represents the high point of Chinese Catholic devotional art, observing that there were "not only orders

---

7. This advice is found in *Sacra Congregatio de. Collectanea Sacrae Congregationis de Propaganda Fide: seu decreta, instructiones, rescripta pro Apostolicis Missionibus.* Vol. 1. (Roma: Ex Typographia Polyglotta, Sacrae Congregationis de Propaganda Fide, 1907), 42. The Latin text reads: "*Nullum studium ponite, nullaque ratione suadete illis populis ut ritus sous, consuetudines et mores mutent, modo non sint apertissime Religioni et bonis moribus contraria. Quid enim absurdius quam Galliam, Hispaniam, Italiam aut aliam Europae partem in Sinas invehere? Non haec, sed fidem importate, quae nullius gentis ritus et consuetudines, modo prava non sint, aut respuit aut laedit, immo vero sarta tecta esse vult . . . Admiramini et laudate ea quae laudem merentur; quae vero laudis expertia sunt, ut non sunt praeconiis, assentatorum more, extollenda ita prudentiae vestrae erit de hit aut iudicium non ferre, aut certe non temere et ultro damnare; quae vero prava extiterint, nutibus magis et silentio quam verbis proscindenda, opportunitate nimirum captata qua, dispositis animis ad veritatem capessendam, sensim sine sensu evellantur.*" The English translation is taken from Peter C. Phan, *Mission and Catechesis: Alexandre de Rhodes and Inculturation in Seventeenth-Century Vietnam* (Maryknoll, NY: Orbis, 1998), 193–94.

8. Celso Costantini, *Church and Chinese Culture* (New York: Society for the Propagation of the Faith, 1931), 10.

for paintings but also for altar pieces and there is an indication that there were even orders for the complete or partial decoration of church interiors."[9]

While some of the artwork of these artists portrayed Jesus in Westernized styles (*xihua*), a significant number of the Furen art professors and their students began expressing their understanding of their Catholic faith and their *sensus* of what Jesus meant to them using the Chinese artistic style (*guohua* 國畫) that incorporated layers of Chinese cultural, philosophical, and spiritual influences. These artists included (Luke) Chen Yuandu 陳緣督, Lu Hongnian 陸鴻年, Xu Jihua 徐濟華, Wang Suda 王肅達, Luke Hua Xiaoxian 華效先, Bai Huiqun 白慧群, Francis Gao Tihan 高褆厂, and others. While many pieces of Chinese Catholic art from this period were irreversibly destroyed or lost during the chaos following the forcible closure of Furen in 1952 and the chaos and destruction of the Cultural Revolution (1966–1975), a number of images are preserved at the Archives of the Society of the Divine Word in Rome, the Ricci Institute for Chinese Western Cultural History at the University of San Francisco, and in museum and private collections around the world.

In an era where Latin, the official language of the Tridentine liturgy, was unknown to a majority of Chinese Catholics, these images in Chinese artistic style (*guohua* 國畫) functioned as "bibles for the poor," narrating aspects of the life and ministry of Jesus Christ and popular Catholic devotions to Mary and Jesus in an accessible manner. Indeed, much of Chinese Catholic art as an emerging genre in the 1930s and 1940s functioned as catechetical aids and devotional objects in churches and homes. More significantly, the artists and students of Furen were themselves converts to Catholicism. Their embrace of art as a tool of catechesis in early twentieth century China enabled them to grasp and express the *sensus* of their Catholic faith through devotional art.

From "Western Art" (*xihua* 西畫) to "Chinese Art" (*guohua* 國畫)

The Chinese Catholic paintings that compose the collection "Icons of the Celestial Kingdom" at the Ricci Institute for Chinese Western Cultural History originated from the 1930s and 1940s and were produced by an artists' workshop that called itself the Fine Arts Department of Beijing Sacred Heart Church at Guanganmen (*Beiping Guanganmen Shengxintang Meishubu* 北平廣安門聖心堂美術部). Not much is known about this collection, which

---

9. Mary S. Lawton, "A Unique Style in China. Chinese Christian Painting in Beijing," *Monumenta Serica: Journal of Oriental Studies* 43 (1995) 479.

was brought to France and subsequently acquired by the Ricci Institute in 1992. There does not appear to be any records indicating any church or chapel at or near Guanganmen. Monica Liu has advanced the hypothesis that this artists' workshop was likely affiliated with Furen's art department.[10]

The Nativity

The nativity of Jesus is a popular subject for the emerging Chinese Catholic artists in the 1930s and 1940s, with many examples by Lu Hongnian, Huang Ruilong, and others. The first image that we are considering is *Birth of Jesus* (耶穌誕生),[11] by Luke Hua Xiaoxian 華效先. The inscription of this painting reads "天主慶賀吾主耶穌聖誕圖; 路加華效先; 北平廣安門聖心堂美術部出品" (God celebrates the Nativity of Our Lord Jesus; Luke Hua Xiaoxian; A product of the Beiping Guang'anmen Sacred Heart Church Fine Arts Department). This painting depicts Mary and Joseph with the newborn Jesus in a cave in the style of a Chinese landscape (shanshui 山水) painting. Of interest is the angels, which are depicted in the style of Daoist immortal maidens playing traditional Chinese instruments. This interreligious engagement is reminiscent of a painting by the Chinese artist Xu Sanchun who produced paintings in St. Luke's Studio (Anglican) in Nanjing under the auspices of T.K. Shen (Shen Zigao 沈子高), the first indigenous Chinese Anglican bishop who advocated for the indigenization of the Anglican Church in China through the use of Chinese art and music. Xu's *Visit of the Three Magi* depicts a kneeling Buddhist monk, a Confucian scholar, and a Daoist with his long beard and gourd of water visiting the baby Jesus with Mary and Joseph under a thatch hut beside a pine tree.[12] Xu's portrayal of the three religions (*sanjiao* 三教)—Confucianism, Daoism, and Buddhism—paying homage to the newborn Jesus is illustrative of how many Chinese converts of that era perceived their newfound faith as a continuation of their ancestral faith traditions.

---

10. See Monica Liu, *Chinese Sacred Art*, internal report for the Ricci Institute, cited in Clarke, *Virgin Mary*, 171.

11. For image, see: http://usf.usfca.edu/ricci/collection/exhibits/celestialicons/icon4.htm.

12. A black and white reproduction of this image may be seen in Daniel Johnson Fleming, *Each with His Own Brush: Contemporary Christian Art in Asia and Africa* (New York: Friendship, 1938) 18.

The Homage of the Three Kings

The painting *Homage of the Three Kings* (三王來朝),[13] by Luke Hua Xiaoxian 華效先, is a fascinating interpretation of the Adoration of the Magi in the context of Confucian China. The inscription reads "三王來朝; 一九四八年七月北平廣安門聖心堂美術部路加華效先敬 繪" (The Homage of the Three Kings; painted by Luke Hua Xiaoxian, Beiping Guang'anmen Sacred Heart Church Fine Arts Department, July 1948). This painting depicts Mary, Joseph, and the infant Jesus in a garden pavilion in a traditional Chinese courtyard, receiving gifts from the three kings. In the background, the kings' horses are being handled by their manservant. This fascinating interpretation of the visit of the three kings melds the classical Chinese portrayal of vassals offering tribute to the emperor with the three kings offering tribute to Jesus, who is depicted with Mary and Joseph in a setting of a garden pavilion that is characteristic of wealthy Chinese households.

The Holy Family

The Holy Family is another popular subject for Chinese Catholic artists. Compared to European paintings of the Holy Family that often present the Holy Family in idealized and otherworldly terms, Chinese artists often contextualized the Holy Family within the idealized Chinese family that is shaped according to Confucian norms. In this regard, *The Holy Family* (聖家),[14] by Bai Huiqun 白慧群, depicts the Holy Family in as a well-to-do traditional Chinese family, with Mary and Joseph around baby Jesus in his crib in a pavilion of the courtyard of a Chinese home. In particular, Joseph is shown as a Confucian paterfamilias watching over his household. This depiction of the Holy Family as an idealized Confucian family can be seen in *The Holy Family with Angels* (天使隊中聖家), by (Luke) Chen Yuandu 陳緣督,[15] where Joseph, the Confucian paterfamilias, gazes at Mary with a standing toddler Jesus, all served by a team of angels as in a traditional and wealthy Chinese nobility family. Hence, Chinese convert artists painted the Holy Family not in abstract theological terms, but as an idealized Confucian

---

13. For image, see: http://usf.usfca.edu/ricci/collection/exhibits/celestialicons/icon6.htm.

14. For image, see: http://usf.usfca.edu/ricci/collection/exhibits/celestialicons/icon7.htm.

15. A black-and-white reproduction of this image is found in Fritz Bornemann, *Ars Sacra Pekinensis: Die chinesisch-christliche Malerei un der Katholischen Universität (Fu Jen) in Peking* (Mödling bei Wein: Druck und Verlag, 1950), 31.

family, integrating Confucian and Christian understandings of family life to convey their understandings of the Holy Family.

The Confucian dimension is also explicitly highlighted in Bai Huiqun's *The Education of Jesus* (耶穌受教育),[16] which highlights the traditional Confucian ideal of the love of learning (*xue* 學) and filial love of one's parents (*xiao* 孝). He depicts this within the traditional Confucian household in a creative reinterpretation of the familial bonds of the Holy Family. This image depicts Jesus as a young boy reciting his lessons in traditional Confucian style to his father, shown as a Confucian *paterfamilias*, with his mother listening to him while engaging in embroidery. The setting of this painting is a pavilion in a garden of a Chinese traditional house. Chinese Catholic converts who gazed at this image would not miss its overt Confucian emphasis on Jesus' filiality (*xiao* 孝) toward his father, as conveyed by his reciting his lessons to an approving father. Moreover, it highlights the preeminence of learning (*xue* 學) in Confucian society, to the extent of showing Joseph as the ideal embodiment of an educated Confucian *paterfamilias* who is able to participate in the learning and education of his son.

The idea of filial submission and obedience can also be seen in the remarkable painting *Jesus Submits to his Parents* (耶穌服從父母),[17] by Wang Suda 王肅達. In this painting, Wang Suda vividly portrays "Jesus was obedient to his parents" (Luke 2:51) in a Confucian context. Set in a simply furnished Chinese home, Joseph, as *paterfamilias* in a Confucian household, sits at a table with carpentry tools beneath it. The table is set for a meal with steaming Chinese dishes, bowls, chopsticks, and bottles of condiments. Mary presents Jesus, who is bringing out a tray filled with bowls of steamed rice to offer to his father Joseph. Here, the Chinese Catholic *sensus* that integrates the Confucian ideals of filiality as outlined in Analects (*Lunyu* 論語) 1:6[18] and 2:5[19] with the commandment to honor one's parents (Exodus 20:12) is portrayed unequivocally.

---

16. For image, see: http://usf.usfca.edu/ricci/collection/exhibits/celestialicons/icon9.htm.

17. A black-and-white reproduction of this image is found in Bornemann, *Ars Sacra Pekinensis*, 127.

18. "子曰: 弟子入則孝" (The Master said, "As a young brother and son, be filial (xiao 孝) at home"). English translation from Roger T. Ames and Henry Rosemont, trans. *The Analects of Confucius: A Philosophical Translation* (New York: Ballantine, 1998) 72.

19. "子曰: 生, 事之以禮; 死, 葬之以禮, 祭之以禮" (The Master replied: "While [your parents] are living, serve them according to the observances of ritual propriety (*li* 禮), when they are dead, bury them and sacrifice to them according to the observances of ritual propriety"). English translation in Ames and Rosemont, Analects, 77.

Madonna and Child

The next set of images is, strictly speaking, the Chinese equivalent of the genre of Madonna and Child. However, the mother-child relation that is expressed in this painting is different than European images of Madonna and Child. "Jesus recites his lessons from memory" (耶穌在背書),[20] by Francis Gao Tihan 高褆厂, develops the Confucian love of learning (*xue* 學) and filial love toward one's parents (*xiao* 孝). In this image, Gao Tihan presents a young Jesus reciting a lesson from memory with his back turned toward his mother, who is seated at a table with an open book. The whole scene is set in a traditional Chinese landscaped garden with a screen at the back of Mary. This painting often elicits differing responses from East Asian vis-à-vis European audiences on the issue of Jesus' apparent submission to his mother on the matter of his education and studies. Whereas the latter might react to the incongruity of this depiction of Jesus having to be tested by his mother in contrast to the Lukan narrative of the boy Jesus knowing more than the learned teachers in the Temple (Luke 2:41–51), East Asians would recognize immediately the traditional posture of learning, that is, reciting lessons from memory for a parent that exemplifies both the quest of learning (*xue* 學) and filiality (*xiao* 孝) toward one's parents.

The evocative image *Our Lady at the Spinning Wheel with the Child Jesus* (紡織中的聖母與孩童耶穌),[21] by Bai Huiqun 白慧群, shows the tender mother-child relation in a Chinese domestic family context. Specifically, Bai Huiqun presents Mary hard at work at a spinning wheel in a traditional Chinese garden while Jesus, who is seated next to hear, reads a lesson from his book. This image expresses the same *sensus* as the preceding image, namely the mother-child relation between Mary and Jesus as understood through the lens of filial obedience and love of learning in the quest to be a noble or perfected human person (*junzi* 君子), the goal of Confucian moral rectification as expressed in the Analects (*Lunyu* 論語) of Confucius.

Likewise, Bai Huiqun (白慧群)'s *Our Lady with the Child Jesus Writing Characters* (聖母與孩童耶穌在寫字)[22] further unpacks the Confucian reception of the mother-child relations of Mary and Jesus. In this image, set in a landscaped garden under a tree, the young boy Jesus holds an ink stone as Mary prepares to write on a scroll. It appears that Jesus is gazing raptly at

---

20. For image, see: http://usf.usfca.edu/ricci/collection/exhibits/celestialicons/icon14.htm.

21. For image, see: http://usf.usfca.edu/ricci/collection/exhibits/celestialicons/icon13.htm.

22. For image, see: http://usf.usfca.edu/ricci/collection/exhibits/celestialicons/icon15.htm.

Mary as she writes characters. The implication here is Mary's show-and-tell on how to write characters. "Our Lady with the Child Jesus" (聖母與孩童耶穌),[23] also by Bai Huiqun 白慧群, continues in a similar vein. Set yet again in a traditional Chinese landscaped garden, Mary is seated on a rock looking lovingly at Jesus with his opened book, as he proudly shows his mother what he has done in his learning (xue 學).

At the same time, this is not the only manner of portraying the mother-child relation. *Our Lady with the Child Jesus* (聖母與孩童耶穌),[24] by Luke Hua Xiaoxian 華效先, portrays Mary leaning on Jesus for support in a traditional Chinese garden that is landscaped with rocks, bamboo, and trees. This image of Mary leaning on Jesus for support as she walks comes out of traditional foot-bound Chinese women who needed the assistance of their servants to hobble on their painful crippled feet. "Jesus helps his mother in her work" (耶穌助母勞作),[25] by Lu Hongnian 陸鴻年, seeks to convey comparable sentiments. Lu Hongnian sets his painting in a Chinese countryside. Jesus, depicted as a young child, is helping Mary with the family laundry, squeezing the newly washed clothes to dry them. Here, we see filiality (xiao 孝) in action as Jesus helps his mother in her daily chores.

Nonetheless, not all Madonna and Child images are stern and serious. A lighthearted example is *Mary and the White Doves* (聖母和白鴿).[26] In this delightful painting, set in a landscaped garden bounded by a wall and gate, Mary and the young child Jesus are playing with flying white doves as Joseph peeks at them through the gate. In particular, Mary holds a bowl of water for the doves to drink while Jesus plays with the doves around him. Instead of overt Confucian precepts, one finds a Chinese family enjoying one another's company in the simplicity of nature.

More importantly, the tenderness and poignancy of this mother-and-child portrayal in the various representations of mother-and-child relations is unmistakable. At a more profound level, this shows the extent to which Chinese Catholic converts perceive and receive the traditional Holy Family and parent-child relations on their own terms, that is to say, through a Confucian familial perspective. The genius of the Chinese *sensus* is that the Holy Family and Madonna-and-Child are not abstract doctrinal contexts

23. For image, see: http://usf.usfca.edu/ricci/collection/exhibits/celestialicons/icon17.htm.

24. For image, see: http://usf.usfca.edu/ricci/collection/exhibits/celestialicons/icon18.htm

25. For a black-and-white reproduction of this image, see Bornemann, *Ars Sacra Pekinensis*, 179.

26. For a black-and-white representation of this image, see Bornemann, *Ars Sacra Pekinensis*, 181.

but realized through a powerful synthesis of Confucian-Christian contextualization where Jesus, notwithstanding his status, is filial toward his parents, submits to their authority, assists in daily chores, and engages in rigorous learning and study under his parents' tutelage. We see a very human Jesus engages in typical Confucian practices of moral rectification—filiality, learning, and studying, as well as assisting and serving parents, exemplifying a low christology from below rather than a high and triumphant christology. We see an explicit endeavor to contextualize Jesus in real, human terms in a creative engagement and synthesis of Confucian and Christian imagery of being human (*ren* 仁) as the highest and perfected embodiment of Confucian moral rectification.

Conclusion

Religious art and imagery as faith expressions of a community often reveal that community's identity construction and sense of belonging in relation to the wider society. Jeremy Clarke's observations, made in the context of Chinese Catholic Marian art, are also applicable here. Specifically, Clarke asserts

> Chinese Christian art was more than just a fad promoted and supported by only a few Westerners. These works, and the reception of them, therefore reveal aspects of the Chinese Christian communities. In the same way, the choice of thematic content illustrates key identifying characteristics of the Catholic communities.[27]

More importantly, Clarke argues that these paintings are more than mere devotional piety of the new waves of Chinese Catholic converts. He points out that these images, which were "used on all manner of church occasions, ranging from prayer cards at ordinations to devotional artwork in family homes," represent a major response to the push and challenge by Costantini to Chinese Catholics to find indigenous ways of "expressing the Chinese Church's emerging individuality" that formed "a critical part of the movement towards a Chinese Catholic identity."[28]

From the foregoing discussion of various Chinese images of Jesus in various settings, one is struck by the creative synthesis of Confucian ethical vision with the artists' sense of the ethical and soteriological significance of Jesus Christ in their artistic oeuvre. As Chen Yuandu (陳緣督) explained:

27. Clarke, *Virgin Mary*, 189.
28. Ibid., 191.

> I believe that when I paint the wonders of Christianity according to the ancient rules of Chinese art, the painted objects exert an externally new and strange effect, so that at the same time I enrich to a marked degree the old laws of Chinese painting . . . If I can represent the teachings of our holy church in pictures according to Chinese art, and by means of such natural impressions draw the Chinese to know God, why should I not render so useful and enjoyable a service?"[29]

The intended catechetical function of these artistic images is clear. As Jeremy Clarke explains, these images were painted primarily to serve as catechetical aids for display in churches and chapels, as well as pious devotional images for adornment in homes.[30] He notes that the images were largely on biblical themes, with a strong preference for infancy narratives and representations of the Madonna and Child.[31] Mary S. Lawton suggests that Chinese Catholic art of this period focused on specific themes because of their intended use, as well as in response to cultural sensibilities of the artists and their audience.[32] As she explains:

> Almost all the compositions are biblical and the majority illustrate the childhood of Jesus and the life of the Virgin. There are very few Ascensions or Crucifixions and, again, these are painted by only one or two men. Such rarity of themes so prevalent in the West is, in part, in deference to the general proclivity of the Chinese to avoid the depiction of physical suffering in art. Moreover, a similar aversion to nudity meant that the image of a semi-clad Christ suspended upon the cross would have offended the traditional sense of decorum and contravened the degree of respect felt to be due to Him. On the other hand, consistent with the requirement for proper reverence are the mandarin settings which serve as the background for paintings of the Virgin and especially scenes of the Annunciation. Indeed, unless introduced into conventional Qing landscape iconography, illustrations of the Holy Family in unbefitting settings of poverty are extremely rare.[33]

Lawton's observations can be seen in the artistic depictions in this selection, which framed the artistic depictions of Jesus within Confucian

---

29. Cited in Fleming, *Each with His Own Brush*, 12.
30. Clarke, *Virgin Mary*, 184–85.
31. Ibid., 185.
32. Lawton, "A Unique Style in China," 474–75.
33. Ibid., 475.

sensibilities. For example, the framing of many images within the norms of traditional Chinese landscape (*shanshui*, 山水) art of mountains, gardens, and nature, as previously discussed, reveals how these artists contextualized their reception of Jesus and the stories from the Christian Gospels about Jesus within the Confucian Doctrine of the Mean (Zhongyong 中庸)'s primordial vision of cosmic union and balance (*he* 和) between the triad of heaven (*tian* 天), earth (*di* 地), and humanity (*ren* 人), as expressed in the traditional Confucian adage—"heaven, earth, and humanity are one" (*tiandi renyi* 天地人一). Likewise, the portrayals of Jesus within a Confucian familial setting that portray the child Jesus as engaging in learning (*xue* 學), as well as showing filiality (*xiao* 孝) and embodying deferential manner of relating (*li* 禮) to his parents, highlight the traditional Confucian themes of moral rectification in the Analects (*Lunyu* 論語) that are used to convey the *sensus* of what Jesus meant to the artists and their audience—a Jesus who loved learning (*xue* 學), who was filial (*xiao* 孝) to his parents, and who modeled the Confucian manner of relating deferentially to one's elders (*li* 禮).

On one level, one could read this as the Chinese artists, as Catholic converts and their audience perceiving their relationship to the God of their Catholic faith as exemplified by the manner in which Jesus related to his parents. On a deeper level, it reveals how these Chinese Catholic artists were able to integrate and synthesize Confucian and Catholic worldviews in response to Costantini's call to root the Catholic faith in Confucian Chinese soil. Nonetheless, the deep Confucian dimensions of these images of Jesus also meant that the traditional Confucian association of poverty, suffering, and death with failure resulted in a paucity of images that dealt with elements of poverty, suffering, and dying in favor of highlighting the relational, ethical, and cosmic aspects in their paintings. Hence, we see the *sensus* of the Chinese Catholic converts that sought to integrate their reception of the Christian Gospel and express what Jesus meant to them within traditional Confucian categories. Thus, we saw how Bai Huiqun and Chen Yuandu portrayed the Holy Family within the context of an idealized Confucian family that combined the best aspects of Confucian and Christian understandings of family life.

Finally, the nascent interreligious aspects of these images should not be overlooked. For example, the Nativity scene by Luke Hua Xiaoxian and the Visit of the Three Magi by Xu Sanchun exemplify these interreligious dimensions, with Hua's inclusion of Daoist immortal maidens as angels and Xu's imaginative reinterpretation of the Three Magi as three wise elders representing the three Chinese religious traditions of Confucianism, Daoism, and Buddhism. Hence, we see an incipient positive perspective that the three great religious traditions of China that emphasizes continuity and engagement, rather than confrontation and absolute break with the past.

21

Discerning the *Sensus Fidelium* in Asia's Narrative Theologies

Edmund Kee-Fook Chia

Stories Reveal the *Sensus Fidelium*

> Theology is often seen as a task of experts who can easily handle abstract explanation and argument . . . Today, however, the awareness is growing that, if theology is asking questions and reflecting over one's experience in the context of one's faith, then anyone who can ask questions and reflect can theologize. They can as well take the form of a story.[1]

NARRATIVE THEOLOGY IS THE thrust of the present article. Though by no means mainstream, it has become more recognized today. While narrative theologians have been with us for centuries and millennia, it is only in the recent decades that their contributions have come to be regarded as theology. In reflecting on the place of story in systematic theology, Paul Fiddes alludes to this and, in fact, demurs theologians who "classify metaphorical and narrative discourse as 'religious speech,' [in order] to reserve 'theology' for conceptual reflection on religious expressions." Instead, he insists, there is "no need to deny the title 'theology' to a mode of talking about God which is characteristic both of everyday speech of the community of faith and of a certain kind of academic thinking."[2]

---

1. Michael Amaladoss, "Foreword," in Wedell D'Cruz, *A Warli-Christian Story: An Experiment in Story Theology* (Delhi, India: Vidyajyoti/ISPCK, 1999), ix.

2. Paul F. Fiddes, "Concept, Image and Story in Systematic Theology," *International Journal of Systematic Theology* 11.1 (2009) 7. Fiddes cites Nicholas Lash, *Theology on the Way to Emmaus* (London: SCM, 1986) 101.

Stories, as the everyday speech of the community, are avenues where we can discern the realities of the people's experience. They are the theology of the people. Narrative theology in Asia, therefore, has the potential for revealing the *sensus fidelium* of the people in Asia. It enables us a peek at what matters to Asians and how they hope to respond in order to live life to its fullest (John 10:10). This article will begin by discussing narrative or story theology in general and will then make a case for its coherence with the Asian theological methodology.[3] The most important part of the article will be the actual doing of narrative theology from an Asian perspective. It will engage in the task of theological reflection using, as starting points, three stories that have arisen from different contextual circumstances and addressing differing themes.

Background Story of Story Theology

The above subtitle is an adapted version of a chapter-title from Terrence Tilley's book on story theology, and its theses guide the following reflections.[4] Tilley begins by observing that story theology is "a thoroughly American movement," an observation that Wentzel van Huyssteen concurs with while adding that it is also a significant "contribution to postmodern anti-foundational theological thought."[5] Tilley attributes the advance of story theology to the rise of the modern sciences, the discovery of new fields of knowledge, as well as to the reform movements taking place within the church in the 1960s.[6] Within Roman Catholicism, the reforms inaugurated by the Second Vatican Council inspired theologians to explore new ways for expressing their faith. Meantime, within Protestantism, the 1960s represented the end of the theological giants and also coincided with the era of social transformation and impending secularism, giving rise in some quarters to the "death of God" theology. It was within these contextual realities that narrative theology emerged, spurred greatly by the following four key factors that Tilley identifies as responsible for the sea change and revolution within theology.

The first is the challenge from the logical positivist philosophers of language who insist that religious and moral assertions must be verifiable

---

3. While "story" is often defined as the sequence of events and "narrative" as the structure of the event, the two terms are often used synonymously.

4. Terrence W. Tilley, *Story Theology* (Collegeville, MN: Liturgical, 1985) 18–84.

5. Wentzel van Huyssteen, "Narrative Theology: An Adequate Paradigm for Theological Reflection?" *HTS Theological Studies* 45 (1989) 768.

6. Ibid., 18.

analytically and empirically. Reactions to this included stories becoming more appreciated as avenues for investigating and expressing Christian faith. A second factor is the realization that human experience is inherently narrative in form. Tilley cites Stephen Crites's classic and groundbreaking article, "The Narrative Quality of Human Experience,"[7] as highlighting the fact that human experience is intrinsically durational in form and thus the need for narratives to report that experience. A third factor is the result of the advent of modern methods in biblical scholarship. The Quest for the Historical Jesus, for example, not only raised questions about sacred traditionally-held beliefs and practices, but also highlighted the fact that the Bible is basically a set of stories and that it is these stories that provide the contexts for appreciating the laws, teachings, and rituals that have developed within the Christian religion. A fourth factor is that our basic notions of what it means to be an autonomous human being, our understandings of how evolution has shaped the world, our knowledge of what is really real out there, and our ability to distinguish scientific knowledge from art have all been shaped largely by the Enlightenment worldview and the myths of modernity. These and especially the myth that modern humans have outgrown the stories of their ancestors had to contend with counter-myths that emphasized that the world which we live in is pluriformly constructed and that there are multifaceted ways for encountering and appreciating it. Primarily these four factors of modernity, Tilley asserts, gave rise to alternative modes for doing theology, one of which is the narrative method.

H. Richard Niebuhr is often regarded as the "father" of contemporary narrative theology. His 1941 essay "The Story of Our Lives"[8] is frequently cited for initiating the conversation: "The chapter emphasises the early Church's storytelling as the locus of revelation."[9] From there the narrative theme spread across most disciplines of theology, with influence coming from "fields as diverse as literary criticism, psychology, linguistics, social ethics and communications theory."[10] By the 1970s, according to Gary Comstock, narrative theology "burst onto the theological scene," with scholarly

---

7. Stephen Crites, "The Narrative Quality of Human Experience," *Journal of American Academy of Religion* 39 (1971) 291–311.

8. Helmut Richard Niebuhr, *The Meaning of Revelation* (New York: Macmillan, 1941).

9. David K. Clark, "Narrative Theology and Apologetics," *Journal of the Evangelical Theological Society* 36 (1993) 499.

10. Gabriel Fackre, "Narrative Theology. An Overview," *Interpretation* 37 (1983) 340.

literature "on narrative in the Bible, narrative and theology, narrative and morality, narrative tradition, narrative practice, even narrative truth."[11]

Asain Theology and the Narrative Method

Before discussing how narrative method sits with Asian theology, it is timely at this juncture to attempt a description of it. For sure, the narrative method begins with stories and not abstract principles, precepts, or doctrinal statements.[12] The stories arise from the immediate experiences of the people and have implications for their lives and well-being. The stories capture the pains and struggles of the community and reveal the beliefs, hopes, and theologies of the people, especially the victims, those who are marginalized, and those at the grassroots. The narrative method is thus inductive in its approach. The trained theologian's role is to assist in systemizing the ideas and relating them to biblical narratives and church teachings, as well as to other theological musings on similar issues. The result of these reflections should inspire transformation and enable change.

Doing narrative theology, therefore, is not so much for the purpose of understanding as for changing minds and converting hearts in view of facilitating concerted action. This resonates well with the Asian theological methodology that steers clear of the Western classical and intellectualist approach. Benigno Beltran, who has been doing theology while engaging in his ministry to those who live in a garbage village in the Philippines, confirms this: "I realized that theology should not only be a *fides quaerens intellectum* (faith seeking understanding), a purely cognitive approach to theological inquiry. In today's world, theology should also be linked to social concerns as *fides quaerens justitiam* (faith seeking justice), *fides quaerens pacem* (faith seeking peace), and *fides quaerens vitam* (faith seeking life)."[13]

This is especially true for Asia where justice, peace, and life are the real and immediate needs of the people. That is why some of the most profound theologies are done not so much by academically trained theologians but by the ordinary people and pastoral workers ministering on the ground. These theologies come to us not so much as grandiose theories but as simple

---

11. Gary L. Comstock, "Two Types of Narrative Theology," *Journal of the American Academy of Religion* 55 (1987) 687.

12. Reference: Alexander Luce-Smith, "Narrative Theology as a New Approach to Theology," in *Narrative Theology and Moral Theology* (Aldershot, UK: Ashgate, 2007) 1; Philip Gibbs, "Narrative and Context in a Practical Theology for Papua New Guinea," *Australian eJournal of Theology* 9 (March 2007) 4–5.

13. Benigno P. Beltran, *Faith and Struggle on Smokey Mountain: Hope for a Planet in Peril* (Maryknoll, NY: Orbis, 2012) 35.

stories of the day-to-day experiences of the people. They are found not so much in tomes or journals but in parish bulletins and newsletters as well as in the oral tradition passed on around dinner tables or in the market square. Asian theologians today are thus beginning to reclaim the narrative method as not only an appropriate but also the preferred way for doing theology. The most recent Asian Mission Congress released a statement that "sought to enflesh many of the challenges found in Pope John Paul II's Ecclesia in Asia (EA): 'narrative methods akin to Asian cultural forms are to be preferred'. . . Pope John Paul II recommends following 'an evocative pedagogy, using stories, parables and symbols so characteristic of Asian methodology in teaching' (EA 20g)."[14]

The narrative method is employed with the conviction that stories function as the potent and critical force for praxis. The indirect, circuitous, and subtle natures of stories are subversive methods consistent with the Asian ways of knowing and acting. Stories are able to accomplish goals that the logical rational discursive discourse may find difficult. Stories are, therefore, means for discerning the issues of concern of the people, as well as for expressing their hopes and fears and plans for action.

Contextual Theology and Theological Resources

As pointed out earlier, a significant feature of narrative theology is its inductive approach. Felix Wilfred discusses the inductive method more specifically by suggesting that Asian theologians make a distinction between experience and context. Both are inherently important for how one does theology but they are nevertheless different. He explains: "Space has been a rediscovery of contextual theologies, and it has been a major source of theological creativity in Asia."[15]

Thus, for Asian theology, space or context is of prime significance, much the same way history has been for Western theology. It is this realization that has shaped much of Asian theology and guides the church's approach to mission and evangelization. That is why the Federation of Asian Bishops' Conferences (FABC) has been insisting that evangelization in Asia is through what they call the Triple Dialogue.[16] This is the dialogue in which

---

14. "Telling the Story of Jesus: Final Message of the First Asian Mission Congress," *Tripod* 27/145 (Summer 2007) http://www.hsstudyc.org.hk/en/tripod_en/en_tripod_145_02.html.

15. Felix Wilfred, *Asian Public Theology: Critical Concerns in Challenging Times* (New Delhi: ISPCK, 2010) 280.

16. Edmund Kee-Fook Chia, *Edward Schillebeeckx and Interreligious Dialogue:*

the church must have with the cultures, the religions, and the poor of Asia. It simply means that Christians must be in contact with the ground realities of the Asian context. In discussing the Asian method for doing theology, Peter Phan emphasizes that the contextual realities of Asia are regarded as resources for theology: "The first resource is the billions of Asian peoples themselves, with their stories of joy and suffering, hope and despair, love and hatred, freedom and oppression, stories not recorded in history books written by victors but kept alive in the 'dangerous memory' (Johann Baptist Metz) of the 'underside of history' (Gustavo Gutierrez)."[17] Phan then goes on to enumerate other resources for doing theology in Asia in which he includes "the sacred texts and practices of Asian religions that have nourished the life of Asian peoples for thousands of years before the coming of Christianity into their lands and since," the "Asian monastic traditions, with their rituals, ascetic practices, and social commitment" and the "Asian cultures in general with their immense treasures of stories, myths, folklore, symbols, poetry, songs, visual art, and dance."[18]

In a keynote address to the Asian Missionary Congress, Cardinal Luis Antonio Tagle suggested that using Asian resources, especially stories, in theologizing can assist in our understanding of the church's mission in a continent that is multicultural and multireligious: "I believe that story telling provides a creative framework for understanding mission in Asia, a continent whose cultures and religions are rooted in great stories or epics."[19] He then spelled out the characteristics of good stories, confirming not only that they are significant resources for appreciating Christian mission in particular but also for discerning the theology of the people in general. Among these, the cardinal notes, is that good stories are based on experience and are best told if they are personal. He then talked about how stories that are common to a community can bind unique individuals into a cohesive body and that stories, when received, can transform the listener, who in turn becomes the new storyteller. However, stories can also be suppressed, either by oneself because it rekindles traumatic memory, shame, or guilt, or by others, especially those who have the power to forbid their retelling.

Perspectives from Asian Theology (Eugene, OR: Pickwick Publications, 2012) 133.

17. Peter C. Phan, *In Our Own Tongues: Perspectives from Asia on Mission and Inculturation* (Maryknoll, NY: Orbis, 2003) 187.

18. Ibid., 188–89.

19. Luis Antonio G. Tagle, "Mission in Asia: Telling the Story of Jesus" *Asian Mission Congress* (Chiang Mai, Thailand, 19 October 2006), http://www.fabc.org/asian_mission_congress/amc.htm.

Story as Matrix of Theology

Stories, therefore, have tremendous potential in the theological realm in Asia. As C.S. Song asserts, "theology and story are inseparable. Where there is story, there is theology." Suggesting that if a good story "grips you in the depths of your heart and mind" and forces you to reflect upon the relationship between yourself, nature, world, and God, then "it is already profoundly theological."[20] Song insists that "story is the matrix of theology." Song is undoubtedly the "father" of story theology among the Christian community in Asia, having authored monographs of that specific genre.[21]

Just exploring C. S. Song's works alone can offer us many more thoughts and guidelines for story theology especially from the Asian perspective. For instance, his critique of the Western-centered nature of theology, his focus on the socio-political challenges to one's faith, and his advocacy for the use of stories external to the Christian tradition are so rich that they warrant many more articles than the present in order to do justice to the themes. Suffice to say that Song has demonstrated not only the legitimacy but also the need for Asians to be doing story theology: "For theology to be theology, it must be story theology."[22] I would, therefore, be seriously remiss if I come to the end of the present article without engaging explicitly in the actual task of doing story theology. The remainder of this article will be an attempt at storytelling in view of using the stories as starting points for theological reflection. Its goal is to discern the people's theology from the stories. I will employ stories that address the three themes which Song has been emphatic about, viz. Western-centric theology, political theology, and interfaith relations.

Border Crossing

> We were standing in line at the immigration checkpoint at Lo Wu, waiting to cross over to mainland China. We were on the Hong Kong side of the border and the year was 1997. The crowd

---

20. C. S. Song, *In the Beginning Were Stories, not Texts: Story Theology* (Eugene, OR: Cascade Books, 2011) 18.

21. C. S. Song, *The Tears of Lady Meng: A Parable of People's Political Theology* (Geneva: World Council of Churches, 1981); C. S. Song, *Tell Us Our Names: Story Theology from an Asian Perspective* (1984; reprinted, Eugene, OR: Wipf & Stock, 2005); C. S. Song, *Believing Heart: An Invitation to Story Theology* (Minneapolis: Fortress, 1999); C. S. Song, *And Their Eyes Are Opened: Story Sermons Embracing the World* (Saint Louis: Chalice, 2006).

22. Song, *In the Beginning were Stories*, 18.

of several thousand queued up in lines which zig zagged all over, guided only by flimsy ropes hung over metal poles that served as dividers. Despite the less than orderly arrangement, everyone waited patiently to have their passports stamped. I then noticed a Chinese man dressed in a Mao Tse Tung-styled traditional costume. He had just arrived and, instead of joining the line from the back, simply made his way to the front by crossing over the ropes and going in between lines. Having reached the front he inched his way forward until it was his turn to go up to the immigration counter. All of a sudden a loud and angry shout rang out from the middle of the lobby. It came from a Caucasian gentleman dressed in business suit and carrying a briefcase. He rushed up to protest the Chinese man's queue-jumping. Using less than polite words he accused the other of cheating and being unfair to everyone else. The commotion brought out the immigration police who, after a few questions, simply ushered the Chinese man to go on ahead to get his passport stamped. Flabbergasted, the Caucasian man uttered profanities, charging now the police for being unfair to the rest of us who were waiting in line. An elderly Chinese woman standing behind me made these remarks, obviously directed at the Caucasian man: "If you yourself are in a hurry, you can always jump queue. Why inflict this commotion on the rest of us?"

On the surface this incident might look like a straightforward case of a transgression and its effects. Who the transgressor was and the nature of the transgression, however, is a matter for discussion. The transition of colonial Hong Kong to Chinese rule in 1997 is the setting for the theological reflection. It is symbolic of the challenges that Asian theology faces as it individuates from its Western forebears. C.S. Song advises: "Theology can no longer be a repetition of what we have inherited . . . We have to assume theological responsibility for ourselves, believing that God has always had other plans for Asia and means to implement these plans that go beyond the experience and knowledge of Western Christians and churches."[23] Asian Christian theologians, therefore, have to engage in theology critically and independently of their colonial masters. They do so within their own context and using local resources and this includes the beliefs, values, and priorities of the people in Asia.

As far as queuing up and orderly conduct are concerned, Asians are known to be relatively at ease with a certain amount of disorder. The situation at the Lo Wu border crossing is by no means out of the ordinary. The

---

23. Song, *Believing Heart*, 57.

lines and dividers serve as guides, just as traffic lights in Asian cities are usually obeyed but also often not. Anyone who has experienced getting on a jeepney in Manila or a boat to go down the River Chao Phraya in Bangkok or a commuter train in Mumbai will know that rushing is the order of the day. Asians are used to dealing with chaotic behaviours not only in public transportation but also in many other aspects of their lives as well.

The Westerner's obsession with rigidity and rules may not necessarily find resonance within the Asian psyche. Appreciation for difference, including one's situation or needs, accounts for the Asian's ability to accommodate differential treatment. This is also the reason why diverse spiritual paths are acknowledged as necessary for leading the diversity of people to truth and salvation. There is no need for any "one and only" religious way nor a singular universal approach to doing theology. This appreciation for pluralism is especially pronounced in Asian theology, according to the Asian bishops, on account of the influence of "certain values that are paramount in Asian cultures arising from the various philosophical traditions and the concrete social-religious-cultural situations in which Asians live." In light of this pluralism the FABC advocates that "what is needed is a vision of unity and harmony, and a language of reconciled diversity."[24]

Thus, unity and harmony and a language of reconciled diversity are priorities for people in Asia. They supersede any rules or principles that insist on one orthodox way for doing things. This applies as much to the way theology is done as to how society is run. The elderly (wisdom? understanding?) Chinese woman at the end of the story spells this out eloquently: breaking of rules is not as bad as disrupting the harmony. The well-dressed (formal? legalistic?) Westerner in the story might disagree with such sentiments. That might be because law and order are to the West what peace and harmony are to Asians. This is another way of saying that if for the Westerner the values of justice, fairness, and rights are important, the Asian prefers the values of serenity, tranquillity, and harmony. Felix Wilfred suggests that this difference arises from different worldviews, whereby the Westerner's is architectonic while the Asian's organic. The architectonic worldview, based upon a reality conceived in terms of individuality and separateness, is emphatic about distributive justice "because there needs to be some kind of balancing among the parts." The organic worldview, with a reality conceived in terms of relationship among the parts, is emphatic about the harmonious integration of the community that "subsumes under it the ethical concern

---

24. "Methodology," in *For All the Peoples of Asia*, vol. 3, 330.

expressed by justice . . . [hence,] organic vision is open to accept the otherness of the other."[25]

We should not underestimate how this difference shapes the way Asians think about life, about God, and about the world. The Asian's worldview interacts with the issues and concerns on the ground to determine the response each person makes in faith. One way we can witness how this faith is expressed is to examine the folktales that have been passed down through the generations. As C.S. Song believes, "reflected in these stories of the people—folk tales—is not only the remote past. Projected in them is the universal struggle of people to be human, free, and authentic."[26] We shall now look at one such story.

The Tears of Lady Meng

Lady Meng lived during the Qin Dynasty at the time of the first emperor. To defend this newly united dynasty, the emperor took young men slaves in order to build the Great Wall of China. Wan Xiliang escaped and hid in the home of the Meng family, who got to know him and realized that he was a good man. They married their daughter, Lady Meng, to him. Three days after their secret but joyous wedding, however, government officials came and took away Wan Xiliang. Lady Meng waited for a year for her husband to return before deciding to look for him. She walked during all day hours and camped wherever she stopped. Finally, Lady Meng arrived at the Great Wall on a chilly autumn day. She asked around about her husband, only to be told that he had died and was buried under the Wall. A great surge of sorrow overcame Lady Meng; she cried and cried on top of the Great Wall, with her tears running like a river. Her cry moved the slaves and the guards, who stopped working and shed tears with her. Suddenly, a loud roaring sound broke out, as a section of the Great Wall collapsed, exposing beneath it piles of human remains, all of slaves who had died. When the emperor heard about Lady Meng he asked to see her. He was instantly struck by her beauty and decided to make her empress. Lady Meng knew she could not avoid her fate and agreed on condition that the Emperor build a terrace forty-nine feet high on the river bank in preparation for her husband's burial. When everything was ready she climbed on the terrace and cursed the emperor and

---

25. Felix Wilfred, "Towards a Theology of Harmony: Some Fundamental Reflections," in *Yearbook of Contextual Theologies* (Aachen, Germany: MWI, 1993) 149.

26. Song, *The Tears of Lady Meng*, 25.

then jumped from the terrace. The emperor flew into a rage and ordered that her body be cut into little pieces. When the soldiers did that the little pieces changed into little silver fishes in which the soul of the faithful Lady Meng lives.[27]

C. S. Song employed an extended version of this story in his presentation of the D. T. Niles Memorial Lecture in Bangalore in 1981 during the General Assembly of the Christian Conference of Asia.[28] The lecture was titled "Political Theology of Living in Christ with People" and delivered against the backdrop of the political scenario around Asia at that time. The Philippines was under the Marcos martial law regime. Suharto was ruling Indonesia with an equally tyrannical fist. Asia was still reeling from the "killing fields" left behind by Cambodia's Pol Pot and the Khmer Rouge, which massacred more than a million of its citizens. The military general Park Chung-Hee had unqualified control over the people and resources of South Korea. There was also the Gwangju May 18 Democratic Uprising in C. S. Song's own native homeland of Taiwan, where the people were attacked by government troops.

In the context of these events, the Great Wall, for Song, is the epitome of power and control, a manifestation of might and grandeur. But it is also a wall that had claimed countless number of innocent lives, especially the lives of the weak and powerless. The many Great Walls around Asia have broken up families, robbed children of their parents, and parents of their children. They are at once a symbol of national pride and honor as well as of subjugation and oppression. Supposedly built to protect the country and its people, these walls have more often been used for the protection of the ruling elites and those in power and, according to Song, is a "savage god of national security."[29] This idolatry of power pervades much of Asia and has resulted in the immense suffering of the ordinary people. It is in reflecting on these issues that Song insists upon the value of folktales in revealing innate political theologies: "In fact, the kind of political theology we find in folktales can be more genuine, more powerful, more heart-breaking and also more heartening than many 'Christian' political theologies."[30]

---

27. Adapted from "Good Stories from China: Lady Meng-Jiang's Tears Made the Great Wall Collapse," *The Epoch Times* (Aug. 2, 2006), http://www.theepochtimes.com/news/6-8-2/44537.html; and also from C. S. Song, *The Tears of Lady Meng*.

28. An expanded version of the lecture was published as a booklet, *The Tears of Lady Meng*. The reflections in this section are from the same booklet.

29. Ibid. 33.

30. Ibid. 29.

Lady Meng's only weapon against the tyranny of power are the tears that flowed down her cheek. The tears, however, seemed ineffective in changing the response of the wall or the power behind it. But Lady Meng's tears did move the slaves as well as the guards to tears. The latter seemed to have switched sides, at least in their unguarded moments, from guarding the powerful to crying with the powerless. Crying together has a solidarity effect among people, as it breaks down the walls that divide them while uniting them in their vulnerability. Song shares in the political theology that the folktale storyteller was attempting to convey: "Our political theology is not a theocratic interpretation of structures of government as ordained by God . . . The source of our political theology in Asia is the people—the people humiliated, oppressed and impoverished. And the power of our political ethic comes from people's tears."[31] He then takes the reader back to the time of Jesus: "We need only recall the confession of the Roman soldier at the foot of Jesus' cross. That Roman soldier, completely armed from head to toe, is completely disarmed by Jesus on the cross, armed with nothing but two pieces of wood, a symbol of shame, wretchedness and death. What moved him to confess that Jesus is the Son of God? Jesus' powerful tears! His undefeatable love!"[32]

The Tears of Lady Meng folktale certainly reveals the heroine's undefeatable love, but it does not end with Lady Meng retrieving her husband's bones. The emperor wanted more, demanding now Lady Meng's own body and soul. Song reminds the reader of King David demanding the same of Bathsheba after killing off her husband Uriah. He points out that hidden behind the Chinese folktale is an alternative theology of authority and power. Such power is autocratic and selfish and knows no bounds. It steals, it rapes, and cares not what happens to its subjects. In the face of such terror Lady Meng had a few options. She could have submitted, she could have rebelled, or she could have launched a revolution. But, like Jesus, she chose to use her wretched fate to speak the truth. It was perhaps the first time the emperor was told to his face how cruel he was to his subjects. Lady Meng was indeed the voice of the oppressed.

While there is no evidence of historical borrowing between this Chinese folktale and Christianity's passion narrative, both have the theme of suffering and death, which then paved the way for the resurrection. Song reflects on what the Lady Meng folktale is proclaiming: "Death is not the end! The power of the emperor, brutal, cruel and inhuman as it is, is not

---

31. Ibid. 43.
32. Ibid. 46.

the final power!"³³ This is the theology that the Lady Meng story, one of China's Four Great Folktales, witnesses to. While by no means a "Christian" story, its political theology turns out "to be a history of the cross and resurrection in Asia."³⁴ In Lady Meng's case, the resurrection took place in the little silver fishes that still live in the rivers of China and all across the world.

As we can see from this folktale, C. S. Song's insistence on the use of narratives from outside the bounds of Christianity is certainly relevant to the task of doing theology in Asia. Christian theologians have much to learn about the people's theology by examining the folktales of Asian cultures. We shall look at yet another story from our neighbors of other faiths, this time a contemporary example.

The Chief Buddhist Monk

> The Venerable Dhammananda, chief monk of his country's Buddhist community, became seriously ill and was hospitalized. As he was in hospital attire the nurse who came on her rounds did not know who he was, except that he was an elderly, bald-headed, smiling gentleman. She looked at his registration form, which read Ven. Dhammananda, and then wrote on the whiteboard behind his bed the short form of what she thought was his first name: Mr. Ven. The next morning a Christian pastor paid him a visit, not knowing who he was, again, except that he was an elderly, bald-headed, smiling gentleman. The pastor introduced himself as one who had come to bring the Good News of salvation especially to those in need and at critical junctures of their lives. He invited Mr. Ven to receive Jesus as Lord and savior. The Venerable Dhammananda accepted, was prayed upon in the name of the Lord Jesus Christ and received the blessings from the pastor. Later that evening, as the pastor was leaving the hospital, he passed by Dhammananda's room again. Imagine the shock when he saw a group of young Buddhist monks clad in saffron robes kneeling by the old man's bedside. They were receiving some sort of teaching and blessing from him. As the monks were leaving the pastor asked one of them who the old man was. "He is our chief," came the reply. Troubled, the pastor rushed into the room and asked for forgiveness: "I am sorry, Sir. I did not know you are the chief Buddhist monk. I didn't mean to insult your religion. Had I known who you are I would not

33. Ibid. 64.
34. Ibid. 65.

have invited you to receive the Lord Jesus Christ." Surprised, the Venerable Dhammananda said: "Young man, I don't know why you have come to apologise. You offered me something good and I accepted it graciously. I thank you for the wonderful gift and blessing of the Lord Jesus Christ. Go in peace."

The teller of this story was the Venerable Dhammananda himself. He related it at a Buddhist-Christian seminar, which means it was a story for both the Buddhist as well as the Christian communities. It was meant to convey a message to both parties. The Venerable Dhammananda, however, did not attempt an exegesis of the story. He left it at that. Everyone had a good laugh. It was indeed a parable, a story with a powerful religious lesson, with an unexpected twist, meant to provoke reactions and facilitate discussions. However, for the benefit of those who were not present and unfamiliar with the context, I will attempt to explain the story here in view of discerning theological thrusts it points to and especially questions it raises.

As a Christian the first question I would be asking is how we evangelize in multi-religious contexts. What guides our mission theology especially vis-à-vis persons of other religions? Many will probably refer to the biblical mandate or the Great Commission. This is usually cited as basis for the door-to-door approach in evangelism.[35] Wesley Ariarajah sees this as problematic, insisting that attributing a missionary practice to scriptural mandate is alien to most peoples of other faiths in Asia. He challenges Christians to not only take note of such scriptural texts integrally and contextually but also "to rethink the exaggerated claims made for its authority and the habit of looking to them as providing the rationale for the mission."[36] That is why Ariarajah believes that while Asian theologians have done much by way of indigenizing aspects of church life, such as music, worship and even theology, much more needs to be done in the field of missiology, especially in religiously plural contexts. He advocates a radically indigenized approach to Christian mission in Asia.

Aside from questions relating to scriptural authority, another question that the story raises is whether the method of aggressive evangelization is appropriate in multi-religious settings. Would Christians be equally welcoming of their children being visited by Muslim or Buddhist or Hindu evangelists at their hospital beds? The Golden Rule or ethic of reciprocity informs this question. This is an especially sensitive issue in Asia for two

35. "The Biblical Mandate for House to House or Door to Door Evangelism," *FAITH SAVES.net,* http://faithsaves.net/biblical-mandate-house-to-house-evangelism/.

36. S. Wesley Ariarajah, "Towards a More Radically Indigenized Asian Christian Missiology," in Wati Longchar ed., *Doing Contextual Theologies in Asia: Essays in Honour of Huang Po Ho* (Kolkota, India: PTCA, 2014), 102.

reasons. On the one hand, many Christians in Asia have been on the receiving end of aggressive evangelization and have had their children converted out of the Christian faith, especially to Islam. On the other hand, numerous charges have been made against Christian missionaries for employing less than ethical methods, some of which border on proselytism. Arun Shourie's book, *Harvesting Our Souls*,[37] exposes a number of these in the Indian context and betrays the negative perception that our neighbors of other faiths have towards Christian mission.

The *Christian Witness in a Multi-Religious World: Recommendations for Conduct* statement is instructive here. Issued jointly by the Vatican's Pontifical Council for Interreligious Dialogue, the World Council of Churches and the World Evangelical Alliance after deliberations over a period of five years, it advises Christians not to use "inappropriate methods of exercising mission." Instead, it exhorts Christians "to build relationships of respect and trust with people of different religions," as well as "to listen in order to learn about and understand others' beliefs and practices."[38] These are loaded statements and certainly rule out the colonial and exclusivist missionary approaches that, according to Ariarajah, focus on how "to 'bring' people to Christ," and that often use "military metaphors, such as 'occupying' the unoccupied areas, 'deployment' of missionaries, 'strategies' of evangelism, sending 'reinforcements,' and conducting 'evangelistic crusades.'"[39]

Returning to the Venerable Dhammananda, while it is probably not a problem for him to be evangelized, one cannot say the same for his flock. The fact that the pastor apologized seems to indicate something was not altogether appropriate in his door-to-door missionary approach. Why did the pastor think it was fine if the "target" was simply an elderly bald-headed man? This raises the issue of power relationship, which would be obviously asymmetrical if the pastor was encountering a lay Buddhist, and an ill and vulnerable one at that. Felix Wilfred points out that this is often an argument used by the Hindu intelligentsia when protesting Christian mission amongst the tribals and Dalits in India: "Their question is why at all do the Christians entice these vulnerable and uneducated segments of society, who will fall easy prey to the Christian allurement? Instead of targeting these

---

37. Arun Shourie, *Harvesting Our Souls* (Delhi: SSA Publications, 1999).

38. "Christian Witness in a Multi-Religious World: Recommendations for Conduct," *Pontifical Council for Interreligious Dialogue* (January 2011), http://www.vatican.va/roman_curia/pontifical_councils/interelg/documents/rc_pc_interelg_doc_20111110_testimonianza-cristiana_en.html.

39. Ariarajah, "Towards a More Radically Indigenized Asian Christian Missiology," 100.

groups for conversion, why are the Christians not attempting to convert the educated, the elite, the upper castes?"[40]

The chief Buddhist monk would certainly fall into this latter category, enabling him to accept the pastor's gestures graciously since he was already well-grounded in his own faith. For him, grace, blessings, and even baptism are transcendental entities, not economic. Accepting one does not necessitate the rejection of another or one's own. There is room for many. An educated Chinese friend of mine once told me: "I don't know why you Christians limit yourself to one God. The more you have the more blessings you receive!" That was perhaps the message the chief Buddhist monk was imparting to his own Buddhist disciples: be open to others and to their blessings but, at the same time, be grounded in your own faith and you don't have to give it up. Comparative theologians may be tempted to see hints of double-belonging here. Of course, such thoughts probably did not cross the mind of the Christian pastor as he would have viewed the Venerable Dhammananda's reception of the Lord Jesus Christ quite differently. Traditional Christianity would not have allowed for faith in more than one savior or allegiance to more than one religious way. That is because it has a coherent and at the same time exclusive soteriology. As Catherine Cornille points out, "the more encompassing a religion's claim to efficacy and truth, the more problematic the possibility of multiple belonging."[41]

We could go on to explore other theological issues from the Buddhist monk's story to discern how Christian faith is expressed in Asia. Suffice it to say that the story has been a critical source for theological reflection and reveals aspects of the people's theology, especially on how to relate across faiths.

Conclusion

In fact, all three stories used in the experiment above, arising from three different contexts, have probably contributed much more to Asian theological reflection than many of the doctrinal propositions that have been promulgated for the church in Asia. Thus, narrative theology is not only a valuable method for doing theology in Asia but is also better at engaging real-life issues that directly affect the people. It is the theology of the people. It is for this reason that Asian theologians are looking towards greater use

---

40. Felix Wilfred, *Asian Dreams and Christian Hope: At the Dawn of the New Millennium* (Delhi: ISPCK, 2003), 234–35.

41. Catherine Cornille, *Many Mansions? Multiple Religious Belonging and Christian Identity* (2002; reprinted, Eugene, OR: Wipf & Stock, 2010), 2.

of the narrative in their theologizing. This is a refreshing change from the traditional classical approach, which is not only abstract and conceptual but also often irrelevant to the peoples' day-to-day hopes and dreams or their pains and struggles.

The late Jesuit priest Anthony de Mello, another master narrative theologian of the Asian Christian community, has often spoken out against such abstractions. De Mello's many books are characterized by the trademark of stand-alone stories. They are self-explanatory and need no commentary. In conclusion, therefore, let us reflect one of de Mello's stories that cautions against theology that does not speak to the people's needs.

The Parachutist

> The story goes that a parachutist was blown off course from where he was supposed to land. Unfortunately, he ended up caught on a tree and hung up there in the middle of nowhere waiting for help. Finally, a gentleman passed by. The parachutist shouted: "Sir, can you help me?" The gentleman replied, "Sure, but please tell me what happened first." The parachutist told his story and then asked, "And, can you please tell me where I am?" The gentleman replied, "Sure, you are up on a tree." The parachutist replied, "Thank you. By the way, you must be a theologian." The gentleman was stunned, taken aback, scratched his head, and then said, "In fact I am. But, how did you know?" The parachutist replied, "Well Sir, what you said is certainly true, but, just as certainly useless."[42]

---

42. Adapted from Anthony de Mello, *The Prayer of the Frog*, vol. 1 (Anand, India: Gujarat Sahitya Prakash, 2003) 88.

22

Storytelling as an Expression of *Sensus Fidelium*

A Korean American Catholic Perspective

HOON CHOI

ACCORDING TO RICHARD R. Gaillardetz, one can trace the fundamental concept of *Sensus Fidelium*—which can be defined as the *consensus omnium*, i.e., the "universal belief of the faithful" or as "the inerrancy of the faith of the whole community of believers"—back to the very origins of Christianity.[1] If Gaillardetz is correct and that the entire body of the faithful today also possesses a supernatural sense of faith, then one is able to discover the manifestations of a particular kind of it in a certain ethnic community within the Catholic Church. In this chapter, I depict and attend to distinctive elements of Korean and Korean American Catholic stories to that end. Through these stories, I demonstrate that the *sensus fidelium* is both handed down and manifested locally with distinctive colors. Consequently, this sense of faith is not passively and simply received but actively nurtured through local experience and expressions.

This chapter shifts in three parts. First, I present a dynamic sense of understanding *sensus fidelium* that places, and discerns a proper role for, Korean American Catholic stories in the context of the wider church. Second, I identify a common thread that weaves through the history of early Christianity and, in distinctive ways, Korean Catholicism that enhances such a dynamic understanding of *sensus fidelium*. Finally, I point to a new story that is traditioning via Korean American Catholics and suggest that it

---

1. Richard R. Gaillardetz, *Teaching with Authority* (Collegeville, MN: Liturgical, 1997), 231; On *consensus omnium*, see Wolfgang Beinert, "Bedeutung und Begründung des Glaubenssinnes (Sensus Fidei) als eines dogmatischen Erkenntniskriteriums," *Catholica* 25 (1971) 275.

contributes positively both to the handing down of the faith and to its development. The wider church can look to such a story to grow and progress toward the fullness of truth.

Sensus Fidelium in Context

Since the early church, there has been continued insistence on the significance of the collective witness of the faithful. One illuminating example is John Henry Newman's study of the Arian controversy, which concluded that the orthodoxy of the Christian faith was preserved "not by the episcopate but by the belief of the faithful."[2] However, as is true of any conceptual history, the emphasis on the significance of *sensus fidelium* has not been seamless. The anti-Protestant polemic between the times of the Council of Trent and Vatican I, along with the preoccupations with questions of papal authority and the manuals' "passive mirroring of magisterial teaching," set back the course that insisted on the collective sense of the faithful observed by early Christians.[3] While hints suggest that the instincts of faithful communities remained very much alive during those periods, it was not until the Second Vatican Council that one clearly sees a return to the *sensus fidelium* that was exhibited by the early church.

The Council in *Lumen Gentium* (12) asserted that by virtue of baptism the entire body of the faithful possesses a supernatural sense of faith, allowing for the manifestation of a universal consensus in matters of faith and morals, that could not be mistaken in belief.[4] Thus, by sharing the same source, namely the Holy Spirit, "the authority of church office and the Spirited insight of the faithful cannot be put in opposition to one another."[5] This view, however, does not signify the facile individual exercise of *sensus fidei*. Rather, it refers to the corporate belief of the universal body of the faithful (*sensus fidelium*).[6] To avoid this confusion, the International Theological Commission in its "*Sensus Fidei* in the life of the Church" makes a distinction between the two manifestations of *sensus fidei*:

---

2. Gaillardetz, *Teaching with Authority*, 232.
3. Ibid. 231–33.
4. Ibid., 233.
5. Richard R. Gaillardetz, *By What Authority? A Primer on Scripture, the Magisterium, and the Sense of the Faithful* (Collegeville, MN: Liturgical, 2003) 108.
6. Gaillardetz, *Teaching with Authority*, 234.

Sensus fidei fidelis, to refer to the personal aptitude of the believer to make an accurate discernment in matters of faith, and *sensus fidei fidelium* to refer to the Church's own instinct of faith.[7]

More importantly, the commission argues that interaction between these two manifestations, which results in a kind of communal consensus (*consensus fidelium*), is vital:

> The *sensus fidei* in this sense is reflected in the convergence of the baptized in a lived adhesion to a doctrine of faith or to an element of Christian *praxis*. This convergence (*consensus*) plays a vital role in the Church: the *consensus fidelium* is a sure criterion for determining whether a particular doctrine or practice belongs to the apostolic faith.[8]

What the commission calls the *consensus fidelium* is the *consensus omnium* of the early church through which "the charism of infallibility is operative."[9] In the most dynamic sense of understanding, then, divine revelation has been *given* to the church *and* the church *looks to* the plentitude of the fullness of truth for the actualization of God's Word in the life of the church (*Dei Verbum* 8).[10] The whole body of the church participates in continually progressing toward that truth.

There are at least two implications to these claims. One, a teaching must not only be proclaimed by the magisterium but also be received by the baptized community who possesses this supernatural instinct. Because the truth revealed in Christ is not something that the Church can possess—rather the truth that possesses the church[11]—the movement toward the plentitude of the fullness of truth is an ongoing process *within* the People.[12] Orlando Espín poignantly points to this movement and says, "Christians believe a Christianity that is what *they* believe Christianity is."[13] Of course,

---

7. International Theological Commission, "*Sensus Fidei* in the Life of the Church" (2014), no. 3. http://www.vatican.va/roman_curia/congregations/cfaith/cti_documents/rc_cti_20140610_sensus-fidei_en.html.

8. Ibid., no. 3; See the discussion on the subject-matter in the context of a global *sensus fidei* in Kevin Patrick Considine, "The Han of the Sinned-Against: A Global *Sensus Fidei* in the Pope Francis Era," *New Theology Review* 27.2 (2015) 38–46.

9. Gaillardetz, *Teaching with Authority*, 234.

10. Ibid., 76, 79 (emphases mine).

11. Ibid., 79.

12. Gaillardetz argues that there is significance in the listing by the Council members of the ways in which the Church grows in the truth, with the role of all believers appearing *before* the preaching of the bishops. Ibid., 42, 78.

13. Orlando O. Espín, *Idol and Grace: On Traditioning and Subversive Hope* (Maryknoll, NY: Orbis, 2014), xxiii.

that does not mean that the bishops are to abandon their unique roles as authoritative teachers. It *does* mean, according to Saint Cyprian of Carthage, that they not only teach but before they teach, they may learn from inquiring into the insights of the faithful alongside Scripture and tradition.[14] This method is what Gaillardetz and Cardinal Newman mean by "breathing together" the holy breath of God.[15] In other words, the magisterium and the baptized community are two participatory poles in one dynamic "traditioning" process.[16] In this sense, magisterium teaching and theology must play indispensable hermeneutical roles with the consensus of the people.[17]

Two, this instinct of faith is actualized within a particular context.[18] Human culture expresses *sensus fidelium* in its own (local) way and it thereby *progresses* toward the fullness of truth (universal). In this sense, according to Gaillardetz:

> Not only is the individual response to Church teaching influenced by social and ecclesial context, but the individual's response also contributes to the Christian community's ongoing appropriation of God's word.[19]

Hence, Espín argues, rather than talking about inculturation that supposes a "canonical something" that "exists independent of a culture and can be ... transmitted into other cultures," one ought to speak of interculturality or "inter-trans-culturation" that discovers and affirms the ever-deepening truth, "through mutual witnessing, contrasting dialogue, and non-colonizing reflection."[20] By paying attention to the plentitude of the fullness of truth in local manifestations of the universal *sensus fidelium* rather than forcefully imposing truth onto a culture, both the magisterium and its believing community can more properly move toward the actualization of God's Word in the life of the Church. Each believer contributes something to the faithful consciousness of the Church "by offering their own imaginative construal of the divine self-gift they have received within the distinctive framework of their own life story."[21] In short, the Catholic Christian faith is both handed down from early Christianity and the ecclesial authorities *and* manifested

---

14. Gaillardetz, *By What Authority?*, 112.
15. Ibid., 111.
16. Gaillardetz, *Teaching with Authority*, 42.
17. Espín, *Idol and Grace*, 24.
18. Gaillardetz, *Teaching with Authority*, 257.
19. Ibid., 257.
20. Espín, *Idol and Grace*, 63.
21. Gaillardetz, *By What Authority?*, 110; cf. *Dei Verbum*, 8.

locally and differently. Thus by examining the local manifestations of the *sensus fidelium*, one can get a sense of the universal faith. To trace back to the root of this sense in Korean American Catholicism, then, I begin with early Christian martyrs.

Stories of Early Christianity

From very early on, one can discover stories of Christians in exile and/or their members becoming martyrs, both in the sense of dying for the faith and in the sense of μαρτυρεῖν, becoming a "witness." This theme of becoming martyrs, often in exile, is the thread that runs through the stories of early Christianity.

On his way to martyrdom in Rome, for example, Saint Ignatius of Antioch wrote several letters and commentaries. In these writings that he gave to his visitors, he indicated his desire to "bear" or become a *witness* (read "a martyr"). He wrote, "I fear your kindness, which may harm me" referring to the rumor that Christians in Rome were considering the possibility of freeing him from death. He went on to urge them to resist their desires to save him, because such efforts would threaten to place an obstacle before his desire "to attain unto God" and by so doing to "become a word of God."[22] He called off all attempts to save him so that he could "seal his witness with his blood."[23] His sacrifice was not only a merely passive acceptance but also an active pursuit.

Years earlier, Ignatius had advised a young Bishop Polycarp of Smyrna also to stay firm in his faith. When conflicts arose years later against Christians who refused to worship the gods under his watch, the angry crowd shouted "Death to the atheists!" (referring to those who had no visible gods) and "Bring Polycarp!" When the now old bishop Polycarp learned about it, he initially went into exile. In an act of accepting God's will, at some point he made the choice to stop fleeing and simply waited to be arrested. Even though he had experienced a lapse in determination, when facing death he boldly upheld his faith during a conversation with the proconsul presiding over the trial. Being tied to the post in the pyre he prayed out loud, "Lord Sovereign God . . . I thank you that you have deemed me worthy of this moment, so that, jointly with your martyrs, I may have a share in the cup of

---

22. Justo L. González, *The Story of Christianity: The Early Church to the Dawn of the Reformation*, 2nd ed. (New York: HarperCollins, 2010) 1:53; Ignatius of Antioch, *Romans* 1.2—2.1.

23. González, *The Story of Christianity*, 53.

Christ."²⁴ His desire to become and join the communion of martyrs, despite some very human temptation or momentary lapse, shows the strength of his conviction.

Another example of martyrdom can be found in the story of Cyprian of Carthage in exile. Cyprian's challenge came shortly after he became a bishop and when the Decian persecution broke out. He went into exile with other leaders for the good of his flock, maintaining that this act was not one of cowardice. The genuineness of his insistence may have been demonstrated both when he was in exile—during which he continued to guide his flock through an extensive correspondence—and when, a few years later, he gave his life as a martyr.²⁵

The last example of martyrdom is of female martyrs. Young Perpetua's father and the slave girl Felicitas's jailer attempted to persuade them to abandon their faith to save their own lives. Perpetua responded by saying that, just as it is useless to give someone a different name when they already had one, she had the name of Christian, and this also could not be changed. Felicitas, who was recovering from giving birth and was facing martyrdom by being thrown to the beasts (in her case a crazed cow), responded by saying that her suffering now was only hers but "when I face the beast there will be another who will live in me, and will suffer for me since I shall be suffering for him."²⁶

One can easily draw parallels from these stories of early Christian martyrs and *Sitz-Im-Leben*, then, with those of the Korean Catholics. A clear example of the similarities is found in the story of Father Zhou in the *Silk Letter*. The *Silk Letter* was written by Alexius Hwang Sa-yŏng in 1801 when he was informed of the execution of the Chinese missionary and the first priest to Korea, Father Zhou Wenmo (K. Chu Munmo). The letter is addressed to Bishop Gouve of Beijing in an effort to request diplomatic relations or even the extreme measure of military intervention to gain approval of foreign missionaries and the establishment of Catholic Church in Korea. It was written on a piece of silk and sewn to the lining of the garment. Fr. Zhou's intention was to secretly pass this letter on to the bishop. His plan failed, however, and fell into the hands of the Korean government.²⁷

---

24. González, *The Story of Christianity*, 54–55; *Martyrdom of Polycarp*, 14.

25. Ibid., 102–4.

26. Ibid., 98–9; *Martyrdom of Perpetua and Felicitas*, 5.3.

27. Franklin Rausch, "Dying for Heaven: Persecution, Martyrdom, and Family in the Early Korean Catholic Church," in Charlotte Horlyck and Michael J. Pettid eds., *Death, Mourning, and the Afterlife in Korea: From Ancient to Contemporary Times* (Honolulu: University of Hawaii Press, 2014) 222–23. Don Baker from University of British Columbia has worked on an English translation of the Silk Letter in its entirety,

It is true that some of the Korean Catholic stories were likely written intentionally to mirror the New Testament (Passion) narratives or early church stories.[28] Nevertheless, one cannot undervalue the consistent theme that appears in all these stories: martyrdom as being central to the survival of often exiled Christians. In the remaining portions of this essay, I will point to manifestations of this theme in early Korean and Korean American Catholic stories and suggest a way forward to the current and subsequent generations of Catholics.

Korean Stories of Catholicism

So as to discover these enriching and faithful manifestations of divine revelation in unique settings with unique elements, one can also look to local experiences of Asian and Asian American communities. The intuitive ways Asians and Asian Americans express their faith is discovered through the act of storytelling. For instance, for Koreans some of the previously silenced stories of the martyrs (especially female martyrs) only came to surface partly from the canonization of 103 martyrs in May 1984 and as a result of Pope Francis's visit to South Korea in August 2014 to beatify 124 Korean Catholic martyrs. Many of these stories, however, were either implicitly silenced or not at the forefront of Korean Catholic theological discourse, as the title of a 2002 dissertation by Jong-Rye Gratia Song, SPC, suggests, "Listening with the Heart to the Echo of Silenced Voices."[29] Nevertheless, these stories of martyrdom endured through oral traditions as well as academic studies, thanks in large part to surviving texts, letters, journals, and prison writings, including the famous *Silk Letter* of Hwang Sa-Yŏng. These resources have helped believers and scholars get glimpses of the early Catholics' *sensus fidelium* in Korea.

Of course, it would be inaccurate to caricature these martyrs as sharing the same sensibility or motivations for their martyrdom. However, there are at least some commonalities among them. These martyrs often spoke of their feelings and motivations "not to disobey the will of God," or "to imitate God," or "to gain heaven."[30] Song focuses heavily on the obedience to the will of God as being important for Korean women because they faced

forthcoming through University of Hawaii Press.

28. Rausch, "Dying for Heaven," 2.

29. Jong-rye Gratia Song, SPC, "Listening with the Heart to the Echo of Silenced Voice," PhD diss., Weston Jesuit School of Theology, 2002.

30. Ibid., 172; see Jong-rye Gratia Song, "Martyrdom and the Autonomy of Korean Catholic Women," *Asia Journal of Theology* 17.2 (2003) 365.

martyrdom "in a distinctly Korean way, flowing from a characteristic of Korean spirituality," which can be seen more properly as a confluence with their Catholic Christian faith.[31] She argues, therefore, that their martyrdom—which was chosen freely as Catholic acts of heroism, revealing their autonomy (ironically in death)—consummated their duties of *Hyo* (filial piety), *Ch'ung* (loyality), and *Ŭiri* (the practice of justice and righteousness), which required women to particularly choose *Chŏljae* (chastity). These concepts strongly demanded obedience, which, when applied to their society at large, resulted in submission and obedience to men in general but when applied to the heavens, resulted in equality of class and gender before God.[32] Thus, it is fair to say that while Catholic women faced their martyrdom in a distinctively Korean and Neo-Confucian way, the Catholic understanding of these Korean concepts is rather different from, and often overriding that of, the late Chosŏn society (which is one reason why Catholics were persecuted). In that sense, these women martyrs, living in a patriarchal culture, were more willing to be obedient to the will of God, thereby embracing their full autonomy and dignity by becoming a martyr.[33]

The story of Columba Kang Wan-suk helps us to locate the distinctively cultural ways in which early Korean martyrs faced martyrdom and yet reserved their final loyalty to Catholicism. After the persecution of 1791, Kang separated from her husband, who was not Catholic, and went into exile in Seoul with her daughter, stepson, and mother-in-law (all Catholic). While in exile, she practiced *Hyo* (filial piety) and continued to take care of her mother-in-law and stepson.[34] While her dutiful commitment to her family that reached even to her in-laws is commendable, more importantly, Catholic Christian spirituality helped her to extend her obedient heart to God, overriding her cultural-philosophical commitment. When, for example, Fr. Zhou Wenmo (Chu Munmo) successfully came to Korea 1795, she hid him, in her firewood storehouse for three months, since in aristocratic families, outside men could not enter the main living room reserved for women, according to the Confucian tradition. She broke away from tradition and asked her mother-in-law to allow him to be brought in to her main room.

---

31. Song, "Listening with the Heart," 173; Song "Martyrdom and the Autonomy of Korean Catholic Women," 365.

32. Ibid., 180, 188; Song, "Martyrdom and the Autonomy of Korean Catholic Women," 369, 374.

33. See Francine Cardman's discussion on women martyrs' focus on embracing their autonomy and dignity in her "Acts of the Women Martyrs," *Anglican Theological Review* 70 (1998) 149; see also Song, "Listening with the Heart," 187; "Martyrdom and the Autonomy of Korean Catholic Women," 374.

34. Song, "Listening with the Heart," 43–44.

For a woman separated from her husband, hiding a fugitive in exile from a foreign land who was a man and approximately of her age, she was risking not only gossip but her life with this decision.[35] Partly as a result of her effort to house Fr. Chu, assist him as the main confidant and translator, and be versed enough to run (appointed by Fr. Chu) a women's group, catechism, and prayer group, Catholics grew from four thousand to ten thousand. Her work was so important that the French Catholic missionary and the author of *The History of the Church of Korea*, Claude-Charles Dallet, credited Kang, even more so than Fr. Chu, for the growth of the church during that period by saying, "In all [Fr. Chu's] efforts, the priest was, in telling effect, second to Columba Kang . . . So should we, in fairness, attribute a large part of this progress of the religion [Catholicism] at the time to her [Kang]."[36] All this was possible initially because of her commitment to the cultural spirituality (*Hyo*). More importantly, however, her Catholic commitment to be a filial servant of God allowed her to be resilient and steadfast in her faith.

Alternatively but related to Song's claims, Franklin Rausch, a historian of pre-modern East Asia, focuses on the stories of the Korean martyrs with a particular attention to their hope for the afterlife in his article, "Dying for Heaven: Persecution, Martyrdom, and Family in the Early Korean Catholic Church."[37] While he acknowledges the influence of the ethos of obedience on the Korean martyrs, he looks for a broader motive in the intentions of Korean martyrs, namely their hopes for entrance into, and ultimately upholding of, their familial obligations in Heaven.[38] He argues that Korean martyrs pursued ways to maintain both their cultural-familial duties and Catholic doctrinal obligations by drawing from both worldviews. He uncovered that many Koreans, including neo-Confucian scholars, found life on earth ultimately dissatisfying. For some neo-Confucian scholars, the fact that life on earth, like everything else, came to an end sooner rather than later seemed to translate to a loss of meaning. When they discovered Catholicism, however, they gained new hope for both eternal life and life on earth. The lower-class "untouchables" sought Catholicism because they were treated like other human beings with equal dignity on earth by other Catholics and taught that they will continue to enjoy this loving commu-

---

35. Ibid., 43–45.

36. Ibid., 48; My translation: "Dans tous ses efforts, le prêtre était très-efficacement secondé par Columba Kang. . . Aussi doit-on, en toute justice, lui attribuer une grande partie des porgrès que fit la religion à cette époque." Claude-Charles Dallet, *Histoire de l'Eglise de Corée*, vol.1 (Paris: Palmé, 1874) 81.

37. Rausch, "Dying for Heaven," 213–35.

38. While Song also wrote of this desire by the martyrs, she does not treat this theme with as much emphasis as does Rausch.

nity after this life, an idea that was certainly threatening the neo-Confucian ethos and caste of the time. For nobility, they sought Catholicism in their journey to find something more fulfilling beyond this world, eventually finding that in the possibility of their survival in the afterlife. As a result he concludes that they reconciled the tension between neo-Confucian morality and Catholic belief *and* encouraged other Catholics to be unwavering in the face of martyrdom by imagining their lives in heaven. In heaven, they will be able to fulfill their cultural-familial duties by helping their earthly family members enter the kingdom of God along with relishing a life that is everlasting. To establish this rationale, archetypical stories are in order.

In the surviving documents of another aristocratic family, that of Matthew Yi Yunha and especially in the prison letters of his daughter, Luthgrade Yi Suni, one discovers the early Korean Catholics' efforts to reconcile their Catholic beliefs with their Confucian heritage in their vision of martyrdom and the afterlife. While waiting for her martyrdom in prison, for example, Yi Suni wrote of her vision of heaven as "a place of family reunion" to her mother, sister, and sister-in-law. She was able to envision this because she, the "worthless child," would be "suffused with unlimited bliss" via martyrdom, would "take your hand and lead you to heaven," where they would enjoy "eternal happiness together."[39] Rather than betraying her Confucian filial duty, martyrdom transformed the meaning of her desire to fulfill her filial duties by helping her family members attain unto God. This particular vision of the afterlife allowed her to be steadfast in her faith along with following through with her cultural-familial duties. Perhaps Father Zhou, the Chinese missionary and the first priest to Korea, had a similar envisioning when he came out of his exile and surrendered to the authorities. With many of his closest followers jailed, tortured, and martyred, and many of his family members dead, "the promise of the new world to come where he would be reunited with his loved ones, would have certainly been attractive."[40]

Whatever their *raison d'être* or motivation—obedience to the will of God or hope in the afterlife—a sense of wanting to become a martyr often in exile exemplify Catholic religiosity in these stories. While the local manifestations of these religious impulses may widely vary—whether they were nobles, old, educated, wealthy, working class, young, uneducated, poor, steadfast in their faith, lapsed, etc.—their instincts of wanting to be a witness to their faith, i.e. a martyr, remain the common thread amidst that diversity. Their belief in the afterlife and their efforts to stay true to their cultural heritage, both of

---

39. Ibid., 225; See also a forthcoming chapter by James K. H. Lee in Simon C. Kim and Francis Kim, eds., *Jubilee Reflections of Korean American Catholics* (Eugene, OR: Wipf & Stock, forthcoming).

40. Ibid., 222.

which contributed to their resilience in exile and in martyrdom, helped early Korean Catholics to form a communal sense of faith.

A Korean American Story of Catholicism[41]

It should be noted that Korean Catholic stories of martyrdom and experiences, while related, are also profoundly different from complex and complicated Korean *American* Catholic stories and experiences. First, it is both obvious and important that these stories occurred in a different region and time period from Korean American communities and their experiences. Second, many of the Korean martyrs were elites themselves or by association via familial membership. Many accounts of Korean Americans origins, however, are stories stemming from their struggles to survive starting at the bottom of the socio-economic ladder. While they may be able to relate to the stories at the level of survival and their status as marginal figures, the privilege and the access to the goods and services that martyrs had as elites would be foreign to many early Korean Americans Catholics who had to survive without those privileges. Third, Korean American Catholic communities *today* are a diverse and ever-changing group. Rather than starting from scratch and working toward the "American Dream," many Koreans immigrating today are already quite affluent and established. Many American-born generations after the first generation of immigrants, and many Koreans immigrating to the States now, are also quite prosperous and successful in their careers; many of them certainly have more socio-economic power than their first-generation immigrant parents and grandparents. Thus, it is necessary to share stories that capture the *American* experience and stories of "crossing the border" into this land. How did my forebears settle in this land? How did they survive? What does it mean to be a descendant of that struggle and survival? How does that help to understand how and who I am today? Sharing these stories is crucial, then, to begin answering some of these questions.

However, similar to Asian experiences, there is not a monolithic Korean American experience that encapsulates who they are. Nevertheless, specific local stories of crossing the border, settling, struggling, surviving, and living certainly do contribute to that end. The distinctive Korean American stories will guide and give a framework for Korean Catholics for understanding who they are precisely as Catholics. More importantly, sharing specifically Korean American Catholic stories moves all members of the

---

41. Revised Romanization transliteration of Korean is used for this section.

church, including the faithful people of God, toward the actualization of the truth in God's Word in the life of the church.

One of these stories starts, not in metropolitan or affluent California or New York, but more appropriately in a remote area in Kentucky at St. Christopher Roman Catholic Church in Radcliff, right outside of a U.S. Army Training Facility in Fort Knox.[42] Margaret Young Sook Ha arrived there with her American (soldier) husband after the completion of his assignment in South Korea in 1964. Being born and raised in Korea and finding no other parishioner of Korean descent when she first entered the door of St. Christopher Church, she was truly "crossing the border" into the unknown. The only connection remaining with her motherland was now Catholicism. In her innermost place her Korean roots were still undergirding her identity. For all intents and purposes, she was effectively living in "exile." The yearning to go back to her origins had never stopped and the Catholic liturgy served to fill both her yearning to be at the ultimate origin of her being, namely God, and her need in exile to stay connected to her land of origin, namely Korea.

After a few years, other Korean military wives began to appear at St. Christopher Church. Initially, there were no efforts to congregate among Koreans despite a steady growth of them. Finally, Korean military brides formed a community of Koreans within St. Christopher Church in 1982. There were not any official activities or concerted effort to bring about a separate Korean Catholic community but the sheer act of taking on a local habitation of this Spirited group was enough for their prayers to be answered and become witnesses of their faith. Meanwhile, fifty minutes up I-65, a separate group was forming in Louisville.

In September 1984, Father Francis Xavier Young Soo Wang from the Cincinnati Korean Catholic Church established a small Korean Catholic community in Louisville. Father Wang also established a Korean Catholic community in Indianapolis in September 1986, paving the way for future Korean priests from Indiana to also assist both communities in Kentucky. In 1990, Father Peter Kyung Yong Choi became the first priest of an officially recognized Korean Catholic Church in Indianapolis. Father Augustine Doowan Kim took the baton from Father Choi and continued to help and celebrate mass with the Kentucky community in the early 2000s.

Coincidentally, back in 1984, Julia "June" Kyung Sook Yoon arrived in Pewee Valley, Kentucky, and attended an American parish, St. Aloysius Roman Catholic Church, with her American husband. She found out about the

---

42. St. Andrew Kim Korean Catholic Community at St. Aloysius Church in Pewee Valley, Kentucky, maintains the following records.

Korean Catholic community in Louisville and about their efforts to bring the Korean Catholic communities together. She, along with others, would eventually request assistance from St. Aloysius Church so that they may celebrate mass regularly there and have a Korean priest to look after them.[43] It was an unlikely request for a community of 50 people or so. Nevertheless, the resilient spirit of becoming a witness to faith that was with the original church in Levant and in the early church of Korea refused to give up.

In the meantime, with the help of St. Aloysius Church, the archdiocese contacted the Catholic Bishops' Conference of Korea. With the raising of his hand, the archbishop of Euijungboo (near Seoul) volunteered to send one of the priests from his diocese to Kentucky. On June 27, 2012, Father Blaise "Blasio" Young Wook Kim celebrated Mass in Korean with Korean Catholic communities from Fort Knox/Radcliff, Louisville, Lexington, and southern Indiana at the auxiliary chapel (which was the original chapel) of St. Aloysius for the first time. As he made his initial procession, many members of the community could not resist their tears of joy for this long-awaited moment and they often recounted the feeling of the presence of the Holy Spirit that day.

Now with regular services and a firm foundation, Margaret Ha and others enjoy sowing the seeds of Korean herbs and greens around St. Aloysius. She says that these seeds have a tendency to spread far and wide and grow in multitudes. The next generations of Korean American Catholics are now able to enjoy the kind of vegetables that she could not enjoy when she first arrived in the States. She has both literally planted the seeds for the next generations as well as planted the seeds of faith (in the land of the *New Seeds of Contemplation*) that will spread the living *sensus fidelium* far and wide and grow in multitudes.[44]

A Future Implication

As poignant and encouraging as this Korean American Catholic story may be, many Korean American Catholics today are assimilated professionals who, unless lapsed, attend an established Anglophone or Korean American Catholic church. It is vital to have stories that can encourage, direct,

---

43. For a time, Father Doo Jin Kim, a student at St. Meinrad Seminary, celebrated mass with them (2007–2010). Their only other access to a comprehensible liturgy after that was from Father Peter Jae Hyun Choi who came down from Indianapolis once a month.

44. Thomas Merton, *New Seeds of Contemplation* (New York: New Directions, 1961; reprinted, 2007).

and reveal to young Catholics of their roles in this traditioning process of their salvation history. What does it mean to be a witness at this moment in history, in America, as a Catholic of Korean descent? What ought I do to contribute to my flourishing and that of my communities? What will be my role in this locality that has universal and Catholic implications? For a story that will help grapple with these questions, it may be helpful to go back to their roots yet again.

The story of Paul Chŏng Ha Sang—after which many Korean American Catholic Churches are named—is one story that will help guide the next generations of Korean American Catholics in their effort to search for initial answer to those questions concerning their roles. Paul Chŏng Ha Sang had previously lost his father Chŏng Yak-chong (the uncle in-law of Alexius Hwang who wrote the *Silk Letters*) in the persecution of 1801. The Korean Catholic Church had been left neglected for thirty-three years. The following generations of Korean Catholics were in dire need for a leader to pick up where their parents' generation left off. Paul Chŏng took up this challenge and crossed the border to China—which entailed collecting enough money from Korean Catholics, including poor individuals, to provide for his traveling expenses, and walking 1,300 miles per trip on foot—no fewer than nine times, in order to request the bishop of China to dispatch a priest to Korea. He must have been aware that the survival of Catholics in Korea, in great part, depended on his effort. After many failed attempts, which included drafting a letter addressed to the Pope in Rome and a death of a priest on his way to Korea, Paul and his friends (Augustine Yu Chin-kil and Carolus Cho Sin-ch'ul) were able to bring Father Pacificus Liu, Father Maubant, Father Chastan and Bishop Imbert to Korea. In 1839, he was caught by the authorities along with his sister and mother and beheaded on September 22 of that month.[45]

Paul Chŏng serves as an important exemplar. After the first generations of Korean Catholics in the US pass on, the Korean American Catholic Churches will be left in the hands of the next generations for its survival. They will have to cross their regional, cultural, and spiritual borders multiple times, just as Paul Chŏng and indeed Jesus did, in order to spread God's message by all necessary means. The American Catholic reality and Korean American Catholic reality in particular, are at a crossroads again. The number of Catholics is declining and the religious "Nones" are on the rise. The decision to take up and continue the efforts that their ancestors undertook

---

45. Joseph Chang-mun Kim and John Jae-sun Chung, eds. *Catholic Korea: Yesterday and Today: 1784–1884* (Seoul: St. Joseph, 1984), 130–131, 160, 169–171. Cf. Won-jae Hui, "Sang-Jaesang-seo," *KIATS Theological Journal: Journal of the Korea Institute Advanced Theological Studies* I.2 (Seoul: KIATS, 2005) 133–47.

so that their communities endured must be made in the present time. This is the kind of instinct that guided Paul Chŏng's faith and the faith of his community. How many borders must we cross? How many times? For how long? If Paul Chŏng and the Korean martyrs, as well as early Christians have taught us anything, they have taught us that the survival of the community requires us to make the necessary sacrifices and be patient and resilient in order to persevere.

Indeed, Christianity depends on and is defined by the lesson from Jesus, of sacrificial love that requires the spirit of sacrifice and martyrdom. However, this sense of faith is not only handed down but also manifested in diverse ways. Ethnic communities, like Korean American Catholics, must continue the work of their Christian ancestors to hand down this faith but do so in their own distinctive ways. They have a wealth of stories from their Christian and Korean pasts by which they are formed and helped. Their American experience will enable them to figure out exactly how that same instinct of faith will be manifested in their context. That way, their Catholic Christian faith will be both universal *and* their own.

Conclusion

Through the Korean and the early Church's stories of martyrdom and the more particular story of a Korean American Catholic community, two elements are brought to the surface. One, that there is a real requirement of martyrdom for the Catholic faith. My intention for highlighting the sacrificial aspect of faith is not to simply accuse the current generations of Korean and Korean American Catholics for "not doing enough" compared to their forefathers and mothers. Rather, being a witness of faith was required for all Catholics of all persuasions and locations. As such, the current and the next generations of Korean and Korean American Catholics have a calling to discover what their contributions to their local and wider communities are as witnesses to faith. For existing first-generation people, martyrdom may come in the form of sacrificing their long-held customs to let in some fresh air to appreciate the signs of the time. Being a martyr, as exemplified by the stories of the instinctual consensus of the faithful in the early and modern stories, is a fundamental quality of the *sensus fidelium* of the Church.

Secondly, listening is a gateway through which many permutations of these stories of martyrdom may come to future fruition. Listening to the stories in the *Silk Letter* and of the Yi family letters points both to where they have been and the poignant nature of these stories (the oral history) that rejuvenated Catholics to be steadfast in their faith, even affecting non-Catholics to take interest. The decision by others to listen to the stories of this small Korean Roman Catholic community in Kentucky was the starting point for this group to endure and survive despite their unlikely chances of survival. Listening to the stories from the people of God is an essential element of understanding the *sensus fidelium* of the Church.

Hence, the successful survival of the Korean American Catholic Church requires martyrdom. The more Korean American Catholics are exposed to the stories of the Korean American experiences as Catholics, the more they will be able to make sense of where they come from, who they are, and where they are going (or ought to go). The wider the church is open to listening to these stories, the better these communities will be able to survive as a group. More importantly for the Church, listening to these stories also will contribute to its own ongoing appropriation of God's Word among the people of God.

More specifically for Korean American Catholics, their becoming witnesses, i.e., martyrs, for their faith means to be in line with both their Christian and Korean ancestries. What is necessary for them, then, is to figure out and discover what becoming a witness means to them in their American context. This discovery, however, is impossible if they simply dismiss their Korean heritage in favor of a "melted" Catholic identity and if they do not share their stories in the trans-American context. What is your story of survival? What is your story of resilience? What sacrifices and contributions should you make as a group to the universal church? Perhaps, a country-wide institution like KAPA (Korean American Priests' Association) or FIAT (a non-profit organization dedicated to developing leadership and the spirit of service among Catholic Korean Youth and Young Adults in North America), or a formulation of a web community or forum can all help in this endeavor and start collecting, listening, and sharing these stories.

The lived experience of the effect and the power of storytelling in Korea enables the imagination to move beyond one's geographic, cultural, and religious locations. It is also the case that the storytelling provides a way for Korean immigrants and Korean Americans of affirming in consciousness and memory their rootedness in geographical, cultural, and religious locations. The newly unveiled stories of martyrs in exile will certainly resonate with the body of the faithful regardless of their current location. The new stories that are traditioning Korean American Catholics will contribute positively to those end. Perhaps they will motivate other ethnic (Asian) groups to follow suit. With the assistance of the Holy Spirit, these stories can help all people of God to evoke and reignite their faith. They also allow the wider church to look to these stories to grow and progress toward the fullness of truth. Margaret Ha and the Kentucky community along with numerous uncovered stories all over the country certainly have already planted those seeds. They received these seeds from deeply rooted tree of their traditions. It is up to the subsequent generations to cultivate those seeds lovingly and bring them to blossom intentionally in their contexts through becoming witnesses, martyrs for their faiths. Indeed, according to Thomas Merton,

> Every moment and every event of every man's life on earth plants something in his soul. For just as the wind carries thousands of winged seeds, so each moment brings with it germs of spiritual vitality that come to rest imperceptibly in the minds and wills of men. Most of these unnumbered seeds perish and are lost, because men are not prepared to receive them: for such seeds as these cannot spring up anywhere except in the soil of freedom, spontaneity, and love.[46]

---

46. Merton, *New Seeds of Contemplation*, 14.

23

The *Sensus Fidei* in the Recent History of the Latin American Church

— Maria Clara Lucchetti Bingemer —

In this reflection about theology, local churches, and the *sensus fidei*, I would like to begin by quoting the recent document of the International Theological Commission, "*Sensus Fidei* in the life of the Church," of 2014. This paragraph treats the relationship between the *sensus fidei* and theology:

> As a service towards the understanding of faith, theology endeavors, amid the *conspiratio* of all the charisms and functions in the Church, to provide the Church with objective precision regarding the content of its faith, and it necessarily relies on the existence and correct exercise of the *sensus fidelium*. The latter is not just an object of attention for theologians; it constitutes a foundation and a locus for their work. Theology itself, therefore, has a two-fold relationship to the *sensus fidelium*. On the one hand, theologians depend on the *sensus fidei* because the faith that they study and articulate lives in the people of God. In this sense, theology must place itself in the school of the *sensus fidelium* to discover there the profound resonances of the word of God. On the other hand, theologians help the faithful to express the authentic *sensus fidelium* by reminding them of the essential lines of faith, and helping them to avoid deviations and confusion caused by the influence of imaginative elements from elsewhere (n. 81).[1]

In this paragraph, the *sensus fidei* and the *sensus fidelium* are identified with that sense, that "feeling," that springs from faith, and is related to

---

1. International Theological Commission, Sensus Fidei *in the Life of the Church* 2014, http://www.vatican.va/roman_curia/congregations/cfaith/cti_documents/rc_cti_20140610_sensus-fidei_en.html.

everything that affects the life of faith and faith experience. Its major source is the Holy Spirit, which allows every faithful person to "feel" and develop an intuitive evaluation of the central contents of faith. The method to attain that "sense" of faith is not rationally deductive nor grounded in formal arguments, but consists of an experience through which we can recognize and discern what does and what does not belong effectively to faith[2].

Different from theology, which is the "science of faith," the *sensus fidei* is not a reflected knowledge of the mysteries of faith, and does not develop concepts nor use rational methods. It is a *sensus*, similar to a vital instinct that causes attachment to the truth and rejection of what contradicts it. As Pope Francis says in the *Evangelii Gaudium*, "The presence of the Spirit gives Christians a certain connaturality with divine realities, and a wisdom, which enables them to grasp those realities intuitively, even when they lack the wherewithal to give them precise expression" (119).

As we see, in spite of not being a science and not expressing itself by rational arguments, the *sensus fidei* can be and in fact has been an important source of inspiration to theology and in particular pastoral theology, the same as to the whole life of the church. In this text, we will take into consideration and into account this intimate relationship, so desirable and accurate, between *sensus fidei* and theology, and will reflect on it in light of the experience of the Latin American Church.

We will reflect upon the recent experience of Latin American Theology of putting itself in "the school of the *sensus fidelium* to discover there the profound resonances of the word of God."[3] I will take three landmarks in the recent path of the Latin American Church during the 70s and 80s, which provide—in my judgment—examples of our local church. These landmarks first presented themselves in the community of the faithful, and were later assimilated not only by the hierarchy and the magisterium but also by theologians in their reflections. As I describe them, I will try to comment on and highlight how they became theology.

They are:

1. Liberation Theology and the Option for the Poor.

2. The popular reading of the Bible.

---

2. See W. Kern and F.-J. Niemann, *El conocimiento teológico* (Barcelona: Herder, 1986) 229; apud Joaquín Silva, *El carácter vinculante del sensus fidei en la vida de la Iglesia*, Presentation in the Seminario de Profesores de la Facultad de Teología, May 26, 2015.

3. In that first section the author relies on material from the the Duffy Lectures, a series of lectures given on Latin American Theology at Boston College, February 2015.

3. The interaction between women theologians and women from grassroots communities.

At the end I hope to have demonstrated that the *sensus fidei* was not only very important to the Latin American Church, but that it molded and configured that church, bringing to fuller, consistent expression the face it has today. In spite of all the difficulties and pressures suffered during the years after the fall of the Berlin Wall and the end of the (false) utopias, the closeness between theology and the *sensus fidelium* remains a powerful element in the configuration of church life at the southern part of America.

Liberation Theology and the Option for the Poor[4]

The topic of human rights, associated with the global effort to confront poverty, emerged emphatically after World War II, especially in the northern hemisphere and in international organizations like the UN. Within the UN, the Food and Agricultural Organization (FAO) was founded in 1945, with the aim of ensuring stable food supplies and nutrition, especially in the poor countries. "Before, poverty and hunger were problems more or less spread everywhere. But today they are serious problems, concentrated in particular parts of the world, to the extent that these regions form, alongside the countries of the capitalist West and the communist East, an underdeveloped Third World, to use the term coined by the French geographer Alfred Sauvy in 1952."[5] At this point, the Third World is emerging simultaneously both as a problem and as a new agent on the international scene.[6]

In 1961, the number of countries participating in the FAO increased, and it now incorporated Latin America, which began to be an important part of the so-called Third World. The Cuban revolution took place, marking the beginning of anti-imperialist struggles to develop marginalized parts of the world, and to break bonds of dependence on First World countries that were perpetuating the legacy of colonialism.[7]

---

4. I follow here closely the excellent article of Paulo Fernando Carneiro de Andrade, "Opção pelos pobresno Magistério: Pensamento Social Católico do Vaticano II à Conferência de Aparecida," *Concilium* 361, junho de 2015, Globalization and the Church of the Poor.

5. See Alfred Sauvy in the French magazine *L'observateur*, on 14 August 1952, apud P. F. C. de Andrade.

6. Ibid.

7. See R. Gil Benumeya, "Tradición y actualidad em la evolución internacional del socialismo árabe," *Revista de política Internacional*, 89 (1967) 37–54; and L. Almeida, "O Pan-Africanismo e a formação da OUA," *Revista geo-paisagem* 6.12 (July–December 2007) 23, http://www.feth.ggf.br/África.htm. Para América Latina:

In the face of this new reality, the question of how the church was to be present in such places and evangelize their peoples became a very controversial one. Since the end of the nineteenth century, the church had been conscious of having lost the working classes. The openness of the church towards social problems, especially manifest in Pope Leo XIII's Encyclical Letter, *Rerum Novarum* (1891), was the fruit of a slow preparation in which lay "social pioneers," activists as well as thinkers, played a major role.[8]

The publication of the encyclical *Rerum novarum* of Leo XIII in 1891 was an attempt to repair the breach that had opened up between the church and the poor, which resulted from industrialization. In the twentieth century, this same church turned to the Third World,[9] eager to hear the cries of the poor and to respond to their fears and aspirations.

On September 11, 1962, one month before the beginning of Vatican II, John XXIII made a broadcast that surprised both the church and the wider world. He affirmed: "Where the underdeveloped countries are concerned, the Church presents herself as she is. She wishes to be the Church of all, and especially the Church of the poor."[10] Thanks to the pope's words, the idea of the church of the poor broke through.[11] The council opened up new paths, and its reception in Latin America led to a structural critique of an evangelization conducted for elites, and servicing stakes.[12]

The Theology of Liberation—a new structural approach to theology as a whole—took as its starting point the following question: "What does it mean to be a Christian in a continent of poor and oppressed people?" What is at stake in a theology seeking to make common cause with the pastoral practice of a church that has intended to make itself freely poor, that places itself at the side of the poor, and commits itself to the processes of liberation from all forms of oppression and marginalization?[13]

This theological movement of liberation theology began with an attentive and careful listening to people from the grassroots who expressed their

---

E. Faletto, "Los años 60 y el tema de la dependência," *Estudos avançados* 12.33 (May/August 1998), São Paulo" p. 5 cited in Paulo Fernando Carneiro de Andrade, "Opção pelos pobresno Magistério."

8. ITC, 73.

9. See the 1974 word of W. Buhlmann, *O Terceiro Mundo e a Terceira Igreja* (São Paulo: Paulinas, 1976).

10. John XXIII, opening speech of the II Vatican Council http://w2.vatican.va/content/john-xxiii/en/speeches/1962.index.html.

11. P. F. Carneiro de Andrade, art. cit.

12. Cf. Pe. H. Lima Vaz, *Igreja Reflexo / Igreja Fonte. Cadernos Brasileiros* (Rio de Janeiro) 46 (1968) 1722.

13. De Andrade, art. cit., 8–9.

feeling of distance from the official church and their desire to find responses to their anxieties regarding the oppression that weighed on them. Also the church listened to the those middle class Christians, lay or religious, who were conscious of the inequality that divided the continent and questioned a pastoral approach that worked mainly with the elite.[14]

In addition, this offered a theology that wants to be listening closely to the culture of the indigenous peoples, to speak the language of these cultures and to appreciate their traditions, their rituals, their worshiping. This theology doesn't want to end up with those traditions as non-Christian ones, but to respect them as they are and extract from them inspiration and material for its reflection. Moreover, where those traditions and cultures live together with Christian culture brought by colonial evangelization, the effort has to be made of integrating them as constitutive parts of the process of church discourse and praxis.

Such integration would be our opportunity, in the view of prominent Brazilian philosopher Henrique de Lima Vaz, for the Latin American Church to make a step from being a church that only projects and reflects European church and theology to a church that is a source of a native and original living of the Gospel, which can generate a new way of thinking and speaking about God, that is, of doing theology that originates in a continent that is poor and oppressed.

Who, however, are the poor? The behavior and praxis of the poor are the center of Christian life. Jon Sobrino came to define what we understand by poor in Latin American liberation theology. "The *analogatum princeps* of the poor, of those by whom the Church made a preferential option in the 60s is, very concretely, those human beings to whom the fundamental fact of living is a heavy burden and a hard struggle in the middle of total insecurity and precarious conditions, even concerning the most elementary and basic human rights: eating, housing, health, etc."[15] Biblically speaking, they are those who are bent, bowed, humiliated for life, together with ignored and despised by society.[16]

That is the understanding of "poor" in Latin American theology. The poor are those who are first of all socio-economically poor. That is not an ideological expression. Poor are those who are stripped of life and happiness,

---

14. Among those, we have to highlight the importance of the movement Ação Católica (Action Catholique), which began in France but became very important in Latin America during the 50s and the 60s.

15. Jon Sobrino, "Opción por los pobres," in *Revista Latinoamericana de Teologia* in *Revista Electrónica Latinoamericana de Teologia* 251, http://servicioskoinonia.org/relat/251.htm.

16. Ibid.

of any kind.[17] Frei Betto, another well-known liberation theologian powerfully describes reality on the continent:

> To speak about human rights in Latin America is a luxury. Here, we are still struggling for the rights of animals, because to eat, to have a roof over the head, to feed and raise, and breed have to do with animals and beasts. I have never seen a veal abandoned in the streets of Brazil or a cow at the corner of the street waiting for someone to give it food. However, there are 8 million abandoned children and thousands of beggars searching something to eat in garbage cans.[18]

Together with this poverty, there is also socio-cultural poverty. This element was very much stressed by the Theology of the People (*Teología del Pueblo*), which became very important for the archbishop of Buenos Aires, Jorge Mario Bergoglio, today Pope Francis. The Theology of the People was, according to Gustavo Gutierrez, a stream with its own characteristics within liberation theology.[19] Among the most important figures of this theology are—according to V. Azcuy[20]—Lucio Gera[21] and Rafael Tello[22] in the first generation, J.C. Scannone in the second, and Carlos Galli in the third. The proper method of this theology is to work with cultural and symbolic mediations as hermeneutical choices.

Scannone defines the steps for this theology as follows:

1. It begins with the Latin American peoples, the original peoples in whose wisdom and religion is frequently enculturated the people of God.

---

17. Ibid.

18. Frei Betto, Direitos humanos ou direitos animais? http://www.correiocidadania.com.br/antigo/ed373/opiniao.htm (translation mine).

19. G. Gutiérrez, *La fuerza histórica de los pobres* (Lima: CEP, 1979) 377.

20. Teología ante el reto de la pobreza una perspectiva latinoamericana, desde las mujeres, texto en elaboración, 2002.

21. Lucio Gera is considered the main inspiration for this Argentinian trend. For more about him beyond his writings, see R. Ferrara and C. Galli, ed., *Presente y futuro de la teología en Argentina. Homenaje a Lucio Gera* (Buenos Aires: Paulinas, 1997).

22. I follow here the contribution of V. M. Fernández: "Creo que nadie se acercó teológicamente al pobre como el padre Rafael Tello. Él es—junto con Lucio Gera—una de las grandes figuras de la 'teología de la cultura popular.' Por eso me parece injusto, aun cuando a él pueda desagradarle todo homenaje, que casi nunca se lo mencione cuando se habla de la teología argentina," cf. *Con los pobres hasta el fondo. El pensamiento teológico de Rafael Tello*, in V. R. Azcuy, ed., *Semillas del siglo XX*, Proyecto 36 (2000) 187 [187–205].

2. The preferential use of historical-cultural analysis as a mediation to interpret and to judge historical and social reality of the poor in the light of faith.

3. To use human sciences in a more synthetic and hermeneutical way as history, cultural anthropology or sciences of religion and also symbols and narratives, without despising more analytical sciences.

4. Since its inception this school of thought made a critique of the use of a Marxist mode of analysis, considered not enough critical, from Liberation Theology. The poor have, nevertheless a special place within the central categories of a *Teologia del Pueblo*: people, popular religion, culture.

Liberation theologians, however, never denied the importance of cultural poverty.[23] Together with socio-economic poverty, there is also the socio-cultural one, equally hard and heavy. There is (also) racial, ethnic, and sexual oppression and discrimination. In addition, very often, the fact of being an afro-descendant, indigenous, or a woman, increases the difficulty of living. These difficulties are not separate from socio-economic reality, but it happens very frequently, at least in the Third World, within it. That is the reason why liberation theology chose to face socio-economical poverty as a central priority. It is what better described both then and now poverty in the world, which is compounded by forms of oppression that originated from other kinds of discriminations.

The entire movement for a new pastoral point of departure that happened on the continent, as well as new priorities and a new way of doing theology, was proposed as a three-point action plan for the church, as proclaimed by the Medellín Conference of 1968: faith and justice together, inseparably united, as priorities; a new way of doing theology, with the method: to see—to judge—to act; a new model of church, starting from how local communities at the base and in poor areas, gathered around the Scriptures, expressed themselves. It was centered on the popular reading of the Bible, which has its own method for approaching the Scripture,[24] and was marked by a desire to be a church of the poor.[25] These points were

---

23. See J. Sobrino, "Opción por los pobres."

24. The popular reading of the Bible had its method composed and developed by the Carmelite Carlos Mesters and has three steps: reality (fact of life); Gospel enlightenment (Bible text); and transforming action.

25. Cf. Documento de Conclusões da Conferencia do episcopado latino-americano em Medellin, Colombia, 1968, http://www.celam.org/conferencia_medellin.php.

confirmed at Puebla in 1979 as a preferential option for the poor, a theology of liberation, and the ecclesial base communities as a new way of being church.

The base ecclesial communities were a very important area where we could feel and experience the *sensus fidelium* in action. Those small communities, gathered usually outside churches and parishes, formed by people at the grassroots, where the Bible could be discussed, and celebration could happen—they were the model of how the poor can find together a path for their liberation.

The Basic Ecclesial Communities (CEBs) spread all over the continent, especially in some countries such as Brazil. There happened to be around 80,000 in the 80s. The reason for their growth is that they offered a simpler and horizontal way of being church, based on the reading of the Bible, confronting the facts of precarious life, which led to transformative actions to benefit the poor. The creator of the method of the so-called Biblical Circles was the Carmelite Carlos Mesters, and those circles were the germ of what would be in the near future the CEBs. In a huge country like Brazil, with not enough clergy to attend the Catholic communities, those communities provided a hope and a way of cultivating faith and linking it with their everyday life. They were led specially by sisters and lay people (mostly women) and began to be several thousand all over the continent, organizing every two years a huge meeting where bishops and leaders prayed, reflected, and celebrated together.

Leonardo Boff, at this point a Franciscan friar, was the one who developed an ecclesiology that came out of those communities. That is the topic of his book *Eclesiogenesis: A New Way of Being Church*. He was one of the great lights of this movement, producing and practicing a theology arising from this option for the poor, called liberation theology, together with the then-diocesan priest Gustavo Gutiérrez.[26]

The communities were especially active in rural parts of Latin America where parish priests were not always available, as they placed a high value on *lay* participation. They suffered also the consequences of all that happened in 1989 with the fall of utopias and the consequences for Latin American theology. As of May 2007, it was estimated that the number of base communities has radically diminished, but in the poorest and more isolated parts of the continent, they are still very active.[27]

---

26. Gustavo Gutiérrez is now a Dominican. Leonardo Boff left the Franciscans and priesthood, despite his continuing to publish on theology and philosophy.

27. Declaration of Don Erwin Kreutler.

Considered a "new way of being church," an alternative to traditional parish life, those communities were and are formed by poor people and by pastoral agents who identified themselves with them and wanted to share their life. This fact shows that liberation theology, despite the endorsement by Gutiérrez, Boff, and others, strove to be a bottom-up movement in practice, with biblical interpretation and liturgical practice designed by lay practitioners themselves, rather than by the orthodox church hierarchy. Many initiatives born of the creativeness of the CEBs were afterwards assumed by the authorities of the church, especially about liturgy, interpretation of the Bible, and even a new way of doing theology.

This work is the *sensus fidelium* in truth and in action. The biblical circles and the embryos of the basic communities confronted the facts on the ground with the Word of God to extract a way of acting that was capable of transforming an unjust reality. And they offered a powerful contribution to deep and beautiful transformations that happened in the church of the continent.

The Biblical Circles: Reading the Bible and Listening to the People

Before Vatican II, Catholics didn´t have much access to the Bible. They received the Scripture through the filter of the magisterium. The openness of the council and the convocation to go back to the sources represented the devolution of the Scripture to the hands of the people.

In Latin America, in particular, where the pre-conciliar pastoral focus was mostly on sacraments, the new emphasis on giving the Bible into the hands of the faithful was a true revolution. The desire to know the Bible inspired many people to more frequently read the scriptural text and to develop a freer interpretation of it. The new translations and the work of the exegetes fostered much of that. Moreover, the growing missionary movement of evangelical churches challenged Catholics to learn more deeply the biblical text.

There have been very many initiatives to promote the reading of the Bible in the church on the continent, with the result that the groups who did it multiplied by hundreds and thousands.

Carlos Mesters was responsible for creating a method to read the Bible in small and poor communities called Biblical Circles. This method has three steps, which is very much in accordance with the *sensus fidelium*, common to each and every community: 1) to see the facts of life; 2) to be enlightened by the Word of God; and 3) to motivate the people and the community to serve and transform reality.[28]

This method is characterized by three criteria. First, the poor bring to the reading of the Bible the problems of their lives. From this perspective, they read the Bible. The reading, then, takes place in community. It is first a communitarian reading, a prayerful practice, an act of faith; it is an obedient reading, listening to God, ready to change and transform life if God wants it so. Therefore, to know the Bible brings more vitality into community; to coexist in community brings about service to the people; to serve the people brings about the wish for a deeper knowledge of the Bible, its origins, etc. A continuous dynamic brought the poor who had this contact with the Word of God to transform not only reality, but also the Church. It inspired, moreover, many theologians who were close to them and listened to their desires and claims.

Biblical Circles and the popular reading of the Bible were the embryos of the base communities. The base communities multiplied everywhere Biblical Circles, together with reflection groups, Gospel groups, family groups, and others, took hold. The communities were gathered around the Bible. During the 70s, these communities were more stable and showed a new face of the church. They decided to promote themselves nationally and internationally. The Intereclesial Encounters of the CEBs started to happen periodically. The communitarian dimension lived by the CEBs starting from the Bible even renewed many parishes that started to organize themselves as a "community of communities."[29]

Especially after 1968, with the results of the Medellín Conference, there was an important step made as a result of this scriptural reading by the poor gathered in communities. The growing knowledge of the Bible and renewed communal impulse provided an incentive to discern more actively the pastoral goal of serving the people and transforming reality. The people of Biblical Circles and of the CEBs had neither the money nor the time to read books about the Bible. Therefore, they started to read the Bible based on the only criterion they had, which is to say, their faith life, lived in community, and their painful life under oppression. Reading the Bible in this way, they discovered what they didn´t know: the history of the people of God, very similar to their history, of oppression and struggle for the same values they desire and sought—land, justice, sharing, fraternity. In short, they came to know the meaning of a human life. The fruit of that discovery

28. See Carlos Mesters, *Círculos Bíblicos* (Petrópolis: Vozes, 1973); *Por trás das palavras* (Petrópolis: Vozes, 1980).

29. See *Comunidade de comunidades: uma nova paróquia* (Community of communities: a new parish) (Brasília: Edições CNBB, Coleção Estudos, 2013).

and the liberating practice that resulted from it was reflected and elaborated by liberation theology and influenced the whole church. It is during this period that faith began to be thought of as inseparable from its political dimension.

In raising churches' consciousness of themselves and their mission there emerged an enlightening evolution: one of struggling for the defense of the life of a people threatened by poverty and oppression. During the 70s the CEBI (Centro de Estudos Bíblicos—Center for Biblical Studies) was established, which promoted a Popular Pastoral approach that has as its goal to articulate, to explain, to deepen, to publicize, and to legitimate the reading of the Bible, which people were already doing in their communities.

Inspired by those poor who dealt with the Scripture and felt at home with it, the whole church was transformed and turned attention to the poor, committed to take part in their liberation process. The spiritual life generated by this commitment was ardent and impressive.[30] In addition, many wanted to share, at least in some measure, the effects of injustice and oppression with the poor and make deep and radical changes in their own lives in order to do so.[31]

Among those engaged in this work, women were among the most important. After the great event of the Second Vatican Council, female voices began to be heard more and more, occupying spaces inside the church and doing so effectively. Women coordinated communities at different levels, questioned the denial of women's access to priestly ministry, produced theoretical reflections about religious experience and the doctrinal contents of Christian faith. The fact is that today it is not possible to do theology or pastoral work, or to lead church life in our continent, without taking into account the contribution of women.

Women Listening to Women and Producing Theology

Vatican II opened a door to the participation of women in the church. The relegation of women to second-class status is virtually everywhere and direct violence against women is a very common phenomenon globally.

---

30. Cf. documento de Conclusões da Conferencia do episcopado latino-americano em Puebla de los Angeles, Mexico, em 1979, http://www.celam.org/conferencia_puebla.php.

31. Pedro Arrupe, Discours d'ouverture à la Congrégation des Procureurs, in J. Y. Calvez, *Foi et justice. Dimension sociale de l'évangélisation* (Paris: coll Christus, DDB-Bellarmin, 1985) 56.

Positively, the twentieth century did see impressive momentum toward the recognition of women's rights as human rights, progress in women's education, and greater employment opportunities for women in virtually all sectors of society. Within the church, women began to come out of an invisibility that had lasted for many centuries and began to participate in the church in a more concrete way. On the other side, such reforms met fierce resistance, and are too rarely implemented at the practical level, even when guaranteed by law.[32]

During the 70s, Latin American women started to explore theology within Latin American churches, interdependently with the poor and motivated by the option for the poor. Their vision and their attentiveness turned towards their sisters in the North, who were opening up discussions about the possibility of thinking and speaking "beyond God the Father," and about the patriarchal approach dominant in theology.[33] They saw, as a strong and beautiful challenge, the possibility to jump-start a theology in which they participated as producers and not only consumers. Nevertheless, Latin American theology done by women is not completely similar to feminist theology done in the northern hemisphere. It is inseparable from the option for the poor, since that is constitutive of its configuration.[34]

The women who, in those years, entered theology courses, and went on the adventure of the elaboration of their own thinking about the mystery of God and His/Her revelation, were not only motivated by their personal desire, although it is clear that at the roots of the act of doing theology there is always a desire. For those pioneers, a desire bigger than themselves allowed them to dare the impossible: to venture into a world that had been dominated by men and, almost entirely, by celibate clergy. This was a world where the thinking and presence of women only had an indirect entry. This was the world where the "crazy" ones of that first moment started to articulate their reflections and dared to take their first theological steps.[35]

However, there was also the challenge of reality. Women who intended to do theology in this initial moment had their eyes turned to the reality of

---

32. See Lisa Cahill, "Journeys of Liberation: Catholic Theological Ethics Beyond Vatican II," conference address to be delivered at the International Symposium for the 50 years of Vatican II and Concilium Journal, Rio de Janeiro, May 26–28, 2015.

33. Cf. M. Daly, *Beyond God the Father: Toward a Philosophy of Women's Liberation* (New York: Beacon, 1973).

34. Cf. S. Suaiden, Questões contemporâneas para a teologia—Provocações sob a ótica de gênero, in SOTER (org.), *Genero e Teologia. Interpelações e perspectivas* (SOTER/Paulinas/Loyola, SP 2003) 147.

35. "Crazy" means *locas*. I allude here clearly to the Mothers of the Plaza de Mayo, in Argentina, called "las locas," by the dictatorship they challenged.

the poor and perceived that theology should be done in close dialogue with social sciences. They also perceived a phenomenon that later on was called "the feminization of poverty."[36] A poor person, who is also a woman, is doubly poor, since her female condition adds to her poor and marginalized condition, making it more complex and more difficult. It was then that a new solidarity emerged in Latin America, one that linked women theologians with poor women who worked at the grassroots in community. The former understood themselves as spokespersons for the latter, and responsible for recovering their rights. The encounters of female theologians and pastoral ministers, in a fertile and revealing progression, demonstrated a collective face of passion and a commitment to struggle for justice, inseparable from the building of the Kingdom of God.[37]

The encounters, colloquia, and congresses among women theologians were repeated at national, continental, and intercontinental levels. The movement realized by them started to receive attention, to raise curiosity and reactions, both favorable and unfavorable. They were at some times full of joy and hope, at other times full of aggression, irony, or sarcasm, and rejecting the uncomfortable novelty. Ecumenical since their beginning, those encounters helped Latin American female theologians to live out—beyond the covenant with the grassroots women—a fertile interaction among Catholics and Protestants, which brought a mutual enrichment and built a solid basis for the future.

Women theologians' struggle in Latin America acquired a new status different from desire or dream. It started to be a concrete reality. Besides their presence in the pastoral grassroots, women developed an open space

36. The introduction of this concept is given by the American Diane Pearce, http://socialworkers.org/feminizationofpoverty/presentations/pearce/Pearce_The%20Feminization%20of%20Poverty_1978%20original%20article.pdf. For her, the feminization of poverty is a process that develops from the moment women with children do not have a husband or partner living in the same household and taking responsibility for the maintenance of the family. In this perspective, the feminization of poverty is when women, home alone, have to take care of their children and provide for their wellbeing.

37. The topics of the meetings, which took place at the national level and Latin American level, attest to this agglutination and organization done by the female pastoral theological community as an active subject in the ecclesial community. The topics include these: "Mujer: la que aprendió a desconocer su lugar ("Woman: the one who learned to ignore her place" (1984), "La mujer en búsqueda de su identidad (Women: in search of her identity") (1985), "Y la mujer rompió el silencio ("The woman broke the silence") (1986), "Haciendo teología en femenino plural" ("Doing theology in the feminine plural") (1987). The leaders were followed by others who maintained the key points of these first steps: the occupation of a different place not assigned to a woman before; the encounter of a new identity given by the other; the breaking of the silence and the access to visibility and audibility in ecclesial space; and the configuration of a theological community in solidarity and plurality.

within faculties and institutes of theology, in a long and laborious effort to obtain academic degrees, which would allow them to gain equal voice vis-à-vis their male companions. This represented a long journey, a search for recognition, presence, and visibility in spaces that had been predominantly male. It was an attempt to attain citizenship and legitimacy through a different and alternative way of doing theology, a way where head, heart, and body are united in a fertile and harmonic dance whose product is a different reflection about faith.

Listening to and observing what happened in the popular layers of the local church, women not only entered the world of theology, but also pastoral work and ministries at the grassroots level of the church. In the 80s, when the fruits of Vatican II began to mature, and the church in Latin America assimilated more in-depth the conferences of Medellín and Puebla and women dared to challenge an ecclesial situation that didn't allow them to have a more visible and effective presence with the people of God. Many of them, both lay and religious women, started to take over ministries in the communities. From the coordination of communities to liturgical celebrations, women led their communities. As they lived out a church model in which power is freely shared and decisions are taken more collectively, they rendered countless services.

The occupation of such an open space began to outline a new paradigm for the church, one that was highly positive and welcomed by the people. In the 90s, these routes were deepened, following new and difficult paths through which Christian woman could find her place in the ecclesial space. The services women rendered testify to the leap that has taken place in their ecclesial consciousness and in the renewal that is being processed in her and from her, as the strength of the Spirit moves her to serve.

The Brazilian Conference of Bishops recognized explicitly the role of women in their participation in and contribution to the preparation of the document for the CELAM conference held at Aparecida.[38] The same document of Aparecida mentions the importance of women in different ecclesial services, stating, for the first time, that they should be actively participating in levels of decision-making in the church.[39]

---

38. Consider the claim "the Church makes the Eucharist and the Eucharist makes the Church." In light of the fact that 80 percent of Brazilian Catholics are prevented from celebrating the Eucharist on Sunday, we must conclude that 80 percent of Brazilian Catholics are deprived of the most important dimension of ecclesiology. It also suggests that the issue of the ordained ministries for lay people should be considered more seriously, together with the possibility of regaining the ministry by married priests.

39. See Documento de Aparecida, 458.

Intuitions of women, starting from the grassroots and coming up to the levels of decision-making, are changing the face of the Latin American Church. It is, again, the *sensus fidelium* that is taking place before our eyes.

Conclusion: Sensus Fidei and its Fruits Today

Today the Latin American Church is experiencing an unexpectedly good moment, thanks to Pope Francis's pontificate. Many signs show that the process that began humbly and discretely, with the deep intuitions and practices of those rescued being reflected upon by theologians and pastoral agents, is again alive and confirmed by the whole Church after a long period of Ecclesial Winter.[40]

The memory of great church leaders is being revived and honored; the sacrifice of bishops and priests killed under military dictatorships is being recognized and venerated; and some theologians once accused of unorthodoxy are being embraced and their achievements newly valued.[41] The first Latin American pope has given the church in his home continent full citizenship in the universal church.

A new day has dawned for the church in Latin America under Pope Francis. Moreover, this new and hopeful moment owes a lot to the experiences that *sensus fidelium* brought in to the Latin American Church between the years 1970 and 1980.

---

40. This is Rahner´s expression. In his last interview, in March 5, 1984, he speaks about a winter in the Church (in *Il Regno* 29 [1984] 286–94).

41. See the article of Gerard O´Connell, http://americamagazine.org/issue/latin-american-revival: "While this attitude first emerged in the last years of Paul VI's pontificate, it flourished under St. John Paul II and, to an extent, also under Benedict XVI. This caused much suffering not only to theologians like Gustavo Gutiérrez (in Peru), the Boff brothers (in Brazil), and others, but also to courageous pastors like Paulo Evaristo Arns, Ivo Lorscheiter and Hélder Câmara (Brazil), Juan Landázuri Ricketts (Peru), Talta Proaño (Ecuador), Óscar Romero (El Salvador), Samuel Ruiz Garcia (Mexico), and many more."

24

Theology as Conversation

Sensus Fidelium and Doing Theology on/from the Margins

Gemma Tulud Cruz

Introduction

The faith of the Christian is always a received ecclesial faith. *Sensus fidelium*, which literally means sense of the faithful, could be described as "collective faith consciousness" of all the faithful that leads to a consensus of faith. Daniel Finucane defines it as the objective or theological expression of what is believed.[1] Vatican II acknowledged this long-held tradition within the church, that is, that the faith is received and transmitted not solely through the teaching magisterium but fundamentally through all the faithful. The oft-quoted line from *Lumen Gentium* lends credence to this long-held tradition: "The body of the faithful as a whole, anointed as they are by the Holy One (cf. 1 John 2:20, 27), cannot err in matters of belief" (LG, 12).

There is a special triad of voices within this "collective faith consciousness," which make up the primary sources of the *sensus fidelium*. These are the *sensus laicorum* (sense of the faith coming from the laity), the *sensus theologorum* (sense of the faith of theologians), and the *sensus episcoporum* (sense of the faith of bishops).[2] By means of the *sensus fidelium*, the people of

---

1. Daniel Finucane, *Sensus Fidelium: The Use of a Concept in the Post-Vatican II Era* (San Francisco: International Scholars Publications, 1996), 227. See also Francis Sullivan, S.J., *Magisterium: Teaching Authority in the Catholic Church* (Mahwah, NJ: Paulist, 1983) 23.

2. Ormond Rush, *The Eyes of Faith: The Sense of the Faithful and the Church's Reception of Revelation* (Washington, DC: Catholic University of America Press, 2009) 251.

God intuitively sense what, in a multitude of ideas and doctrines presented to it, actually corresponds to the Gospel and can, therefore, be received.[3] Hence, a theology rooted in the *sensus fidelium* carefully investigates the various levels of reception that occur in the life of the people of God.

It is, in a sense, easy to assert that one's theology is vigorously challenged by the *sensus fidelium*. To claim, however, that one's theology is deeply informed by it is another matter. As we shall later see, cultural differences, diversity of languages, and all sorts of other contexts make the theological study and interpretation of the faith of real Christian people a very difficult task. What complicates the task further, argues Orlando Espín, "is precisely its being a 'sense' that relies on a 'bet' and a 'hope' . . . [that] is never discovered in some kind of pure state" and expresses and traditions itself in extremely varied ways."[4] To do theology, therefore, in dialogue with the *sensus fidelium* is about sensing intuitively what is of God and what is not of God, and this needs interpretation and discernment that necessarily involves trying "to ascertain the authenticity of the intuitions (i.e. their coherence and fundamental agreement with the other witnesses of revelation) and the appropriateness of the expression (i.e., their validity as vehicles for the traditioning of revelation)."[5]

Sensus fidelium is arguably not autonomous and self-sufficient. To function as it should depends upon pastors and, to a certain extent, theologians who authoritatively present the word of God as contained in Scripture and tradition. The fact, however, is that lay people, which includes many theologians, constitute the vast majority of individuals who are active and committed Christians. In what follows, I wish to examine how theologians are challenged and informed by the *sensus fidelium* in the global and local church, especially by the *sensus laicorum* from the margins. In particular, this essay explores three areas in which doing theology is affected by the *sensus fidelium*, namely vision, sources, and method. I argue that the vision, sources, and method in doing theology are rooted in ordinary people's lives, engaged in dialogue, and oriented towards justice and hope when they are challenged and informed by the *sensus fidelium*, especially by the *sensus laicorum* from the margins.

---

3. International Theological Commission, *Sensus Fidei in the Life of the Church*, 82. http://www.vatican.va/roman_curia/congregations/cfaith/cti_documents/rc_cti_20140610_sensus-fidei_en.html.

4. Orlando Espín, *Idol and Grace: On Traditioning and Subversive Hope* (Maryknoll, NY: Orbis, 2014) 23–24.

5. Ibid., 24.

Theology and *Sensus Fidelium* from the Margins

In the document *Sensus Fidei in the Life of the Church* the International Theological Commission (hereafter ITC) points out that theologians have a two-fold relationship to the *sensus fidelium*. On the one hand, theologians must place themselves in the school of *sensus fidelium* so as to discover there the profound resonances of the word of God that are animated by the Spirit and integrate these resonances in their research. On the other hand, theologians help the faithful to express the authentic *sensus fidelium* by reminding them of the essential lines of faith, and helping them to avoid deviations and confusion caused by the influence of imaginative elements from elsewhere.[6] Rush points to a few elements that engage the productive imagination of the theologian as far as *sensus fidelium* is concerned. These include the *sensus laicorum* of a theologian's community, which is an important starting point of inquiry; the particular chosen theological method; and the use of foundational texts and practices emerging from the tradition process of the church's life through history such as Scripture, creeds, magisterial definitions, theological, liturgical, and spiritual classics. In this section I condense and discuss these elements into three organizing principles—namely sources, method, and vision—on the basis of the argument that theologies challenged and informed by *sensus fidelium*, particularly the *sensus laicorum* from the margins, cannot but engage in a multilevel dialogue with the faith of the people in its various contexts in view of building and sustaining hope and justice.

Sources: Theology from the Heart of the People

John Henry Newman explains that the tradition of the apostles was committed to the entire church *per modum unius* but in different times and places. Newman contends, therefore, that the channels of tradition are many and diverse. These channels of tradition could sometimes be through the mouth of the episcopacy, sometimes by the doctors, sometimes by the people, sometimes by liturgies, rites, ceremonies, and customs, by events, disputes, movements, and all those other phenomena that fall under the name of history.[7] Theologians believe that "ordinary believers, when they articulate their faith, do have a real teaching authority, which comes from

---

6. *Sensus Fidei in the Life of the Church*, 81.

7. See John Henry Newman, *On Consulting the Faithful in Matters of Doctrine* (1859; reprinted, New York: Sheed & Ward, 1961).

their dignity as recipients of God's prime revelation."[8] Ordinary believers' secular context and, in particular, their application of the Gospel to daily life in new and secular contexts and cultures constitute an important contribution to the traditioning of revelation in general and the teaching office of their sense of the faith as lay people, in particular.

The reality, however, is that what is written in Church documents or preached in the pulpit do not necessarily speak to or connect with those who sit on the pews, particularly ordinary believers. Karl Rahner, for instance, points to a gap or discrepancy between what the church officially teaches and what the people actually believe. In view of this Rahner posits that the actual faith of the People of God is a crucial part of the work or theologumena of theologians.[9] As *Lumen Gentium* 37 states: "In accordance with the knowledge, competence or authority that they possess, [the laity] have the right and indeed sometimes the duty to make known their opinion on matters which concern the good of the church." Rush eloquently summarizes the ways in which the *sensus laicorum* could challenge and inform theology:

> In their witness to the world, lay people, therefore have a special sense of how to bridge "story" and "significance." Through the exercise of their particular charisms, they are able to see things with the eyes of faith that others, not given that charism, cannot see. Within the daily challenges of family life, work, and civic life, they attempt to sense what signs of the times are in harmony with the Gospel, and those which impede it. In the light of those signs of the times they can intuitively and prophetically raise the consciousness of the church to address new questions in order that the church might be a more effective sacrament of salvation in the world.[10]

When I went to the Netherlands to do my doctoral studies, I went with all the passion and idealism of a young budding theologian and put forward an ambitious topic, only to be brought down to earth by my supervisor who asked me to think if I really want to write about the topic or whether I could narrow it down. Fortunately, shortly after I arrived in Nijmegen and long before the proposal defense, I got invited to a conference in Thailand and

---

8. Herbert Vorgrimler, "From *Sensus Fidei* to *Consensus Fidelium*," *Concilium* 180.4 (1985) 8.

9. Karl Rahner, "What the Church Officially Teaches and What the People Actually Believe," in *Theological Investigations*, vol. 22 (London: Darton, Longman & Todd, 1991) 165, 171.

10. Rush, *The Eyes of Faith*, 260.

took the opportunity to go home to the Philippines for a visit. I took the taxi from the airport. The taxi driver and I got talking during the ride and, at some point in the conversation, he shared how overseas migration has broken his marriage and family and how, despite all that had happened, he is planning to work overseas, too. The introduction of my dissertation actually begins with this story of encounter, with this taxi driver, as that conversation planted the seed for my research interest in migration.

Looking back on this experience and on my various encounters with other migrants from around the world, it is my belief that a theology challenged and informed by *sensus fidelium*, especially one that is done with *sensus laicorum* from the margins, involves engaging the faithful themselves. As Rush notes: "Listening to the varied *sensus laicorum* within a local community is an essential task for a theologian. This fundamental source, capturing contemporary experiences of salvation, constitutes the lens through which the theologian, in a hermeneutical circle of inquiry, can interpret Scripture and the tradition's interpretation of God's salvific work through Jesus Christ."[11] Cardinal Antonio Tagle further illustrates the point I am making here in a speech at Catholic Theological Union when he said he has "seen many worlds," from dehumanizing poverty, the havoc left by corruption and injustice, trafficking of women and children as slaves, and the horrible typhoons in the Philippines and Asia. "As I enter these worlds," Cardinal Tagle opined, "theology happens, theology beckons."[12] Paying attention, indeed, leads to noticing; noticing leads to recognition; recognition leads to disclosure.

Doing theology that is informed by encounters with people is a recognition of the fact that theological ideas have real roots and consequences in the lives of ordinary, even illiterate Christians.[13] This fact has implications for our theological sources and how we engage our sources. This does not simply mean doing interviews and all forms of research that directly engage people but, more importantly, not forgetting that the texts we work with in our theologizing, whether it is the Bible, the classics, or the work of our contemporaries, are not abstract materials but the work of real faithful people or communities in conversation with the faith of a particular people/community in a particular time and place. This means that the major philosophic development of our time, that is, the shift from epistemology

11. Ibid., 265.

12. Grace Garcia, "Cardinal Tagle gets Chicago Theological Union doctorate," http://globalnation.inquirer.net/123591/cardinal-tagle-gets-chicago-theological-union-honorary-doctorate.

13. Roger Bergman, *Catholic Social Learning: Educating the Faith That Does Justice* (New York: Fordham University Press, 2011) 61.

to hermeneutics and from the idea to language must be taken into account if the *sensus fidelium* is to serve as an effective principle for relating the catholicity of faith to its inculturated forms.[14] For those who do theology from the margins, where theology or power may be expressed orally or in creative, unconventional ways, it also means using the arts and digging deep into popular piety as possible theological sources.

Rahner, for example, believes that theology should be considered mystagogical, that is, theology cannot exist merely in the abstract but must be experienced concretely in one's life. In this sense, theology shares with art a concern for living out human transcendence in concrete reality as art forms can teach us to "hear" truths of human experience that point us ultimately to a holy mystery.[15] As Rahner writes near the end of his life, "true art always embodies a very definite, particular and historical instance of human transcendence."[16] Thus if, as Rahner claims, an experience of art can also be an experience of transcendence, we must explore how it is possible for human activities, such as the arts, to open us to an encounter with grace. Creativity is not simply permissible for the church, it is an irreducible facet of the Spirit's operation in the church.

Popular religiosity, in the meantime, refers to the great variety of manifestations of Christian belief found among the people of God in the church. Latin American bishops describe it as "the Catholic wisdom of the people" as it "creatively combines the divine and the human, Christ and Mary, spirit and body, communion and institution, person and community, faith and homeland, intelligence and emotion" and is also for the people "a principle of discernment and an evangelical instinct through which they spontaneously sense when the Gospel is served in the Church and when it is emptied of its content and stifled by other interests."[17] Pope Francis echoes the significance of popular piety in *Evangelii Gaudium* by noting how it is the "manifestation of a theological life nourished by the working of the Holy Spirit" (EG, 125) and that it is an important part of the process by which "a

14. Paul Crowley, "Catholicity, Inculturation and Newman's *Sensus Fidelium*," *Heythrop Journal* 33 (1992) 168.

15. Gesa Elsbeth Thiessen, "Karl Rahner: Toward a Theological Aesthetics," in *The Cambridge Companion to Karl Rahner*, eds. Declan Marmion and Mary E. Hines (New York: Cambridge University Press, 2005) 229, 230.

16. Karl Rahner, "Theology and the Arts," *Thought: A Journal of Philosophy* 57 (1982) 29.

17. CELAM, Third General Conference (Puebla 1979), Final Document, 448, as quoted in *Sensus Fidei in the Life of the Church*, 108. Espín, for example, makes a case for popular Catholicism as an expression of *sensus fidelium* on account of its strong cultural basis. See Orlando Espín, *The Faith of the People: Theological Reflections on Popular Catholicism* (Maryknoll, NY: Orbis, 1997).

people continuously evangelizes itself" (EG, 122). Francis insists that to underestimate this "active evangelising power . . . would be to fail to recognise the work of the Holy Spirit" (EG, 126).[18] *Sensus fidelium*, the ITC affirms, both gives rise to and recognizes the authenticity of the symbolic or mystical language often found in the liturgy and in popular religiosity. Hence, theologians need to critically examine not only new currents of thought and new movements in the Church but also expressions of popular piety. To do this the ITC recommends that "the theologian needs actually to participate in the life and liturgy of the local church, so as to be able to grasp in a deep way, not only with the head but also with the heart, the real context, historical and cultural, within which the Church and her members are striving to live their faith and bear witness to Christ in the world of today."[19]

Generally speaking, the sense of the faithful will be most reliable in matters that are close to the experience and behavior of the average Christian, such that the laity would have a lot to say about the order of worship or matters of personal and family morality. In fact, Rahner contends that "the actual faith of the people would have a 'normative' significance for the church's official faith and teaching" and that "this actual faith must certainly not be the whole of what is taught (but) it should serve as a starting point."[20]

Doing theology that is challenged and informed by *sensus fidelium* from the heart of the people also means making daily life or *lo cotidiano* as *locus theologicus*, for it is in the midst of the concrete realities of daily life that marginal(ized) people, individually and communally, experience revelation and encounter God. It is where sin is experienced as well as compassion and grace. Daily life is the context of all other contexts and hence the one existential space and ever-present moment in which God reveals God's self and humans respond in faith (or not).[21] It is in the ordinariness (not necessarily redundancy) of the everyday that the depths of salvific encounters with God are to be found.[22] Indeed, the present context, as it is expressed in the daily grind of life, in which the Christian community seeks

---

18. Rahner points to this creative and normative function of popular religion in the church alongside other normative sources of revelation in "What the Church Officially Teaches and What the People Actually Believe," 145, 147.

19. *Sensus Fidei in the Life of the Church*, 82.

20. Rahner, "What the Church Officially Teaches and What the People Actually Believe," 175.

21. Espín, *Idol and Grace*, 35–36.

22. Fortress Press' series "Compass: Christian Explorations of Daily Living" reflects this theological perspective. See, for example, Elizabeth Groppe, *Eating and Drinking* (Minneapolis: Fortress, 2010); and Darby Kathleen Ray, *Working* (Minneapolis: Fortress, 2011).

to appropriate, practice, and develop the Christian tradition is an important ingredient in the work of the theologian insofar as the true nature of Christians' response to church teaching is interwoven in their daily lives as part of a community of believers.

Christians are people born into a community, that is, the family, and brought into a community, that is, the church, by a God of community, that is, the Trinity. It makes sense, therefore, that theology is done in and with a community as a source for doing theology. In practical forms community involves relationships—connecting with others, learning from others, sharing with others, rejoicing with others, and struggling with others. We need the church to be a hermeneutical community that seeks to understand God's word to it in its particular contexts. This corporate nature of the church as a community of interpretation extends not only to the church in every culture but also to the church in all ages.[23] Through community hermeneutics, we seek a growing understanding, if not agreement, on key theological issues that can help us test our theologies and our practices.

Method: Theology as Dialogue

All human reality is historical and cultural. All experience, therefore, is interpretative experience. We are always coming from somewhere else, whether it be from the past or in the present. How we see things depends on where we have been and where we are now standing, with its own unique perspective. Both our framework of interpretation and perspective are, at the same time, enabling and limiting. Hence, as Giorgio Agamben contends, there is no method or logic valid for every context.[24]

When I began writing my dissertation a Dutch professor asked me what I was writing on. When I said "migration," he replied with raised eyebrows, "migration? In Theology? Isn't that under the social sciences?" His reply was one of the reasons that set me on a path of dialogue with other disciplines as a part of my theological method.

Within the works of Rahner[25] and the Vatican II Fathers, one can see the idea that a theology challenged and informed by *sensus fidelium*

23. Paul Hiebert, "The Gospel in Human Contexts: Changing Perceptions of Contextualization," in *Missionshift: Global Mission Issues in the Third Millennium* (Nashville: B & H, 2010) 96.

24. Giorgio Agamben, *The Signature of All Things: On Method* (New York: Zone Books, 2009), 7.

25. Rahner sees *sensus fidelium* in terms of communal consensus-building and stresses the need for engaging in both dialogue and experiment within the pilgrim Church of God precisely because as far as Rahner is concerned, the communal process

involves dialogue with history, cultures, and contexts. One way to do this is by engaging in dialogue with disciplines outside of and within theology itself. Theology encompasses a broad range of interrelated disciplines, but theologians sometimes fall into the trap of exclusively working within the confines and comfort of their areas of specialisation when the divisions of the various areas are not always precise. Moral theology, for example, needs both the breadth of systematic theology and the sensitivity of the pastoral or practical theologian. Moreover, systematic theology, as constructive theology, often examines a given issue in terms of its biblical foundations, historical development, expression in the teaching of the magisterium, and in the views of contemporary theologians. Hence, John Paul II encourages theologians in *Fides et Ratio* "to be sure to reflect in their work all the speculative and practical breadth of the science of theology."[26]

Moreover, it is good for theology to engage other academic disciplines. Rush notes that the theologian not only engages with works from the past but also searches for resonances of the Gospel in relevant background theories from related non-theological disciplines such as philosophy, psychology, cosmology, sociology, culture studies, gender studies, literary studies, and the natural sciences, based on his or her own experience of the Christian Gospel, which enables him or her to synthesize that Gospel in the fresh categories of the background theories that s/he selects.[27] While a theological statement cannot necessarily be "proved" according to the methods of the physical or social sciences, good theology should be, at least, consistent with what is known from other sources of knowledge. In talking about some of the more urgent duties of Christians with regard to culture, for example, *Gaudium et Spes*, 62 points out that while harmonizing culture with Christian thought can be difficult, far from harming the faith, the difficulties "stimulate a more precise and deeper understanding of that faith." The text also notes that research and discoveries in various disciplines "bring up new problems which have an important bearing on life itself and demand new scrutiny by theologians." In pastoral care, for example, theologians are asked to make use not only of theological principles but also of the findings of secular sciences, especially psychology and sociology, to assist others to come to a more mature faith life. Another example is the use of deconstructive readings of the Bible and Christian doctrine, which reflect the influence that literary theory, linguistic philosophy, and hermeneutics have exerted

---

of deciding the truth can never be achieved in theory but only in praxis. Rahner, "What the Church Officially Teaches and What the People Actually Believe," 140–47.

26. John Paul II, *Fides et Ratio*, no. 105, http://w2.vatican.va/content/john-paul-ii/en/encyclicals/documents/hf_jp-ii_enc_14091998_fides-et-ratio.html.

27. Rush, *The Eyes of Faith*, 263.

on theology over the last decades. All of these call for collaboration with experts in many fields.[28]

The Christian tradition is a living faith that is rooted in history. Ever interpreted and understood anew, it extends into mystery. Theology, therefore, needs to be done squarely in the midst of inescapable human contexts and time's transience. Indeed, while it must safeguard God's self-revelation in Jesus, theology must, at the same time, help ensure that the language used by the church to proclaim such revelation remains intelligible in different cultures and new historical contexts. As indicated in *Mysterium Ecclesiae,* every expression of revelation is historically conditioned and, consequently, limited.[29] This is echoed in *Gaudium et Spes,* which reminds us that the Christian message must be expressed today, as it was in the past, "in the concepts and languages of different peoples" and "to clarify [that message] in the light of the wisdom of their philosophers" (GS, 44).

One of the tasks of a theologian, therefore, is to help make the church's language and proclamation up-to-date by making them intelligible in new historical contexts and re-examining the Church's tradition to enable it to shed its light on new questions. These days, however, at least based on my experience, navigating contemporary language alone could be tricky. Take, for example, the list of 6,500 new words that Collins Dictionary has added to the word game Scrabble. The list, which Collins Dictionary said, "was influenced by all parts of life including social media, slang, technology and food, plus English from around the world" would probably render many theologians puzzled at best and clueless at worst. There's cakehole (synonym for mouth), sexting (the act of sending sexually explicit messages, primarily between mobile phones), twerking (as in Miley Cyrus's sexually provocative dance), bezzy (for best friends), emoji (for expressive digital icons), ridic (short for ridiculous), and lolz. I thought I was already "cool" for knowing what lol stands for. So I thought to myself what does lolz mean? Laugh out loud what? Apparently lolz is not just laughing out loud, it means laughing out loud like a maniac, something like the plural of lol.[30] As a theologian

28. Mary Ann Donovan, "The Vocation of the Theologian," *Theological Studies* 65 (2004) 11.

29. *Mysterium Ecclesiae* noted four ways in which expressions of revelation can be limited: by the expressive power of the language of the times, by the limited knowledge of the times, by the specific concerns that motivated the definition or statement, and by the changeable conceptualities (or thought categories) of the time. Sacred Congregation for the Doctrine of the Faith, *Mysterium Ecclesiae,* 5, http://www.vatican.va/roman_curia/congregations/cfaith/documents/rc_con_cfaith_doc_19730705_mysterium-ecclesiae_en.html.

30. Faith Karimi, "Scrabble dictionary adds ridic list of new words," http://edition.cnn.com/2015/05/22/us/scrabble-new-words/.

who does some work on the idea of laughter and dance as everyday forms of resistance, I wonder how contemporary language such as lolz and twerking could figure in my work or in theology in general. Pushing the envelope further, How might theologians, for example, make sense of sexting and twerking in a contemporary theology of sex or sexuality? Imagine a book title with *Toward a Theology of Bezzy* instead of *Toward a Theology of Friendship*? Isn't that, as the new Collins dictionary puts it, "ridic"?

Nevertheless, theology should not underestimate nor ignore social media. It seems to me that it is a new frontier for a theology challenged and informed by the *sensus fidelium* because, in some ways, it has (1) "globalized" *lo cotidiano* and the quest for well-being, peace, and social justice by, and on behalf of, individuals and local communities worldwide; (2) transformed human relationships and; (3) become an important means and battleground for the expression, propagation, and transmission of the Christian faith. Transformational theology takes people seriously, in the particularity of their persons, societies, cultures, and their ever-changing histories. It integrates cognition, affectivity, and evaluation in its response to biblical truth, and it defines faith not simply as mental affirmations of truth or as positive experiences of God but as beliefs, feelings, and morals that lead to response and obedience to the Word of God. It rejects the division between pure and applied theology.[31]

The role of the Holy Spirit in *sensus fidelium* also means that *poiesis* (creating, making, or doing) is theology's primary mode of operating such that doing theology becomes an exercise of the creative Christian imagination. The text, context, and the Holy Spirit, therefore, form a kind of hermeneutical circle. We are able to hear what the Spirit is saying as we engage with our context in the light of our text and the illumination given to us as a community of believers.[32] Hence, whether it is done in the comfort of our homes or offices or in the midst of the forgotten people and places in our struggling communities, the idea of theology as a conversation among God's people across generations foregrounds the theological process.

Vision: Theology as a Hermeneutic of Hope

Doing theology is a hermeneutical exercise and, as an exercise in hermeneutics, it includes those that might fall under the contemporary theological

---

31. Hiebert, "The Gospel in Human Contexts," 101.

32. Melba Maggay, "Early Protestant Missionary Efforts in the Philippines," in *Asian Church and God's Mission*, eds., Wonsuk and Julie Ma (Manila: OMF Literature, 2003), 40.

rubric of "praxis," or what is said and done. To be sure, a theological statement that has no relevance to the life of Christian peoples, even if true, will not be an effective expression of the community's faith.

As a theologian born and raised in the global South, who has done some volunteer work and overseas travel beyond touristic places, I have seen various forms and degrees of suffering in different cultures and contexts. These have influenced me in the way I understand and do theology not only in terms of my research but also in my teaching. In 2014, for example, I brought 16 Australian postgraduate Theology students on a study-trip to the Philippines where stories of struggle and hope in a different context came to life for them. At the heart of this endeavour is a hope for my students to experience and learn theology from the heart of the people with a view to expanding Anselm's classic definition of theology from "faith seeking understanding" to "faith seeking empowering understanding."

Such experiences are a reminder that theology is also about *phronesis*, or practical wisdom, insofar as it is about discovering a sense of the collective faith knowledge applied in the concrete realities of everyday life, bridging theory and praxis, doctrine and life. In this phronetic vision of theology, the poor play a special role, for as Pope Francis says, "they have much to teach us. Not only do they share in the *sensus fidei* but in their difficulties they know the suffering Christ. We need to let ourselves be evangelized by them."[33] They and the countless Christians who "reveal Christ to others principally through the [injustice and] witness of their lives," along with the sinners and the saints or "those who are resplendent in faith, hope, and charity" (LG, 31) are valuable sources in doing theology in conversation with the *sensus fidelium*.

This is true, in particular, among the "disposable poor" because, as Espín writes, it is a duty of Christian traditioning to keep alive the memory of those—including Jesus himself—whom the dominant regard as disposable, and whose lives and faith are deemed as unimportant and forgettable. Faithfulness to history and tradition is also faithfulness to the meanings and hope constructed by their victims. For Espín, this subversive hope is the core and ground of revelation. Thus, expressing and traditioning the *sensus fidelium* "must somehow be congruent with Christianity's necessary proclamation and practice of compassion, justice, peace, liberation, and reconciliation as indispensable dimensions of a world according to God's will."[34] In this regard one could argue that liberation theology is an example

---

33. Pope Francis, *The Church of Mercy: A Vision for the Church* (Chicago: Loyola, 2014), 24.

34. Espín, *Idol and Grace*, 25.

of translating the theological value of the *sensus fidelium* into real social and historical terms. As Paul Crowley writes, it is

> a theological and a pastoral movement which arose within the churches, but which has been influenced by elements of the theological and pastoral tradition of the church in other locales, notably Europe . . . The theology of liberation rests upon an assertion of a church model that begins with the *sensus fidelium*, not with hierarchical structures. It challenges other theological streams within the church, including those expressed by the hierarchical magisterium, to listen to and become engaged with the legitimate mediations of the faith tradition that have taken place within the local church contexts.[35]

Indeed, since the traditioning of the *sensus fidelium* needs to facilitate the People of God's participation in the construction of a world according to God's compassionate will, it "demands an awareness of culture and of economic and political reality, as well as awareness of hidden (but certainly present) class and ethno-cultural biases and interests which may blind the People of God, and their ministers and theologians, to dimensions of revelation present in the faith-full sense of the People."[36] The theologian's aim in this case is to prophetically express the Christian community's hopes.[37] Therefore, a theology challenged and informed by *sensus fidelium*, particularly by the *sensus laicorum* from the margins, cannot but be a hermeneutic of hope.

In 1 Peter faith is presented as the reason for our hope. Consequently, "true theology," Gustavo Gutierrez contends, "must interpret the reasons for hope in whatever way possible" and this locus of hope "must have the capacity, freedom, and commitment to pay attention to the smallest of things."[38] Gutierrez writes,

> In a personal note, I do not like to speak only about the suffering of the poor because they have also experienced joy, and have projects and intentions. These may be nothing more than little hopes and short moments of joy. Perhaps these small things are too little for those who are not excluded, but no hope is too

---

35. Crowley, "Catholicity, Inculturation and Newman's *Sensus Fidelium*," 171.

36. Espín, *Idol and Grace*, 25.

37. Rush, *The Eyes of Faith*, 262.

38. Gustavo Gutierrez, "Poverty, Migration and the Option for the Poor," in *A Promised Land, A Perilous Journey: Theological Perspectives on Migration*, eds., Daniel Groody and Gioacchino Campese (Notre Dame: Notre Dame University Press, 2008) 84.

small to go unnoticed. Without hope there is no personhood and hope is present even if surrounded by suffering.[39]

One of the criteria for assessing the adequacy of a theological statement relates to efficacy, that is, its ability to speak to the concerns of contemporary people. Efficacy, in this regard, relates to how theology builds and nurtures hope among people and how that hope translates to Christian witness, particularly in view of social justice. This transformative dimension makes doing theology a vocation[40] because, as a member of the people of God gifted with a charism for teaching, the theologian is called to exercise that gift for the renewal and building up of the Church.[41] Ultimately, theology is about giving an account of that which and whom we hope for as a Christian community in a particular time and place.

As a hermeneutic of hope, theology that is challenged and informed by the *sensus fidelium* from the margins means that theologians are in touch with their own contexts, too. To be sure, theologians do not theologize in isolation nor complete ignorance of the contexts of the People of God, not simply because they are members of it but also because, as human beings, theologians are members of families and communities. They are part of struggling or flourishing relationships whether as a spouse, a parent, a child, a sibling, a co-worker, among others. Moreover, they deal or wrestle with the realities and challenges of daily life whether it is sleeping or eating, health or old age.

As a hermeneutic of hope, theology that is challenged and informed by the *sensus fidelium* from the margins also requires humility and prophetic critique in doing theology. It means, for example, recognizing the fact that our work is not necessarily relevant in socio-cultural and historical contexts outside our own. More importantly, it means being cognizant of the constructs, biases, and, consequently, incompleteness and possible deficiencies in our theologies. As such the "contents of tradition" are not and cannot be simply reduced to propositional doctrinal statements. Espín argues,

> The contents that are traditioned by Christians have been and still are molded and affected by human histories and human cultures, by power asymmetries and conflict, by ethnic bigotries

---

39. Gutierrez, "Poverty, Migration and the Option for the Poor," 84.

40. The Congregation for the Doctrine of the Faith itself understands the work of the theologian as a vocation in service to the Word within the Church. Congregation for the Doctrine of the Faith, "The Ecclesial Vocation of the Theologian," 6, http://www.vatican.va/roman_curia/congregations/cfaith/documents/rc_con_cfaith_doc_19900524_theologian_vocation_en.html.

41. Donovan, "The Vocation of the Theologian," 9; see also LG, 12.

and social prejudices, by racism and gender biases, as much as by courageous attempts at compassion and truthfulness, by dogged hope and self-giving, and by a faithfulness to revelation that is far greater than mere obedience or repetition of orthodoxies. All contents traditioned by Christians, in other words, are shaped by the same dynamics and processes that mold and impact all things human. It cannot be otherwise.[42]

The *sensus fidelium* clearly both shapes and reflects the historical faith of the Church. Theologies that are informed by it, particularly from the margins, best exert such influence on the faith of the church not only when they eloquently name the injustice done to the "crucified people"[43] in contemporary times but also the resilience and hope that can be found in these people's lives. To be sure, "crucified people" embody a luminescent faith, hope, and communal solidarity that have helped desperate communities to survive in the face of overwhelming odds.[44] The extent that theology is able to shed light on this double-edged experience is the extent to which it becomes an authentic and effective reflection on the Christian faith.

Conclusion

Theologies that are challenged and informed by the *sensus fidelium* drive home the point that theology is a vocation and that theologians need a creative, dialogical, and prophetic imagination. These theologies are a reminder to us, as theologians, that because we are human beings, sinners and saints, our theologies are, ultimately and inescapably, contextual, perspectival, historically- and culturally-bound, expressive of asymmetric power relations and, therefore, always provisional and incomplete. Our only hope is that our theology today would authoritatively speak to current and future generations who themselves would come to understand the tradition within the horizons of their own particular experience. This is what theology as a conversation is all about. In the words of Bonaventure, it is

---

42. Espín, *Idol and Grace*, 8–9.

43. Coined by Ignacio Ellacuria and further developed by Jon Sobrino, "crucified people" refers to that collective body that, as the majority of humanity, owes its situation of crucifixion to the way society is organized and maintained by a minority that exercises its dominion through a series of factors that, taken together and given their concrete impact within history, must be regarded as sin. See Ignacio Ellacuria, "The Crucified People," in *Mysterium Liberationis: Fundamental Concepts of Liberation Theology*, ed. Ignacio Ellacuria and Jon Sobrino (Maryknoll, NY: Orbis, 1993) 590.

44. Robert Lasalle-Klein, "A Postcolonial Christ," in *Thinking of Christ: Proclamation, Explanation, Meaning*, ed. Tatha Wiley (New York: Continuum, 2003) 135–36.

about recognizing the inadequacy of "reading without repentance, knowledge without devotion, research without the impulse of wonder, prudence without the ability to surrender to joy, action divorced from religion, learning sundered from love, intelligence without humility, study unsustained by divine grace, thought without the wisdom inspired by God."[45]

---

45. As quoted in John Paul II, *Fides et Ratio*, 105, http://w2.vatican.va/content/john-paul-ii/en/encyclicals/ documents/hf_jp-ii_enc_14091998_fides-et-ratio.html.

25

How Are Theologians Challenged and Informed by Their Engagement with the Sense of the Faithful in the Local/Global Church?

Anne Arabome, SSS

Nairobi is one of Africa's most vibrant cities and the capital city of the country that loaned the word "safari" to the English lexicon. For hundreds of thousands of tourists who flock to Kenya's popular game reserves, national parks, and exotic resorts the country is synonymous with happy animals on display in carefully managed habitats. As far as the eye of any visitor can see, high-rise office and residential apartment blocks sprout across Nairobi's downtown Central Business District like elephant grass while the riotous sounds of its chaotic traffic defy the logic of civilized commute. People who know and live in Nairobi are accustomed to navigating its contours by sight and by sound.

For visitors endowed with a keen sense of smell and who are not averse to a little bit of adventure, it is easy to detect another "Nairobi"—the Nairobi of the slums. A total of thirty-six slums ring the city like barricades of distressed human existence. I know one of them: it is called Kibera or Kibra. Home to an estimated one million slum dwellers, Kibera is a detritus of what Pope Francis calls "an economy of exclusion and inequality."[1] Such is the legendary notoriety of Kibera that it is actually listed as a tourist attraction, a must-see item on a bucket list of "to do" in eastern Africa. Safaris are conducted to this dingy edge of human existence, where poverty presides unchallenged over the lives of countless women, men, and children.

---

1. Pope Francis, *Evangelii Gaudium*, 53. https://w2.vatican.va/content/francesco/en/apost_exhortations/documents/papa-francesco_esortazione-ap_20131124_evangelii-gaudium.html.

What I find most remarkable about Kibera is the slum's singular capacity to assault all five human senses at once—the smell of putrid open sewers, the sight of naked hordes of children, the endless cacophony of energetic voices and activities, the acrid taste of dust mixed with charcoal, the unforgiving heat of the midday sun with hardly a tree shade for cover. This is Kibera, home to Josephine Opondo, Josephine Otieno, Fiona, Cynthia, Dinah, and Violet—six teenagers who I now consider my daughters.

Over the last couple of years, I have made a modest attempt to journey with these young women by offering a listening ear and a willing shoulder for them to lay down their cares and challenges. I strive to mentor them and instil in them a sense of confidence and hope in their potential to become women of conscience, compassion, and competence. They call me mother, obviously not in any biological sense, but as a woman who has freely chosen to birth in them positive alternatives to the closed existence imposed on them by the accident of their birth and life in Kibera. It is in this concrete sense that I concur with Leonardo Mercado's incisive observation that "the role of the theologian is to function as a midwife to the people as they give birth to a theology that is truly rooted in a culture and moment of history."[2]

These young women and thousands of others who are quarantined in Kibera by poverty do not possess the benefit of a supernatural theological insight or spiritual instinct capable of receiving or rejecting, contesting or querying, exalted magisterial teachings, as we usually like to define *sensus fidelium*. What they have are *senses* native to their context; *senses* that allow them to smell, taste, hear, feel, and see the action of the Spirit at work in their broken milieu. The truth of the faith that the magisterium proclaims and theologians discourse is filtered through these *senses*. Like most women of color that I have come to know and in whose lives I have become engaged, the experience to which their *senses* bear witness is one of pain and exclusion, manifested in multiple forms of injustice and abuse, including domestic rape, gender-based violence, female genital mutilation, limited access to education, and poor sanitation, maternal, and child health.

Through the lives of these women, I have made a fundamental discovery that *sensus fidelium* is not a concept to be understood in the singular. *Sensus* is not mere insight or instinct affirming or rejecting a truth minted in abstract and extraneous context; *sensus fidelium* represents a *plurality of senses* of the people of God by which they perceive and live the reality of their faith, vocation, and ministry. In the best tradition of the *Spiritual*

---

2. Stephen B. Bevans, *Models of Contextual Theology: Faith and Culture*, rev. and exp. ed. (Maryknoll, NY: Orbis, 2002) 18–19.

Exercises of St. Ignatius of Loyola, *sensus fidelium* calls for an application and discernment of the senses.[3]

For this reason, I consider inadequate the customary approach to the question of *sensus fidelium* from the perspective of a trichotomy that distinguishes and separates faithful, hierarchy, and theologians. In this hierarchical construct, relevance and influence either increases or decreases in function of the position of a particular group or category within this unequal relationship. Credit goes to the architects of Vatican II for attempting to dismantle this skewed relationship, first, simply by recovering for the church its original theological self-understanding as the people, the faithful, the communion, or the body of the Risen Christ, ahead of functional differentiations of roles and tasks, and, second, by insisting on the irreplaceable character of the faithful in their local context for an authentic understanding of the world church. Many are the theologians who have truly understood this dynamic dialect of the local and the global. Robert Schreiter conceptualized it as "glocality," Stephen Bevans rendered it as "contextuality," theologians of the global south celebrate it as inculturation, and liberation theologians prioritize it as praxis.

In my ongoing quest for theological authenticity and relevance I have discovered Kibera not as a place but as a metaphor for the intriguing reality called *sensus fidei* or *sensus fidelium*. However we choose to define or understand it, the sense of the faithful is filtered through the senses of the context or condition of people of God. Even Pope Francis has recently acknowledge the vital importance of the olfactory organs in the evangelizing mission of the church as the community of the people of God, for a true shepherd must "take on the 'smell of the sheep.'"[4]

Thus, drawing on my experience in Kibera, I now understand that to be challenged and informed by the *senses* of the faithful is to get "involved by word and deed in people's daily lives . . ." to embrace "human life, touching the suffering flesh of Christ in others . . . [S]tanding by people at every step of the way, no matter how difficult or lengthy this may prove to be."[5]

If we believe in the centrality of the principle of *sensus fidelium*, as a charism of the Spirit, we affirm also the communality of the faith and the shared responsibility we bear for witnessing to, celebrating, and elaborating this faith as gift and task. In this optic, the faithful, no matter how well-flattered, are not a category apart—fictionalized or reified matter for

---

3. International Theological Commission, "Sensus Fidei in the Life of the Church," 83.

4. *Evangelii Gaudium*, 24.

5. Ibid.

theological disquisition or hierarchical patronization. If we had more open forums of synodality, consultation, communication, and conversation, at various levels of church life and governance, from Rome to the slums of Kibera—where hierarchy, theologians, and laity can exercise their shared responsibility for the function of ecclesial magisterium as integral rather than episodic dimension of the church—we would be engaging practically with the senses of the faithful in our local church and in the world church.

Engaging the *sensus fidelium* is as much a mental shift as a spatial relocation. I confess that the theology in which I have been schooled in the academia over the last decade leaves little or no room for engaging the *sensus fidelium*, as a lived reality, that is, one that is not merely outsourced to or monopolized by a specialized group of academicians and ecclesiastics. To engage with the senses of the faithful is to effect a radical pairing of discourse with action, and to my knowledge few are the theologians within this sorority and fraternity that successfully achieve such conjugation of "word and deed," creating thereby a theology brewed in the gritty reality of human life. Few are the theologians who seek to be part of the solution, practically, thinking globally but acting locally one step at a time.

Consequently, as to the "how" of engaging the *sensus fidelium*, I propose as a methodological approach of listening-in-dialogue. Integral to this process is consultation, conversation, and respect for difference. In Africa we say that when you listen carefully you can hear a crab cough. If we engage with the senses of the people of God and allow ourselves and our theologizing to be immersed in their reality, we can hear more distinctly what the Spirit is saying to the church through their laments and narratives, and we can appreciate more profoundly their struggles against the multitude of evils that traumatize them. We become in this way, Elochukwu Uzukwu's "listening church," rather than patrons, patronesses, and purveyors of a distilled theology, too concentrated for local consumption, yet prized for its inebriating effect on its elite corps of members-only theologians. What I propose, then, is an art, not a technique.

As I have stated earlier on, Kibera is a metaphor, a medium for recognizing and engaging the senses of the faithful, or what the International Theological Commission aptly refers to as "the school of the *sensus fidelium*."[6] There are other metaphors and mediums. Listening and engaging the senses of the faithful happen when—like Kristin Heyer and Daniel Groody—we theologize at the frontiers and borders that separate kith and kin from the privileges of developed nations. Listening and engagement

---

6. International Theological Commission, "*Sensus Fidei* in the Life of the Church," 81–82.

happen when—like Bryan Massingale and Shawn Copeland—we deconstruct the foundations of centuries-old racial inequality and injustice. Listening and engagement happen when—like Elizabeth Johnson, Ada Maria Isasi-Diaz, Linda Hogan, Teresa Okure, Margaret Farley, Lisa Sowle-Cahill . . . to name but a few—we expose the ideological fanaticism that wreaks havoc on women and our bodies in church and society under the guise of practicing and preserving the traditions of the fathers. Listening and engagement happens when, following the lead of Brad Hinze, we practice a form of theological communication that is inclusive of all voices, no matter how different from or how strange they may sound to our cultural biases.

To listen to and engage the senses of the faithful is to strive to create and empower local networks capable of harnessing the wisdom of the local church in order to enrich the theological, doctrinal, and evangelical profile of the global ecclesial community. I mean by this cross-cultural networks, such as those initiated by Jim Keenan, David Hollenbach, Agbonkhianmeghe Orobator, Mercy Amba Oduyoye, Stan Chu Ilo and others, aiming to redefine how we do theology, giving voice to colleagues, and pressing for inclusivity at the table of mutuality.

Furthermore, listening and engagement of the senses of the faithful occur when theologians of the Catholic Theological Society of America, in solidarity with the oppressed, speak out against a macabre culture of targeted killing of unarmed black men in a country that prides itself as the most powerful nation on the globe.

I could continue this inventory of engagement with the senses of the faithful, but the point is clear: both in our local churches and in the world church, as theologians, we need a well-developed, complete, and attuned set of senses to discern the truth of the faith that theology seeks to understand—in and around us, in our locale, for the edification of the global community of the faithful. The truth that the church's hierarchy and official magisterium oftentimes grudgingly predicate of the people of God is not a thing possessed merely and exclusively of the intellect. It embodies a reality filtered through multiple senses.[7]

To conclude this brief presentation, in my relatively short lifespan as a theologian, three key issues have taken on greater significance, first, for an accurate understanding of the senses of the faithful, and second, for a deeper appreciation of the true sense of the local church.

Women. Women. Women. To speak out of my local African-Nigerian context, women are the church. It is that simple. Although centuries of doctrinal aberration and ecclesiastical abuse of power have actively conspired

---

7. Ibid., 39.

to undermine our dignity and limit our participation in the local church and world church, the resilience of African women in acts of charity and worship, ritual and celebration, service and compassion, validates the monumental claim of Pope Francis that women—as modelled in the person, faith, and ministry of Mary—are "more important than the bishops."[8] Nowhere would this declaration be truer than in the church in sub-Saharan Africa. On this issue I want to underline the position that *sensus fidelium* is not an instinct or a privatized intuition; it is not static reproduction of tradition; it is not conformity for the sake of unity; it is a communion in mutuality; a praxis of subsidiarity and inclusion. As women we constantly point up the disvalue of such lack of ecclesial inclusion locally and globally. In this context, and in this church that boldly and confidently honors the senses of the faith, Bishop Libby Lane would be an African Catholic woman; naming women to the International Theological Commission would be a routine not a token, and leadership would be exercised as a function of the combination of charism and competence, call and compassion, not a by-product of gender, race, status, power, or privilege.

Authority. Authority. Authority. A sacramentally and hierarchically stratified ecclesia commands the faithful to show subservience, loyalty, and obedience. This practice is the direct antithesis of the principle of *sensus fidelium*. We have historical and contemporary contested questions in theological ethics and institutional leadership that illustrate the virulence of this command and control exercise of authority in the church. Yet, if we are to engage the senses of the faithful authentically, such senses, intuition, or wisdom ought to be recognized, valued, and received as active expression of the evangelizing and teaching mission of the church as the people of God. In this light, over and above all else, to engage the *senses of the faithful* amounts to a rediscovery of the *imago Dei*—that inalienable and supernatural gift conferred on every baptized Christian and sustained by the creative Spirit of the risen Christ.[9] It is anything but a privilege selectively conferred by the authoritative teaching of the church. *Sensus fidelium* is an affirmation of the points of divergence and convergence around the multiple dimensions and expressions of the faith in the one communion of Christ.

Theologians. Theologians. Theologians. As theologians we are constantly tempted by the lure of academia. The very notion of *sensus fidelium* locates the source of our research and scholarship in the practiced wisdom of the community of the people of God. In line with what I have consistently

---

8. *Evangelii Gaudium*, 104.

9. See *Lumen Gentium*, 12. http://www.vatican.va/archive/hist_councils/ii_vatican_council/documents/vat-ii_const_19641121_lumen-gentium_en.html.

maintained, to do theology, therefore, requires that we see ourselves first as learners—women and men learning from those we seek to teach and recognizing their role as legitimate stewards of the word of God and custodians of the apostolic traditions.[10] To borrow the terms of Jean-Marie Roger Tillard, we are practitioners of communion in a manner that is symbiotic, mutually respectful, and compassionately in solidarity with those voices relegated to the margins of social, political, ecclesial, and economic insignificance. To learn is to recognize *sensus fidelium* as a theological source or *locus theologicus*.[11]

Back to the question. "How are theologians challenged and informed by their engagement with the sense of the faithful in the local and global church?" I can only speak for myself. Much of my research has engaged with issues concerning African women in both the diaspora as well as women with whom I am in contact in various African settings, in particular my six daughters in Kibera. Because I am an African-Nigerian woman, I acknowledge my own biases—first, as an African Black and, then, as a Black woman. I approach the issues through these lenses. My heart responds to the pain and struggles of women as expressed in their lives. I strive to listen to voices from the margins, orient myself toward the unappealing frontiers of the human condition, and prioritize deeds of justice, mercy, and compassion mandated by the Risen Christ—and these over and above desiccated notions of truth and tradition that are oftentimes the prized possession of a self-conceited ecclesiastical hierarchy. This theological option to listen to the senses of the faithful has convinced me that the binary proposition of reception and rejection of church teaching—that developed over a long period in theology—does not exhaust the deepest meaning of *sensus fidelium*.[12] I believe that what I have identified as the senses of the faithful constitutes a source of theological truth; the senses of the faithful represent a teaching authority, too, inspired by the Spirit of the Risen Christ, in our local churches and in the world church.[13]

In prayerful conclusion, dear colleagues, may the senses of the people of God *prophetically* speak to us, challenge us, inform us, teach us, and call us forth.

---

10. See *Dei Verbum*, 10. http://www.vatican.va/archive/hist_councils/ii_vatican_council/documents/vat-ii_const_19651118_dei-verbum_en.html.

11. Ibid., ¶81.

12. Ibid., ch. 2.

13. Ibid, ¶74.

Selected Bibliography

Albert the Great. *Commentarii in IV Sententiarum (Dist. I–XXII)*. Opera Omnia 29. Paris: Vives, 1894.

Astell, Ann W. *Eating Beauty: The Eucharist and the Spiritual Arts of the Middle Ages*. Ithaca, NY: Cornell University Press, 2006.

Baggett. Jerome P. "Becoming Absence-Minded: Sociological Reflections on the Sense of the Faithful." *Proceedings of the Catholic Theological Society of America* 70 (2015) 1–26.

———. *Sense of the Faithful: How American Catholics Live Their Faith*. New York: Oxford University Press, 2009.

Bergman, Roger. *Catholic Social Learning: Educating the Faith That Does Justice*. New York: Fordham University Press, 2011.

Burkhard, John J. "*Sensus fidei*: Meaning, Role and Future of a Teaching of Vatican II." *Louvain Studies*, vol. 17 (1992) 18–34.

———. "*Sensus Fidei*: Theological Reflections Since Vatican II: I. 1965–1984." *Heythrop Journal* 34 (1993) 41–59.

———. "*Sensus Fidei*: Theological Reflections Since Vatican II: II. 1985–1989." *Heythrop Journal* 34 (1993) 123–36.

———. "*Sensus Fidei*: Recent Theological Reflection (1990–2001), Part I." *Heythrop Journal* 46 (2005) 450–75.

———. "*Sensus Fidei*: Recent Theological Reflection (1990–2001), Part II." *Heythrop Journal* 47 (2006) 38–54

Bynum, Carolyn Walker. *Christian Materiality: An Essay on Religion in Late Medieval Europe*. New York: Zone Books, 2011.

Chia, Edmund Kee-Fook. *Edward Schillebeeckx and Interreligious Dialogue: Perspectives from Asian Theology*. Eugene, OR: Pickwick Publications, 2012.

Comstock, Gary L. "Two Types of Narrative Theology." *Journal of the American Academy of Religion* 55 (1987) 687.

Congar, Yves. *Lay People in the Church: A Study for a Theology of the Laity*. Translated by Donald Attwater. Westmister, MD: Newman, 1957.

Cooke, Bernard J. *The Distancing of God: The Ambiguity of Symbol in History and Theology*. Minneapolis: Fortress, 1990.

Cornille, Catherine. *Many Mansions? Multiple Religious Belonging and Christian Identity*. 2002. Reprinted, Eugene, OR: Wipf & Stock, 2010.

Crites, Stephen. "The Narrative Quality of Human Experience." *Journal of American Academy of Religion* 39 (1971) 291–311.
Davis, Cyprian and Jamie Phelps, eds., *'Stamped with the Image of God': African Americans as God's Image in Black*. American Catholic Identities. Maryknoll, NY: Orbis, 2003.
D'Cruz, Wedell. *A Warli-Christian Story: An Experiment in Story Theology*. Delhi: ISPCK, 1999.
Doyle, Dennis. *Communion Ecclesiology: Vision and Versions*. Maryknoll, NY: Orbis Books, 2000.
Duffy, Eamon. *The Stripping of the Altar: Traditional Religion in England, 1400–1580*. 2nd ed. New Haven: Yale University Press, 2005.
Dulles, Avery. "Authority in the Church." In *The Cambridge Companion to John Henry Newman*, edited by Ian Ker and Terrence Merrigan, 170–88. Cambridge Companions to Religion. New York: Cambridge University Press, 2009.
———. "Sensus Fidelium." *America* 115 (Nov. 1, 1986) 240–42.
Espín, Orlando. *Idol and Grace: On Traditioning and Subversive Hope*. Maryknoll, NY: Orbis, 2014.
———. *The Faith of the People: Theological Reflections on Popular Catholicism*. Maryknoll, NY: Orbis, 1997.
Finucane, Daniel. *Sensus Fidelium: The Use of a Concept in the Post-Vatican II Era*. San Francisco: International Scholars Publications, 1996.
Francis, Pope. *Evangelii Gaudium*. http://w2.vatican.va/content/francesco/en/apost_exhortations/ documents/papa-francesco_esortazione-ap_20131124_evangelii-gaudium.html #The_joy_of_the_gospel.
———. *Laudato Si': On Care for Our Common Home*. Vatican City: Libreria Editrice Vaticana, 2015.
Gaillardetz, Richard. "The Reception of Doctrine: New Perspectives." In *Authority in the Roman Catholic Church*, edited by Bernard Hoose, 95–114. London: Ashgate, 2002.
Gutiérrez, Gustavo. *Las Casas: In Search of the Poor in Jesus Christ*. Translated by Robert R. Barr. 1993. Reprinted, Eugene, OR: Wipf & Stock, 2003.
———. "Poverty, Migration and the Option for the Poor." In *A Promised Land, A Perilous Journey: Theological Perspectives on Migration*, edited by Daniel Groody and Gioacchino Campese, 76–86. Notre Dame, IN: Notre Dame University Press, 2008.
Hershberger, Michele, *A Christian View of Hospitality. Expecting Surprises*. Scottdale, PA: Herald, 1999.
International Theological Commission. "The *Sensus Fidei* in the Life of the Church." 2014. http://goo.gl/ievbTI.
———. "Theology Today: Perspectives, Principles and Criteria." March 2012. http://www.vatican.va/roman_curia/congregations/cfaith/cti_documents/rc_cti_doc_20111129_teologia-oggi_en.html.
Jennings, Willie James. *The Christian Imagination: Theology and the Origins of Race*. New Haven: Yale University Press, 2010.
John Paul II, Pope. Encyclical Letter, *Fides et Ratio: On the Relationship Between Faith and Reason*. Vatican City: Libreria Editrice Vaticana, 1998.
Küng, Hans. *Infallible?: An Unresolved Inquiry*. Translated by John Bowden, Edward Quinn, and Eric Mosbacher. New York: Continuum, 1994.

Lakeland, Paul. *A Council That Will Never End: Lumen Gentium and the Church Today*. Collegeville, MN: Liturgical, 2013.

Lonergan, Bernard J. F., SJ. "Prolegomena to the Study of the Emerging Religious Consciousness of our Time." In *A Third Collection*, edited by Frederick E. Crowe, SJ, 55–73. Mahwah, NJ: Paulist, 1985.

———. *Grace and Freedom: Operative Grace in the Thought of St. Thomas Aquinas*. Edited by J. Patout Burns. New York: Herder & Herder, 1971.

———. *Insight: A Study of Human Understanding*. 3rd ed. New York: Philosophical Library, 1970.

———. "Natural Knowledge of God." In *A Second Collection*, edited by William J. F. Ryan, SJ and Bernard J. Tyrell, SJ, 117–35. Toronto: University of Toronto Press, 1974.

———. "Natural Right and Historical Mindedness." In *A Third Collection: Papers by Bernard Lonergan*, edited by Frederick E. Crowe, SJ, 169–83. Mahwah, NJ: Paulist Press, 1985.

———. *Method in Theology*. New York: Herder & Herder, 1972.

———. "The Subject." In *A Second Collection*, edited by William J. F. Ryan, SJ and Bernard J. Tyrell, SJ, 69–87. Toronto: University of Toronto Press, 1974.

Lubac, Henri de. *Corpus Mysticum: The Eucharist and the Church in the Middle Ages*. Translated by Gemma Simmonds. Notre Dame: University of Notre Dame Press, 2006.

Macy, Gary. "The 'Dogma of Transubstantiation.'" In *Treasures from the Storeroom: Medieval Religion and the Eucharist*, 81–120. Collegeville, MN: Liturgical, 1999.

———. *The Theologies of the Eucharist in the Early Scholastic Period: A Study of the Salvific Function of the Sacrament according to the Theologians c. 1080–c. 1220*. Oxford: Clarendon, 1984.

Mannion, Gerard, Richard R. Gaillardetz, Jan Kerkhofs, and Kenneth Wilson, eds. "Part 3: Synodality and Collegiality—The Dynamics of Authority." In *Readings in Church Authority*, 149–218. Aldershot, UK: Ashgate, 2003.

Maxwell, John Francis. *The History of Catholic Teaching on the Moral Legitimacy of Slavery*. Chichester, UK: Rose, 1975.

Newman, John Henry. *On Consulting the Faithful in Matters of Doctrine*. 1859. Reprinted, New York: Sheed & Ward, 1961.

Noonan, John T., Jr., *A Church That Can and Cannot Change*. Notre Dame: University of Notre Dame Press, 2005.

Phan, Peter C. *In Our Own Tongues: Perspectives from Asia on Mission and Inculturation*. Maryknoll, NY: Orbis, 2003.

Pohl, Christine D. *Making Room: Recovering Hospitality as a Christian Tradition*. Grand Rapids: Eerdmans, 1999.

Rahner, Karl. *Theological Investigations Vol. 22*, "What the Church Officially Teaches and What the People Actually Believe." In *Theological Investigations* 23 vols. London: Darton, Longman and Todd, 1961–1992: 165–175.

Rush, Ormond. *The Eyes of Faith: The Sense of the Faithful and the Church's Reception of Revelation*. Washington, DC: Catholic University of America Press, 2009.

Schroeder, H. J., trans. *Canons and Decrees of the Council of Trent: Original Text with English Translation*. St. Louis: Herder, 1941.

Song, C. S. *Believing Heart: An Invitation to Story Theology*. Minneapolis: Fortress, 1999.

———. *In the Beginning Were Stories, not Texts: Story Theology.* Eugene, OR: Cascade Books, 2011.
———. *The Tears of Lady Meng: A Parable of People's Political Theology.* Risk Book Series 11. Geneva: World Council of Churches, 1981.
———. *Tell Us Our Names: Story Theology from an Asian Perspective.* 1984. Reprinted, Eugene, OR: Wipf & Stock, 2005.
———. *And Their Eyes Are Opened: Story Sermons Embracing the World.* Saint Louis: Chalice, 2006.
Snoek, G. J. C. *Medieval Piety from Relics to the Eucharist: A Process of Mutual Interaction.* Studies in the History of Christian Thought 63. Leiden: Brill, 1995.
Sullivan, Francis A. *Magisterium: Teaching Authority in the Catholic Church.* Mahwah, NJ: Paulist, 1983
———. "The Sense of Faith: the Sense/Consensus of the Faithful." In *Authority and Roman Catholicism*, edited by Bernard Hoose, 85–94. Aldershot, UK: Ashgate, 2001.
Thomas Aquinas. *Summa Theologica.* Translated by Fathers of the English Dominican Province. 5 vols. Westminster, MD: Christian Classics, 1981.
Tilley, Terrence W. *Story Theology.* Theology and Life Series 12. Collegeville, MN: Liturgical, 1985.
Wilfred, Felix. *Asian Dreams and Christian Hope: At the Dawn of the New Millennium.* Delhi: ISPCK, 2003.

Topical Index

Africa, xvi–ii, 3, 94, 159, 186, 189–90, 214, 220, 231–34, 248, 286, 360, 363, 365
African-Americans, xvii, 54,61–4, 187, 230–31, 234, 237–41, 243–47, 250, 252–54
Asia Minor, *see* Turkey
Asia, 220, 286, 296, 298–303, 305–10, 318, 320, 348
Asian Americans, 318
atheism, 108
atheists, 316

baptism, xv, 6–7, 15, 23–6, 42, 45, 48, 143, 150, 205, 235, 244, 310, 313
Baptist Church, 64. See also Baptists
Baptists, 231, *see also* Baptist Church
Bakongo, *see* Kongo (African people)
Bible, *use for* Scripture, xxi, 4, 14 18, 24, 28, 31–2, 59, 72, 74, 76 107, 118, 138, 149–54, 197, 199, 201, 216, 221, 225, 244, 268, 285, 297–98, 313, 330, 335–39, 345–46, 348, 352. *See also* Hebrew Bible *and* New Testament
Buddhism, 223, 286, 293
Buddhists, 286, 307–10

Canada, 231
Canon law, 31, 33, 128, 132–33, 186
Caribbean, xvii, 203, 230, 240, 249, 251–52, 277

Catholic Church, 60-6, 97, 104–5, 111, 114, 118, 127, 132, 137, 143, 146, 149, 154, 168, 171, 174, 197, 202, 216–17, 221, 224, 228, 231, 239, 246, 253, 259, 281, 282–84, 312, 317, 320, 323–25, 327, 344
Catholic Theological Society of America (CTSA), 28, 90, 93, 108, 127, 155, 180, 225 234, 364
Catholics *use for* Roman Catholics, xv, 49, 54, 57–8, 62–6, 87, 90, 100, 102–13, 117–20, 125, 138, 148, 151, 168, 175, 178, 180, 185–87, 216, 224, 230–31, 237–38, 241–43, 245–47, 253–54, 285, 291, 312, 317–22, 324, 325, 326–27, 337, 341–42
Chinese, 59–60, 281–93, 302–3, 306, 310, 317, 321
Christ, *see* Jesus Christ
Christianity, xvi–ii, 8, 30, 79, 98, 149, 155, 166, 180, 185, 192, 203, 214–16, 218–25, 228, 244, 249, 276, 280, 283, 292, 300, 306–7, 310, 312, 314, 316–17, 326, 355
Christology, 46, 219, 225, 291
civil unions, 182. *See also* same-sex marriage
collegiality, 83–84, 132
Commissio Theologica Internationalis *use for* International Theological

371

Commission (ITC) xvi, 3–4, 7, 15–17, 27–9, 40–41, 43–44, 47–48, 50, 53, 57–58, 60, 65, 69–71, 73–78, 82–84, 86–87, 89, 128, 135–36, 139, 155, 167, 181, 184–86, 188, 192–93, 196, 198, 201, 203–7, 209, 213–14, 218–19, 221–24, 227, 255–59, 261, 264, 266, 268, 273, 313–14, 329, 345–46, 350, 362–63, 365
Communion, *see* Eucharist
Confucianism, 223, 286, 293
Congregatio pro Doctrina Fidei, *use for* Congregation for the Doctrine of the Faith (CDF), 50, 73, 76, 82, 87, 140, 171–74, 177, 197, 200, 206, 208, 283, 353, 357
Congregatio pro Institutione Catholica, *use for* Congregation for Catholic Education, 171, 173–74
Congregation for Catholic Education, *see* Congregatio pro Institutione Catholica
Congregation for the Doctrine of Faith (CDF), *see* Congregatio pro Doctrina Fidei
Consejo Episcopal Latinoamericano (CELAM), *use for* Latin American Episcopal Conference, 201, 335, 339, 342, 349
contraception, 49, 100–101, 105
Council of Ephesus (341), 215, 219
Council of Nicaea (1st : 325 : Nicaea, Turkey), xvi, 97, 219
Council of Trent (1545–1563), 37, 47, 70–71, 313
curia, 75, 222, 227, 233, 235

Dalits, 222, 309
Dei Verbum [Dogmatic Constitution on Revelation], 71, 85, 146, 151, 153–54, 264, 268, 314–15, 366
Dignitatis Humanae [Declaration on Religious Freedom], 167–68
Dignity USA, 180
Directory on Popular Piety and the Liturgy, 202
divorce, 86, 117, 125, 177
doctrines, xv–xvi, 4, 7–8, 10, 12, 17, 19, 28, 42–43, 45–48, 50–51, 54, 59–60, 65–66, 70–71, 76, 77, 79–82, 87, 89, 90, 96, 98, 105, 107, 108, 113, 114, 117–18, 126, 140, 144–45, 147, 153, 155–57, 159, 166, 167, 168, 170, 175, 177, 179–81, 197, 200, 203, 205, 207, 214–19, 223–24, 226, 246, 256, 264–65, 268–69, 272, 274, 276, 280, 293, 314, 345–46, 352, 355
Dogmatic Constitution on Catholic Faith, 217
Dominicans, *use for* Order of Preachers, 18, 36–7, 188, 246, 336

Ecclesia in Asia (EA) [The Church in Asia], 299
ecclesiology, 44, 45, 48, 56, 73, 75, 86, 90, 102, 107, 110–11, 126, 128–30, 132, 134, 141, 144, 147, 155, 225, 264, 266, 336, 342
ecumenism, 197
Eucharist *use for* Communion *or* Lord's Supper, 11, 27–39, 48, 65, 96, 177, 246, 342
Europe, 37, 40, 49, 192, 220, 233, 282, 356
Evangelii Gaudium (EG) [Joy of the Gospel], 43, 77, 85, 144–45, 151, 202–3, 236, 330, 349–50, 360, 362, 365
excommunication, 108, 119

fasts and feasts, xvi, 27, 30, 32, 35–9
Feast of Corpus Christi, xvi, 27, 30, 32–33, 35, 37, 39. *See also* fasts and feasts
Fides et Ratio, 61, 352, 359
Fourteenth Ordinary General Assembly of the Synod of Bishops, *see* Synod on the Family (2015)
Fourth Lateran Council, *see* Lateran Council (4th: 1215)
Gaudium et Spes [Pastoral Constitution on the Church in the Modern World], 78, 153, 242, 352–53

TOPICAL INDEX

gays, 170–71, 173–76, 178–80, 182. *See also* homosexuality *and* lesbians *and* LGBTQ
gender, xv–xvii, 38, 57, 155–58, 160–68, 236, 243, 319, 352, 358, 361, 365. *See also* transgender
God, xv, 4–6, 8–17, 19–24, 29–31, 35, 38–39, 41, 43, 47–49, 54–58, 60–63, 65, 66, 69, 71–76, 79–85, 87, 96, 99, 101, 111, 117, 127–33, 135–36, 138–39, 142–48, 150–53, 161, 166, 168, 174–75, 177, 185–86, 188–92, 196, 199–206, 208, 215, 222, 228–30, 235, 243–44, 246, 248, 259, 262–63, 266, 268–69, 274, 279, 286, 292–93, 295–96, 301–4, 306, 310, 314–16, 318–21, 323, 325, 327, 329, 330, 333–34, 337–38, 340–42, 345–51, 353–57, 359, 361–66
grace, 5, 11, 13, 17, 19, 21–22, 24–26, 51, 55, 58, 95, 107, 125, 139, 151, 155, 174, 176, 186–89, 195, 200, 224, 257, 262–63, 266–69, 310, 314–15, 345, 349–50, 355–56, 358–59
Guadalupe, Our Lady of, 158, 274–77, 278–79

Hebrew Bible, *use for* Old Testament, 16, 72, 219. *See also* Bible
heresy, 42, 218
hermeneutics, xvii, 83, 145–50, 153, 214, 265, 349, 351–52, 354
Hinduism, 223
Hindus, 308–9
Holy See, 63, 161. *See also* Papacy
Holy Spirit, *use for* Spirit, xv, 4–5, 10–13, 16, 18–21, 26, 29, 47–48, 53, 55–57, 65–66, 71, 80, 85, 95–96, 101, 127, 129, 135, 138, 143–47, 150–54, 179, 184–86, 189, 190–92, 201–3, 206–8, 221, 227–29, 234, 236, 243, 247, 249, 254, 257, 269, 275, 279, 313, 324, 327, 330, 342, 346, 349–50, 354, 361–63, 365–66
homosexuality, 100, 171, 176. *See also* LGBTQ *and* gays *and* lesbians
Humanae Vitae, 49, 100–101

Immaculate Conception, 46, 49, 126, 274, 276
India, 140, 309
Institute for Black Catholic Studies, 237–38, 244–45, 246
International Theological Commission (ITC), *see* Commissio Theologica Internationalis
interreligious dialogue, 224–25, 267, 299, 309
Islam, 228, 309

Jesuits, *use for* Society of Jesus, 189
Jesus (of Nazareth), 22, 29, 30, 34, 37, 56, 147, 151, 153, 202, 226, 246, 253, 260–61, 269, 280, 284–93, 297, 299–300, 306–7, 325–26, 353, 355
Jesus Christ, *use for* Christ, xv, 4–6, 8–9, 13–4, 18, 21–26, 29, 33–34, 36–38, 43, 45, 47–48, 50, 54, 56, 58–59, 66, 74–75, 77, 130–31, 143, 146–47, 150, 153, 163, 168, 173–75, 179, 180, 187, 205, 207, 214, 218–19, 228–29, 234–36, 243–44, 249, 259, 272–73, 280–81, 285, 291–92, 305, 307–10, 314, 317, 348–50, 355, 358, 362, 365–66
Jews, 150

koinonia, 227, 229, 235, 249
Kongo (African people) *use for* Bakongo, 239, 250–52
Korea, 220, 305, 317–21, 323, 325, 327
Korean-Americans, 312, 316, 318, 321–22, 324–27

laity, 5–7, 28, 29–30, 33–34, 36, 42–46, 50–53, 56, 62, 76, 77, 79–80, 100–108, 113–15, 117–18, 125, 129–31, 134, 143, 178, 186, 193, 197, 205–6, 214, 229–30, 235, 246, 254, 274, 344, 347, 350, 363
Lateran Council (4th: 1215), *use for* Fourth Lateran Council, 33–35
Latin America, xvi–xvii, 186, 204, 277–78, 280, 331–34, 336–37, 341–43
Latin American Episcopal Conference. *See* Consejo Episcopal Latinoamericano (CELAM)
Latino/a, xvi, 40, 245, 257, 259–62, 267–68, 270
Laudato Si, 41, 161
Leadership Conference of Women Religious (LCWR), 119
lesbians, 170–71, 174–76, 178–80. *See also* gays *and* homosexuality *and* LGBTQ
LGBTQ, *includes* LGBT, 117, 170, 179–82
liturgy, 29, 34–5, 65, 74, 95–6, 186, 202, 223, 245, 248, 274, 285, 323–24, 337, 350. *See also* worship
Lord's Supper. *See* Eucharist
Los Angeles, California, 228–30, 234
Lumen Fidei, 15–16
Lumen Genitum [Dogmatic Constitution on the Church], xv, 3–7, 43, 47, 53–58, 60–61, 63, 65–66, 70–71, 73, 76, 79, 85, 89–90, 94, 96–97, 131, 143–46, 202, 235, 255, 264, 313, 344, 347, 355, 357, 365

magisterium, 48–50, 52–3, 69–76, 78, 80–88, 99, 101–2, 107, 115, 117, 127, 132, 140–41, 143, 152, 166, 167–68, 174, 178, 181, 185, 186, 189, 197–201, 206, 222, 224, 227, 244, 255, 265, 274, 279, 313–15, 330, 337, 344, 352, 356, 361, 363–64
Marian devotion, 276, 279
marriage, 8, 31, 50, 61, 86, 101–2, 105, 134, 147, 163, 164, 172, 176–77, 180–81, 231, 251, 348. *See also* same-sex marriage
Mary, Blessed Virgin, Saint, 5, 47, 125–26, 159, 248, 261, 282, 285–92, 349, 365
medieval history, *see* Middle Ages
Middle Ages, *use for* medieval history, 3, 16, 31, 33–35, 38, 204
Missale Romanum, 32
missiology, 220, 308, 309
missionaries, 61, 189, 220, 231, 283, 309, 317
Muslims, 60, 184, 189, 192, 308
Mysterium Ecclesiae, 199, 200, 206, 353

National Conference of Catholic Bishops, *see* United States Conference of Catholic Bishops (USCCB)
Nestorius, Patriarch of Constantinople, 215, 219
New Orleans, 237–40, 247
New Testament, 16, 89, 143, 147–49, 151, 219, 318. *See also* Bible
Nigeria, 228, 232–33, 250
North America, 49, 54, 63, 186, 220, 228, 233–34, 257, 327
Nostra Aetate [Declaration on the Relation of the Church with Non-Christian Religions], 224
nuns *use for* sisters *and* women religious, 31, 37, 60, 63–4, 72, 119, 238, 241, 243, 251, 336

Old Testament, *see* Hebrew Bible
Order of Preachers, *see* Dominicans
orthodoxy, 44–5, 52, 119, 204–5, 213–15, 217, 219–21, 225, 313

Papacy, 84, 97. *See also* Holy See
philosophy, 11, 93, 162, 198, 238, 251, 253, 336, 340, 349, 352
Pontifical Council for Culture, *see* Pontificium Consilium pro Cultura
Pontifical Council for Interrelgious Dialogue, *see* Pontificium

Consilium pro Dialogo inter
    Religiones
Pontificium Consilium pro Cultura
    use for Pontifical Council for
    Culture, 156–57, 162–65, 309
Pontificium Consilium pro Dialogo
    inter Religiones *use for* Pontifical
    Council for Interrelgious
    Dialogue, 309
popular piety, 74, 202–3, 209, 349, 350
prayer, 30, 95–6, 136, 186, 194, 202, 208,
    246–48, 252, 274, 246, 291, 311,
    320, 323
priesthood, 31, 130–31, 173–75, 229,
    233, 234, 243, 336
Protestants, 62, 101, 148, 186, 341

Quakers, *use for* Society of Friends, 186

race, xv, 58–60, 62–3, 66 131, 236, 239,
    243, 253, 279, 365
Reformation, 139, 147, 316
Rerum Novarum, 332

sacraments, 14, 22, 24–25, 32–37, 55,
    95–96, 105, 107, 114, 119, 128,
    131, 173, 235, 238, 261, 337, 347
salvation, *use for* soteriology, 5–6, 11,
    20–21, 31, 60, 85, 104, 145, 148,
    155, 174 215, 272–73, 278–80,
    303, 310, 307, 325, 347–48
same-sex marriage, 180–82. *See also*
    civil unions *and* marriage
Scripture, *see* Bible
Second Vatican Council, *see* Vatican
    Council (2nd: 1962–1965)
secularism, 296
sexual orientation, xv, xvii, 171–72,
    175–76
sin, 5, 11, 24, 32, 36, 38, 155, 158, 165,
    174, 187, 278, 350, 358
sisters, *see* nuns
slavery, 58, 62, 180, 186–87, 240, 247
social sciences, 90–1, 93–4, 102, 341,
    351–52. *See also* sociology
Society of Friends, *see* Quakers
Society of Jesus, *see* Jesuits

sociology, 94, 97, 112–13, 115–16,
    118–19, 129, 266, 352. *See also*
    social sciences
soteriology, *see* salvation
Spirit, *see* Holy Spirit
Summa Theologiae (ST), 18–23, 26, 38,
    188, 258
Syllabus of Errors, 167–68
Synod on the Family (2014), 50–51, 86,
    125, 147, 170, 171, 175, 177–79,
    181–82
Synod on the Family (2015), 85–6, 125,
    147, 150
synods, xvi, 50–1, 85–6, 133, 147, 150,
    171, 175–79, 181, 206, 229, 230

Third Extraordinary General Assembly
    of the Synod of Bishops, *see*
    Synod on the Family (2014)
transgender, 180. *See also* gender
Trinity, 10–1, 36, 55, 129, 219, 351
Turkey, 219

United States Conference of Catholic
    Bishops (USCCB), *use for*
    National Conference of Catholic
    Bishops, 133, 171, 235
United States of America (USA), xvi,
    58–59, 61, 63, 133, 158, 171,
    226–31, 233–35, 239, 243, 245,
    247, 260, 275, 278
Ut Unum Sint, 208

Vatican Council (2nd: 1962–1965), *use
    for* Vatican II *or* Second Vatican
    Council, xv–xvii, 3–6, 43–44,
    47, 50, 53, 57, 60, 70–71, 73–75,
    77, 79, 81, 83–84, 87, 89, 98,
    105–6, 107, 125–32, 134–36,
    138, 141, 144–45, 150, 154, 186,
    206, 224, 241, 255–56, 258, 264,
    268, 273–74, 279, 280, 296, 313,
    331–32, 337, 339, 340, 342, 344,
    351, 362
Vatican Councl (1st: 1869–1870), *use
    for* Vatican I, 95, 97, 139, 188,
    217, 313

Vatican I, *see* Vatican Council (1st: 1869–1870)
Vatican II, *see* Vatican Council (2nd: 1962–1965)
Vatican, 55, 73, 83, 93, 105, 119, 128, 156, 175–76, 195, 205, 207, 242, 309

women religious, *see* nuns
women, 31, 34–35, 37–38, 54–55, 57, 61, 63–64, 105, 117, 119, 138, 156, 159, 162–65, 167–68, 173, 175, 177, 195, 222, 224, 234, 239, 242, 251–54, 262, 274–78, 280, 290, 318–20, 331, 336, 339–43, 348, 360, 361, 364–66
World Council of Churches, 197, 301, 309
World Evangelical Alliance, 309
worship, 30, 39, 135, 166, 173, 202, 221, 226, 241, 244, 274, 308, 316, 350, 365

Yoruba (African people), 239, 250, 252

Personal Name Index

Adamson, Matthew, 109
Agamben, Giorgio, 140, 351
Alberigo, Giuseppe, 129, 132
Albert the Great, 38
Alexander VI, Pope, 60
Almeida, E., 331
Alszeghy, Zoltán, 258
Amaladoss, Michael, 295
Ambrose of Milan, Saint, 36, 219
Ames, Roger T., 288
Andrade, Paulo Fernando Carniero de, 331–32
Ani, Marimba, 247
Aquino, María Pilar, 259–61, 267–68
Aquinas, Thomas, Saint, *see* Thomas Aquinas, Saint
Ariarajah, Wesley, 308–9
Aristotle, 12, 20
Armah, Ayi Kwei, 232
Armstrong, Regis J., 136
Arns, Paulo Evaristo, 343
Arrupe, Pedro, 339
Ashley, J. Matthew, 244
Astell, Ann W., 38–9
Athanasius, Bishop of Antioch, 205
Augustine, Saint, Bishop of Hippo, xvi, 3–17, 22–3, 62, 70
Ayres, Lewis, 10–11
Azcuy, V. R., 334

Baggett, Jerome P., 90–93, 95, 97–98, 103–14, 116, 118–20, 155

Baker, Dan, 317
Baldisseri, Lorenzo, 177
Barr, Robert, 249
Bass, Dorothy C., 246
Beinert, Wolfgang, 126, 132, 135, 140–41, 312
Bellarmine, Robert, 47
Beltran, Benigno P., 298
Benedict XV, Pope, 282
Benedict XVI, Pope, *use for* Ratzinger, Joseph, 15, 73, 78, 135, 153–54, 162, 197, 205, 343
Benton, Thomas Hart, 59
Benumeya, R. Gil, 331
Berengar, of Tours, 33, 35
Bergman, Roger, 248
Bergoglio, Jorge Mario *see* Francis, Pope
Berman, Harold J., 190–92
Bettelheim, Barbara A., 249
Betto, Frei, 334
Bevans, Stephen B., 361–62
Bhaskar, Roy, 93–4
Blackshear, Juanita, 247
Boff, Leonardo, 336–37, 343
Bonaventure, Saint, 358
Boniface VIII, Pope, 31
Bonino, Serge Thomas, 72
Bornemann, Fritz, 287–88, 290
Boulaga, F. Eboussi, 249
Bourdieu, Pierre, 104, 106–7, 109–13, 115–19
Bowman, Thea, 241–42, 251

Brennan, Patrick McKinley, 188
Brown, Peter, 98
Bruce, Steve, 99
Buber, Martin, 193
Buhlmann, W., 332
Burkhard, John J., 70–1, 90, 105, 140, 258
Butler, Sara, 72, 197
Bynum, Carolyn Walker, 38, 40

Cahil, Lisa, 340, 364
Calvin, John, 130
Câmara, Hélder, 343
Campese, Gioachinno, 356
Cano, Melchior, 47, 126
Cardman, Francine, 319
Carey, Patrick W., 245
Castellano, Antonio, 72
Castillo, Ana, 275
Chambers, Donald, 247
Chia, Edmund Kee-Fook, 299
Chŏng Ha Sang, Paul, 325–26
Chong, Francis, 282
Chung, John Jae-sun, 325
Cixous, Helene, 162
Clark, David K., 297
Clark, Emily, 239
Clark, Henry, 63
Clark, Thomas, 247
Clarke, Jeremy, 282, 286, 291–92
Clausen, John A., 95
Cohen, Will, 134
Collier, Andrew, 94
Comstock, Gary L., 297–98
Congar, Yves, 6, 28, 48, 80, 153, 197, 243
Considine, Kevin Patrick, 314
Cooke, Bernard J., 29–30, 35
Copeland, Shawn, 245, 364
Copernicus, Nicolaus, 157, 166
Cornet, Joseph, 250
Cornille, Catherine, 310
Costantini, Celso, 282–84, 291, 293
Coulson, John, 42, 44
Crites, Stephen, 297
Crowe, Frederick E., 94, 98–99, 127, 188–91
Crowley, Paul, 264–65, 349, 356
Curtin, Philip, 250

Cushman, Robert, 12
Cyprian, Saint, Bishop of Carthage, 5, 219, 315, 317

Daly, Mary, 340
Damian, Peter, Saint, 31
Dash, J. Michael, 240
Daston, Lorraine, 40
Davis, Cyprian, 58, 61–62, 243, 245
Day, Dorothy, 202
Decastello, A., 277
Deferrari, Roy J., 6
Denaux, Adelbert, 72
Dhammananda, Venerable, 307–10
Díaz, Miguel H., 261
Dihle, Albrecht, 11–12
Dillon, Michele, 106, 117
Donovan, Mary Ann, 353, 357
Doran, Robert M., 94, 98, 189, 190, 194
Doyle, Dennis M., 44
Drexel, Katharine, Saint, 238, 248
Duffy, Eamon, 34–35, 40
Dulles, Avery, 43, 46, 101, 137
Dunne, George H., 189
Dykstra, Craig, 246

Egbulem, Nwaka Chris, 248, 250
Ehlers, Tracy, 277
Ekpo, Anthony, 131
Ellacuria, Ignacio, 358
Elliott, Dyan, 31
Espín, Orlando O., 40, 257, 259–64, 266–70, 274, 275, 314–15, 345, 349, 355, 357
Eusebius, Bishop of Caesarea, 221
Eusebius, of Vercelli, 205
Evans, Carolyn, 190

Fabre, Geneviève, 240
Faggioli, Massimo, 149, 156
Faletto, E., 332
Fanon, Franz, 241
Farley, Margaret, 179, 364
Fernández, V. M., 334
Fernando, Paulo, 331–32
Ferrara, R., 334
Ferré, Rosario, 274–75, 277–80
Fiddes, Paul F., 295

Finn, Daniel K., 186
Finnis, John, 91, 92
Finucane, Daniel, 344
Fiorenza, Francis Schüssler, 145
Fisch, Thomas J., 30
Fitzgerald, Allan D. 6
Fitzmyer, Joseph A., 32
Flannery, Austin, 127, 255
Fleming, Daniel Johnson, 286, 292
Ford, John, 49
Francis, of Assisi, Saint, 136
Francis, Pope, *use for* Bergoglio, Jorge Mario, xvi, 15, 41, 43, 50, 77, 79, 84–7, 125 128, 144–46, 149, 151, 156–71, 174–79, 181–82, 184, 192–93,197, 202–6, 208, 235–36, 257, 314,318, 330, 334, 343, 349–50, 355, 360, 362, 365
Freud, Sigmund, 162

Gadamer, Hans-Georg, 145
Gadoua, Renee, 60
Gaillardetz, Richard R., 43, 71, 107, 110, 115, 128, 140, 201, 276, 312–13, 315
Galilei, Galileo, 166, 168
Gallagher, Michael, 242
Galli, C., 334
Garcia, Grace 348
García, Samuel Ruiz, 343
George, Francis E. (Francis Eugene), 187
George, William P., 190, 194
Gera, Lucio, 334
Gibbs, Philip, 298
Gibson, David, 165
Gibson, Otis, 59
Gilroy, Paul, 250
Ginsburg, Ruth Bader, 60
Glissant, Edouard, 240
Godzieba, Anthony, 201
Goizueta, Roberto S., 259–61
Golden, Willa Ellis, 247
Gonzalez, G. M. James, 253
González, Justo L., 220–21, 316
Gordon, Lewis R., 253
Gregory VII, Pope, 31
Greshake, Gisbert, 133
Grimes, Katie, 243

Grisez, Germain, 49
Groody, Daniel, 356, 363
Groppe, Elizabeth, 350
Guarino, Thomas G., 214, 217, 219
Gutiérrez, Gustavo, 187, 300, 334, 336–37, 343, 356

Habermas, Jürgen, 145
Hadewijch, of Brabant, 38
Hahnenberg, Edward P., 110, 272, 274–75
Haimo of Auxerre, 32
Hall, Gwendolyn Midlo, 239
Haquin, André, 34
Harrold, C. F., 265
Hart, Columbia, 38
Hasler, August Bernard, 101
Hayes, Diana L., 58, 245
Heidegger, Martin, 151
Hershberger, Michele, 226
Heurtley, C. A., 213
Hiebert, Paul, 351, 354
Hilary, of Poitiers, 205
Hines, Mary E., 349
Hinze, Bradford E., 111, 127, 364
Hipskind, Timothy, 247
Hirsch, Arnold R., 239
Hoebel, Thomas, 137
Hogan, Linda, 364
Hollenbach, David, 364
Hoose, Bernard, 71, 132, 259
Horlyck, Charlotte, 317
Hugh of Saint-Cher, 36
Hugh of Saint-Victor, 16
Hur, Wonjae, 325
Hwang, Alexius Sa-yŏng, 317–18, 325

Ignatius of Loyola, Saint, 144, 195, 247, 316, 362
Ilo, Stan Chu, 364
Innocent III, Pope, 33
Irigaray, Luce, 162
Isasi-Diaz, Ada Maria, 364
Ivančić, Tomislav, 72
Ivereigh, Austen, 203

Janis, Mark W., 190
Jennings, Willie James, 58

Jerome, Saint, 193
John Paul II, Pope, *use for* Wojtyła, Karol, 61, 155–56, 162, 164, 168, 178, 224, 299, 343, 352, 359
John XXII, Pope, 37, 39
John XXIII, Pope, 85, 127, 151, 206, 208, 332
Johnson, Elizabeth, 364
Jordan, Mark D., 182
Juliana of Cornillon, *see*
Juliana of Liège, Saint, *use for* Juliana of Cornillon, 35–7, 39

Kaplan, Sara, 252
Karimi, Faith, 353
Kasper, Walter, 137, 149, 203
Keenan, Jim, 364
Kerkhofs, Jan, 71
Kern, W., 330
Kim, Doo Jin, 324
Kim, Doowan, 323
Kim, Francis, 321
Kim, Joseph Chang-mun, 325
Kim, Simon C., 321
Kim, Young Wook, 324
King, Martin Luther, Jr., 64, 202
Kinkupu, Leonard Santedi, 72
Klein-Lasalle, Robert, 358
Knight, Kevin, 213
Koehlinger, Amy, 64
Komonchak, Joseph, 90, 99–102, 129, 132
Kotsko, Adam, 140
Kreutler, Don Erwin, 336
Kristeva, Jula, 162
Kuhn, Thomas S., 157
Küng, Hans, 49

Lacan, Jacques, 163
Lafferty, Maura, 30
Lakeland, Paul, 56
Lam, Anthony, 282
Lamberts, Jef, 34
Lash, Nicholas, 265, 295
Lawrence, Frederick G., 92, 102
Lawson, Stephen, 48–49
Lawton, Mary S., 283–85, 292
Lee, James K. H., 321

Leo XIII, Pope, 332
Lerch, Joseph R., 139–40
Levada, William, 197
Liesen, Jan, 72
Lima Vaz, H. 332–33
Liu, Monica, 286
Liu, Pacificus, 325
Logsdon, Joseph, 239
Lohfink Gerhard, 128
Lombard, Peter, 3
Lonergan, Bernard J. F., xvii, 91–92, 94, 97–99, 102, 127, 130, 184, 185, 187–95, 241
Lorscheiter, Ivo, 343
Lubac, Henri de, 33, 36
Luce-Smith, Alexander, 298
Lukken, Gerard, 34

Ma, Julie C., 354
Ma, Wonsuk, 354
MacIntyre, Alasdair, 92–94, 97
Macy, Gary, 33
Maggay, Melba, 354
Mahoney, Roger, 228
Majozo, Estella Conwill, 251–52
Makowski, Elizabeth, 31
Maloney, Linda M., 128
Manning, Henry Edward, 44
Mannion, Gerard, 70–71, 132
Marinucci, Mimi, 157
Marmion, Declan, 349
Marquard, Odo, 147–48
Martin, August, 58
Massingale, Bryan, 364
Maxwell, John Francis, 186
McCann, Pamela, 198, 200
McElwee, Joshua, 156
McGreevy, John, 63–64
McLoughlin, David, 132
McPartlan, Paul, 72
Mello, Anthony de, 311
Mercado, Leonardo, 361
Merton, Thomas, 324, 328
Mesters, Carlos, 335–38
Metz, Johann Baptist, 244, 300
Milhaven, John G., 179–80
Miller, Edward Jeremy, 45
Miller, Vincent, 201

PERSONAL NAME INDEX

Mitchell, Nathan, 30
Möhler, Johann Adam, 47, 89, 126
Mosely, LaReine-Marie, 245, 247
Moten, Fred, 240
Mouroux, Jean, 139
Moxon, Reginald Stewart, 213
Mudge, Lewis S., 70
Mulder-Bakker, Anneke B., 35
Muller, Earl C., 245
Müller, Gerhad, 197
Müller, Mogens, 148
Murray, Paul D., 197, 201

Nanko-Fernández, Carmen, 40
Nearon, Joseph, 238, 251
Neuner, Joseph, 217
Newcomb, Steven, 59
Newman, Barbara, 35–37
Newman, John Henry, xvi, 5, 17, 28, 42–47, 50–52, 81, 89–90, 96, 126, 193, 205, 217, 219, 222, 256, 264–65, 273–74, 279, 313, 315, 346, 349, 356
Nichols, Aidan, 43
Nickoloff, James B., 267
Niebuhr, H. Richard, 297
Niemann, F.-J., 330
Noonan, John T., 180–81, 186
Nora, Pierre, 240
Norris, Pippa, 99
Nutt, Maurice J., 242

O'Connell, Gerard, 343
O'Connor, James T., 36
O'Gara, Margaret, 127
O'Meally, Robert G., 240
Oduyoye, Mercy Amba, 167, 364
Okure, Teresa, 364
Orgad, Liav, 60
Ormerod, Neil, 90, 94, 99
Orobator, Agbonkhianmeghe, 364
Osabu-Kle, Daniel Tetteh, 231

Parker, Kenneth, 48–49
Patel, Eboo, 194
Paul IV, Pope, 156
Paul VI, Pope, 49, 101, 159, 237–38, 343

Paul, the Apostle, Saint, 11, 18, 21, 23, 31–2, 34, 37, 45, 147, 149, 163, 192
Pearce, Diane, 341
Pelikan, Jarslav, 3
Perrone, Giovanni, 47, 126
Peter, the Apostle, Saint, 56, 149
Pettid, Michael J., 317
Phan, Peter, 284, 300
Phelps, Jamie T., 62, 243, 245–46
Phillips, George, 130
Pinn, Anthony, 240–41
Pius IX, Pope, 46, 62, 101, 126, 167
Pius XI, Pope, 101, 282
Pius, V, Pope, 32
Pius, XII, Pope, 47, 101, 125–26
Pohl, Christine D., 228
Posey, Thaddeus, 238, 251
Potts, Richard M., 247
Proaño, Taita, 343

Rahner, Karl, xvii, 98, 151–52, 196–209, 244, 280, 343, 347, 349–52
Ratzinger, Joseph, *see* Benedict XVI, Pope
Rausch, Franklin, 317, 320
Ray, Darby Kathleen, 350
Raymond, Gino, 109
Rey, Terry, 117
Ricci, Matteo, 202
Ricketts, Juan Landázuri, 343
Ricoeur, Paul, 145, 148
Rodriguez, Ismael, 276
Rodríguez, Jeanette, 262
Romero, Óscar, 343
Rosemont, Henry, 288
Rotelle, John E., 6
Rouwhorst, Gerard, 34
Rubin, Miri, 33, 35–7, 40
Rush, Ormond, 71, 90, 105, 114–15, 121, 147, 153, 196, 201, 205, 206, 258, 273, 276, 279–80, 344, 346–48, 352
Ruthizer, Theodore, 60
Ryan, William J. F., 188, 193

Sargent, Aaron Augustus, 59
Sauvy, Alfred, 331

Savage, John J., 36
Scannone, Juan Carlos, 203, 334
Schaff, Philip, 213
Schneiders, Sandra M., 149
Schrift, Alan D. 145
Schroeder, H. J., 37
Seitz, John, 109
Serra, Junipero, 158
Shea, John J., 111
Shourie, Arun, 309
Silva, Joaquín, 330
Simmonds, Gemma, 33
Slusser, Michael, 51
Smith, Christian, 93
Smith, Janet E., 49
Smith, Mark, 27
Snoek, G. J. C., 30
Sobrino, Jon, 333, 335, 358
Söding, Thomas, 72, 197
Song, C. S., 301–2, 304–7
Song, Jong-rye Gratia, 318–20
Standaert, Nicolas, 283
Stevens, Evelyn, 277
Suaiden, S., 340
Sullivan, Francis A., 70–71, 85, 259, 344
Szymik, Jerzy, 72

Tagle, Luis Antonio, 150, 300, 348
Talbot, George, 44
Tanner, Kathryn, 91
Tanner, Norman P., 143
Tertullian, 31
Tetteh, Daniel, 231
Thiessen, Gesa Elsbeth, 349
Thiong'o, Ngugi wa, 231
Thomas Aquinas, Saint, xvi, 15, 18–20, 34, 37–39, 188, 258

Thompson, Harriet, 62, 248
Thompson, John B., 109
Thompson, Robert Farris, 249–53
Thompson, William M., 7
Ticozzi, Sergio, 282–83
Torre, Miguel de la, 277
Tronier, Henrik, 148
Turner, Michael, 139
Tyrell, Bernard, J., 188, 193

Urban II, Pope, 31
Urban IV, Pope, 36–37

Vertin, Michael, 127, 189–90
Vincent, of Lérins, 89, 213–20, 222–23, 225, 256
Vitale, Dario, 128
Vorgrimler, Herbert, 43, 153, 179, 347

Wace, Henry, 213
Wacquant, Loïc J. D., 112–13, 115–16, 118–19
Walters, Barbara R., 35
Weakland, Rembert G., 170
Weeramantry, C. G., 194
Weil, Simone, 38–39
Wenmo, Zhou, 317, 319
Wiederkehr, Dietrich, 136
Wilfred, Felix, 299, 303–4, 309–10
Wilson, Kenneth, 71
Wojtyła, Karol, *see* John Paul II, Pope
Wyntar, Sylvia, 240

Yak-chong, Chŏng, 325
Yong Choi, Peter Kyung, 323

www.ingramcontent.com/pod-product-compliance
Lightning Source LLC
Chambersburg PA
CBHW071231290426
44108CB00013B/1366